D1591612

YEMEN

Titles in ABC-CLIO's *Latin America in Focus Series*

Venezuela   Elizabeth Gackstetter Nichols and Kimberly J. Morse

Titles in ABC-CLIO's *Africa in Focus Series*

Eritrea   Mussie Tesfagiorgis G.

Ethiopia   Paulos Milkias

Titles in ABC-CLIO's *Asia in Focus Series*

China   Robert André LaFleur, Editor

Japan   Lucien Ellington, Editor

The Koreas   Mary E. Connor, Editor

Titles in ABC-CLIO's *Middle East in Focus Series*

Saudi Arabia   Sherifa Zuhur

Egypt   Mona Russell

YEMEN

Steven C. Caton, Editor

ABC-CLIO

Santa Barbara, California • Denver, Colorado • Oxford, England

Library of Congress Cataloging-in-Publication Data

Yemen / Steven C. Caton, editor.
    p. cm. — (Middle East in focus)
  Includes bibliographical references and index.
  ISBN 978-1-59884-927-1 (hardcopy : alk. paper) — ISBN 978-1-59884-928-8 (ebook)
1. Yemen (Republic).   I. Caton, Steven Charles, 1950–
  DS247.Y4Y44   2013
  953.3—dc23   2012042489

ISBN: 978-1-59884-927-1
EISBN: 978-1-59884-928-8

17   16   15   14   13   1   2   3   4   5

This book is also available on the World Wide Web as an eBook.
Visit www.abc-clio.com for details.

ABC-CLIO, LLC
130 Cremona Drive, P.O. Box 1911
Santa Barbara, California 93116-1911

This book is printed on acid-free paper ∞
Manufactured in the United States of America

Contents

4 THE ECONOMY, 113

Charles Schmitz

Introduction

The news about Yemen these days is almost always negative.

Ask most Americans where the country is and they probably will not be able to tell you, but they think they do know (because newspaper articles assert it over and over again) that "it is the homeland of Osama bin Laden" and therefore "a hotbed of terrorism in the Middle East." Never mind that Osama bin Laden grew up in Saudi Arabia not Yemen; never mind that it was his father who came to Saudi Arabia from Yemen many decades ago to become enormously wealthy in the construction industry during the oil boom years of the 1960s and 1970s; never mind that most Yemenis hardly think of the bin Ladens as one of their own: The connection has been made in the U.S. mind between Yemen and terrorism that seems natural or ineluctable rather than a very recent phenomenon due to a number of international as well as domestic circumstances, some of which were beyond Yemen's control.

Another powerful stereotype is that Yemen has a "weak state" and as such there is "no rule of law" in the country. Never mind that Yemen has had a state (for all of its supposed weakness) for thousands of years, one that has ruled either outright or has depended on tribal groups to guarantee local peace through their own customary laws; never mind that in addition to state and tribal laws, religious law or Sharia has also been a powerful means through which justice has been served; never mind that historically the state has had its own army but has also depended on local militias to patrol its borders and confront external aggression and thereby maintain national sovereignty. These are not the way our states work, let alone our armies, and therefore what is to be found in Yemen must be backward and unworkable, the "survival," if one will, of "traditional" or "primitive" or at least "nonmodern" political systems that cannot possibly work in the contemporary world and therefore have to be changed.

The danger of this sort of narrow reporting is not only that it reduces a complex reality to certain simple-minded and ill-informed generalizations, but it also fuels a kind of paranoia that can then be used to argue for various U.S. foreign policies toward the country, including military intervention, that are not only unnecessary but could also have ruinous consequences, both for Yemen and for ourselves. If we are told that Yemen is yesterday's Afghanistan (and we went to war there), then it follows that we should go to war in Yemen too, a haven for terrorists and a country on the "brink of chaos." Never mind that the number of terrorists in Yemen number in the hundreds not the thousands and are not mobilized along ethnolinguistic lines like the Taliban; never mind that Yemen like Afghanistan is a mountainous country with a terrain almost impossible for occupying armies to control; never mind that Yemen's history, like Afghanistan's, is full of examples of great imperial powers from the ancient Romans to the Ottoman Turks that have tried to control the country's terrain and failed: These superficial analogies lead us into quagmires from which we seem unable to extricate ourselves (or else we are comforted by the false hope that "this time it will be different").

In short, our encounter with Yemen these days is reduced to nothing more than terror, insecurity, and loose talk about war. This is a shame, for there is a lot more to learn about this fascinating, beautiful, and ancient land, one that is arguably the most different or unique of all the Arab countries in Middle East and North Africa (MENA). Ask people who have traveled widely in the region and been to Yemen, and they will inevitably tell you that they have never encountered a country quite like it, because of its beautiful landscape, its people, its culture, and its history. And yet among Middle East specialists, there is an often unstated assumption that there are four civilizational or political centers in the region (Egypt, Iraq, Syria, and possibly now also the Gulf), and that other areas (be they the Maghreb or North Africa; the Levant that would include Lebanon, Jordan, and Israel; and Afghanistan) are on the periphery of influence and power. Yemen is seen as being at the periphery of the periphery, the poorest of all the MENA countries, the weakest in terms of its state-structure, and the least developed or modernized. In other words, it may be unique and fascinating, but it is not important in world historical terms.

This is to forget that what made Yemen unique was also what made it historically important. Like Oman, it is situated on one of the "corners" of the Arabian Peninsula, that wedge of land that looks like an axe, with its handle sticking out into the Mediterranean world and Central Asia. The tip of the axe head that Yemen is on abuts the Red Sea (which connects it to Africa, especially Egypt) as well as the Indian Ocean, thus linking it simultaneously to three continents: Africa, Europe, and Asia. Geographically speaking, then, Yemen is not so much on a periphery as it is strategically located at a hub or corridor, and this fact has been profoundly important for its history.

Bearing this geography in mind, consider the following.

It is now assumed to be true that earliest man crossed over into Europe and the rest of Asia by two routes: one was by heading north along the African coast of the Red Sea and then crossing over the bridge of land that is Sinai into the European and Asian worlds; the other was by crossing the narrow straight of land that connected the horn of East Africa with southwestern Arabia (the Straight of Mandab) during one of the ice ages when that body of water would have been frozen, and then migrating along the Arabian coasts into Asia. In relation to the spread of earliest man out of Africa, Yemen was hardly at the periphery but one of the "bridges."

While it is true that great agricultural and urban-based civilizations arose in Egypt, Iraq, and Turkey, it is false to assume that agriculture and civilization did not exist in ancient Yemen because it had no rivers upon which flood irrigation depended as in ancient Egypt and Mesopotamia. The greatness, even the genius, of ancient Yemen is that its people learned how to produce great agriculture by harvesting rainwater that came twice a year during the monsoon seasons, and they did so in two ways. One was dam-irrigation works, and Yemenis built the largest dam known in the ancient world (Marib dam) whose construction began sometime around 2,000–1,500 BCE. (So strong is the belief in civilizational centers outside Arabia having the real clout and significance that historians have argued until only quite recently that such greatness could only have come about through outside influence rather than local ingenuity.) The other was based on the fact that Yemen is a very mountainous country, and they created a vast mountain-terraced agricultural system, fed by a complex network of underground and above-ground channels that carried water by gravity from large cisterns to terraces that abutted the mountain sides, all the way from their tips to their bottoms in fertile wadis for hundreds, if not thousands, of feet.

But Yemen was not only a fertile country but was also a trading and commercial empire from at least the beginnings of Marib Dam, carrying frankincense that was highly coveted in funerary rituals of the ancient Europeans from the coasts of Arabia across the great deserts of the peninsula's interior into the Mediterranean world and Central Asia. Ships crossed the Indian Ocean bearing textiles, spices, and semiprecious gems from Asia and landed at one of the many natural harbors on coastal Arabia, from which those same goods were then transported overland along with the frankincense to destinations all over the ancient world. (What is becoming clearer in recent historiography is the extent to which Yemen looked toward Asia and the East as much as, if not more so, than it did Europe and the West.) It hardly makes sense to talk here of center and periphery as opposed to hub and spoke, and because of its trade, Yemen saw the emergence of some of the richest, most powerful, and most fabled kingdoms of the ancient world. The Queen of Sheba, who is mentioned in the Bible and the Qur'an and is a storied figure in both Western and Islamic art and literature, came from the land of Yemen. Yemen came to be known by the Romans as "Arabia Felix" because of its wealth and productivity, and for that reason also a target of their imperial ambitions. Their attempt to annex it as a colony in the rule of Emperor Augustus was perhaps the first example of imperial overreach in Yemen. The Romans got as far as Marib and then were either picked off by the locals or died of thirst; in any case, it was as if they had been swallowed by the desert.

Even less well-known than Yemen's ancient past is the achievement of its medieval Islamic societies. It is true that by this time (and although Yemenis were among the first converts to Islam and fought in the early wars of Islamic conquest), Yemen was seen as a land to be annexed to the great early caliphates rather than as an empire or a power center that could rival them. But partly because it was remote and inaccessible, it became the haven for many a religious or political refugee from caliphate excess or repression, some of whom founded lasting dynasties that would rule Yemen for hundreds of years. At the same time, as already noted, Yemen continued to be at the hub of vast trading networks that stretched from the Indian Ocean into the European world. Not only did Islamic empires outside the peninsula try to control that trade by conquering the land (though never for very long) or by establishing proxy powers there (all of whom became virtually independent precisely because of Yemen's remoteness), but also local dynasties arose to achieve great wealth, power, and distinction. During the reign of the Rasulids, for example, not only did Yemen monopolize the world's coffee trade (through which it became enormously wealthy), but it also became a leader in Islamic art, science, and political administration. It was during this time, too, that one of the great cultural manifestations of Jewry emerged in Yemen, one that would leave a lasting impact on Yemen's art and architecture. As this was the time of the Mongul conquests that cut off the overland trading routes across Asia to Europe, trade by ship across the Indian Ocean became even more important, and much of it had to go through Yemen because of the latter's many natural harbors where ports like Aden thrived. Yemen traders took the opportunity to spread Islam to India and Southeast Asia, and a vibrant exchange of people, goods, and ideas took place between Southwestern Arabia and Southeast Asia that has lasted for over 900 years.

One of the reasons that these historical facts are not as well known as they should be, aside from the sort of center-periphery thinking that has tended to marginalize and downplay Yemen's history, is that it was not until the 1980s and 1990s that modern archaeology (Russian, German, Italian, and American) made truly significant strides in unearthing that history and interpreting it for us. That work has been stalled from time to time because of political events within the country, with so much more yet to be done to clarify Yemen's rich and complex history; publication has also been slow, as it almost always is in archaeology, because of the nature of excavation, material processing, and analysis. But there is enough of it now to suggest that we can never look at Yemen's history with the same lenses as we did in the past. Another reason that it has taken a while for Yemen's history to become better known is that for the medieval period, although there is a rich trove of manuscripts to base it on, it is not conveniently accessible. Many manuscripts have been collected in the national library in Sana'a, but many also exist in private hands (scholarly families in Yemen pride themselves on owning libraries with hundreds, if not thousands, of handwritten manuscripts dating back hundreds of years). It has taken time (and it will continue to take time) for these manuscripts to be unearthed by interested scholars, read, and analyzed. When they are, it is likely that they will alter our understanding of the Islamic medieval period completely. This volume is the most up-to-date synthesis of that data, archaeological and historical, presented in a language that is accessible to the nonspecialist.

If Yemen was great in the ancient and medieval periods, it went into steep decline in the modern period, from roughly the late 18th century until the present, for reasons that seem at one and the same time obvious and obscure. New routes and new forms of transportation dependent upon them made Yemen less important in the global flow of goods and ideas. By the end of the 18th century, for example, Portuguese Brazil and Dutch Surinam grew a coffee deemed by European tastes to be nearly as delicious as Yemen's and certainly much cheaper, and Yemen not only lost its monopoly but also eventually could not even compete. Today's "Yemen Mocha" brand, readily available in most coffee emporia, is more likely to have been imported from Ethiopia than Yemen. It has also been said that Yemen became more inward-looking (though what this means exactly is hard to say) at the same time that it became more internally driven by strife (which, sorry to say, we know exactly what that means), the combination along with its economic decline leading to its marginalization and poverty. When oil was discovered in the 1980s, it was hoped that things now could finally be turned around and Yemen might once again reclaim its past importance and stature, but the reality is rather different for reasons this book will attempt to explain. It is not that the country is unimportant, but its influence in the foreign arena has less to do with power or economic wherewithal in its own right than with it being able to play a delicate balancing act as middle man in great power politics, whether it was between the United States and Russia during the Cold War, or now between militant Islamic forces and the U.S. global war on terrorism.

We are fortunate that we know more about Yemen's modern period than we do any other, thanks to the unending stream of social science scholarship, Euro-American as well as Russian, that has come out since the early 1970s. Indeed, we perhaps know more about modern life in Yemen than we do most other MENA countries, which may seem ironic given how the country is sometimes described as a "blank slate" or "peripheral." That is due to the fact that after the 1962 revolution, it opened itself up to researchers, in fact welcomed them in most instances, which cannot be said of Iraq or Syria. Practically, every discipline has been involved in that highly productive research effort—political science, economics, anthropology, religious studies, linguistics and literature, archaeology, and art history. Without the superb efforts of those scholars, this book certainly would not have been possible. But it is also true that this vast information has never been synthesized before in one volume, making it easier for those who know nothing or little about the country to access it.

Despite this wealth of information on modern Yemen, it has not (or not until quite recently) become more widely known in the corridors of power, let alone the general U.S. public, which is one reason that the overheated generalizations with which this introduction began can be so long-lasting and devastating. Perhaps, this book would correct that; that is certainly the hope of its authors.

Other generalizations that need to be qualified or contextualized are that Yemen is the poorest country in MENA. In some sense, this is correct, but only because the region's mean standard of income has been driven up by the oil economy. When one compares Yemen to other developing countries, it ranks somewhere at the bottom of the middle tier. Another generalization has to do with its despotic government, and that one has to look elsewhere to see democracy at work. Yemen's former president Ali Abdullah Saleh was justly criticized toward the end of his 33-year rule for having become an autocrat, but what is not emphasized in the same breath is that Yemen is also the most democratic country in the peninsula, and arguably was so even in the region, with the exception of Turkey and Israel, until only recently. To add to the irony, when Yemen went through its own "Arab Spring" recently, its long-term president eventually stepped down from power and a nationally elected transitional government was installed in his place, one that is basically secular and committed to republicanism. Compare this with the outcome of the "Arab Spring" in other countries of the region, and Yemen would seem almost the best-case scenario as far as political change is concerned. And, finally, though in world terms Yemen is an underdeveloped country—when one compares what is in place there in terms of a national road system, a public health system, and a universal educational system, to what existed before 1962—one can say that it has made enormous strides that only slowed down or faltered in the last decade. Illiteracy is still a major problem, but since the 1970s, that rate has diminished—and continues to decline—at a relatively rapid rate. While women are still greatly disadvantaged, by comparison to men, there are more women graduates of Sana'a University (the national university in Yemen) than there are men. Access to sufficient and safe drinking water has now become an acute problem in Yemen, a tragedy painfully ironic for a country that was a master of water sustainability in ancient times. The same people who see Yemen as unworkable for this or that reason (only to find that the country in fact manages just fine) now predict a crisis of such existential proportions that the country surely seems doomed. That also remains to be seen, of course.

It serves certain political interests at times to characterize Yemen in such-and-such a way; these simple (and sometimes simple-minded) generalizations do not capture the complex realities of this country as they exist on the ground. Western and Yemeni scholars have joined forces in this book to give a sense of that complexity. Its contents or information is hopefully useful, but that information without being placed in context and properly analyzed is not.

I first came to Yemen in 1978 to do dissertation fieldwork on oral tribal poetry. I spent three years there at that time. I did not return to the country again for another 20 years, a few months before the bombing of the U.S.S. *Cole* in October 2000, the event that changed the U.S. relationship to Yemen to one focused on (even obsessed by) security. When I returned, I was struck by how large the cities had grown and how extensive the national infrastructure had become, and yet in many ways, the people had not changed at all. They were still as hard-working, hospitable, and enterprising as I had remembered them being. But in so far as one can judge anything like a collective attitude, it seemed they were less hopeful about their country's prospects than they were when I left the country in 1980. Then there was an exuberance about being able to realize the goals of the 1962 revolution, an exuberance that flagged and turned sour by the time I returned.

Now Yemen has undergone another revolution, led by a new generation of committed and idealistic youth. They face daunting problems to be sure, but I am not at all certain that they are any more daunting than what the country faced after its first revolution. It is time to be hopeful again.

Geography

Charles Schmitz

What is now called the Republic of Yemen (RoY) is located in the southwest corner of the Arabian Peninsula, a large landmass attached in the north to western Asia (Iraq and Jordan) and surrounded by water on the other three sides. To the west lies the Red Sea, to the south the Arabian Sea, and to the east the Arab Gulf (or sometimes called the Persian Gulf). The RoY has a northern border with the Kingdom of Saudi Arabia and an eastern border with the Sultanate of Oman. Because of its strategic location at the Straight (or *Bab* in Arabic) of Mandab, the country has a long coastline with the Red Sea and another long coastline with the Arabian Sea. It is thus a country that geographically faces two bodies of water that have been historically important in terms of migration to and from Africa, as well as trade routes to the Mediterranean world in one direction and South Asia in the other. But the rest of the country is characterized by geographic features that link it up with the interior of the Peninsula: a central spine of highland mountains running north to south (that link it with Saudi Arabia); and an eastern desert that links it up with the great interior desert of the Arabian Peninsula, the Empty Quarter, and with the interior of Oman. It has no rivers or lakes, being an arid region like the rest of the Peninsula (though not without precipitation).

THE LAND

Lands and seas are shaped primarily by the movement of great tectonic plates pushed along, broken apart, and crushed together by the molten energy at the earth's core. The movement of tectonic plates distributes landmasses across the globe and lifts great landmasses into mountain ranges. The erosive power of weathering aided by the force of gravity sculpts the landscape into the physical forms familiar to us. Weathering and erosion breaks apart primary materials, and gravity transports them downward, scouring valleys and depositing layers of sediment in alluvial plains and coastal shelves.

Yemen provides a striking example of tectonic forces at work. The western and southern coast of the Arabian Peninsula fits like a puzzle piece into the northeastern coastline of Africa, much like the western coast of Africa, which closely corresponds to the eastern coast of South America. Africa was once the inland center of a much larger continent from which India, South America, and Europe all broke away. In recent geological time (40 million years ago), upwelling of magma in the Afar area of Ethiopia has created a triple juncture of divergent fault zones, meaning that the continental crust is continuing to break apart and separate. The famous East African rift valley, the Red Sea, and the Gulf of Aden are all divergent fault zones that converge in the Afar region of Ethiopia. Seafloor spreading associated with divergent fault zones under the Red Sea and the Gulf of Aden is pushing the Arabian plate northwestward away from Africa at a rate of about 2 centimeters (cm) per year.

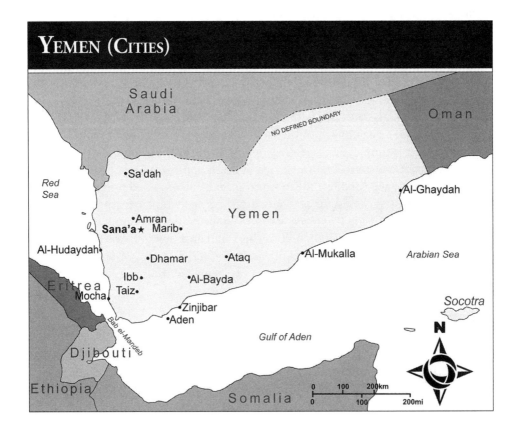

The contemporary configuration of the continental plates is of immediate significance to Yemen for three reasons. The first is Yemen's relative distance from the equator, which is a primary factor in climate. Yemen is located in the subtropical belt just north of the equatorial zone where the sun's energy is concentrated. While Yemen experiences some seasonal difference in the sun's energy, the climate is mostly quite warm. Were it not for the high altitude of Yemen's highlands—capital city Sana'a at 7,200 feet (ft; 2,195 meters [m]) above sea level is much higher than "mile high" Denver (1,609 m or 5,280 ft)—the country would be very hot like the Persian/Arabian Gulf. Second, Yemen long served as a land bridge between Africa and Eurasia. Archeologists today suggest that southern Arabia was a link in the human migrations out of Africa and that there were many migrations into this region and through it to Asia, in particular. While the land bridge to the north in the Sinai Peninsula was more continuous and may have been the preferred route for migrations, Yemen apparently also served as a link in some of these migrations out of Africa at Bab al-Mandab (about 40 kilometers [km] or 25 miles [mi] of water currently separates Africa from Yemen), and during periods of glaciations when sea level was much lower and the distance was minimal. Recent research points even to multiple migrations out of Africa and some evidence of migrations back into Africa again. Yemen not only served as a land bridge between Africa and Eurasia, but it also served and serves as an important link between the Mediterranean and the Indian Ocean. The Red Sea and the Gulf of Aden have long been strategically important waterways connecting the trading networks of the Indian Ocean and farther east with the Mediterranean, Europe, and North Africa. The ancient Egyptians

Socotra Island with dragon blood tree. (Jan Krejza/Dreamstime.com)

SOCOTRA ISLAND

Socotra (also spelled Soqotra) is an island in the Arabian Sea about 220 mi from Yemen's eastern coast. Its extinct volcanic peaks rise to about 5,000 ft above sea level and at night, are shrouded in mist. Lying at the crossroads of Africa, Asia, and Europe, it has experienced biological cross-fertilizations over millennia that have resulted in some of the most exotic plants and animals found anywhere on earth. It is home to hundreds of endemic species, including plants, reptiles, and snails. Among the most legendary of these is the "dragon blood" tree, so named because of its sap that is blood-red in color. UNESCO made Socotra a World Heritage Center to help protect and preserve the island's unique habitat. Its inhabitants speak a language, Socotran, that is entirely distinct from Arabic and may be related to South Arabic that was spoken in Yemen long ago. Because of its pristine beauty, there has been talk of developing the island as an ecotourism destination (which it already is to some extent), but such plans raise fears among islanders and environmentalists alike about the possible dangers to the island's pristine environment.

---

connected the Nile to the Red Sea providing a direct water link, and the Suez Canal serves the same purpose in the modern era. Today, about 40 percent of the oil transported in the world passes through the Bab al-Mandab (www.eia.gov). Land routes through the Arabian Peninsula from one sea to the other have been just as important as water routes during much of human history, and one of the more important overland trade routes followed the western mountains through Sana'a, Mecca, and north to the Levant and the Mediterranean. The ancient Egyptians, the Portuguese, the Ottomans, the British, the Italians, the Russians, and now the Americans are among those that came to Yemen to control and police these trade routes.

GEOLOGY AND TOPOGRAPHY

The most important topographic feature on the Arabian Peninsula is the east-west tilt of the Arabian plate. The Arabian plate is raised in the west and submerged in the east. The eastern portion of the Peninsula is flat and extends under the Persian/ Arabia Gulf and eastern Iraq where it collides with and submerges under the Eurasian plate, lifting the high mountains of western Iran. The uplift of the western portion of the Arabian Peninsula is only the latest in a much longer history of tectonic movement. At one time, what is now Yemen was submerged under the sea. Eroded material carried by rivers was deposited in great layers of sediment on the bottom of the sea. Sea shells now found in rocks high atop mountain peaks attest to this history as does the presence of oil and gas that were formed in the period when what is now Yemen was under the sea.

Western coastal Yemen (also called the Tihama) is a narrow strip of alluvial plains that are formed from very recent deposits eroded by the fluvial action of rain and

Port city of Aden. (Karim Sahib/AFP/Getty Images)

rivers descending from Yemen's western and southern highlands. These are the hot and dry narrow coastal plains where Yemen's famous ports such as Al-Hudaydah, Mocha, Aden, and Al-Mukalla are located. The distinctive natural harbor of Aden is a caldera, a collapsed volcano with the city of Aden sitting on a remnant of the rim that juts into the sea. The coastal area is anywhere between 20 and 50 km wide (from approximately 12 to 30 mi) and consists of a variety of microenvironments including marine, mudflat, and marshes.

From this plain rises precipitously and dramatically a spectacular range of mountains extending north from the southern tip of Yemen all the way to Jordan. Along the western ridge, no more than 24 mi inland from the Red Sea, the peaks of Yemen rise abruptly to heights of more than 9,843 ft (3,000 m) above sea level. The highest peak on the Arabian Peninsula is Jabal al-Nabi Shu'ayb west of Sana'a at 12,033 ft (3,666 m) above sea level. These mountains contain many large *wadis* (or valleys) that flood during the monsoon rainy season; their waters flow eventually into the sea unless they are harvested by irrigation works. The geology of the western mountains of Yemen is dominated by igneous rock formed by cooling magma in the form of intrusive basement layers, volcanic eruptions, or surface basalt flows. Most of the highest elevations around Sana'a and south to Aden are dominated by recent basalt flows. To the far north of Yemen into modern Saudi Arabia and the region southeast of Sana'a to Abyan and western Shabwah are exposed basement rocks, some of pre-Cambrian age—the oldest rocks exposed on the surface of the earth.

Eastern Yemen is dominated by layers of sedimentary rocks deposited during this period, when this area was covered by seas. Separating the sedimentary rocks of the eastern region from the west is a large graben, or block depression that has fallen between parallel faults, that runs from the Al-Jawf southeastward toward Marib and through Shabwah to the Gulf of Aden. It is in this depression on the eastern flank of the Yemeni highlands (sometimes also called the Sayhad region, after the desert by that name on the outskirts of the Empty Quarter) where the ancient Yemeni civilizations of Ma'in and Saba took root. Northeast of Marib begin the high rolling sands of the Empty Quarter that extends across the Arabian Peninsula to the United Arab Emirates.

CLIMATE

Temperature

Climate is the long-term average of precipitation and temperature. Weather is what we experience from day to day; climate is the average of weather conditions over many decades or centuries. Temperature is most strongly related to distance from the equator: the equatorial zone receives the greatest energy from the sun, and the poles receive the least. Yemen lies in the northern hemisphere between the latitudes of 12 and 19 degrees, which means that Yemen is in the subtropical zone well north of the equator but south of the Tropic of Cancer. Subtropical regions receive a large amount of the sun's energy and generally are quite warm throughout the year, as in Yemen. They are some distance from the equator, and thus, like Yemen, these zones do experience some seasonality. In the summer the sun passes directly overhead, and in the winter it is lower on the horizon, lowering temperatures. In 2005, the mean July temperature in Sana'a was 74.1°F (23.4°C), whereas December's mean in Sana'a was 55.6°F (13.1°C). Sana'a's old houses were built with the sun's movement in mind; southern sides of the houses have lots of glass that allows the sun's rays to warm the rooms in the winter, whereas the northern sides of the buildings have fewer windows to keep the summer sun's rays out.

Temperature is also determined by elevation above sea level. Yemen's capital Sana'a at 7,200 ft (2,195 m) above sea level has pleasantly mild weather, whereas the port cities of Aden and Al-Hudaydah along the narrow alluvial plain of the coast experience very warm temperatures most of the year. During the winter months, mean low temperatures in Sana'a are just above freezing, while on the coast in Aden and Al-Hudaydah, they are closer to 68.0°F (20°C). Average summer highs on the coast are 104°F (40°C), whereas in the highlands and Sana'a, they are a much more pleasant 90.0°F (32.0°C). Yemen's high mountain elevations provide more than mild temperatures; the mountains also play a key role in precipitation.

Moisture

Moisture, the second element of climate, is provided largely by the seas. Yemen is close to water, but its location within the largest belt of aridity on the planet, stretching from Mauritania across the Saharan Desert, the Arabian Peninsula, Iran, and into Central Asia, makes Yemen very dry. The Arabian Peninsula, in particular, is extremely dry. The Empty Quarter is a vast sea of sand that receives little rainfall, and the coastal areas of the Persia Gulf are similarly dry. The coastal regions of Yemen and the northeastern deserts rarely receive more than 100 mm (4 in.) of rain per year and will typically only receive trace amounts of rain.

View of Shibam, Wadi Hadhramawt. (Vladimir Melnik/Dreamstime.com)

What makes Yemen unique on the Arabian Peninsula is the rain that falls in the highlands. The southern highland cities of Ibb and Taiz receive close to 1,200 mm (47 in.) of rain per year, similar to the East Coast of the United States where, for example in Baltimore, Maryland, an average of 990 mm (39 in.) of rain falls per year. Nowhere else in the Arabian Peninsula is there significant rainfall, and Yemen's rain has nourished settled populations who developed complex civilizations in eastern Yemen more than two thousand years ago. Yemen's tribesmen in the highlands have long been settled agriculturalists, whereas in the rest of the Arabian Peninsula, desert Bedouins dominated until recently.

The rain in Yemen's highlands is caused by a seasonal shift in prevailing winds that draw moist tropical air over the high Yemen mountains in the spring and summer. The Asian monsoon is caused both by an extreme low pressure cell that develops over central Asia in the summer months and the seasonal movement of the intertropical convergence zone (ITCZ), the zone of intense insulation where the sun's rays are perpendicular to the earth. The Asian low pressure draws air toward the continent from the relative high pressure cells forming over the cooler water of the oceans. In Yemen, it is the movement of the ITCZ that is the dominant factor in producing the onshore shift in prevailing winds. The fishing season ends in Yemen when the monsoonal winds begin in April or May, because the onshore winds produce rough seas and make fishing in small boats, the vast majority of fishing vessels, impossible.

The lift provided by the wind pushing the moist air over the highlands (orographic lift) causes the air to cool, the water to condense, and the rain to fall. The moist air drops most of its rain on the southwestern portions of the Yemeni highlands. As the wind carries the air northeast over the highlands and down toward Marib and the Al-Jawf into the central desert regions, the air descends, warms, and absorbs moisture, causing a rain shadow in the northeastern portions of the country. Thus, Yemen's rainfall is concentrated in the southern highlands where the summer months are very green. Little or no rain falls on the narrow coastal plains of Yemen along the Red Sea and the Gulf of Aden, though these plains receive water in the form of intermittent rivers during the rains in the highlands whose floods carve deep wadis in the mountains on their way to the coast.

Yemen's rainy season is on a tropical cycle associated with the northward shift of the sun in the summer, rather than a winter rainy season like in the northern portions of the Middle East such as the Atlas Mountains in Morocco and Algeria, the Zagros Mountains in Iran, or the Taurus Mountains in Turkey. (The traditional flood cycle of the Nile before the construction of Nasser Dam shared Yemen's tropical seasonality, because the headwaters of the Nile are in the nearby highlands of Ethiopia, Kenya, and Uganda.) Ibb and Taiz receive most of their rainfall between April and August. These cities in the southwestern highlands are the wettest cities in Yemen, and they are the heart of what are known as the "middle" regions of Yemen, located between Aden and Sana'a, the two central urban poles of Yemeni national identity. The "middle" regions produce the greatest agricultural wealth in Yemen.

Yemen and the Arabian Peninsula have not always been as dry as they are today. In the ten thousand years since the last glaciations, Yemen has had periods of much greater precipitation, even to the extent of lakes forming and the development of soils associated with marshes, which indicates that the water balance was positive rather than strongly negative as it is today. Archeologists have found prehistoric settlements in Yemen associated with old lakeshores. Human migrations out of Africa or from Eurasia into the Arabian Peninsula occurred in wetter periods, when the southern Arabian Peninsula was quite hospitable to human habitation.

ECOLOGICAL ADAPTATIONS

ARABIA FELIX

Southern Arabia was called Arabia Felix (Latin for "Happy Arabia") by the Greeks and Romans, because they found green mountains where they were expecting only desert and high civilizations where they were expecting barbarians. Yemen stood in contrast to the rest of the Arabian Peninsula with its large-scale agriculture (the Dam of Marib) in the outskirts of the great central desert of Arabia known as the Empty Quarter and its literate kingdoms with their monumental architecture that flourished as a result of the trade in spices, incense, precious metals, and textiles that were brought overland by caravans, wending their way from the coasts of Oman and Yemen northwestward to the Mediterranean world.

Yemen is rich in water and arable land relative to the rest of the Arabian Peninsula, but that only means that Yemen is less desolate than some of the more desolate places on earth. The Ministry of Agriculture estimates that only about 3 percent of Yemen is arable, but the extent of cultivated land varies considerably each year depending upon rains. In the last few years, Yemen's land under cultivation has varied between 1.3 and 1.5 million hectares (ha) out of a total area of 45.5 million ha. In the United States, about 18 percent of land is arable, in Morocco about 14 percent, and in Syria 28 percent. By comparison, the rest of countries of the Arabian Peninsula have smaller percentages of arable land than Yemen. And though it really rains in Yemen unlike in the rest of the Arabian Peninsula, water is still scarce. Yemen today has one of the lowest per capita freshwater supplies in the world. This is a result of rising population and limited water supplies. Yemen's water comes only from the rain that falls in the highlands. It has no rivers bringing water from other areas such as the Nile in Egypt, the Tigres and Euphrates in Iraq, or the Hindus in Pakistan. And it does not yet have the capital to invest in desalination plants. The surrounding oil-rich countries with smaller populations can invest in capital- and energy-intensive desalination plants that increase their freshwater supply and mask the true scarcity of natural water.

Yemenis have had to innovate in order to adapt to their arid environs. Fortunately, they are very innovative. Over the millennia, they built ingenious systems of sustainable agriculture, made use of marginal lands with livestock, utilized the wealth of the sea, engaged in trade with the wider world, and went in search of additional sources of wealth outside of Yemen in order to make a living. In general, there are two agricultural systems in Yemen: one adapted to use the rain that falls in the highlands, and the second designed to utilize the runoff that comes rushing down the wadis from the highlands across the coastal plains toward the sea or into the desert in the east where the first civilizations arose. Both systems have long been supplemented by shallow hand-dug wells, where possible. Livestock in Yemen has been an important means of utilizing scarce resources on marginal lands, particularly in the more arid desert regions of the east. Yemenis have also made good use of the sea for fishing and for transport of people and goods. About a third of Yemenis still work today in agriculture, livestock, and fishing. The scarcity of natural resources in Yemen makes trade and migration with the wider world an important factor in the Yemeni economy. In various periods of history, Yemen has possessed an important resource sought by the world; it was frankincense in antiquity, coffee in the 1600s, and oil in the last two decades. In other periods, Yemenis went abroad to seek their fortunes: sometimes as laborers as in Saudi Arabia and the Gulf in the 1970s and 1980s, sometimes as merchants as in East Africa and Southeast Asia, and other times as religious leaders as in the case of the Alawis from south Yemen who have emigrated to South and Southeast Asia over the last five centuries. Yemenis from the Hadhramawt were the palace guards of the Moghuls of India in Hyderabad.

HIGHLAND AND LOWLAND AGRICULTURE

In the highlands, Yemenis have ingeniously captured the rain that falls by terracing the mountain slopes. Stone walls built across the slopes of the high mountains and in the rocky valleys capture surface runoff from the rain. When the rainwater slows or pools behind the walls, it drops its sediment load that gradually develops into soils behind the walls. Over many centuries, the rocky slopes of the mountains became bands of fertile soils held in place by the rock-terrace walls. In the higher elevations of Yemen, people have often laid rocks across a small crevice or depression in the solid rock of the mountainside in the hopes of creating a new terrace. Contrasting a line of few small rocks lain across a bare area of solid rock with the fertile soils further down the mountainsides lends an appreciation of the incredibly long history of labor investment in Yemen's fertile lands.

The terrace system not only allowed soils to develop but also ingeniously utilized scarce water by recycling the runoff from one terrace to the next. Drainage holes at the base of the terrace walls allow water that has percolated through the soil of one terrace to flow onto the surface of the soil in the next terrace below, thus maximizing soil and plant absorption of rainwater.

Rain-fed agriculture is still the dominant form of agriculture in Yemen today. The Ministry of Agriculture estimates that today just under half of the cropped area depends upon rain for its water. These fields are all in the highlands of the governorates of Taiz, Ibb, Dhamar, Raymah, Sana'a, 'Amran, Mahwit, Hajjah, Sa'dah, and Al-Hudaydah. Al-Hudaydah is by far the most productive agricultural area of all governorates, because it comprises the greatest portion of the western slopes of the highlands and the entire coastal plain along the Red Sea where spate irrigation (see below) predominated in the past and mechanized wells predominate today. Almost one-quarter of the land under cultivation in Yemen's 21 governorates is located in Al-Hudaydah.

Agricultural terraces in Wadi Al-Ahjar, circa 1980. (Steven C. Caton)

The second system of agriculture in Yemen depends upon capturing the floods of water that descend the valleys from the highlands on the way to the sea. These waters are little understood by outsiders. Yemen has no permanent rivers. The wadis that lead down from the highlands to the sea are washes where rains in the highlands collect in powerful floods that can last for about 20 hours or as little as a few hours. During this period, large quantities of water flow like huge rivers through the valleys, but for most of the year, no water flows at all in the wadi.

For lowland coastal areas of Al-Hudaydah, Taiz, Lahaj, Abyan, Shabwah, and in the eastern side of the highlands where the mountains descend into desert such as in Marib, the Al-Jawf, or the Hadhramawt, capturing rainwater floods and making use of them are essential to survival. Yemenis have developed a system of spate irrigation that is able to effectively utilize large amounts of water over a short period of time. At the mouth of the wadi where it enters the alluvial plain, a series of canals are dug that branch laterally from the mouth of the wadi. Off each canal, a series of small fields are surrounded by dirt walls or bunds that are about 2 m high. Each field is usually no more than a quarter or half acre. More canals are dug further down the wadi on the alluvial plain, and more small fields with high surrounding walls are built. In the rainy season, farmers watch for storms in the highlands, and when it appears that water is coming, farmers post themselves along the upper portions of the wadi with guns to use as signals that the water has reached them. As the water arrives, it is diverted into the channels closest to the wadi's mouth first, and each field is filled to about a meter high and then closed. When all of the fields on a channel have been filled to a meter depth, the channel is closed and water flows to the next series of channels where the process is repeated. The meter of water is allowed to soak into the soil, and then the fields are plowed and planted. This water is sufficient to grow most crops over a full

---

SAYLA OR FLOOD WATERS

Sayla is an Arabic word that is used in Yemen to refer to streambeds as well as the bodies of water they contain (hence, "stream" or "flood" might be another translation). Visitors to Sana'a during the rainy season can experience the power and spectacle of these floods by watching the Sayla in the Old City. In the late 1990s, a foreign development project paved the road and lined the banks of the riverbed with cut-rock walls. On most days, the Sayla is full of taxis, trucks, motorbikes, and cars in a crush of rushing traffic. But at the sound of thunder, people immediately get their vehicles out of the Sayla, because very quickly, it converts into a rushing river of water 5–8 ft high. Vehicles caught in the flood are smashed against bridge supports or washed like sewage toward the city outskirts. Often within a couple of hours, the Sayla returns to normal, and cars and trucks once again take to the road on their business.

season. Any less water and crops will die; thus, the critical factor is the meter depth. The Yemeni system of multiple channels with a myriad of small fields is uniquely adapted to maximize the area that receives a full meter depth of water in any given season. When the Soviets ran South Yemen in the 1970s and 1980s, they tried to rationalize the Yemeni system by creating large parcels of land that could be efficiently mechanized. But a large area of land is difficult to fill at a depth of a meter when the source of water is so unpredictable. As the local Yemeni irrigation administrator explained, the Russians thought the wadi flowed like the Volga! The Soviet projects were returned to the Yemeni system shortly after the Russians left.

CROPS AND THEIR GEOGRAPHY

Yemenis adopted crops suited to the various climatic zones. Some crops do well in highland rain-fed agriculture, whereas other crops are better suited to spate irrigation in the hotter climates of the coast and lowland interior. In the past, Yemen's staple crop was sorghum whose drought-tolerance is well suited to arid and semiarid environments, and whose leaf and stems are very useful as fodder. Even today, sorghum is the most widely cultivated cereal in Yemen. Most cereals are cultivated in the rain-fed highland terraces and comprise about half of the total area cultivated. It makes up about 60–70 percent of the land devoted to cereal production, and the majority of land dedicated to fodder and sorghum is cultivated on almost half the agricultural land in Yemen (Republic of Yemen, Ministry of Agriculture). Other cereals are cultivated in Yemen in lesser quantities: Wheat and millet are the most widely cultivated cereals after sorghum; barley and corn are less extensively cultivated.

After cereals, the most widely cultivated crop is fodder due to the high value of animal feed. The dominant fodder crop is again sorghum, followed by nitrogen fixing clover (berseem) and grasses. The lowland arid regions of Yemen in the governorates of Marib, Abyan, Lahaj, Al-Hudaydah, Al-Jawf, Hadhramawt, Shabwah, and Al-Mahrah, all have a much higher percentage of their arable land cultivated in fodder, because livestock are more important to these regions. In desert regions, rains are intermittent and geographically dispersed. Unlike planted crops, livestock are mobile and can go to where the rain has fallen and forage has sprouted. Fodder is cultivated in these regions to supplement foraging. The main livestock in Yemen are goat and sheep (Republic of Yemen, Ministry of Agriculture). Goats are hardy and can handle the heat, so they are more prevalent in the hotter and more arid regions. Hadhramawt accounts for almost a quarter of all goats, followed by Shabwah and Abyan. These three governorates produce almost half of all goats in Yemen. Sheep are less hardy and are more vulnerable to heat, but are a major food source. Sheep are more predominant in the highlands where it is cooler, but Hadhramawt, Al-Jawf, and Shabwah are still major producers of sheep. Al-Hudaydah is the largest producer of sheep along with Sa'dah and Hajjah.

Farmers pruning a qat tree. (Khaled Fazaal AFP/Getty Images)

Qat is almost as widely cultivated as fodder with about 12 percent of total land area (Republic of Yemen, Ministry of Agriculture). It is also a tropical highland crop like coffee and does not grow in the lowlands below about 3,280 ft (1,000 m) above sea level, so qat in Aden and Al-Hudaydah must come daily from highland areas. There is far less qat in Hadhramawt because its climate is not conducive to its production. The Governorate of Sana'a surrounding the capital city of Sana'a is by far the largest producer of qat followed by nearby 'Amran. A quarter of all the land cultivated with qat is in Sana'a Governorate, and Sana'a and 'Amran together possess 40 percent of all land cultivated with qat (Republic of Yemen, Ministry of Agriculture).

The other "cash" crops—nonfood items—cultivated in Yemen are coffee, tobacco, and cotton. Coffee was at one time a major source of wealth in Yemen. In the 16th and 17th centuries, Yemen was the major source of the world's coffee. But coffee production has declined, and now it is cultivated on about a quarter of the land dedicated to qat. Sana'a cultivates almost a third of Yemen's coffee, followed by Raymah. Cotton needs a warmer climate and more water, since it takes a full eight months to mature. Yemen's cotton is cultivated in Al-Hudaydah, Abyan, and to a lesser extent in Lahaj.

Yemen also produces in smaller quantities a variety of fruits, vegetables, and legumes, mostly for the domestic market.

QAT CHEWING

The shrub *Catha edulis* is known in Yemen as *qat*. Only the topmost succulent leaves of this plant's branches are chewed for the "buzz" or slightly euphoric high their juices effect. This is due to an alkaloid called cathinone, an amphetamine-like stimulant. (The U.S. government has banned qat in the United States.) There are certain negative physiological effects associated with its consumption over time, including insomnia, acid buildup in the stomach and esophagus, mild constipation, temporary impotence, and suppression of appetite. It is difficult to know precisely how many people in Yemen, both men and women, chew qat, though it is reasonable to suppose that it is a large majority. Its leaves are chewed fresh, and its markets are usually near urban markets. Chewing of qat is a social activity that takes place mostly at home, during which politics, business, and all manner of social issues are debated and even decided upon. Qat cultivation consumes a fair amount of water in a land with water shortages and is therefore deemed wasteful by donor countries that would like to see it banned. A more realistic approach to the problem is to improve the efficiency of water use among qat farmers.

RESOURCES

Groundwater

In the past, both the terraced system of the highlands and the spate irrigation system of the lowlands were supplemented by shallow wells. Human labor was used to dig wells to a depth of 200 ft or more in order to gain access to groundwater. Wells supplemented flood irrigation or rain-fed highland fields and allowed crops to be cultivated with long maturity such as cotton, or that required more water such as fresh fruit and vegetable crops, or permanent crops such as trees. Reliance on human labor limited the depth at which groundwater could be exploited for most of human history in Yemen. In the last 50 years, however, the introduction of drilling rigs and mechanized pumps has dramatically changed Yemeni agriculture. Drilling rigs and mechanized pumps allow people to gain access to water at much greater depths than hand-dug wells. Yemenis now can draw upon much more water than before, and until recently, this has led to significant improvements in agricultural productivity because water supplies were now more regular. They have abandoned to some extent the flood irrigation techniques and relied more upon well water. The Ministry of Agriculture indicates that today 32 percent of the cropped area in 2009 relied upon wells, whereas 17 percent relied upon flood or spate irrigation. In the past, much more of the cropped area was irrigated exclusively by spate irrigation and less by wells.

    The improved productivity, however, has come at a heavy cost in terms of the de-
pletion of groundwater supplies. The FAO's "Aquastat" (FAO stands for Food and
Agriculture Organization of the United Nations) estimates that Yemen is drawing
160 percent of its annual groundwater recharge, meaning that Yemenis are pumping more water out of the ground than the rain replenishes each year. Yemenis have
known this for some time because groundwater has been falling. Wells have to be
drilled deeper in order to produce more water. Those that have the capital to hire a
drilling rig and run a pump win, and those that don't lose. Until recently, there has
been little regulation of the new drilling technology, and consequently, groundwater
levels have dropped significantly, leaving most of the hand-dug wells without water.
The major urban area of Taiz has essentially run out of water. Residents receive water
through the municipal system one day per week, and the rest of the time purchase
water from trucks or local vendors, but agriculture uses the bulk of Yemen's water.
About 90 percent of water is used for agriculture and the rest for urban areas. Of
the water used for agriculture, about 40–60 percent is used for the cultivation of qat.

Groundwater and Qat

The impact of qat is controversial. It consumes a large amount of water, almost
all of which is drawn from groundwater. It is a perennial plant that is harvested
by intense watering, followed by cutting the tender shoots that sprout a few days
after watering. Farmers flood the area around the qat plants to force the new sprouts.
Both the conveyance of the water from the well to the field or plot and the flooding
of the plot are wasteful, and better practices such as using pipes to convey water
and other means of water conservancy would make the use of water more efficient.
Adopting better conservation practices requires both knowledge and the financial
means to invest in supplies. In recent years, both knowledge and new technologies
have begun to spread in Yemen (and not just in qat production), but not nearly
at the pace to make a significant difference in the overall water balance. For now,
qat production consumes a large quantity of valuable water.

    In terms of the economy, qat is a very valuable cash crop and an important source
of income for rural families. Though qat production uses only 12 percent of cultivated land, it accounts for about a third of the value of agricultural production in
Yemen. Agriculture constitutes about 10 percent of GDP (gross domestic product),
and qat accounts for about another 3 percent of GDP (Republic of Yemen, Central
Statistical Organization). Yemen is a poor country, and poverty in Yemen is concentrated in the rural areas. In this context, qat can be seen as an internal income
transfer from urban areas where the primary markets are located to the surrounding
rural highland regions where it is produced. Income is a strong correlate to micro
food security, and qat production therefore increases rural food security—defined
as access to regular and sufficient food supplies—by increasing rural income. In
Yemen's macro food security situation, qat plays a different role though, consuming
water and land that could be used to increase Yemen's domestic food supply and
decreasing food imports to some extent.

NATIONAL FOOD SECURITY

Whereas sorghum was the staple crop in Yemen for most of its history, now the staple grains are rice and wheat, both of which are imported. All of Yemen's rice is imported as well as the vast majority of its wheat. In 2009, cereal imports alone constituted 12 percent of the value of imports, and food was a quarter of imports by value (Republic of Yemen, Central Statistical Organization). Yemen's population is growing, and its demand for food has increased tremendously. Water and arable land in Yemen are limited, and so increasing amounts of Yemen's food supply must come from imports. Importing food is not unusual; this is the benefit of international trade. Many countries, particularly in the arid Middle East, are dependent upon imports to satisfy their food needs. But reliance on food imports means that food is dependent upon income from exports and international trade. If there is a sudden rise in food prices, such as that happened in 2007 when global wheat prices doubled, or there is a decline in export revenues, which happens when a country is highly dependent upon just a few commodities (e.g., oil) for the bulk of its exports, then the food bill will consume a larger proportion of the hard currency earned from exports or in the national reserve.

In this context of the macroeconomic role of food imports, many observers both Yemeni and foreign lament the fact that qat has largely replaced coffee, a cash export crop. Coffee exports would help reduce Yemen's trade deficit, and reducing qat production would conserve water as qat cultivation techniques are particularly water intensive (though this is not without controversy; see "Water Crisis" in Chapter 7), but relying upon agricultural exports may not be the wisest choice for Yemen given its water scarcity.

VIRTUAL WATER

Food is stored in water or what water experts call "virtual" water, a concept created by John Anthony Allan (King's College, London School of Oriental Studies, London). Crops take a certain amount of water to produce, depending on the biological makeup of the crops themselves as well as soil and climatic conditions. It may be more economical for countries like Yemen, which are relatively water "poor," to import certain crops like rice or sugar rather than to grow these crops themselves. Yemen must not only consider the role of food in its international trade strategy, but also include the impact of virtual water in its macroeconomic calculations. Yemen's domestic water scarcity suggests a trade strategy in which Yemen imports "virtual" water in food and exports "dry" goods that do not use much water. But depending on food imports for crops considered essential to the daily diet as rice, sugar, and wheat might also make a country food insecure. A country like Yemen must measure such insecurity against the insecurity of an unsustainable water supply made ever more precarious by growing water-thirsty crops.

EMIGRATION

An additional Yemeni adaptation to scarce land and water has been to leave the country. Yemenis have long emigrated in search of fortunes elsewhere, but they maintain a connection with their ancestral home, and their earnings have always been an important part of the Yemeni economy. At the conclusion of the civil war between the Royalists and the Republicans in the north, Yemenis entered a period of rapidly increasing income, eating better, living longer, and reproducing more. Yemen's postwar blossoming in the 1970s and 1980s, in both the north and the south, was a result of additional wealth from remittances sent back to Yemen from workers abroad. Resource scarcity in Yemen has always pushed Yemenis to look for opportunities abroad to make income. Yemenis have gone overseas in search of business opportunities, in the service of empires, as religious leaders, and in recent history as laborers.

For centuries, Hadhramis have migrated to South and Southeast Asia, where they are important civic, business, and political leaders. Money from these Yemenis maintained the spectacular palaces of the Wadi Hadhramawt. Hadhramis and Yemenis from other parts of Yemen, particularly the Taiz region, have become important business leaders in other countries as well. In Saudi Arabia, some of the wealthiest business people are Yemenis. The Bin Mahfouz family, for example, are extremely influential business leaders in Saudi Arabia, and they are of Yemeni stock. Yemenis came to the United States in the 1920s and settled in the agricultural fields of California and in the Detroit region to work in the auto industry. Detroit and Dearborn are still centers of Yemeni culture in the United States, and large numbers of Yemenis now reside in Oakland, California, as well. During the oil boom in the Gulf States in the 1970s, they flocked to the new centers of construction, and the money they sent home transformed the Yemeni economy. Remittances sent back by Yemenis abroad are still an important contributor to the economy. Remittances have held steady at about 1.2 billion U.S. dollars over the last 20 years. This is an important source of foreign exchange for Yemen, and households at all income levels benefit substantially—about 8 percent of income on average—from remittances. A key to Yemen's current economic transition is the ability of Yemeni workers to migrate in large numbers again to the Gulf Cooperation Council (GCC) countries.

IMMIGRATION

In spite of Yemen being a relatively poor country, it has received refugees from other countries in recent years. Fleeing war and depressed economic conditions in Somalia, thousands of young people, mostly male, have been welcomed in Yemen, though the conditions in the refugee camps located in southern Yemen are wretched and hardly better there than what life provided in the home country. These refuges are not likely to find a permanent home in Yemen and await relocation to Somalia once conditions improve there or to another country that will receive them. Meanwhile, security fears on the part of the United States have led to suspicions that the ranks of younger

Somali refugees have been infiltrated by al-Shabab, an Islamist force in Somalia, who may hope to spread their fight against the U.S.-backed government in Yemen.

Rural to urban migration is also an important demographic trend in the last 40 years, due in part to an agricultural system under stress from drought and groundwater depletion (due to a number of factors). This migration has led to very rapid urban growth in recent years. Sana'a, the capital, is one of the fastest grow-ing cities on earth, not only due to national population growth rate but also due to migration from the economically depressed countryside. This phenomenon places great pressure on municipalities to provide adequate public services such as housing, electricity, and water, and on the local economy to absorb essentially farmwork-ers with relatively little education and few employable skills in an urban context. Poor people and beggars were infrequent sights in Sana'a 40 years ago, but now are ubiquitous, especially older people and young children.

ETHNIC GROUPS

Yemen is made up of several ethnicities, whose particularities will be described in detail in Chapter 5. It is important here to understand how these ethnic groups have adapted differently to the environment, both natural and social.

Tribes

Though tribes will be discussed in detail in Chapter 5, broad outlines of their orga-nization are mentioned here as it pertains to the natural environment. Part of the tribes are Bedouin, located in the foothills of the Empty Quarter in the eastern part of the country. (They are known by the Arabic term "*badu*" in Yemen.) Traditionally, they herded their camels on pastures fed by rainwater during the winter months and congregated in oases settlements when water becomes scarce and pastures wither in the hotter summer months, but now many have taken to a mixed mode of livelihood, with many of them owning and working farmland outside of Marib. The percentage of Bedouin is a tiny fraction of the overall population, and yet they are important politically on the eastern borders of the country. Heavily armed, they sometimes have served as a battle-seasoned force for the government in times of national defense. Because of their location in the border zone between Saudi Arabia and Yemen, they have also been active in trade and smuggling.

The other tribal group, known as *qaba'il* (sing. *qabilah*), is far greater, and the fact that these tribes are settled is an important feature: tribesmen elsewhere in the Peninsula are thought of as badu, and they are distinguished from peoples called settled (or *hadar* in Arabic) who live in oases, towns, and cities. But in Yemen, settled tribesmen are in the majority. The exact figures are hard to come by and controver-sial in any case (depending on whether one sides politically for or against the tribes): they range as high as 50 percent to as low as 12 percent, with a figure around 35 per-cent being more likely for the population as a whole. Tribesmen have traditionally lived in the countryside, close to their agricultural fields, but in the decades since the 1962 Revolution, they have increasingly come to populate the rapidly growing towns and cities, partly because of changing economic opportunities as they left their farms to join the army (in which tribesmen are by far the majority) or have taken on piece meal work in the cities as taxi drivers, guards of private residences, and sellers of qat, or because of the troubled agricultural system that can no longer sustain the rates of growth seen in the 1990s. As a result of these economic trends, tribes have come more and more to live in urban rather rural settings, and they have also changed in their outlooks, become more modern and educated.

Other Groups

Though the *saadah* or descendants of the Prophet Muhammad were once the ruling elite of Yemen, their political power has greatly diminished since the 1962 Revolution that overthrew the Zaydi Imamate and established the Republic. Because of their education, especially in the technical professions such as engineering and medicine, they retain influence, and some have also been very successful in business. The greatest threat to their identity, however, came not with the Revolution but with rise of the Wahhabi Salafi movement in Yemen from the 1990s until the present. This movement denigrated Zaydi spiritual leaders as Shia "unbelievers," further undermining saadah legitimacy and authority, especially in the northern parts of the country like the City of Sa'dah and its environs, and leading eventually to a populist uprising fighting for recognition of its rights. This now has morphed into a full-scale confrontation with the central government, the details of which are described in Chapter 7.

On the opposite end of the status hierarchy in traditional Yemen were the servants, known as *khaddam* and *akhdam.* The *khaddam* hardly exist any longer as a viable group, there no longer being much demand for their traditional services as butchers, circumcisers, masters of ceremonies at weddings and other public gatherings, or town criers and praise singers. Most have "assimilated" into other ways of life. It is the akhdam, presumed to be descendants of slaves because of their African racial phenotypes, who have grown in population (though exact figures are again hard to come by) and for the most part are found in the large towns and cities of Yemen, living in slums on their outskirts, and barely making a living as street cleaners or beggars.

Religious differences are another important marker in the Yemeni population. Sunnis are a little over 50 percent of the population, with various denominations of Shias (mostly Zaydis and a few Ismailis) making up the rest. A small population of Sufis can be found in Sana'a and in the Hadhramawt.

THREE FACETS OF YEMEN'S POPULATION: SIZE, DYNAMICS, AND URBAN–RURAL DIVIDE

The first important facet of Yemen's population is its relative size on the Arabian Peninsula. According to official numbers, Yemen's population today is just over 24 million people (CIA 2011). That makes Yemen's population about equal to that of all of the GCC countries combined.

GULF COOPERATION COUNCIL (GCC)

The GCC is composed of Kuwait, Bahrain, Qatar, the United Arab Emirates, Oman, and Saudi Arabia. It was founded in 1981. The general aim of the GCC is to foster economic, technological, and scientific cooperation among its member states; but the most important function of the GCC is its security alliance with the United States. The only country in the Arabian Peninsula not included in this economic union is Yemen, ostensibly because it does not border the Arab Gulf (or Persian Gulf as it is called in Iran). However, neither do Jordan and Morocco, and they have been invited to join the GCC in recent years. It is difficult to explain Yemen's exclusion except on political grounds (i.e., all the GCC countries—and that would apply as well to Jordan and Morocco—are monarchies, whereas Yemen revolted against its monarchy in 1962 and replaced it with a democratic republic, making its action perhaps threatening to the regimes of the other member countries). Whatever reservations member states might have about including Yemen in the GCC, it is nevertheless considered an "associate" (as are presently Iraq, Jordan, and Morocco).

This comparison depends upon how one counts, and counting is not straightforward in the Gulf. Citizenship is not awarded by territory in the Gulf States. In contrast to the territorial basis of citizenship in most countries today, a person born in the territory of the state in the Gulf is not a citizen. Citizenship in the Gulf is awarded on the basis of blood relationship to those resident in the territory before the advent of oil wealth. This is because the Gulf States are in the unique position of having very large guest-worker populations, so large that in the extreme case of the United Arab Emirates a mere 10 percent of the population are citizens. The dependence of the economies of the Gulf upon a large number of noncitizen workers is a very sensitive political issue, and as such the Gulf States are shy to publish population statistics. Nevertheless, what figures are available points to the fact that Yemenis are equal in number to the citizens of all of the GCC countries combined.

Yemen is the only country on the Peninsula with a large settled population since before human history. Yemenis have a long history, whereas the GCC countries do not. Yet, the GCC countries possess great wealth today, and Yemenis are relatively quite poor. The relationship between the GCC countries and Yemen is similar to the relationship between the United States and Mexico, except that the demographics of the Arabian Peninsula are quite different from that of the NAFTA countries. Poverty-ridden Yemen is quite populous relative to the wealthy GCC states, and this is another politically sensitive issue. Saudi leaders, in particular, are very wary of a populous but poor Yemen on the edge of their wealthy kingdom. There are other reasons the Saudis are wary of Yemenis, but a fundamental element of the complex relationship between Saudi Arabia and Yemen is demographic.

The second facet of Yemen's population that is important to note is its dynamics. On the one hand, Yemen's population is growing very fast. In fact, it is growing at one of the fastest rates in the world. According to World Bank data, only 12 countries had faster growth rates than Yemen in 2009. Most of these countries are sub-Saharan African countries like Tanzania, Eritrea, Uganda, and Liberia. Yemen's annual growth rate is just less than 3 percent. If Yemen's growth rate were to hold steady at this pace, its population would double every 21 years. It has almost doubled since the two Yemens unified in 1990. The Yemeni Arab Republic reported a population close to 10 million, and the People's Democratic Republic of Yemen had about 2 million inhabitants at the time that the unified RoY was created (Yemen Arab Republic, Central Statistical Organization; People's Democratic Republic of Yemen, Central Statistical Organization). This means that today half the Yemeni population was born after unification. This is a very rapid rate of demographic change. In general population, growth rates are strongly related to income levels. High income countries have low or even negative rates of natural increase (excluding immigration and emigration). The poorest countries, the sub-Saharan African countries, have the highest growth rates. There are some significant exceptions to this trend and Yemen is one of them. Like all the other Gulf states, Yemen has a higher growth rate than would be expected at their income level. At Yemen's level of income, we would expect a growth rate of about 2.3 or 2.4 rather than its current 2.9 percent. High growth rates in the Gulf States are usually attributed to the high value placed on families whose marriage ages are lower, fertility rates higher, and growth rate higher than countries with similar income levels. We might note as well that Gulf wealth is not related to industrialization, which is an important proximate factor in the reduction of fertility.

Population in Yemen today is a controversial issue. Many commentators both Yemeni and foreign have conjured the specter of a Malthusian population explosion. (Thomas Robert Malthus (1766–1834) was an English demographer and political economist who predicted that the rate of population growth would outstrip the increase in consumable resources made possible by human industry, resulting in fame, disease, and war.) But one has to put these population trends in context. While Yemen's population is growing rapidly, it is important to realize that the rate of growth is falling, which is in line with the trend across the globe toward much lower growth rates during the last 20 years. Like the rest of the developing world, Yemen is experiencing the "third phase" of the demographic transition, in which population continues to grow but at a slower rate as fertility begins to decline. Using World Bank data, Yemen's growth rate was close to 5 percent in the early 1990s and then fell to just less than 3 percent by the early 2000s, where it has held for the last few years. The World Bank data conforms quite well to what would be expected over the long term given Yemen's history. Growth rates were low in the 1960s, when Yemen was torn by civil war, but then, as security was established and incomes began to rise rapidly in the 1970s and 1980s, the population growth rate rose at the same time that people were better fed and rudimentary medical supplies like antibiotics became widely available. In the 1990s and the first decade of this millennium, the Yemeni economy began to change, education levels rose, even for women, and urbanization increased.

These combined to lower growth rates. This is a very rough approximation, and data on Yemen should always be treated with a great deal of caution because, though improving, data on Yemen is often of poor quality, but it follows closely the pattern of other developing countries in the "third phase" of the demographic transition.

Another important reflection of Yemen's slowing population growth is the fertility rate, the average number of children born to women. Yemen was famous for its fertility rates of 7 and 8, but recently the fertility rate has fallen to just less than 5. According to the *2009 Statistical Yearbook,* in urban areas, the rate fell from 5 in 1994 to 4.2 in 2004; and in rural areas, where we would expect the rate to be higher, the rate was 6.2 in 1994 and fell to 5.3 in 2004. These combine to make the overall total fertility rate 4.9 in Yemen in 2004. The fall in growth rates and fertility rates correspond, as we would expect, with higher life expectancies (62 years), lower infant mortality (72 per 1,000), and rising age of marriage (23.8). These are all good trends for Yemen. Amidst Yemen's current crises, many analysts and observers seem to lose sight of the longer historical achievements and trends in Yemen.

A third facet of Yemen's population is its spatial distribution. Yemen's population is concentrated in the highlands. The governorates of Ibb, Taiz, Sana'a, and the highlands of Al-Hudaydah have the largest populations. A dot density map shows population closely follows precipitation in Yemen as it does in the rest of the Middle East. People follow water, and the water is in the highlands of Yemen. Rainfall and rain-fed agriculture also contribute to Yemen's patterns of settlement. Yemenis

Sana'a (Old City), capital of Yemen. (Zanskar/Dreamstime.com)

live in dispersed villages, and small settlements scattered around the highlands. The dispersed population pattern is not simply a result of scattered farmlands, but also a result of Yemen's social organization. Yemeni settlements are dispersed because farmers following the rain spread out through the highlands, but the settlement pattern is also a result of Yemen social organization that focuses on very small communities, local identities, and solidarities. Villages in the highlands are often located on the top of hilltops and mountains that are easy to defend. Rather than accessibility to transport routes, which is often an effect of urbanization, Yemeni settlement patterns in rural areas are strongly shaped by defense needs.

Yemen is one of the more rural countries in the world. In general, higher incomes imply greater urbanization. It is relatively poor, and so it is not surprising that today 70 percent of Yemenis live in rural areas. (Care must be taken in comparing statistics on urbanization, because the definition of urban and rural change by country. Japanese rural areas would be considered urban in the United States, and in World Bank data, for example, Lichtenstein is one of the most rural countries in the world.) But there is no doubt that Yemen is very rural. For the majority of Yemenis, life is still the life of the village, and local community identities are very strong, often even stronger than the national state. Yemenis often identify themselves as belonging to a particular tribe, for example, before they declare that they are Yemeni.

Using the latest World Bank data, Yemen is among the 40 most rural countries in the world. With 69 percent of its population living in what are defined (by Yemen) as rural areas, Yemen is in the company of countries like Vietnam, Laos, and Madagascar on the charts of urbanization. As with all developments in Yemen, trends in urbanization must be placed into context in order to make sense of the data. The largest city in Yemen is Sana'a, the political capital with more than 2 million inhabitants in 2009. In 1968, Sana'a was the scene of a historic siege when royalist tribes surrounded the city expecting to starve the Republican forces holed up inside the city's walls and reestablish the Zaydi Imamate. The Republican forces held, however, and republicanism defeated monarchism in Yemen. People who were around then like to point out that the city barely extended beyond the walls of the old city in those days and that the inhabitants numbered in the tens of thousands. There were few paved roads; most of the roads leading in and out of Sana'a were unpaved dirt. Today, Sana'a is a sprawling metropolis with highways circling the city for as far as the eye can see. So while Yemen is still largely rural, its cities are growing very fast and urban life is rapidly taking shape in Yemen today.

Yemen's largest city is Sana'a, the political capital, with about 2 million inhabitants, followed by Aden with about six hundred thousand, and Taiz and Al-Hudaydah with about a half million each. Aden and Al-Hudaydah are port cities, and Taiz is the administrative center of the productive "middle regions" of Yemen. Taiz was the seat of government under the last Zaydi Imam Ahmed, and Colonel Ali Abdullah Saleh was commander of the military in Taiz before he became the county's president in 1978. In Yemeni historiography, Sana'a was founded by Sam, son of Noah, and thus while Sana'a has always been an important political center and a center of trading routes, it also plays an important symbolic role in the heart of Yemeni identity.

WHAT IS YEMEN?

What we know as Yemen today is a modern territorial state, meaning that it is sovereign over the territory within its borders that are recognized by other states (formally in membership in the United Nations).

It was not always so. The Yemeni state today comprises a much smaller portion of what the Yemeni geographer Hussein al-Waisi refers to as "Greater Yemen," or what al-Haddad refers to as "natural Yemen," or what others call "historical Yemen." These terms refer to southern Arabia, everything from Mecca to Aden and from the Red Sea to the Persian/Arabian Gulf where the southern Semitic tribes live. But in the last 5,000 years, the people in this region developed a kind of cultural affinity born of a shared history. A Semitic culture (defined in terms of language) emerged that sent multiple waves of migration northward into northern Arabia, the Levant, Egypt, and North Africa and westward into what is now the Horn of Africa. South Arabia had a writing system known as Musnad, and inscriptions in Musnad are found throughout the entire Arabian Peninsula as well as the Mediterranean, Egypt, and the Horn of Africa. The modern Ethiopian script is only a slightly modified form of Musnad. The Arabic script Yemenis use today was the writing of the northern Arabs that was adopted in Yemen during the lifetime of the Prophet when Yemen converted to Islam. According to al-Haddad, the name Yemen is mentioned in the 10th century BCE in a text describing a battle between what is believed to be the Ma'in state in Yemen (referring to themselves as the south) and northern tribes. Yemen is also thought to indicate the region south of the Kaaba in Mecca. In this sense, Yemen was a region within which were various states and peoples that shared some common version of a South Arabian culture and identity.

THE MODERN STATE VERSUS THE MODERN NATION

A modern definition of the state would be an administrative apparatus that has control over a delimited territory and that can secure that territory's boundaries through an army as well as secure the safety of the population through a police force. For these reasons, it is sometimes said that a state has a "monopoly" over the means of force within its territory, and in so far as it may not, it may be said to be "weak." Modern states are thus about territory. One is subject to the law of Yemen simply by being present on Yemeni territory, regardless of citizenship. The nation is different from the state. The nation is a cultural idea about who the people within the territory are and what the state represents. National identity is not fixed but is continually redefined. Yemenis have different ideas about what being Yemeni means and about what the state should do in different periods of time. The important point here is that the debate about what it means to be Yemeni is now more or less contained within the territorial borders of the Republic of Yemen.

Yemen's modern territorial state began as two states: the British colony of Aden and its hinterland of South Arabia in the south and the Mutawakkilite Kingdom of Yemen founded by the Zaydi Imam Yahya Hamid al-Din after the withdrawal of the Ottoman Empire in 1918. The Imam of Yemen claimed sovereignty, in the manner of a premodern king, over the Ismailis and the Zaydis living in these territories. He was claiming sovereignty not over territory but over people based upon their religious status, in the style of royalty of past. A coup by military officers led to the establishment of the modern Yemen Arab Republic in 1962 in the north.

The British occupied Aden in 1839 to secure trade routes to India, and subsequently extended their influence into the "hinterland" of southern Yemen and the Hadhramawt in order to secure British Aden from Ottoman and later north Yemeni advances. The British tried to shape this region into an independent state called the "Federation of Southern Arabia," but failed when nationalists in the south forced the British to evacuate in 1967. They relinquished power in the south to nationalists who understood themselves as "Yemeni," not "South Arabian," and they formed the People's Republic of South Yemen, which became the People's Democratic Republic of Yemen in 1970.

In 1990, the two states unified, and in spite of elections in 1993, the question of power was only resolved by a civil war in 1994. Only in the last 10 years have border agreements with Oman and Saudi Arabia settled disputes over the territorial division of the desert between them. These recent agreements in effect renounce any aspirations of the modern Yemeni state for a "Greater Yemen," particularly the territory lost to the Saudi kingdom in 1934.

WHO ARE YEMENIS?

A different question than the extent and nature of the territory of the state is the nature of the people in it. Often modern states like to imagine that they rule in the name of the original inhabitants of a region. The blood of the people is rooted in the soil, they assert. This gives a sense of great historical continuity to a political state that is actually very new in the long march of history. The modern Egyptian state claims the Pharaohs, the Italians claim to be the sons of ancient Rome, and the Turks are the descendants of the Hittites. The national museum in each country figures prominently these original peoples and their achievements.

Yemenis are the descendants of the ancient civilizations of South Arabia, Yemen. They are proud of the Ma'in, the Sabaean, and the Himyarite civilizations that are featured in their national museum in Sana'a. They see themselves as pure Arabs, living descendants of the original Arab tribes and upholders of local tribal honor. They say that they are descendants of Kahlan bin Saba of the greater family of descendants of Sam bin Noh (Sam of Noah, hence Semitic) who populated the Arab Peninsula. In Yemeni national statistics, there are three categories of nationalities: Yemeni, Arab, and foreign. Arabs are citizens of other Arab states, and they are not considered foreigners but fellow Arabs, but then again, not Yemeni.

Yemenis are also Muslim, and they have made important contributions to the faith. They were early converts to Islam who declared allegiance to the Prophet Muhammad in his lifetime. Yemeni tribes served in the Arab armies of conquest, and people today who are descendants of Yemenis and carry Yemeni names live as far away as Mauritania and even Spain. Yemen is home to the 1,000-year reign of the Zaydi Imams, to the 500-year tradition of the Alawi in south Yemen, and home to a long tradition of religious scholarship in many different schools within Islam including Shafi'i, Ismaili, and Sufi. Yemenis are quite active in the debates over what it means to be Muslim in today's world. Yemen's membership in the Arab League and the Organization of Islamic States reflects a modern manifestation of their Muslim and Arab loyalties.

Yemenis also see themselves as part of a new modern world of nation-states in which Yemen is not powerful or wealthy. Many Yemenis have seen or heard first-hand of the wealth in neighboring Gulf States. They have worked and studied in Europe, the United States, and in the former Soviet Union. They are aware that they are far from the centers of power and wealth in the modern world, and they want to take their place in the modern world with all its benefits.

Development is an important value for Yemenis, and they are keen on improving their lives and the lives of their children. They rely on a tradition of innovation, judiciousness, and tenaciousness that comes from surviving in a rugged arid environment.

Yemenis also have a certain cosmopolitan tradition of traveling afar for business, for trade, in search of knowledge, and in the service of religion. Though most Arabs consider Yemen today as backward, Yemenis consider themselves quite modern in many ways in spite of sharing the lower tier of the UN Development Programme's development indicators in the Arab world, along with Mauritania and the Sudan. Yemenis are innovators and believe in the promise of modernity. Far from being slaves of tradition, Yemen is where the tribesmen and saadah of the south took to reading Rosa Luxemburg and Karl Marx and established the only communist state in the Arab world. Yemenis today are proud of their republicanism and democratic traditions (in a region where monarchism prevails), and at the same time, they are aware of its weaknesses, both domestic and international. The Yemeni press is active and relatively free. Parliament is the scene of lively debate. Being a weak state in the international system, Yemenis are strong supporters of justice, equality, and rule of law in the international system, and they are quite wary of foreign intervention in their affairs. They would very much like to determine their own fate in their own modern style.

BIBLIOGRAPHY

Al-Haddad, Muhammad Yahya. *The General History of Yemen: The History of Yemen before Islam* (in Arabic). Lebanon: Manshurat al-Madina, 1986b.

Al-Haddad, Muhammad Yahya. *The General History of Yemen: Yemen in the Pageantry That Is Islam* (in Arabic). Lebanon: Manshurat al-Madina, 1986a.

Al-Waisi, Hussein Bin Ali. *Greater Yemen: Geography, Geology, History* (in Arabic). Lebanon: Maktabat al-Rashad, 1991 (second printing).

Cheung, Catherine, Lyndon Devautier, and Kay van Damme. *Socotra: A Natural History of the Islands and Their People.* Hong Kong: Odyssey Books and Guides, 2006.

CIA. *The World Factbook: Yemen, People and Society.* https://www.cia.gov/library/publications/the-world-factbook/geos/ym.html, 2011.

Collier, Paul. *The Plundered Planet: Why We Must—and How We Can—Manage Natural Resources for Global Prosperity.* New York: Oxford University Press, 2010.

Dresch, Paul. "Debates on Marriage and Nationality in the United Arab Emirates," in *Monarchies and Nations: Globalization and Identity in the Arab States of the Gulf,* edited by Paul Dresch and James Piscatori, 136–157. New York: I.B.Taurus & Co., 2005.

Harrower, Michael J. "Is the Hydraulic Hypothesis Dead Yet? Irrigation and Social Change in Ancient Yemen." *World Archaeology* 41, no. 1 (2009): 58–72.

Held, Colbert, and John Cummings. *Middle East Patterns: Places, People, and Politics.* Boulder, CO: Westview Press, 2011.

Ho, Engseng. *The Graves of Tarim: Geneology and Mobility across the Indian Ocean.* Berkeley: University of California Press, 2006.

People's Democratic Republic of Yemen, Central Statistical Organization. *Annual Yearbooks.*

Petraglia, Michael D., and Jeffrey Rose, eds. *The Evolution of Human Populations in Arabia: Paleoenvironments, Prehistory, and Genetics.* New York: Springer, 2009.

Pollastro, Richard M., Amy S. Karshbaum, and Roland J. Viger. *Maps Showing Geology, Oil and Gas Fields and Geologic Provinces of the Arabian Peninsula.* Denver, CO: U.S. Department of the Interior, Geological Survey, 1999. http://pubs.usgs.gov/of/1997/ofr-97-470/OF97-470B/arbnprov.pdf.

Republic of Yemen, Central Statistical Organization. *Statistical Yearbooks.* http://www.cso-yemen.org/index.php?lng=english.

Republic of Yemen, Ministry of Agriculture. *Agricultural Statistical Yearbooks.* http://agricultureyemen.com/page.php?&id=371.

Republic of Yemen, Ministry of Planning and International Cooperation and International Food Policy Research Institute. *National Food Security Strategy Paper.* Sana'a: MOPIC, 2010.

Republic of Yemen. *The National Strategy for the Sustainabiliy of the Environment* (in Arabic). Sana'a: Ministry of Environment and Water, n.d.

World Bank. *Project Appraisal Document on a Proposed Grant in the Amount of SDR 57.9 Million to the Republic of Yemen for a Water Sector Support Project.* Report No: 4680 1-YE, January 2009.

World Bank. *Yemen: Mineral Sector Review.* Report No. 47985-YE, June 2009.

World Bank Statistics. http://data.worldbank.org.

Yemen Arab Republic, Central Statistical Organization. *Annual Yearbooks.*

History

Steven C. Caton

CHRONOLOGY

Prehistoric

100,000–10,000 BCE—(Paleolithic and Mesolithic stone tool industries)—50,000 BCE shows the earliest evidence of Paleolithic stone tools in Yemen, Mesolithic not attested so far.

10,000–2000 BCE—(Neolithic stone tool industry)—Development of agriculture and urbanism in Yemen.

3300–1200 BCE—Agriculture, settlements, ceramics, and metallurgy.

Ancient

1500 BCE—Rise of the Sabaean Kingdom, capital at Marib and development of South Arabic scripts, monumental architecture, and long-distance trade in spices and incense.

1000 BCE—Queen of Sheba.

600 BCE—Marib Dam completed; Sabaeans control nearly all of Yemen.

400 BCE—Ma'in, Hadhramawt, and Qataba kingdoms vie for control of Yemen.

110 BCE—Rise of the Himyarites, capital at Zafar.

29

25–21 BCE—Under Aelius Gallus, the Romans invade South Arabia but fail to conquer the Sabaeans.

240 CE—Abyssinians (Ethiopia) invade Yemen.

270–280—Abyssinians conquer the Sabaeans with the help of their allies, the Himyarites, who now become the dominant power in Yemen.

500—Christianity begins to be powerful.

517–525 (?)—Reign of last Himyarite king, Yusuf Dhu Nuwas (convert to Judaism).

520—Christian Aksumite Empire invades Yemen and defeats Dhu Nuwas in 525.

530—Abraha becomes ruler of the Aksumite Kingdom in Yemen, with capital at Sana'a.

550 (?)—Abraha besieges Mecca but fails to conquer it.

570—Uprising against Aksumite Kingdom led by Sayf bin Dhi Yazan; Yemen becomes a vassal state of the Persians (Sasanids); birth of the Prophet Muhammad in Mecca.

630 (?)—Ali ibn Abu Talib brings Islam to Yemen.

Medieval Period

820—Ziyadids establish their dynasty in the Tihama; it lasts until 1018.

897—Imam Yahya al-Hadi establishes the Zaydi state, with Sa'dah as its capital; it lasts until 1962.

1047—Sulayhid dynasty establishes, with its capitals in Sana'a and then Jibla; it lasts until 1138.

1067–1138—Reign of Sulayhid Queen, Arwa (1048–1138).

1173—The Ayyubid Turanshah conquer southern Yemen, with Taiz as the capital.

1228–1454—Rasulid dynasty

1455—Beginning of the Tahirid dynasty; it lasts until 1547.

1489–1517—Reign of Tahirid Sultan Amir ibn al-Wahhab.

1497—Portuguese enter Indian Ocean.

1504—Completion of the 'Amariyyah school and mosque complex.

1506—Portuguese conquer Socotra.

1511—Portuguese attack Aden but fail to conquer it.

1547—Ottomans take Sana'a from the Tahirids and establish control over Yemen; First Ottoman Occupation lasts until 1629.

1597–1620—Reign of Zaydi Imam al-Qasim bin Muhammad "The Great" begins (rules until 1620), founds the Qasimid dynasty; proves victorious against the Ottomans.

1620–1640—Reign of Zaydi Imam Mu'ayyid Muhammad; defeats the Ottomans in 1629.

1760–1823—Muhammad al-Shawkani, brilliant Muslim scholar and jurist.

Modern Period

1839—The British seize the port of Aden and found a colony.

1872–1918—Second Ottoman Occupation of Yemen.

1904–1948—Reign of Zaydi Imam Yahya bin Muhammad Hamid al-Din, establishes control over all of Yemen except for the British Aden Protectorate, and founds the Mutuwakkalite Kingdom, with capital at Sana'a.

1933—Yemen loses 'Asir and Najran to Saudi Arabia.

1948–1962—Reign of Imam Ahmed.

1962—Imam Badr comes to power and is overthrown; Yemeni Revolution begins and the Yemen Arab Republic (YAR) is formed.

1962–1970—Yemeni Civil War.

1967—Independence of the Aden Protectorate; founding of the People's Democratic Republic of Yemen (PDRY)

1974–1977—Presidency of Ibrahim al-Hamdi.

1978—Presidency of Ali Abdullah Saleh begins.

1984—Discovery of oil in Marib.

1990—Unification of YAR and PDRY to form the Republic of Yemen.

1994—Civil war between northern and southern forces; the north wins.

1999—First presidential election; Ali Abdullah Saleh wins.

2004—Houthi conflict heats up in Sa'dah.

2006—Second presidential election; Saleh wins but opposition parties make gains.

2007—Emergence of the Southern Movement (eventually calling for secession).

2011—Change Revolution ("Arab Spring").

2012—Saleh steps down through a Gulf Cooperation Council–brokered agreement; Abd Rabbuh Mansur al-Hadi becomes president in a special election.

Arab historiography tends to privilege certain "centers" in the Islamic world—Egypt, Syria, and Iraq—as having been the most important in shaping events, with places like Afghanistan, Pakistan Morocco, and Yemen considered "peripheral" or "marginal." Yet, Yemen's history is as ancient as any country's and more illustrious than most.

Part of the reason for this is its geographic location. In the southwest corner of the Arabian Peninsula, it connects East Africa across the Red Sea with the rest of the Peninsula, and because of its long coastline that faces the Indian Ocean, it has been an important conduit for the flow of trading goods such as spices, incense, and precious metals as well as ideas between Asia and the European world. Another reason for its historical importance has to do with its climate and soil. Though an arid land, it is nonetheless fertile and has since earliest times been an important agricultural producer. Thus, it is not only a place people have passed through but have also settled in. The land of Yemen has been continuously inhabited since earliest man crossed over from Africa into Europe and Asia and developed agriculture. Yemen produced some of the earliest, richest, and most fabled civilizations of the ancient world. Though it went into decline briefly in the two centuries before the rise of Islam, it once again became an important center of trade, learning, and artistry during the Islamic medieval period (roughly from the 10th century CE until the 18th century), when at one time it held a monopoly over the coffee trade. These kingdoms, most of them centered in the middle of the country, are still not as well known as they deserve to be, and they await a new generation of Arab scholars to illuminate the complete range of their power and cultural significance. It is only in the modern period that the country can be said to have gone into decline, partly a function of changing trade patterns but also of internal politics, torn apart by factionalism and by inward-looking rulers who kept the country from being Westernized and developed. Though now poor, Yemen remains an important country politically. It is the only country with a democratic, republican government on the Peninsula, and it remains important because of its strategic geographic location, a potential threat to its northern neighbor, Saudi Arabia, and a haven for refugees from the conflicts in East Africa.

To do justice to this sweep and complexity of history, this long chapter is divided into four main sections: prehistory (from earliest man until the dawn of civilization, around 1000 BCE), the ancient period (from 1000 BCE until the rise of Islam), the medieval period (from 900 CE until 1832, or the arrival of the British in Aden), and the modern period (from 1832 until the present).

PREHISTORY

If the ancestors of *Homo sapiens* originated more than 1.5 million years ago in Africa, as is widely believed, then it is possible that they crossed into Yemen at a time when the eastern portion of the continent and the Arabian Peninsula were either one landmass or more likely were separated by a much narrower body of water than the present Red Sea, one that moreover was mostly frozen during the glacial period of the late Pleistocene. To date, no early hominid remains have been found in Yemen, however.

What has been established archaeologically is the existence of human beings in Yemen as early as the Paleolithic period, about 50,000 years ago. At that time, the Arabian Peninsula was a different place from the harsh and arid land of today. The climate was cooler and wetter, creating a savanna dotted by lakes and marshes, with possibly even some rivers running through it, where shellfish, birds, and wildlife of various sorts abounded. Humans inhabiting this landscape led a hunter-gatherer way of life, following the migrations of the animals that they hunted while collecting wild fruits in mangroves along the coasts. They used stone tools such as arrow heads, spear points, hide scrapers, and vegetable choppers made from obsidian and flint extracted from nearby sandstone formations.

Peoples eventually transitioned into food production and a more settled way of life in what archaeologists call the Neolithic period (8000–2000 BCE). In the coastal Tihama as well as the plateau regions of what is now Khawlan al-Tiyal (east of the capital, Sana'a), there is ample evidence of a later Bronze Age culture (roughly 2700–2000 BCE). Excavations on the plateaus have revealed stone foundations of what were tiny dwellings (presumably for single family households), some with the ashy remains of a hearth, and clustered into small settlements. Nearby are the remains of larger structures that might have had a more public or communal function. All foundations were built of large blocks of stone, squared off as much as possible, with walls of smaller stone above them, held together with mud. Such building material was easy to find as rock and stone are abundant in the area. The roof was probably made of thatch.

Along with obsidian stone tools, a distinctive pottery was found, both on the surface and in excavations, exhibiting two ceramic styles, one more refined than the other, and suggesting specialization of use. Wild and domesticated animal remains

THE ARCHAEOLOGICAL AGES OF EARLY MAN

Archaeologists characterize the history of early man to the beginning of written literatures, according to ages (or stages of development). The Paleolithic, dating back to the Australopithecines around 1.5 million years ago in Africa, is marked by the development of the oldest-known worked (or knapped) stone tools. Humans were probably organized into bands and hunted or scavenged for their food, and by around 200,000 years ago had spread from Africa to Europe and Asia. The Paleolithic lasted until roughly 10,000 years BCE when it was followed by the Neolithic stage, believed to have first begun in the Near East. This is generally considered the last of the "Stone Age," and is marked by the development of farming (sometimes referred to as the Neolithic Revolution), the domestication of animals, and pottery. Following the Stone Age are periods characterized by the smelting of metals like bronze (the Bronze Age), followed by iron (the Iron Age). Writing was invented during the Bronze Age of several important cultures (hieroglyphs in Egypt, cuneiform in the Near East, and Linear B in the Mediterranean). During the Iron Age, writing advanced beyond mere literacy and record keeping to the creation of whole literatures.

were found nearby, along with stone tools that might have been used in working their flesh and hides as well as in harvesting (though of what it is impossible to say precisely). Despite the fragmentary material evidence, it appeared that these small communities were dedicated to animal husbandry and small-scale farming.

That they had a gift for water management, which became all important in the next period of Yemeni history, is evidenced by these villages' location in areas with a reliable water supply. They were also situated beside what must have been trade routes, of which they took full advantage to judge from bronze, seashells, and semi-precious stones that are not local to the area. Clearly, these villages were producing a surplus of some sort, possibly of meat and grains, which was exchanged for these foreign goods. Except for one male statuette, archaeological research has revealed no artistic works associated with this culture, though whether this means they were uninterested in art or that aesthetic artifacts have not been unearthed yet is hard to say.

It appeared that this Bronze Age culture lasted undisturbed for more or less a thousand years, with the Khawlan villages not being abandoned until around 1800 BC. The cause was likely to have been environmental changes due to a tectonic shift that gradually changed the gradient of the slopes along which the villages were located and heavy rainfall that eroded away rich alluvial deposits that affected arable soil. Evidence suggests that the villagers tried to stem the loss of these deposits but without apparent success. What they lacked was the knowledge to control large-scale water action that was one of the hallmarks of the next period.

THE ANCIENT KINGDOMS

The next dominant period in Yemen, the Iron Age, saw the emergence of four major kingdoms that lay on the eastern desert of the country (also known as the Sayhad). These were the Sabaean Kingdom with its capital at Marib, the Minaean Kingdom with its capital at Qarnaw, the Qatabanian Kingdom with its capital at Timna, and the Hadhrami Kingdom with its capital at Shabwah. A fifth major kingdom, the Himyarite Kingdom with its capital at Zafar, emerged in a different part of the country (Dhamar in the central highlands) and much later in time, between the first century BCE and the sixth century CE. Of these ancient kingdoms, the Sabaeans and the Himyarites were the most significant and therefore receive the lion's share of the overview to follow.

The Sabaeans

The most important of these kingdoms were the Sabaens, a rich and powerful civilization, whose origin is more mysterious than that of their predecessors. Did they develop out of the preexisting Bronze Age culture or did they come from outside South Arabia and live alongside the earlier culture? Did their civilization begin sometime in the beginning of the second millennium (when the Bronze Age culture in Yemen appears to have experienced environmental stress) or much later?

Among the scholars who hold to the hypothesis that the Sabaeans arrived on the scene much later are philologist historians (led by the Belgian scholar Jacqueline Pirenne), who base their conclusions on stone inscriptions in the Sabaean language (a dialect of South Arabic, a Semitic language with historical connections to Arabic and Ethiopian) and a chronology of kings listed in them. According to their reading of the inscriptions, the advent of the Sabaeans is a little earlier than 500 BCE. This chronology did not go uncontested even among epigraphers, but it was not until the 1980s when Italian archaeologists managed to excavate one of the Sabaean Kingdom's major cities, Yalaal-Durayb (in eastern Khawlan). Carbon-14 dating of charcoal remains found at the city's lowest levels yielded dates from between 1400 and 800 BCE, supporting the view that the Sabaeans already existed in South Arabia by the middle of the second millennium BCE—in fact, earlier than most scholars suspected. These archaeological remains also revealed marked differences in architectural design and structure as well as types and methods of ceramic production from those of the Bronze Age settlers, suggesting an external origin for the Sabaeans. Perhaps, they migrated to the outskirts of the Empty Quarter from the northern part of the Arabian Peninsula because of political upheavals that were quite common in the Near East in the 13th century BCE. This explanation also accounts for certain marked resemblances in Sabaean writing, pottery, and architecture to Bronze Age Syrian and Palestinian cultures.

A different view about the origins of the Sabaeans has emerged since the early 1970s, one that maintains that Iron Age civilizations generally in southwestern Arabia arose from local origins. Ostensibly, the first scholar to advance this hypothesis was a Saudi archaeologist, Abdullah Masry, who argued that environmental conditions existed in this part of the Peninsula that were conducive to agriculture at the

Ancient city of Marib. (Eric Lafforgue/ArabianEye/Corbis)

THE QUEEN OF SHEBA

Little, if any, archaeological evidence exists to substantiate the existence of this legendary queen. She was surely a historical figure, though whether as a contemporary of the Jewish Solomon, as legend would have it (which would place her reign somewhere around 1000 BCE), remains up in the air. Adding to the mystery is that even the Ethiopians have a Queen of Sheba whom they claim visited the Jewish Solomon.

The Queen of Sheba is prominently mentioned in several important texts and has an iconic status in both the Western and Islamic imagination. The story of her meeting with Solomon is mentioned in the First Book of Kings and the Second Book of Chronicles, Matthew and Luke. Her story is recounted in the Qur'an in the Sura of the Ant, 27, lines 16–45. Her meeting with Solomon fascinated many artists—among them Holbein, Veronese, and Hieronymus Bosch—and also fired the imagination of Arab, Persian, Turkish, and Moghul miniature painters, to whom we owe some of the greatest masterpieces of Islamic art. Later, Arab historians and writers gave the Queen a new name "Bilquis," which is how she is known in Yemen today.

time (around 2000 BCE) and that this propelled development locally. At the time the author was writing, there was little, if any, archaeological evidence for this view, but since the 1980s, archaeologists have found much more evidence to support it.

The peoples of Yemen have always depended on trade for their livelihood, and the Sabaens were no exception. The story of the Queen of Sheba arriving in Jerusalem at the head of a great caravan laden with precious goods encapsulates that way of life. Though at the outskirts of a desert, the Sabaean capital, Marib, was nonetheless strategically located at the confluence of several important overland routes: one of which led to Egypt, another to the Mediterranean, and yet a third to Mesopotamia. (It was perhaps to secure markets for one of these lucrative trading routes that the Queen of Sheba paid a visit to Solomon, a powerful monarch whose influence was widely felt in the Levant.) Marib became rich on the high prices it could charge for these luxury goods, and it grew from an insignificant settlement into the equivalent of a global trading city of today, acclaimed by Greek and Roman geographers and historians such as Strabo, Pliny, and others.

INCENSE AND SPICE ROUTES

For centuries, if not millennia, textiles, spices, and semiprecious stones were brought by ship from Asia to the Omani coast, where aromatic resins such as frankincense and myrrh were also manufactured. They were then transported to three destinations: ancient Egypt, Greece and Rome, and Mesopotamia. Frankincense (Arabic *lubaan dhakr*) was the most prized incense of all. It is a white gum that exudes from a cut in a tree (*Boswelliua sacra*) that grows wild in Hadhramawt and Dhofar (Oman). It burns with a pure white and fragrant smoke and is used to fumigate the house. Myrrh (which means "bitter" in Arabic) is darker and more oily and was used for embalming in ancient Egypt and as a valuable additive to perfumes. Frankincense and myrrh along with Indian spices such as mustard, saffron, and ginger and semiprecious gems were loaded on camels and transported overland. One might think that taking a sea route would be less arduous than trekking by camel over a desert steppe, but the prevailing sea winds made a boat journey hazardous, if not impossible. The circumnavigation of the Peninsula would not be figured out until much later.

To support an urban population of this size, food was needed, and to this end, massive dams and sluices were built, the earliest traces of which date from the third and second millennia BCE. Even more than the Bronze Age peoples before them, the Sabaens had to manage their relatively meager water resources carefully if they were to survive in a region that had grown increasingly more desiccated since the Paleolithic, and they did so by regulating rainwater flow during the monsoon seasons (fall and spring).

The surrounding Marib area was naturally conducive to such an irrigation scheme. The Wadi Dhana, whose outlet is near Marib, is the largest in northern highland Yemen, its water catchment or basin measuring around ten thousand square kilometers (km²; just over 3,800 square miles [mi²]) It stretches westward as far as the watersheds east of Sana'a and is fed by countless, small wadis along the way. It is narrowest at its upstream outlet, but harnessing the water there presents an engineering challenge, for rainwater cascading down the mountain slopes rushes at such breakneck speed that it is difficult to stop or control.

At first, the Sabaeans built small, primitive barriers that diverted water to cultivatable land on either side of the wadi basin, a feat made possible by the fact that most of the stream's force had been spent by the time it reached these barriers and would not knock them down. However, greater volume of rainwater could have been captured—and thus utilized—had there been a way to block the water's flow at the wadi's outlet and then through a series of sluices allow it to discharge into cultivatable fields below at a controlled rate of flow. Solving this difficult hydraulic problem did not occur overnight, and it is clear that the Sabaeans embarked on a series of trials and errors lasting several centuries, resulting in ever larger and more complicated irrigation structures, until Marib Dam, one of the engineering marvels of the ancient world, was completed sometime in the mid to late sixth century BCE.

Marib Dam was 650 meters (m; 2,132 feet [ft]) long, closing Wadi Dhana at its narrowest point, and by the end of its construction turned out to be 15 m (50 ft) high, with sluices at each end built on the rocky mountain tops. The dam's function was more than to contain the water flowing down the mountains and rushing toward

Section of the ancient Marib Dam, about 1980. (Steven C. Caton)

Wadi Dhana; it was also to calm its turbulence and then divert it immediately to the cultivatable plain below. There was no reservoir behind it in the way we associate with modern dams, for the large amount of debris that came down the mountain-sides in the rains would have sedimented behind the dam and quickly filled up the reservoir, making it unusable and requiring arduous dredging operations. Instead, at the very moment the water arrived, it was gathered inside massive basins in which it slowed its rate of flow and then was released through the sluices to channels that took the water by gravity to the fields below. The smaller, distributory channels formed an intricate and far-flung network that irrigated two huge oases, one to the north of the town and one to the south, comprising an area of just under 10,000 hectares (ha; equivalent to 24,700 acres [ac]) when the operation of the dam was at its height. But this does not even give the full scope of what was involved, for the water flow had to travel for a distance of 11 km (6.8 mi) in the northern direction and 21 km (13 mi) in the southern direction, in order for the full extent of the irrigable area to be covered, and the propulsion or forward movement of water had to be accomplished by gravity alone. The whole system also had to be kept clear of mud and debris, and of course maintenance of the actual structures was constant. Such work required some sort of voluntary or corvée labor, supplied by the surrounding tribes and organized by a state bureaucracy (see below).

Agricultural produce from this elaborate and extensive irrigation system was enough not only to feed the inhabitants of the Sabaean capital, but also to provision the caravans that crossed the desert, with perhaps enough surplus for export to neighboring lands as well. So legendary did the Dam of Marib and the gardens it irrigated become, that it was mentioned in the Qur'an, though the emphasis is on its destruction by Allah as a punishment to the Sabaeans for having grown insatiable in their search for wealth:

> There was, for Saba, aforetime, a Sign in their home-land-two Gardens to the right and to the left. "Eat of the Sustenance [provided] by your Lord, and be grateful to Him: a territory fair and happy, and a Lord Oft-Forgiving!" But they turned away [from Allah], and We sent against them the Flood [released] from the dams, and We converted their two garden [rows] into "gardens" producing bitter fruit, and tamarisks, and some few [stunted] Lote-trees. That was the Requital We gave them because they ungratefully rejected Faith: And never do We give [such] requital except to such as are ungrateful rejecters. (Qur'an, 34:15–17)

In the Qur'anic story, the downfall of a mighty civilization is brought about by a rat that gnawed its way through the dam wall and caused its collapse, an allegory of corruption that ate away at society's moral foundation.

But what can be said about the historical causes for the dam's destruction? Inscriptions in the dam itself, dating from roughly 350 to 558 CE, mention a series of four repairs to the dam, with its final bursting coming sometime between 558 and the death of the Prophet Muhammad (b. 570) in 632. Perhaps, the principle reason the dam fell into increasing disrepair had to do with the decline of Sabaean power at this time, a story we have yet to delve into; but there are other, more structural reasons having to do with the shortcoming of the materials used in the original construction consisting of lava rocks, piled shoddily on top of each other, and cemented into place with mortar. This is a bit surprising, given how expertly crafted much of the other monumental architecture of Sabaean civilization was, but perhaps it was thought too much trouble to rebuild the dam from scratch even after its compositional flaws were fully appreciated.

According to the Qur'an (27:17–24), King Solomon first heard about the Sabaeans from the hoopoe bird (still extant) who flew all the way from Yemen to tell him about a queen who reigned over a land of incredible wealth in which the people worshipped the sun. In fact, the religion of the Sabaens was richer and more complex than sun worship. As the capital city of a great civilization, Marib consisted of more than the Great Dam and the oases it irrigated.

In the oldest inscriptions unearthed from Marib, five deities are named: Athtar (resembling the Babylonian Ishtar) who was worshipped throughout South Arabia, as well as Hawbas, Almaqah, dhat-Himyam, and dhat-Badanum who were worshipped only by the Sabaeans. Hawas was the female counterpart of Athtar. Almaqah, a moon god, was the most important, and while the last two are presumably female (based on the grammatical gender of the "dhat-" prefix), nothing else is known about them. In Middle Sabaean times, they were replaced by a goddess of the sun called Shams. Without any description of these deities in Sabaean inscriptions, let alone any sort of written mythology to illuminate their characters or deeds, their exact nature remains obscure.

Sabaean alabaster statuette. (DeAgostini/Getty Images)

The Sabaens built Awam Temple (known in Yemen today as Mahram Bilquis, or Bilquis's Place of Worship) near Marib, the largest pre-Islamic religious structure in Arabia. The Sabaeans called it Bayt Almaqah or the House of Almaqah. (The temple has been excavated twice, once in the early 1950s by the oil explorer and amateur archaeologist Wendell Phillips and again in the 1980s and 1990s by his American Foundation for the Study of Man, directed by his sister Merilyn Phillips Hodgson.) Its complex consists of eight enormous pillars in front of a large, square-shaped hall, inside of which are grand staircases and monumental pillars that were probably lined with beautiful bronze and alabaster sculptures. This hall is the entryway into an enormous oval temple, excavations of which have revealed a treasure trove of ceramics, bronzes, coppers, and alabasters, including what well may be best valuable of all, the first Sabaean fresco unearthed to date. It is clear, however, that the temple has more secrets for future archaeological research to unearth.

This was not the only temple to Almaqah the Sabaens constructed; not far from it at a place called Baran is another one, which has been almost completely excavated by German teams since the 1980s. The temple consists of one enormous rectangular building, built with very finely worked stone, inside of which are five large pillars on top of a raised stage or platform that can be approached by ceremonial staircases. What look like sacrificial troughs for slain bulls and other animals were found inside.

Next to these impressive temple complexes, there are cemeteries filled with tombs, gravestones, and accompanying grave goods. Inscriptions on the tombs and gravestones record the names of the deceased and their families as well as tribal affiliations. Sometimes, they utter a warning in the name of Athtar, slayer of whoever desecrated the graves. Funerary stella consisted of a long, rectangular, and smoothed stone of alabaster, gypsum, or limestone, the upper portion of which was hollowed out to form a niche, inside of which an alabaster head rested, presumably a representation of the deceased. Tombs were built close to one another, with carved images of the heads of the deceased on their outer façades. Objects to accompany the dead included goblets, small animal sculptures, incense burners, and some anthropomorphic statuary. We can only surmise that the reason people were buried near the temples was that they believed their afterlife would be assisted by proximity to them.

Marib was not the only great city in what became the Sabaean Kingdom. At 40 km (25 mi) west is the ancient city of Sirwah, the most important center of the Sabaean Kingdom after its capital in the first millennium BCE. Its archaeological remains are even more impressive than those of ancient Marib, largely because it has remained relatively immune from destruction or damage over the centuries. For example, the unusual curvilinear wall of its Almaqah Temple still stands over 8 m (26 ft) in height, and a wall inscription tells us that it was built by a particular ruler in the mid-seventh century BCE. The stones of its façade are carefully smoothed and fit exactly, demonstrating a very high level of masonry. Inside this structure was the longest Sabaean inscription found to date, recording the deeds of the great Sabaean ruler Karibil Watar, the first to unite large parts of what are now Yemen in the Sabaean Empire. To the north of the temple is a large administrative building, perhaps a palace, dating to the same period, the seventh century BCE. There are also residential dwellings nearby. The city of Sirwah, covering about 3 ha (7.4 ac), was surrounded by an enormous wall, fortified by towers at several points, with the unusual feature of the monumental structures such as the Almaqah Temple and the ruler's palace built into it. Many segments of the wall still stand today. Like Marib, Sirwah's population depended on a complex irrigation system for its food, consisting of barrages, locks, and canals, but no dam anywhere near the size of the dam at Marib has been found.

Many of the statues as well as the walls of monumental architecture at Marib and Sirwah have inscriptions on them, but the earliest form of Sabaean writing is to be found at neither of these metropolises but at another Sabaean city by the name of Yalaal-Durayb, excavated by the Italians in the 1980s. This earliest writing is in the form of brief inscriptions incised on ceramic vessels, apparently to mark the names of their owners, and dates to the 10th century BCE. Later inscriptions are to be found carved in stone, dating to a time three centuries later. There are thus two kinds of scripts: one in the form of independent block letters, indelibly executed in stone or bronze, meant for public display, which either commemorated rituals in gratitude of certain deities or determined property rights and established various laws; the other is a cursive script scratched on more perishable materials such as pottery, sticks, or palm fronds and was used for personal correspondence or business contracts. It is difficult to know how much of the population was actually literate and able to read or write, or whether literacy was confined to a small scribal elite, but what is certain is that writing as a material trace was ubiquitous on walls and at the base of statuary.

In order for long-distance trade to be regulated and secured across potentially hostile territory and in order for water systems to be built and maintained for urban centers such as Marib, some sort of state authority probably existed. Sabaean inscriptions mention mostly the names of rulers known as *mukarrib,* "federator" (rather than *malik,* "king," that came in use around 400 BCE), suggesting that the Sabaean sovereigns exercised authority over a confederation of tribes. According to one theory, a mukarrib was head of a tribe that had become dominant in a region, with the other tribes obeying their (and his) authority, but there is no a priori reason to think that such a hierarchical tribal system was in fact in place. (These tribes were sedentary for the most part and practiced agriculture; it is likely that only a fraction of the peoples that identified as tribal were pastoral nomads. This pattern was not unique to the Marib region either but characterized the tribes elsewhere in highland and coastal Yemen.) It could have been possible for a mukarrib to have been appointed with the consensus of the head of each of the confederated tribes, his role being to execute decisions made jointly by some kind of assembly of elders. He was thus less autocratic than, say, an Egyptian pharaoh or an Assyrian king. His duties included mobilizing men for building works such as defensive walls or towers

SOUTH ARABIAN LANGUAGES AND WRITING

South Arabian (or South Arabian Epigraphic) is the term used to designate the South Arabian inscriptions. It was comprised of four dialects: Sabaean spoken in the Marib region, Minaean spoken in the Wadi al-Jawf, Qatabanian in the Wadi Bayhan, and Hadramautic in the Wadi Hadhramawt. While they are usually classified as a Semitic language with close ties to Arabic and the languages of Ethiopia, they also show affinities with Ugaritic and Aramaic, ancient languages spoken in the Levant. The phonological system is nearly identical to Arabic (with the addition of one more phonemes), and like Hebrew and Arabic, it is formed morphologically on consonantal root patterns. The origins of the Sabaean alphabet are now thought to be in the Fertile Crescent, though why or how it spread to South Arabia remains a mystery. With the arrival of Islam to South Arabia in the seventh century CE, Classical Arabic replaced these written languages, and spoken South Arabic generally survived in only a few isolated pockets in what are today known as the regions of Mahrah (in southern Yemen and Oman) and the island of Socotra.

and water infrastructures, carrying out religious activities in the many temples built by the Sabaeans, leading troops in war, and heading up a council of ministers and executing the laws of the land.

Whatever the reality of his authority, it is important to bear in mind that a powerful state emerged in the midst of a tribal society. Too often it is assumed that state and tribe are antithetical to each other or work at cross-purposes, with the state supposedly always attempting to centralize power in its hands and the tribes presumably attempting to defend their autonomy in the face of state dominance. A much more symbiotic relationship in all likelihood characterized these two powerful forces. The Sabaean state, rather than maintaining a standing army, was dependent upon the tribes for defense of its territories as well as supplying the men and camels needed for its lucrative overland trade, while the tribes, in turn, remained loyal to the Sabaean state as long as they grew wealthy from trade and agriculture. As we shall see, this state–tribe dynamic is one that persisted throughout Yemeni history until the present. Sometimes this dynamic worked well, at other times it worked less well, and the fortunes of both state and tribe waxed and waned accordingly, but it is impossible to understand the contemporary Yemeni state without bearing this dynamic in mind, and that it has a very long history.

There were many important mukarribs during the long time period of Sabaean history but none more so than Karibil Watar (the Great) whose reign began sometime around 775 BCE. Through bloody military campaigns initiated by his predecessors but completed by this mukarrib, the Sabaean Kingdom expanded into an empire whose outright territorial control or influence spread northward to Najran (now in southwestern Saudi Arabia), westward to Sana'a (where the legendary Ghamdhan Palace was built) and the Red Sea coast, and southward as far as the Wadi Hadhramawt and the outskirts of the present port of Aden. In spite of the fact that there were preexistent political entities in each of the places the Sabaeans conquered, they managed to impress their own language and culture upon the local populations, more or less unifying all of South Arabian under their control. This was a huge territory, the equivalent in square miles of the state of New York. Sabaean colonies were even established in Abyssinia (present-day Ethiopia) as proved by inscriptions found there. Just what prompted this expansion is not exactly clear. Perhaps, it had to do with economic control over the lucrative trade routes, of which there were several stretching hundreds of miles across South Arabia. Perhaps, it had to with acquiring slave labor from among the conquered peoples who built and maintained at this time such monumental works such as the Great Dam at Marib and the Almaqah temples at Marib and Sirwah. What is clear is that Sabaean hegemony over this territory lasted a few hundred years, until the rise of rival kingdoms began to challenge it.

Three kingdoms rival to the Sabaeans became prominent in South Arabia, at roughly the same time, 400 BCE. There was Ma'in in what is now the Wadi al-Jawf (northwest of Marib) with three important cities: Qarnaw, Yathil (present-day Baraqish), and Nashan (Al-Sawda'). It never reached the confederation level of political integration enjoyed by the Sabaeans and therefore was never controlled by a mukarrib (only a malik). But Ma'in was nonetheless famous for its perfume trade. It established emporia in northern Hijaz (in present-day Al-'Ula, Saudi Arabia) and was known worldwide in Phoenecia, Egypt, Palestine, and Rome. Eventually, it grew emboldened to attack the Sabaeans, though never managed to conquer its great competitor. In fact, this commercial kingdom collapsed around 100 BCE, possibly due to Sabaean aggression. Another great kingdom was founded in the Wadi Hadhramawt, with its capital at Shabwah (the name also of the present-day site), and in its heyday spread as far south as the Indian Ocean. Because of the paucity of archaeological investigations, little is known about this kingdom. Sabaean inscriptions refer to it as an ally or vassal of its empire until the fourth century BCE, but after this time, it gained increasing importance and independence, primarily because of its possession of Dhofar in Oman, the center of frankincense and myrrh production. The third important kingdom was Qataban (known to the Roman author Pliny as the Gebbanites), located south of Marib in Wadis Bayhan and Harib, with Tamna as its capital (present-day Hajar Khulan). At its height, the Qataban area of influence might have extended southwestward to the Red Sea straits (Bab al-Mandab), and like the other power centers of South Arabia, its wealth was based on the incense and spice trade. (Pliny maintains that the Qatabans held a monopoly on cinnamon.) Its decline was evident by the first century BCE, and it came to an end in second century CE when it was annexed by the Kingdom of Hadhramawt. Other parts of Qataban fell to the Sabaeans. By the first century BCE, only the Sabaean and Hadhramawt kingdoms remained serious power centers in Southern Arabia, and the region as a whole was fearfully divided.

The Sabaeans now faced a new threat, an imperial invasion from Rome, arguably the first attempt by a "foreign" power to conquer and occupy Yemen—though it was not the last. The incense trade seems to have been the cause. The Emperor Augustus (63 BCE–14 CE) was tired of paying exorbitant prices for the incense used in Roman funerary rituals that came from Southern Arabia, and he decided it was time to annex this land, fabled as one of the wealthiest in the world (which the Romans referred to as Arabia Felix or Happy Arabia). He sent the Roman governor of Egypt, Aelius Gallus, to defeat the South Arabian kingdoms. The expedition began in 25 BCE and lasted for about a year. The southwest corner of what is now Saudi Arabia, Najran, was conquered, and the Roman army had no trouble vanquishing

ORIGIN OF YEMENITE JEWS

There are many origin myths, Arab and Jewish, for the presence of the Jews in South Arabia but few reliable historical accounts. One version is that the Yemenite Jews were one of the tribes of Israel that wandered in the wilderness following the Exodus led by Moses from Egypt into the Promised Land. They eventually rebelled against Moses and turned southward to Yemen where they settled. The legend goes that it was from these Jews that the Queen of Sheba learned about Solomon and his great wisdom. By contrast, another legend has it that it was after the Queen of Sheba's visit to Solomon that Jews emigrated from Palestine to Yemen, accompanying her caravan back to Marib. The most persuasive tradition, however, is that the earliest emigration of Jews to Yemen took place just before the destruction of the First Temple in Jerusalem (587 BCE), and it is this story that seems to be historically the most plausible.

the Kingdom of Ma'in in the Wadi al-Jawf, but the Sabaeans were a different matter. Marib withheld the Roman siege, primarily because Aelius Gallus's troops ran out of water and succumbed to disease. They were forced to retreat, and weakened by the arduous journey, they were ready targets for enemy attacks. In the end, it is questionable whether any survived. The campaign was a catastrophe, one of the worst defeats in the history of the empire, and Rome never attempted to conquer Arabia Felix again.

The Himyarites

We have seen that South Arabia was in a state of crisis in the first century BCE. One of the casualties of this period was the Kingdom of Qataban, and from it broke away a group of tribes called the Himyarites. They extended their power southward, competing for control of the incense trade with the Kingdom of Hadhramawt, until they ended up controlling the port of Aden and the southern Tihama. With access to the Indian Ocean, the Himyarites had a way of competing with the Sabaeans, especially at a time when sea routes were becoming ever more important and would eventually supplant overland routes for trade between Asia and the Mediterranean. Eventually, they moved their capital to Zafar, in the central Yemeni highlands, having been pushed out of the southern coastal areas by the power of Hadhramawt. Thus, by the second century CE, there were three great rival powers in Arabia: the Sabaeans, the Hadhramis, and the Himyarites.

Shortly afterward, another invasion of South Arabia occurred, that of the Abyssinians (from Ethiopia). They took over the Tihama in the second century CE where they established a Christian enclave. They marched on the Himyarite capital, Zafar, and conquered it around 240 CE, compelling the Himyarites to enter into an alliance with them. The Sabaeans did not lay idle but chased the Abyssinians out of Najran and engaged them again in the highlands, though the outcome was ambiguous, and the Sabaeans continued to do battle with the Abyssinians and their proxies, the Himyarites, for several more decades. This warfare only served to disrupt the caravan routes and therefore reduce their income, while the Himyarite commerce flourished because of their access to the Indian Ocean. The enemies of the Sabaeans were closing in: Arabs from Central Arabia (concerned about the drying up of their profits from the caravan routes), the Hadhramis from the east, the Abyssinians from the west, and the Himyarites from the south. Around 270–280 CE, the Sabaean Kingdom collapsed and was annexed by the Himyarites. Shortly afterward, their king also conquered Hadhramawt. By the beginning of the third century CE, the Himyarite Kingdom, with the exception of Tihama, which was still under Abyssinian control, was ruler of South Arabia.

The last ruler of the Himyarite Kingdom was Yusuf Dhu Nuwas (ruled 517–525 CE), a controversial figure in Yemeni history. The story of his ascendancy to power is murky, but according to one legend, widely repeated in the Arab sources, he was a handsome youth and the object of unwanted attention by the immediately preceding monarch. In order to escape his attentions, Dhu Nuwas murdered him. The Himyarite aristocracy placed him on the throne. He converted to Judaism, for reasons that remain obscure, and adopted the surname Yusuf.

To understand the politics of Yemen in his day, it is necessary to bear in mind its wider geopolitical context and to step back a bit in time to the African Kingdom of Aksum.

Though Aksum began to exert power over Yemen in the fourth century, this was limited to the Tihama, and even there, its influence was intermittent and fitful. By the sixth century, however, Christian power in Arabia had greatly increased. The central highland town of Zafar was a Christian stronghold and the region of Najran in present-day southern Saudi Arabia. As an attempt to counteract Christian influence in Arabia, Dhu Nuwas launched a deadly campaign against the Christians and their local Arab allies, slaughtering the garrison in Safar and eventually occupying Christian Najran sometime between 518 and 523 CE. There, Dhu Nuwas put to death thousands of Himyarite Christians (according to some sources, the number of dead was as high as 20,000) who refused to convert to Judaism, and he then called on the Persian kings to do the same to the Christians in their realms. As word spread of

---

THE KINGDOM OF AKSUM

The Kingdom of Aksum emerged in the third century CE as a major commercial and military power in East Africa. It encompassed a vast territory, including present-day northern Sudan, Eritrea, and Ethiopia, and eventually spread to territories across the Red Sea in Yemen and present-day southern Saudi Arabia (the province of Najran). For the Aksumites to have maintained an empire that reached to the Upper Nile and across the Red Sea into southwestern Arabia, a territory encompassing well over a million square miles meant that it had formidable land and naval forces. Aksum grew wealthy on trade, exporting agricultural products from the Upper Nile region as well as ivory, tortoise shell, gold, and emeralds from the African interior to Rome and Byzantium. It imported silks and spices from South Asia. The kingdom converted to Christianity sometime between 325 and 328 CE (before its conversion, the religion was mostly polytheistic), when it began minting coins with the sign of the cross.

the fate of the Najran Christians, Byzantium had to act or lose all credibility as protector of "eastern" Christianity; in alliance with the Christian Aksumite Kingdom, it launched a counterattack against Dhu Nuwas.

One of the commanders of the army of the Aksumite king who led the expedition was an Aksumite Christian viceroy in southern Arabia by the name of Abraha, thought to have been of Ethiopian ethnicity (another legend has it that he was of slave origin). Abraha led an army that according to tradition numbered a hundred thousand men, including hundreds of elephants. The Himyarite forces of Dhu Nuwas were no match for them, and in the end, the latter is supposed to have committed suicide by riding his horse into the Red Sea (though a South Arabian inscription may indicate that he perished in battle). His death occurred sometime in 525–530 CE. Abraha seized power in his own name, taking over Sana'a as the capital of his kingdom. The Aksumite king sent over a general to depose Abraha, and the two met in a duel in which Abraha killed his opponent by a shameful ruse, though not without having had a terrible gash inflicted on his own face in the fight, earning him the sobriquet "scar face." Abraha promoted Christianity in Arabia, and, according to tradition, built a great church in Sana'a by the name of al-Qullays (from the Greek "Ekklesia"), which in scale and importance was meant to rival the Kaaba in Mecca. (Its presumed foundations are pointed out by Yemenis to this day in the heart of the Old City.) It was to smash his commercial rivals in Mecca that he invaded the Hijaz around 550 CE, an event commemorated in the Verse of the Elephant in the Qur'an, so named because of the elephants Abraha used in his military campaign. Had it not been for a miracle in which it is said that hundreds of birds took up pebbles in their mouths and bombarded the elephants with them, the defenders of Mecca might have met the same fate as the forces of Dhu Nuwas. According to Islamic exegesis, Abraha perished in this battle, though no independent evidence exists to corroborate this. What is certain is that if he did not die in this battle, he certainly did so shortly thereafter. One inscription dates his death to 553 CE. If correct, this would mean that Abraha's rule, though spectacular in the annals of Arabian history, lasted only about three years. The Christian kingdom he founded and that his two sons continued to rule after his death did not outlast him by many years.

In 570 CE, an uprising began against the kingdom Abrahama founded in Yemen that, even though it was spearheaded by the Persian (Sasanid) Empire, forever after has been associated with the legendary figure of Sayf bin Dhi Yazan, who asked the Persians for help in getting rid of the Aksumites. A Persian mercenary expedition sailed from the head of the Gulf, continued on down and around the Straits of Hormuz and along the southern Arabian coast where it landed, and then fought its way upland to Sana'a, defeating and killing the Aksumite governor. Sayf bin Dhi Yazan was installed as the Persian's vassal ruler over Yemen, but he was on the thrown for only a brief time before he was killed in an Aksumite insurrection. The Persians returned to Yemen and managed to quell the Aksumite revolt, installing Sayf's son on the throne. For the next 70 years, Yemen came under Persian control until Islam made its way into the region in 630 CE, when the Persian vassal state converted to the new religion en masse.

The Coming of Islam

When the tribes of Yemen declared their fealty to the Prophet Muhammad, the latter appointed a governor in Sana'a, the most important city in Yemen since the fifth century CE, to rule in his name. The succeeding caliphs, the Umayyads of Damascus and the Abbasids of Baghdad, adopted the same practice, though these governors exercised little direct control over the territories outside the city, depending instead on the tribes to manage their affairs in the hinterlands. This is a pattern we have seen before, of course. To the extent that a central government has existed in Yemen, it has always depended on the tribes to help govern the territories the state claims in its name. The situation is more or less the same today.

By the middle of the ninth century, Zaydis, fleeing persecution in Iraq, began to settle in the northern town of Sa'dah where they established a polity under their imam, Yahya al-Hadi, in 897. He claimed descent from the Prophet Muhammad through his daughter Fatima, on the basis of which he legitimated his authority among the tribes. This was the beginning of the Zaydi state in Yemen whose power waxed and waned for a thousand years. At times, the imams retreated to their stronghold in the northern city of Sa'dah, having little else over which to claim authority; at other times, especially under the Sharaf al-Din and Hamid al-Din families, they managed to rule practically the entire country, though never for very long periods of time. The central part of Yemen was also becoming restive in reaction to the administrative incompetence of the caliphal governors in Sana'a and rebellions started to take hold. The caliphal governor was often absent, being called away because of political problems elsewhere in the empire, and leaving a deputy in his stead. This absence pro-

---

ISLAM AND THE PROPHET MUHAMMAD

Islam is considered one of the three great monotheistic religions of the Near East (the other two being Judaism and Christianity). Its founder is the Prophet Muhammad (570–632 CE), and its followers are known as Muslims. He is not considered a divine figure, like Jesus, but a human mortal—though not ordinary in any sense of the word. He had revelations later in life in which the Archangel Gabriel was supposed to have relayed the words of God (Allah) in Arabic, presumed to be also a divine language. These revelations were compiled into what would become the Qur'an, Islam's holy book. Muhammad's sayings and deeds, as reported by trustworthy eyewitnesses and companions of the time, were also compiled into what are known as the Hadith. Together the Qur'an and the Hadith became the source of Islamic law or Sharia. Perhaps, the most fundamental tenet of Islam is that there is only one God (Islam literally means "submission" and in this context implies submission to the will of God) and that the Prophet Muhammad is His Messenger. To accept this tenet, as in the declamation of faith or *shahadah*, is to convert to Islam.

THE SUNNI CALIPHATES: UMAYYADS, ABBASIDS, AND OTTOMANS

Caliphate is the term for a government created to rule the Muslim community after the Prophet Muhammad's death. The head of this government was the caliph. The Umayyads (671–750 CE) were the first caliphate (capital in Damascus) and waged the Islamic conquests that led to an empire stretching from Spain, across North Africa, and through western Asia (including the Arabian Peninsula, the Levant, and what are present-day Syria, Iraq, and Iran). The Umayyads were succeeded by the Abbasids (750–1519), with their capital in Baghdad, whose most famous caliph was Harun al-Rashid (ruled from 786 to 809). Under his reign, classic Islamic civilization reached its apogee. The rule of the Abbasid caliphs was interrupted in 1258 when the Mongols destroyed Baghdad, but after only three years, the Abbasids resumed their rule. In 1519, the Ottomans who originated in Turkey and ended up conquering much of the territory held by the Abbasids declared themselves the next Islamic caliphate. It effectively came to an end at the conclusion of World War I in 1918 when the Ottomans and the Germans were defeated by the Allied Powers. The dream of restoring the caliphate is harbored by some present-day Muslims.

---

voked the restive tribes and the northern Zaydis to raise arms against Sana'a, which, in turn, required the caliphs to send an army to quell the insurrections.

THE MEDIEVAL KINGDOMS

The Ziyadid Dynasty (820–1018 CE)

This was a medieval dynasty that arose in the Tihama in the early medieval period. Unfortunately, little can be said about it that is based on firm evidence. It appears to have been quite vast, based in the Tihama, but extending into the highlands and both the Red Sea and Indian Ocean coasts. This was the period when the early Islamic caliphates were concerned with establishing control over their dominions in the heartlands of the empire, and southwestern Arabia was considered to be on the periphery. Nevertheless, when a revolt broke out among a group of tribesmen in the Tihama, the Abbasid caliph at that time was concerned enough to send an emissary Muhammad ibn Ziyad in 820 CE to quell the rebellion. Ibn Ziyad, however, after having accomplished his mission decided to break away from the Abbasids and establish his own independent dynasty, after his name, the Ziyadids. He founded the town of Zabid, which became his capital. Zabid is one of the storied towns of Yemen, later to become a major center of learning and commerce in the medieval Islamic world. In 1018, the Ziyadid ruler was assassinated by a former black slave by the name of Najah, who in turn founded his own dynasty in the Tihama. But their rule did not go unchallenged and in the end was replaced by rivals.

The Sulayhid Dynasty (1047–1138 CE)

It was into this power vacuum that a dynastic family of Ismaili persuasion (see religion) stepped in, the Sulayhids (1047–1138), whose seat of power was in the Heraz mountains northwest of Sana'a (and which today is dominated by the town

---

THE FATIMID AND AYYUBID CALIPHATES

The Fatimids were a dynasty of Shia Arabs who created their own caliphate (909–1171) and challenged Abbasid power in the east. Their great commercial empire extended over an enormous territory (encompassing North Africa, Egypt, the western flank of Arabia, and portions of the Levant). They built Cairo as their capital. Though their branch of Shia Islam was the Ismailis, they were known for religious tolerance of non-Ismaili sects, as well as Sunni and even non-Muslim groups such as the Christian Copts. In 1171, the Fatimid dynasty was defeated by a general of Kurdish origins, Salah al-Din (or Saladin as he is known in Western histories of the Crusades), who founded his own dynasty, the Ayyubids (1171–1250). They too rivaled the Abbasids in the east and like them fell in the Mongol invasion. Ayyubid power was centered in Egypt though their influence extended well beyond it, including Yemen. They tended to strengthen the economy and the arts in the societies they ruled. A Sunni dynasty, they also strengthened Sunni doctrine throughout their realm by establishing madrasahs or religious schools.

The mosque and tomb of Queen Arwa in Jibla. (Herve Collart/Sygma/Corbis)

of Manakhah). With the help of the Egyptian Fatimids, the Sulayhids began the slow process of unifying Yemen under their rule. Their greatest monarch was a queen by the name of Arwa (1048–1138), one of the most interesting and significant figures in the history of Yemen, possibly even the world. Her importance certainly equals that of another great queen of Yemen, Sheba, though she is not as well known. Arwa had a reputation for being highly intelligent and learned as well as politically shrewd. Legend has it that she was also beautiful. Her husband, Ahmed al-Sulayhi, became ruler of the Sulayhid dynasty of Yemen in 1067; but being an invalid and weak, he handed over power to his able wife, making her the de facto ruler of the realm. She had her name mentioned in the Friday mosque sermons, right after the name of the Fatimid caliph, and in that way secured her legitimacy in the eyes of the people.

The Sulayhid capital was at first in Sana'a, but it proved far too fractious for the court, and one of the first things Arwa did as regent was to move it to Jibla, a beautiful town in central Yemen near Ibb. It had a strategically important location near the sources of her kingdom's wealth, the agricultural lands of the central highlands, and it was within easy reach of the southern portions of the country, especially Aden, a port that did a brisk and profitable trade with India and beyond. From that location, she was also able to send armies to the Tihama to quell uprisings that flared up periodically. In Jibla, she built a great administrative palace and a mosque named after her. The mosque is simple and graceful in its proportions, as unpretentious as apparently the queen was herself.

Upon the death of her husband, the Fatimid caliph insisted that Arwa remarry, which she reluctantly agreed to do, though by this time she had become so powerful that her second husband was no more than a figurehead. Indeed, legend has it that she did not even permit the marriage to be consummated. After 10 years' time, this second husband also died, after which Arwa never remarried, ruling Yemen alone and in her own name.

Her rule did not go unopposed, however. In 1119, an envoy was sent by the Fatimid caliph to take control of her realm, which she successfully resisted by mobilizing the tribal sheikhs and dynastic princes who supported her. She sent the Fatimid envoy packing from her court. Obviously, this affront did not endear the audacious queen with Cairo. When the latter was thrown into turmoil over a succession to the dynasty's head, Arwa supported one candidate, an infant son of the previous caliph, over another. The latter, in revenge, rallied Arwa's enemies to overthrow her. Once again, however, she prevailed and continued to reign securely until her death in 1138, having lived to the ripe old age of 90. She strengthened the agricultural economy, enriched the treasury, and built schools throughout her realm, which extended from Sana'a in the north all the way to Aden, effectively uniting the northern and southern regions of the country into a politically unified state for the first time since the Sabaeans. Besides being a patroness of schools, Arwa was also a significant religious leader of the Ismailis in Yemen. She sent Ismaili missionaries to Gujarat, India, where a significant Ismaili community, the Dawoodi Bohra, was formed that exists to this day. The burial site of the Yemeni founder of this community, located in a small town near present-day Manakhah in Yemen, has become an important annual pilgrimage site for Indian Ismailis.

For her good works in the religious sphere, Queen Arwa became a deeply beloved figure and remains so to this day. She is buried in a simple, whitewashed crypt alongside the mosque she commissioned in Jibla, and as one goes by it, one can see a simple wreath of flowers lying humbly on top of it, a token of esteem left by the wayward pilgrim.

Relatively soon after Queen Arwa's death, the unity of the country she had worked so hard to preserve collapsed. Among those who wanted to carve it up were the Zaydi imams in the north who tried to extend their power beyond Sa'dah; a dynasty of slave origins, the Najahids, who tightened their grip on the Tihama; and various tribal sheikhs who created rival fiefdoms in the south. The country was eventually thrown into mayhem.

As happened before and would happen again with almost tiresome regularity, a strong man stepped into the power vacuum to reassert control. That man was Turanshah, brother of the famous and redoubtable Salah al-Din al-Ayyubi, founder of the Ayyubid caliphate, and it was he who conquered central Yemen in 1173. In Taiz, he built an almost impregnable fort on a hill that overlooks the main water source of the Old City (proving the adage that whoever controls the water supply in such an arid land controls the country), and girdled it with a high, thick wall (bits of which are still extant). As the fortifications might suggest, however, Ayyubid rule was constantly challenged. Part of the reason might have been that the Ayyubids had no historical roots in Yemen (their predecessors, the Sulayhids, at least came out of the western highlands), and outside rule has always been fiercely opposed in Yemen, as the Roman Empire knew only too well and the Ottoman Turks knew again in the 16th and 19th centuries. Administrative negligence on the part of the Ayyubid governors of Yemen had just as much to blame, however. Starting with Turanshah and every Ayyubid governor who succeeded him, the head of the government was constantly being called away to help with political affairs in Egypt or Syria or with military campaigns elsewhere in the empire, and while they were distracted from administrative affairs, the old insurrections flared up again.

The Rasulid Dynasty (1228–1454)

It was different for one man who was appointed governor by his predecessor when the latter had to leave Yemen on business to Egypt; he was known as al-Rasul (not his real name). In 1228, al-Rasul broke with the Ayyubids, and his grandson declared himself an independent Sultan, though it is not clear how he managed it; ostensibly, he received the allegiance of the heads of the most important towns and tribes in central Yemen. The Rasulids were a relatively long-lived dynasty (1228–1454), and thanks to a succession of talented and intellectually gifted rulers ended up spearheading a glorious efflorescence of learning and culture in Yemen. The "medieval" period in Islam, unlike that in European Christendom, was a time of enlightenment and civilization, and in many ways, the Yemeni Rasulids were outstanding exemplars of it. Unfortunately, to this day, research on this important dynasty is slant compared to other medieval Islamic states, though the irony is that it was perhaps unique in the Muslim world at that time in the extent to which it kept meticulous administrative records (a treasure trove for any historian).

Glass and enamel bottle, Rasulid dynasty. (Detroit Institute of Arts/The Bridgeman Art Library)

Not since Queen Arwa had the entire country from Sana'a in the north to Aden in the south and from the Tihama in the west to Hadhramawt in the east been unified under one government. The latter governed its territory through fiefdoms, control over which was granted to loyal supporters, a system adopted from the Ayyubids. The capital was in Taiz, already heavily fortified by Turanshah. The state's army was needed in order to put down periodic incursions by the Zaydi imams and the recalcitrant tribes in the Tihama, but the Rasulids did not rule by brute force alone. From the fort built by Turanshah, one looks down on the old city of Taiz and what one sees are two large mosques with schools or *madrasahs* adjacent to them. They are the Ashrafiya and the Mu'tabiya, which are still standing in Taiz today and are slowly being brought back to their old grandeur and beauty by international teams of conservators and restorers. These grand structures were built by Rasulid rulers (one of whom was a powerful queen of one of the rulers), the idea being that the head of the state was also the protector of Islam, whose beliefs and rituals was properly instructed in the religious schools. Thus, state rule was indirectly propagated through the educational system. The complex of fort–mosque–school was not just serendipitous but a potent symbol of Rasulid legitimacy and authority. No wonder this complex became a signature architectural style or urban plan of the Rasulids and their successors, the Tahirid dynasty.

For two centuries, Yemen experienced a period of relative prosperity, thanks to the efficiency of Rasulid administration. The agricultural sector was strengthened by restoring and expanding irrigation works, the fiscal policy of the government was stabilized, taxes were more or less fairly imposed and systematically collected, and, perhaps most important of all, the Indian Ocean trade network to India, China, and Southeast Asia was protected and expanded. Through the exchange of ideas and artistic objects that this trade facilitated (including also links with Egypt and the Mediterranean world), a renaissance in handcrafts and building took place in Yemen, along with an efflorescence in scientific learning (agricultural calendars and treatises), literature, and historical writing. Because of its geographical location, Yemen continued to play a pivotal role in Indian Ocean trade. Deepwater ports in Aden and Mocha became both a landing place for cargo from the east and a launching pad for trade to the Mediterranean world. It was during this period that coffee became a lucrative cash crop in Yemen, greatly in demand in the Muslim world and Europe.

About a hundred years into their reign, the Rasulids lost control of Sana'a to the Zayid imams in 1323–1324. A hundred years later, because of family quarrels and a series of incompetent rulers, they lost control of the rest of their realm. As befitting the historical pattern, sensing the weakness of the dynasty, strong men stepped in and seized power, this time tribal sheikhs from southeastern Yemen known as the Banu Tahir.

HISTORY OF YEMENI COFFEE

The Rasulid dynasty introduced coffee as a drink from Ethiopia sometime in the 15th century, and the Yemeni Sufi brotherhoods were the first to use it in their dhikr ceremonies. Around 1475, coffee consumption spread from Yemen to Cairo, and it was the Ottoman conquest of Egypt (1516–1517) that led to the rapid diffusion of the drink to Istanbul, Damascus, and other towns of the Ottoman Empire. Under the Ottomans in Yemen, Mocha became an important Red Sea port, largely because of the coffee trade. The English sent their commercial vessels there in the early 17th century, followed soon thereafter by the Dutch (the French would not arrive until 1709). So great was the demand for coffee that by the 1600s, it had supplanted the spice trade in revenue. That good fortune was short-lived; for in the early part of the 18th century, the European colonial powers such as the Dutch, Portuguese, and English introduced coffee production on their plantations in Java, Surinam, Jamaica, and Brazil. By the mid-19th century, Yemen produced only a tiny fraction of the world's coffee supply, though it still dominated a connoisseur niche market.

The Tahirid Dynasty (1455–1547)

The Banu Tahir were tribal sheikhs from the Rada' area of Yemen. Tahir ibn Sheikh al-'Ummawi, the founder of the Tahirid dynasty, was a vassal of the Rasulid sultan and sent tribal troops to fight the rebellious tribes in the Tihama and in Aden's hinterland in the name of his lord. In turn, when this vassal's territory was attacked by the Zaydi Imam, the sultan sent troops to the Banu Tahir's aid.

Like all important tribal dynasties, the Banu Tahir owned extensive landholdings in and around Rada', such as terraced agricultural fields, fruit orchards, and grazing pastures. To increase the productivity of these holdings, they were industrious in building up the region's irrigation infrastructure, water works such as small dams and cisterns that harnessed the rains during one of the two annual monsoon seasons as well as underground canals that conducted reservoir water to the agricultural fields. To pay for these structures, the Banu Tahir used the proceeds from the sale of their agricultural goods as well as the taxes they levied on the tribal tenant farmers.

But there was probably another income stream, the lucrative Indian Ocean trade. The Banu Tahir were not only landholding sheikhs, but were also important merchants with large trading establishments in Aden. In fact, this may well have been the major source of their wealth. They owned ships that plied the Indian Ocean and rented space to other merchants in their holds. No doubt the daily routines of such businesses were left to agents or merchants working closely with the shipowners. Trade consisted in luxury goods such as the proverbial incense and spices, textiles, gold, and precious gems coming from Asia as well as food staples such as rice, dates, and nuts—many of which were grown in the Tihama or in Lahaj just north of Aden on plantations and oases the Banu Tahir, among others, built for purposes of trade. Sugarcane production might well have been introduced in Yemen by the first Tahirid sultan. These ships also carried human cargo, pilgrims to and from the holy places in Mecca and Medina, and slaves.

When one understands the sources of their wealth and how interconnected and far-flung these sources were, one can appreciate the Banu Tahir's concern that the Rasulid state was no longer able to maintain social order over its realm and that they had to do something to protect and consolidate their economic holdings, especially in Aden and its agricultural hinterland. Accordingly, two sons of Tahir, Amir and Ali, went down with a tribal contingent and conquered the port city of Aden in 1455. As important as the port city was, however, the trading routes that extended from it northward overland through the Tihama to the Red Sea port cities of Mocha and Al-Hudaydah were not less so, and if these were not secured, the far-flung trading network that brought goods from Asia to Aden and from Aden to the Mediterranean would be disrupted. Taking Aden was thus inevitably a prelude to a wider military campaign. Amir and Ali launched their tribal armies northward, taking Zabid, Taiz, and Al-Hudaydah. By that point it was clear to the last Rasulid sultan that his vassals had become overlords, and he departed for Mecca in a nonbloody transfer of power. Perhaps he was happy to go; ruling such a fractious country must have been dangerous and unendingly tiresome and of little gratification, except to the most power hungry.

SLAVERY IN ARABIA

Slavery is a controversial and complex topic in Arabian history. In many ways, the status of slaves was quite different from and better than what it was in the United States until their emancipation in the Civil War. Slaves had rights enshrined in the Qur'an, including that of adequate food and shelter, and they could also be manumitted by their masters upon marriage to the latter or be set free in their wills. Historically, many men of slave origin rose to become powerful ministers and even heads of state. Nevertheless, there are many examples of slaves having been badly treated in spite of protections under religious law. The great "slave trading" power in the Arabian Peninsula was Oman, but slaves were brought into the peninsula from Africa, Persia, and even Circassia (Russia) through multiple routes. One of the controversies surrounding slavery in Arabia is that it was not legally abolished until relatively recently—not until the 1960s for most countries in the region.

Amir was declared sultan in 1460, but worked closely with his younger brother Ali to consolidate the Tahirid dynasty's power and control. Their hold remained tenuous, however. Eventually, Ali was killed in a battle against the Zaydi Imam in the north. The sultan, meanwhile, was busy quelling tribal rebellion in the Tihama when he died in 1478. His handpicked successor, al-Wahhab, was his nephew who ruled only 11 years before he died, having spent his entire reign either putting down conflicts in his own family or tribal insurrections in the Tihama. His son, Amir, became sultan in 1489.

Sultan Amir ibn al-Wahhab (1489–1517) was in many respects an important and able ruler, though he eventually fell victim to forces larger than himself, ones Yemen had not seen before, the Portuguese. Having inherited a situation in which nearly every part of his realm was up in arms, he spent the first years of his reign defeating his opponents one by one until he became master of central Yemen, with his court in Taiz. The state treasury became rich from the spoils of these wars, and he used the funds to subvent military expeditions against his old enemies in the north, the Zaydi imams. It was not easy, but eventually he conquered Sana'a in 1504. According to eyewitness accounts, Sultan Amir ibn al-Wahhab depended on 80,000 foot soldiers and 3,000 horsemen for his final assault on the city. Sana'a was defended by tribal troops from Sa'dah, loyal to the Imam, but they could not hold out against such a large and well-equipped force and eventually surrendered. The sultan was now ruler of a kingdom roughly the size that the Rasulids controlled in their heyday.

Due on the one hand to their extensive agricultural holdings and trading interests and the other to their treasury amassed from taxes and military spoils, the Tahirid rulers became enormously wealthy, and they—but especially Sultan Amir ibn al-Wahhab—used this wealth to benefit the realm, not just their personal fortunes. They continued repairing and building irrigation systems, a practice they had begun in their homeland region of Rada', not to mention roads, mosques, and schools. They also constructed major monuments; the most significant of which from an artistic point of view was the complex of mosque and school in Rada' known as the 'Amariyyah, which, as the name suggests, was built by the Sultan Amir (ibn al-Wahhab), the most prolific patron of monumental architecture of all the Tahirid sultans.

Visiting the site today, one immediately notices a large, elegant fort, dating probably from Himyarite times, built on a hilltop overlooking the city and below it the magnificently restored 'Amariyyah (see "Yemeni Architecture" in Chapter 6). The urban pattern is the same as that established by the Rasulid monarchs, and arguably for the same reasons, it was important for the state to be seen not only as a military force but also as the producer of learning through an educational system it generously supported. If along the way, it was also a patron of those arts and handcrafts that went into the construction of these monumental works, so much the better for the dynasty's symbolic power.

The building was completed in 1504. It is in the form of a massive rectangle (120 ft by 69 ft) and three storeys in height. (For more details of its layout as well as its interior and external façades, see the section on "Yemeni Architecture" in Chapter 6). To be noted here is the fact that there are many design elements that resemble earlier Rasulid structures in Taiz (a multidomed prayer hall, on either side of which are walkways, colonnaded courtyard, and one or two minarets), which is not surprising given their magnificence. Perhaps more interesting, however, are the resemblances to Islamic monumental architecture in India, reminding us once again of the powerful influence of Indian Ocean culture in Yemen due to long-distance trade. The result was a remarkably harmonious fusion of elements resulting in one of the most beautiful buildings in the world. Legend has it that the sultan, upon visiting his ancestral city of Rada', would order his servants to place a candle in every doorway and window, in every nook and cranny, until the building was ablaze with light. He would then gallop into the hills at night with one of his daughters to gaze at the spectacle and wonder in delight at the beauties of the edifice he had built. The sultan might have sensed that he was gazing at the end of his own world, for the Indian Ocean trade that had made much of this munificence possible was in serious jeopardy by the time the 'Amariyyah was completed, due to the arrival of the Portuguese in the Indian Ocean at the beginning of the 16th century.

Indians and Arabs had been trading peacefully in the Indian Ocean for centuries, there seeming to be enough for everyone, but the Portuguese were not content merely to be partners in this trade, they wanted to dominate it. With their powerful weaponry and ships, they hoped to take over the shipping lanes and be the sole trading agents in the Indian Ocean, an ambition that required military occupation of a far-flung network of ports or colonies. In East Africa, Oman, the western coast of India, and Southeast Asia, they set up trading posts. In Goa (western coast of India), they issued a trading permit or license that every ship had to purchase if it were to trade in the region without being harassed by the Portuguese fleet. If the trading ship refused to pay for the license, it risked being sunk with all men onboard. In earlier days, traders in the Indian Ocean could move back and forth without being stopped or hindered, except by pirates; now they were told that the ocean was effectively owned or controlled by a foreign power to which they owed obeisance—a Christian power no less, not a Muslim one. It was only a matter of time before the Muslim polities in the Indian Ocean rose up to fight this intruder.

To the Mamluks of Egypt, the Portuguese posed an immediate threat to the lucrative Indian Ocean trade; and in 1507, the Mamluk Sultan of Egypt dispatched an expeditionary force to confront them. It sailed to Aden to replenish supplies before heading out into the Indian Ocean. In 1508, supported by an Indian Muslim sultan, the Egyptian fleet confronted the Portuguese and won the first round, but in the next year, the Portuguese fought back and devastated the Muslim forces. Their retreat was beset by violent winter storms and heavy winds, compounding the damage to the trading ships suffered under military bombardment, so that in the end only a few made it back to Aden in one piece. The Portuguese followed up their naval victory with a sweeping conquest of nearly all of the major Indian Ocean ports, with the exception of Aden and the ports of Mocha and Al-Hudaydah on the Red Sea. As Sultan Amir ibn al-Wahhab was the ruler of these ports, he was naturally the man who now had to face the Portuguese onslaught. In 1511, the Portuguese sailed from Goa to Aden. Eyewitness accounts of the attack on the port and the subsequent failure of the Portuguese paint a fascinating picture.

As a result of their failure to take the port of Aden, the Portuguese never succeeded in completely monopolizing the Indian Ocean trade. Nevertheless, their ability to greatly curtail it could not be overestimated, and the Mamluks continued to be alarmed. In 1515, the Mamluk Sultan of Egypt sailed down the Red Sea to the island of Kamaran off the coast of Yemen, recently sacked and burned by the Portuguese, and began diplomatic talks with Sultan Amir for money to pay for the ships and men as well as the provisions to feed them that would be needed for this *jihad* or holy war against the infidel Portuguese. Given the wealth of Tahirid dynasty, such a request was not outlandish, and it appeared as though Sultan Amir

---

THE MAMLUKS

Mamluk comes from the Arabic meaning "owned," because this caste of soldiers, drawn mainly from Turkish tribes, was of slave origin. Because they had no fealty to tribal sheikhs or noble families other than the caliphs, they were thought trustworthy and were employed as soldiers. In time, their status rose far above that of ordinary slaves. They enjoyed power particularly in Egypt where they were instrumental in supporting the Ayyubid dynasty of Salah al-Din (Saladin) and his successors. So reliant upon the Mamluks were the caliphs that they were eclipsed by the slaves who had once served them. The Mamluks eventually founded their own sultanate in the 14th century that lasted into the 19th century.

was prepared to comply when his most trusted minister dissuaded him. It was not wise counsel.

What was supposed to have been a sideshow turned into the main historical event, with disastrous consequences for the Tahirids. Instead of moving on to confront the Portuguese, the Egyptians, who were running out of food and water, had no choice but to land their fleet on the Yemen coastline and harass Tihama villagers for what they needed. In response, Sultan Amir sent one of his sons to confront the Egyptians at the head of an army. They lost Zabid to the Egyptians who pillaged and destroyed the town, and, according to rumored accounts, raped both young girls and boys. Clearly, the conquering army had run amok and the Egyptian Mamluk ruler appointed a governor in Zabid to restore order. Why hostilities did not cease at this point and the Tahirids sued for peace, agreeing to Egyptian conditions that would allow the war against the Portuguese to proceed, is unclear. Perhaps, the Egyptian Mamluk sultan, realizing how wealthy the Tahirid realm was, decided to conquer it. From Zabid, the Egyptians laid siege to Aden, and though they damaged or sunk some ships left in the harbor, they were unable to capture the port. They next turned their attention to Taiz, the capital of the Tahirid realm, which they succeeded in taking by badly defeating Sultan Amir's army. He had to retreat with his wives and treasury to a mountain fastness north of Aden in tribal Yafi'ah territory, where he was protected. Meanwhile, the Mamluks marched on Sana'a. The sultan came down from his mountain fastness, rallied the troops, and confronted the Egyptian invading force but to no avail. His troops fled in the middle of battle, abandoning him to his fate. He managed to escape up the high mountain that dominates the city, and the next morning hoped to make good his escape by going down and making his way to a Tahirid-controlled fort not far away, but was caught by Mamluk troops who killed him then and there, cutting off his head and impaling it on a pike. Thus was the ignominious end of one of Yemen's more accomplished rulers. Seeing the head of his sovereign displayed on the pike above the walled city of Sana'a, the governor of the city lost all hope and surrendered. The town became a scene of pillage and wanton destruction for nearly two months.

The Mamluk victory turned out to be short-lived. A month later, the Ottomans marched into Egypt and conquered it, hanging the last Mamluk sultan in Cairo. A new power had now emerged in the Red Sea, one far more formidable than the Mamluks and with far greater consequences for Yemen. The Ottomans sent a fleet to fight the Portuguese and sailed to Aden. The last Tahirid sultan negotiated a deal with the Ottomans in hopes of gaining their help with his fight against the Zaydi Imam Sharaf al-Din who had gained control over central Yemen after the Mamluks, far from their base in Egypt and without popular support, failed to make good on their military victories in the north. The leader of the Ottoman forces pretended to agree only in order to land his troops in Aden, that port which had withstood so many sieges and invasions in the past and was the commercial center of the country. He summoned the sultan to his ship and promptly had him and five of his aides and companions hanged as a warning to the populace should it contemplate rebellion. Taking the rest of the country would not be that easy, with Sana'a, as usual, posing

---

THE OTTOMAN EMPIRE

The Ottomans were a group of Turkish-speaking tribes that migrated from Central Asia to Anatolia, where they founded a powerful state that eventually spread into what is now Eastern Europe as far as the gates of Vienna and across North Africa, and included parts of the Arabian Peninsula as well. They conquered Byzantine Constantinople in 1453, which became their capital, Istanbul. The empire reached its height under the reign of Suleiman the Magnificent (reigned 1520–1566), when it was arguably the most powerful state in the world. The Ottoman Empire was socially and politically complex, encompassing many different ethnic groups and scores of different languages. One reason it managed to last 600 years (being abolished in 1922 when the Turkish Republic was founded) was the so-called millet system, according to which distinct ethnic, religious, and linguistic minorities were allowed to regulate their own affairs as long as they pledged loyalty to the Ottoman sultan.

---

the most daunting obstacle, but it too finally fell to the Ottomans in 1547, largely though not entirely due to bitter infighting and intrigue within the imamate family. The period of Tahirid rule had come to an end, and Ottoman control over Yemen had begun.

The Zaydi Imamate (911–1962)

The first head of the Yemeni Zaydi state was Imam Yahya bin Hussein al-Hadi (859–911). According to Arab historical sources, he was called to Yemen from the Hijaz (where he had risen to prominence as a great scholar) to mediate a tribal conflict in northern Yemen. As such, he was reenacting a model of Islam's spread that goes back to the earliest example of the Prophet who had migrated from Mecca to Medina to mediate a tribal feud, in gratitude for which the Medinese tribes swore an oath of allegiance to him as their spiritual guide and political leader. In similar fashion, the tribes paid fealty to Yahya al-Hadi as their imam after he had succeeded in getting them to resolve their conflicts peacefully.

The fortunes of the northern Zaydi state waxed and waned but mostly waned in opposition to the strong sultanate states that grew powerful in lower Yemen (the Sulayhids, Rasulids, and Tahirids) until the arrival of the Ottomans and their defeat of the Mamluks in the 15th century. When the Ottomans momentarily retreated from the Yemeni field, they allowed Imam Yahya Sharif al-Din—a family with roots in Kawkaban, a mountaintop village northwest of Sana'a—to enter Sana'a in 1517, from which base the Zaydi state was rebuilt. But this triumph was short-lived. Worried about Portuguese expansion in the Indian Ocean, the Ottomans knew that occupying or at the very least controlling Yemen was crucial in thwarting Portuguese ambitions, and so the Ottoman conquest of Yemen began that changed the fortunes of the country for the next 200 years.

Landing on Kamaran Island on the Arabian coast in 1538–1539, the Ottomans besieged Taiz in 1539–1540 and moved up the central highlands until they reached the gates of Sana'a in 1547. One reason for their success against Imamate forces was their use of cannon (for the first time apparently in Yemen) against impregnable stone fortresses, but another had to do with the Achilles heel of the Imamate state—namely, the incessant dynastic family quarrels and intrigues that weakened its defenses against the Ottoman advance. Sana'a was besieged (the present fort on top of Jabal Nuqum overlooking the city dates from this period), and due to treachery on the part of one of its defenders, the Ottomans entered clandestinely at night and terrorized its inhabitants with murder, rape, and pillage. Meanwhile, the Zaydi princes managed to escape to their fortified mountain hilltops, where they rallied their tribal defenders to face the Ottomans and their cannons. It was one of the Imam's sons, Mutahhar, who in the next 20 years slowly regained Zaydi foothold over the highland region to the north of Sana'a, in large measure because of tribal anger at their harsh treatment by the Turks. In 1566, the city surrendered to Mutahhar, and the Turkish garrison was allowed to retreat unharmed, in marked contrast with the way the Turks had brutalized the population nearly 20 years earlier. The Ottoman sultan responded with a massive counterforce, determined to put down this Yemeni insurgency, but this time, its army was urged not to treat ordinary citizens oppressively. Restraint prevailed, when the Ottoman army entered the city and left the populace unmolested. (The Ottomans did not so much rule Yemen as allow surrogates like Mutahhar's sons to do so while sowing the seeds of dissension among them.) Mutahhar's forces entrenched themselves behind a string of heavily armed forts to the northwest of the city and put up a stiff resistance against enemy bombardment. Unable to dislodge them or to surround them, the Ottomans eventually were obliged to sign a truce, and the Zaydis reclaimed Sana'a. The Jews of Yemen were accused of helping the Ottomans in their fight against the Zaydi state and in 1569, were ordered to be rounded up and sent into exile in Mowza' (southern Tihama). Many perished on the way or under conditions of extreme heat and lack of water once they arrived, but they were allowed to return when tribal sheikhs and other notables complained to the Imam that Jewish economic services were indispensable to the country's well-being.

The depressed state of Zaydi fortunes did not lift until the jihad of Imam al-Qasim bin Muhammad al-Kabir ("The Great," 1559–1620) began the struggle against the Turks in the 16th century. He successfully rallied the tribes around his call (da'wah) to become the Imam and rid Yemen of the Turkish yoke once and for all, and while the insurgency started by him and then carried on by his sons took many twists and turns—and nearly collapsed at one point—it proved victorious in the end. Sa'dah, the historic stronghold of the Zaydi Imamate, was finally retaken in 1619, partly because the Yemenis were now fully armed and could withstand Turkish artillery fire.

In 1620, al-Qasim "The Great" died, and his son al-Mu'ayyid Muhammad (1620–1640) became Imam. He took over the strongholds in the north and began a siege of Sana'a. Meanwhile, lower Yemen became vulnerable to his incursions

THE TWO YEMENS: UPPER AND LOWER

There are, in a sense, two geopolitical "centers" in the country. Sana'a is the geopolitical center of the north, with the northwestern region (Jabal Razih and Sa'dah) and the northeastern region (Al-Jawf and Marib) tribally organized. The Tihama and lowland Yemen (from Taiz to Aden) are largely village-based with relatively weak tribal affiliations. Historically, the lowland coastal Tihama has been vulnerable to invasion by foreign powers, and Taiz, by being linked to it, has been vulnerable in turn; nevertheless, Taiz (or Jibla, Ibb) was a powerful center during the medieval period. The 12th-century Sulayhids essentially abandoned Sana'a and the north in favor of controlling lower Yemen at Jibla. Both Ottoman occupations proved unable to fully secure the northern highlands and retreated to the Tihama, and the same was true of the Egyptians in the 1960s when they fought on the side of the Republic, abandoning the northern reaches of the country to the royalists. Whichever state hopes to control the country must do so through these two centers.

when the Ottomans, harassed by the Persians in Iraq, became distracted from their defenses inside the country. Sana'a surrendered to the Imam in 1629, and Taiz in the same year. The resolve and courage of al-Qasim, his son al-Mu'ayyid, and their tribal supporters are not to be underestimated, but the defeat of the Turks is hard to understand in the face of their initial supremacy in weapons and trained men.

The next Imam to follow al-Mu'ayyid was al-Mutawakkil 'ala Allah Ismail bin Qasim (1644–1676), whose rule is considered the high watermark of the Zaydi Qasimi state (and arguably even the Imamate as a whole). During his time, the agricultural system was restored to prosperity (in part because of years of bountiful rains), the treasury was made solvent, and people were treated evenhandedly. Nevertheless, criticisms flared up over his taxation policies, which he vigorously debated with his *'ulama* (the learned elite). It was in al-Mutawakkil's reign that the territory of the Zaydi state was expanded by force of arms into Hadhramawt, which it eventually conquered. But this move brought the Imamate into conflict with the Sultanate of Oman.

Imamate rule following al-Mutawakkil was marred by internal dynastic feuds, intertribal wars, and antistate rebellions for most of the 18th and 19th centuries, until the ascendancy of al-Mahdi Abbas al-Qasim (1748–1775), who proved to be one of the great imams of Yemen. He was apparently the son of a slave woman of African origins, and though this may seem remarkable in our eyes, it was not uncommon in the Imamate (or in the history of Islamic states, for that matter). (One of the great travelers to Yemen, the Danish Carsten Niebuhr, had an audience with this Imam in 1763). Al-Mahdi ruled with a firm but just hand and was quick to punish any government official for lax or tyrannical practices. He managed to bring

THE OMANI EMPIRE

The Sultanate of Oman managed to drive the Portuguese from its coast in the 17th century and went on to establish a maritime empire that stretched from present-day Oman and southern Iran down the eastern coast of Africa to the island of Zanzibar and as far west as Goa in India. It controlled the lucrative slave trade coming out of Zanzibar as well as the export of cloves, whose world market it controlled. Slaves were transported by ship to the Omani coast, where they were taken by caravan to desert oases like Al Buraymi (located at the present-day border between the United Arab Emirates and Oman) and sold to tribes all over central Arabia. The Omanis were, like the Turks, an experienced maritime power and attacked and plundered both the Arabian Sea and Red Sea coasts almost at will, and the Zaydi Imamate could do little to stop them.

the tribes to heal, more or less, through a combination of payments and military punishments and mobilized them skillfully in both the defense and expansion of his realm, sometimes taking the field of battle himself. There is some question as to whether the state treasury was depleted by these expensive military ventures, but the Imam never seemed to lack for money. Highly intelligent and learned, he was the ideal Zaydi model of an Imam: a wise and just ruler who was at the same time a redoubtable soldier.

CARSTEN NIEBUHR (1733–1815)

Carsten Niebuhr was a German explorer and mathematician who joined a Danish expedition to Yemen in 1760. He was its sole survivor. The expedition concentrated mainly on the Tihama, especially the area around the port of Mocha, and the highlands up to Sana'a. Niebuhr published his account of the expedition in 1772, *A Description of Arabia,* which remains one of the classic travel books of Arabia. Particularly rich are his descriptions of customs and personalities he encountered en route, a veritable treasure trove of ethnological information that remained indispensable to Yemen researchers until the country opened up to ethnographic work in the 1970s. After he returned from the expedition to Denmark, he settled down to a quiet married life in Copenhagen, Denmark, devoting himself to his family, writing, and scientific pursuits and never again embarking on such an adventurous experience as he had in Yemen.

BIBLIOGRAPHY

Al-Radi, Selma M. S. *The 'Amiriya in Rada': The History of Restoration of a Sixteenth-Century Madrasa in the Yemen.* Oxford: Oxford University Press, 1997.

Beyin, A. "The Bab al Mandab vs. The Nile-Levant: An Appraisal of the Two Dispersal Routes for Early Modern Humans out of Africa." *African Archaeological Review* 25 (2006): 5–30.

Crassard, Rémy. *La Préhistoire du Yémen.* BAR International Series 1842. Oxford: Arcahaeopress, 2008.

Daum, Walter, ed. *Yemen: 3000 Years of Art and Civilization in Arabia Felix.* Innsbruck: Pinguin, 1987.

De Maigret, Alessandro De. *Arabia Felix: An Exploration of the Archaeological History of Yemen.* London: Stacy International, 2002.

Durrani, Nadia. *The Tihama Coastal Plain of South-West Arabia in Its Regional Context c. 6000 BC–AD 600.* BAR International Series 1456. Oxford: Arcahaeopress, 2005.

Edens, Christopher, and T.J. Wilkinson. "Southwest Arabia during the Holocene: Recent Archaeological Developments." *Journal of World Prehistory* 12, no. 1 (1998): 55–119.

Gunter, Ann C., ed. *Caravan Kingdoms: Yemen and the Ancient Incense Trade.* Washington, D.C.: Arthur M. Sackler Gallery (Smithsonian Institution), 2005.

Ho, Engseng. *Graves of Tarim: Geneaology and Mobility across the Indian Ocean.* Berkeley, CA: University of California Press, 2006.

Margariti, Roxani Eleni. *Aden & the Indian Ocean Trade: 150 Years in the Life of a Medieval Arabian Port.* Chapel Hill, NC: The University of North Caroline Press, 2007.

Masry, A. "Factors of Growth in the Civilization of Southwestern Arabia: An Ethno-ecological Approach." *Bulletin of the Faculty of Arts* 3 (1973): 41–65.

Newton, Lynne S. *A Landscape of Pilgrimage and Trade in Wadi Masila, Yemen: Al-Qisha and Qabr Hud in the Islamic Period.* BAR International Series 1899. Oxford: Arcahaeopress, 2009.

Piotrovsky, M. B. "The Fate of Catle Ghumdan," in *Ancient and Medieval Monuments of Civilization of Southern Arabia,* 28–38. Moscow: Nauka, 1988.

Rose, Jeffrey I. "The Question of Upper Pleistocene Connections between East Africa and South Arabia." *Current Anthropology* 45, no. 4 (2004): 551–55.

THE MODERN PERIOD

The two decades or so after Zaydi Imam al-Mahdi died (1775) were not distinguished by great successors, but this does not mean that intellectual life stagnated. This period saw the likes of such great Islamic jurisprudents and reformers as Muhammad al-Shawkani (1760–1823), a brilliant scholar of the Qur'an and Hadith who believed in reinvigorating Sunni doctrine through *ijtihad* (innovation). But it was events in Saudi Arabia that had a ripple effect on Yemen: the rise of the Wahhabi Islamic reform movement spearheaded politically by a Najdi princely house, the Al Saud. The first Saudi state was formed (1744–1818), expanding out from

Al-Dir'iyah in Najd northward to Iraq, eastward to the Hijaz and the holy cities of Mecca and Medina, and southward toward northern Yemen and the Tihama. It appeared as though the Wahhabis saw nothing less than the entire Peninsula as their "natural" polity. Alarmed at what this might mean for their foothold in western Arabia, the Ottomans sent the Pasha of Egypt, the redoubtable Muhammad Ali, to confront the Al Saud forces. Eventually, the Ottomans defeated their opponents, raising their capital at al-Dir'iyah in 1818 (after which the Al Saud moved their capital to neighboring Al-Riyadh).

The British Protectorate in Aden, the Second Ottoman Occupation of Yemen, and the Rise of the Hamid al-Din Imams

Located on the tip of the southwestern part of the Arabian Peninsula, Aden has one of the finest natural harbors in the world, and unsurprisingly, it has been a working port for millennia. The impressively large water harvesting cisterns in the hills to the rear of the port were built long ago (some say they are at least as old as the Himyarite Kingdom), and when the British discovered them, they rehabilitated a portion to provide freshwater for their military outpost. The port's strategic location near the Strait of Mandab—the gateway into the Red Sea and the Egyptian and the Mediterranean worlds beyond, as well as the Indian Ocean and the lucrative South Asia trade—made it desirable to many a maritime power, but the British did not become interested in it until it appeared that the Ottomans—fresh from their conquest of the Najd where they suppressed Saudi/Wahhabi power (1811–1819)— were seemingly poised to take control of southern Arabia by moving southward into Yemen. Alarmed at the prospect of Ottoman expansionism, the British decided to seize the port in 1839, declaring it a British colony. When the Suez Canal was opened in 1869, the importance of Aden as a coaling station for the British fleet on its way to and from India increased, and the British colony was expanded beyond the port to include the hinterland, forming what became the Aden Protectorate. The British signed individual treaties with tribal sheikhs and sultans in the hinterland granting them "protection" so long as they did not alienate their territories from British control (or at least not without the latter's permission), creating what became the *Pax Britannica* that survived for 130 years. In 1905, the British and the Ottomans signed a treaty that established the boundary between the British colony and Ottoman dominions in Yemen (which by default remained the boundary between "northern" and "southern" Yemen until unification in 1990).

With immigrants arriving from Africa, South Asia, and Southeast Asia who worked in its prosperous port economy (into which also the British sank a sizeable annual subsidy), Aden grew into a "world" city. The Ottomans in their turn responded to the opening of the Suez Canal by entrenching themselves in the Yemeni highlands, occupying Sana'a in 1872 and the areas southward to and about Taiz and the Tihama, though their control over the rest of the country was tenuous at best. Yemen was in effect partitioned into three "areas of influence" during the mid-to-late 19th century: the Ottomans in the central highlands with their capital in Sana'a,

Main street of Aden, circa 1880. (Hulton Archive/ Getty Images)

the Zaydi Imamate (calling itself the Mutawakkilite Kingdom) retreating northward from the Ottomans to their historical center in Sa'dah, and the British colony in the south in and around Aden.

For the Zaydi Imamate, the 19th century was a period of steep decline. The Qasimi state had imploded, due to unending feuds between contending factions, and with the collapse of the coffee trade, a large revenue stream was lost, leaving the treasury all but depleted. In 1904, the Imamate passed into the hands of Yahya bin Muhammad Hamid al-Din (a descendant of the founder of the Qasimi dynasty) who promptly launched a jihad against the Turks, mobilizing tribal levies loyal for that purpose. Thus began the long reign (d. 1948) of one of the modern Yemen's most important rulers.

When Sana'a was retaken by Imam Yahya in 1905, the Turks responded by sending in more troops into this far-flung province of their empire, recapturing Sana'a and moving northward, where they encountered stiff resistance in and around Sa'dah and then again in Idrisi-controlled 'Asir, losing as many as 30,000 men all told during their campaign. Yemen came to be known as the Ottoman's "graveyard" and is commemorated as such in several mournful songs heard in Turkey to this day. The Tihama and the region around Taiz did not rebel against Ottoman authority, in spite of Imam Yahya's prompting to do so, and so he signed a peace treaty with his enemies. When World War I broke out, the Imam bided his time until the Ottoman Empire's defeat in 1918, whereupon he pushed southward to reclaim the abandoned territories in the name of the Imamate and challenged the British on Aden's doorstep. In his view, the Zaydi state had legitimate religious as well as historic claims over the entire southern portion of the Arabian Peninsula extending all the way to the Omani border. The British did not see it this way, of course, and they were fortunate that the complex web of treaties they had put into place in Aden's hinterland held in the face of the Imam's jihad to throw out the Christian infidels.

Meanwhile, there was another power center emerging in central Saudi Arabia, one that had enormous repercussions on the Imamate. In Najd, the fortunes of the House of Saud, allied with the Wahhabi religious elite, were revived by a young, ambitious, and charismatic prince Abdul Aziz Al Saud, who in 1902 had retaken his ancestral home Riyadh from his family's archenemies and long-term Ottoman allies al-Rashid, a dynastic house based in the northern city of Ha'il. Through a combination of armed aggression and intricate diplomacy over the following quarter-century, he took possession of almost all of what is now Saudi Arabia, having proclaimed himself sultan in 1926 and then king in 1932. The 'Asir had thrown off the Saudi yoke in 1920, siding with Imam Yahya instead, but the Saudis struck back, decisively beating the combined Idrisi and Imamate forces in 1933. Imam Yahya had no choice but to agree to a peace, ceding to Saudi Arabia all of 'Asir and most of Najran, though these are considered historically "Yemeni" domains and from time to time have been subject to political contestation with Saudi Arabia. (The northern border with Saudi Arabia was not "finally" settled until 2000, and incursions of Houthi fighters across the border into Najran in 2009 revived Saudi fears of Yemeni irredentism.)

Imam Yahya maintained peace over his territory through a hostage system called *kafil,* whereby the son(s) of a sheikh were kept as "guests" in the Imam's palaces, or in some grim dungeon somewhere, in return for the sheikh's loyalty. Most hostages were treated reasonably well and received a religious education (for a fictional account, see the superb Yemeni novella *The Hostage,* by Zayd Mutee' Dammaj). Imam Yahya was criticized for keeping his people backward by not opening up his country to Western development, the reason sometimes being given that he feared modern reforms would usher in democratic and particularly un-Islamic ideas as well as make Yemen dependent upon outside imperial forces. In actual fact, he was not averse to all modernist reforms and instituted important administrative and educational changes borrowed from the previous Ottoman administration—as long as these did not weaken his grip on the state. And it was in his reign that a standing army was built, albeit a very small one that was ill-trained and poorly equipped. But complaints began to mount that there were insufficient roads, modern schools, and clinics, in spite of onerous taxes, and resentment against the ruler grew. Imam Yahya did not help his cause by appointing his son, Ahmed, as crown prince, hence turning the Imamate into a family succession rather than, as was expected in Zaydi doctrine, an appointment by a council of saadah and other notables. While the religious elite were inspired by reading the works of modernist Arab writers like Muhammad Abduh and Jamal al-Din al-Afghani and dreamed of social and political reforms, other Yemenis who had been sent abroad for their education came back with radical ideas of their own. In the mid-1930s, they formed an Adeni-based group calling itself the Free Yemeni Movement, which was composed of many of the same intellectuals and activists like Muhammad al-Zubayri and Muhammad Nu'man who became prominent in the 1960s revolutionary period.

In 1948, the Imam fell victim to a coup, planned by rival *sayyid* houses such as the al-Wazir, and was assassinated by Nasir Ali al-Qarda'i, head sheikh of the eastern al-Murad tribe (see his poem commemorating the murder in "Tribal Oral Poetry" in Chapter 6). Abdullah al-Wazir had himself proclaimed Imam and pledged immediate reforms, yet the "revolution" collapsed in just four months. The murder of an Imam was unforgiveable in the eyes of many tribesmen (even though Yemen's history is replete with Imamicide), and the countermobilization of the tribes by Crown Prince Ahmed against the internally conflicted and ill-organized plotters was decisive. The "counterfeit" Imam, along with many members of the al-Wazir house, was executed, his severed head reportedly displayed before the ululating females of the Hamid al-Din household before being flung onto a garbage heap. Ahmed

Palace of Imam Yahya (ruled 1904–1948) at Wadi Dhahr. (Alexey Bazykin/ Dreamstime.com)

had himself declared Imam and decided to move the capital from Sana'a to Taiz where he held court. His son al-Badr was declared crown prince.

Imam Ahmed's outlook or tendencies might have been reformist (he was educated in modern Arab political thought), though in practice, aside from abolishing slavery and allowing the Russians and Chinese to build roads connecting Sana'a to Taiz in the south and to Al-Hudaydah on the coast, he did little to change the country. He believed in ruling by instilling fear in the populace (his face alone, with its huge bulging eyes, made the timid quake) by cultivating an almost occult aura about his person. One story has it that he would appear on his palace balcony before the naïve populace and have a servant creep up behind him and plunge an axe in the side of his head (it was in fact a rubber toy) with the Imam seemingly unaffected by the blow, thereby appearing invincible. There was one aborted coup, which the Crown Prince al-Badr helped to squash, but Ahmed was spared having to face further dissension by dying, of natural causes, in 1962.

Al-Badr succeeded to the head of the Imamate, announcing badly needed social and political reforms to be put into effect immediately, but he was not in power a month before he fell victim to a military coup. He managed to escape to the north where he rallied the tribes in defense of the imamate, while a republican government, strongly supported by the Egyptian military, took over the reigns of government in Sana'a headed by an obscure butcher's son who had risen in the Imam's army to the rank of colonel. Al-Salal became the first president of the newly named Yemen Arab Republic (YAR).

The Aden Protectorate during the post–World War II period was in societal and economic respects the antithesis of its neighbor to the north. British Petroleum set up a refinery in Little Aden and shipping increased, which required an expansion of the port facilities. By the late 1950s, the port was the second busiest in the world, rivaling New York City. A modern education system had been built up by the British, one that served both men and women; modern hospitals were created; and its political public sphere was lively and sophisticated. But that was in the port city. The hinterland, ruled by sultans and sheikhs, was another story, and it remained underdeveloped and often impoverished.

Interestingly, the British encouraged the creation of what today would be called "civil society" associations, most powerful in the form of labor unions, not anticipating that these would become the hotbed of anticolonial activity. At first, these unions struck for higher wages and better working conditions, but these actions coalesced with pro-Nasser pan-Arab nationalism, and the course was set for an anticolonial stance and demands for self-rule. The politically active, educated class in Aden set up networks with peasant groups in the hinterland to spread the revolutionary call for change, and some of the sultans sympathetic to their cause declared themselves anti-British (as did the important sultan of Lahaj). The British insisted that the port colony was too important to give up (despite the huge outlays of money from Whitehall to keep it going), and the colonial administration dug in its heels while protests and insurgency actions surged. Several rival resistance groups led the struggle against the British, but in time, the National Liberation Front (NLF) came out on top.

The Yemeni Civil War (1962–1970) and British Withdrawal from Aden (1967)

The YAR was plunged into a bitter and protracted civil war from 1962 to roughly 1970, pitting republicans with their Egyptian troops and Nasserite allies against the Royalists abetted largely by tribal levies paid for with arms and money from Saudi Arabia. In spite of the fact that Saudi Arabia had been hostile to the Yemeni Imamate, it drew the line where intervention on the part of Egypt in the latter's affairs were concerned, fearing what a Nasserite foothold in the Peninsula might bode for its oil fields. Like other local conflicts in the world, this one too became embroiled in Cold War politics, with the United States providing arms to the Saudis to be funneled to Royalist fighters and the Soviets doing the same via the Republic through its clients, the Egyptians. Losses were heavy on both sides, with the Egyptians, like the Ottomans before them, remembering Yemen as their graveyard.

Yet, fighting remained inconclusive until 1967 when the Arab–Israeli War in which Egypt suffered a humiliating defeat, forced the Egyptians to withdraw their troops from the Yemeni conflict, seemingly leaving the battlefield open to the Royalists. Sallal fled to Moscow (eventually "retiring" in Iraq), while Qadhi Abdul Rahman al-Iryani assumed the presidency. That year, the epic "siege of Sana'a" took place, with the Royalist army surrounding the city and cutting it off from fuel and other badly needed supplies, while republican defenders, greatly augmented by volunteers from Aden and southern Yemen, dug in and determinedly held on. The siege went on for 70 days before the capital was relieved by republican forces. They followed this up with a string of victorious battles that made it clear the Royalists could not prevail. By the late 1960s, it appeared that hostilities would cease on the major condition that al-Badr retreat into exile. By 1970, the civil war was over, with the exception of desultory fighting in more isolated pockets of the country.

The other event of 1967 was the withdrawal of the British from Aden, something that was helped by the revolution in the north. They did not leave quietly, however. Starting in 1966, insurgent attacks on British police and military instillations as well as a few British civilian sites increased in intensity and ferocity, and the colonial authorities struck back, often with brutal force. A revolution had begun, and in spite of deadly fighting between various insurgent factions, it was clear they would prevail nonetheless. And so on November 29, 1967, the last British troops were airlifted from Aden.

YAR and PDRY (1970–1990)

The two regions of the country, both having undergone revolutions, ended up going separate ways. Southern Yemen became the People's (or Popular) Democratic Republic of Yemen (PDRY), a strong Marxist state (the only one in the region) militarily supported by the Soviet Union, though the bulk of its financial aid came from Kuwait, Abu Dhabi, and the World Bank. Besides a powerful army and a ruthlessly efficient state police, it could justly boast of having decent educational and public health systems, thanks to the British. It was also progressive on women's issues:

They were educated, entered professions, and were given rights through a new family law. Soviet interests in this part of the world were obvious: the economic importance of the port city and the strategic location of the country between the Red Sea (and the Suez Canal, nationalized by President Nasser of Egypt in 1956) and the Indian Ocean with its naval access to India and beyond. More indirectly, the PDRY offered a possible foothold into the rest of the Peninsula, to destabilize its conservative monarchial regimes.

Northern Yemen, or the YAR, which had lagged behind other third-world nations in terms of basic goods and services, was recovering from a devastating civil war. So in the 1970s and 1980s, Saudi Arabia and Kuwait along with U.S. Agency for International Development (USAID) and European donor agencies like the Dutch, Germans, and British poured in large quantities of money and technical assistance to develop the country. Saudi Arabia committed millions of dollars to the Sana'a government (mostly into the treasury to pay for the state administration and also to buy the loyalty of certain powerful tribal sheikhs and leaders exiled from the PDRY). Kuwait opted for more public or visible development projects such as the University of Sana'a (the largest university in the country) and a number of hospitals. But perhaps the most important source of development money was remittance payments from Yemeni migrant workers, especially in Saudi Arabia and the Gulf where they worked in the booming construction industry. All through the country, but especially in the central and southern regions as well as the Tihama, "local development associations" (LDAs) were set up with these payments that funded various "self-betterment" projects such as roads, schools, irrigation works, and clinics. Indeed, Yemen was somewhat unique in this respect among developing countries, relying more on local or grassroots self-help than on the central government to provide basic goods and services. The extensive networks of roads and many public facilities in the nation today stem from this period of development.

The early period of the YAR was dominated by the presidency of Ibrahim al-Hamdi, a high-ranking military officer who replaced al-Iryani in 1974. He was a charismatic figure (who fancied himself, and was often hailed, as the next Abdel Nasser) and widely beloved. One of the cornerstones of his presidency was to seek greater ties with the PDRY while at the same time, perhaps paradoxically, appointing Abdul Majeed al-Zindani, a Salafi scholar, to high religious office funded by the Saudis, presumably in order to counteract the influence of the Marxist National Liberation Force in the country (see below). (This style of governing, which amounted to a delicate system of pulls and pushes or balances between countervailing political forces, was also to become the hallmark of al-Hamdi's eventual successor Ali Abdullah Saleh.) Before he became president, he had been elected head of an organization that brought all the LDAs into one administrative body, signaling the centralization process that he would foster in his presidency as a way of boosting state authority (and, of course, ultimately also his own power). Perhaps, it was this same centralizing impulse that led al-Hamdi into oppositional stances to the country's northern tribes, but they proved far more intractable to his machinations than the LDAs (which did not prove that easy to mobilize either). It is not clear what strategy he intended to use to get the tribes, famously independent, to submit to central

Ibrahim Al-Hamdi, President of the Yemen Arab Republic, 1974–1977. (Keystone/Getty Images)

authority, besides paying them off (something the Saudis were doing already), and he was not in office long enough in any case for his policy to have had much impact. He was assassinated in October 1977. Many reasons were given for his demise, ranging from paranoia that made him distrust everyone to tribal leaders upset with his efforts to marginalize or subsume them within state authority. The killers were never found. After a year of further assassination (al-Ghashmi who immediately succeeded al-Hamdi) and counterassassination (of a southern leader), another young military officer Major Ali Abdullah Saleh, whose capabilities had caught al-Hamdi's attention and led to his being rapidly promoted in the military ranks, became president. He came from a relatively insignificant tribe at the time, the Sinhan, part of the Hashid Confederation, and had little formal education and therefore, practically no credentials or legitimacy on the basis of which to govern. The general view was that he would be assassinated like his predecessors, and though several coups were attempted, he managed to thwart them all and cling to power (earning him the sobriquet, "the cat," because of its nine lives). His turned out to be one the longest presidencies not only in the two Yemens but also in the Middle East.

It is hard to imagine that the early period of the PDRY was even more turbulent politically than that of its northern neighbor, but consider this brief presidential history. The initial regime, headed by Qahtan al-Sha'bi, was overthrown in 1969 by the NLF, which consolidated its Marxist influence within the country over the next decade (and extended it into its neighbor to the north). In 1971, the successor to al-Sha'bi, Muhammad Ali Haytham was in turn overthrown and replaced by Salim Rubai Ali. Though the country had become ever more radically Marxist, under Ali, it leaned more toward Beijing than Moscow (he actually favored nonalignment); and in 1978, he was overthrown and executed, and a new president, Abdul Fattah Ismail, came to power who leaned more toward Moscow. Though he lasted only two years, it was under him that a Marxist–Leninist party, the Yemeni Socialist Party (YSP), was established with the help or encouragement of the Soviet Union (and remains on the scene of Yemeni politics, though without its hard-line Marxist–Leninist approach). Ismail fell victim to a coup and resigned (being exiled to Moscow) and was replaced by Ali Nasir Muhammad in 1980, who lasted longer than his predecessors but had no less a violent end. When in 1986 the returned former president Ismail rallied supporters for an armed struggle inside the country, it claimed the lives of thousands of people, including that of Ismail. Ali Nasir was promptly replaced by a new leader, Haydar Abu Bakr al-Attas. In other words, 6 presidents in a little more than 15 years, with transitions to power that were more violent and ruthless than anything the YAR had seen. In this early period, the country was also a haven for several international terrorist groups including the Red Brigade, the Baader Meinhof "gang," and the Irish Republican Army, though their operations were eventually shut down in the 1980s by Ali Nasir Muhammad (partly to reassure the country's northern neighbors—particularly the Gulf states, on whom he was counting for badly needed economic assistance—that there would be no meddling in their internal affairs). Like the YAR, the PDRY balanced different and sometimes competing political interests in the Cold War: Soviet presence versus Chinese influence and Western financial aid versus Soviet military weapons and advisers. But on the whole, it leaned as much toward the Communist bloc as the YAR leaned toward the capitalist and U.S.-dominated sphere.

During the entire period from 1970 to 1980, the PDRY made repeated efforts to influence the YAR, both by spreading its ideology through the NLF and by periodic military incursions across the border in which the YAR was badly outclassed. It was in the last of these in 1980 that the YAR agreed to a treaty with the PDRY, one of whose conditions was the unification of the two countries by 1990. This was greeted with scorn by many northern tribes, especially ones with grievances against the south dating back to the civil war, and by Saudi Arabia, which feared the combined strengths of these countries on its southwestern flank, and with skepticism by the diplomatic community that thought unification was a long shot.

Development and Growth in the YAR (1980–1990):
Agriculture, Oil, and Gas

While the PDRY seemed stalled economically, for the YAR the 1980s was a period of development and economic growth, though admittedly not unproblematic. Yemen has long been the "bread basket" of the Arabian Peninsula; and despite the fact that earlier states—in part to enhance their power—had embarked on agricultural improvement schemes (e.g., see the Rasulids and Tahirids), these had been, with the important exception of coffee, largely for subsistence production and internal markets. In the 1980s and 1990s, that trend changed dramatically. As in other developing countries at the time, Yemen's government was being encouraged by the World Bank, the International Monetary Fund (IMF), and donor countries to capitalize sectors of the economy that had the potential of entering regional and global markets. In Yemen, that largely meant the agricultural sector. If the venture proved successful, the country would become less dependent upon foreign assistance, while its economy would be penetrated further by the global market system (presuming that that is a good thing). The other side of this development strategy (and some might argue in contradiction with the first or market strategy one) was to strengthen the central state that would be in charge of this development. President al-Hamdi had begun the process of subsuming the LDAs within the state's authority, in line with classic theories of the state as the main provider of goods and services for the people, so this ambitious plan was in keeping with it.

The government imposed an import ban on fruits, with the aim of stimulating fruit cultivation within the country. Oranges and limes were now cultivated in the highlands for a higher monetary return than was formerly to be had from tomatoes and onions, and bananas, mangoes, and melons were harvested in the Tihama, where practically none such crops had been seen before. These items were sold mainly in regional markets, though there was hope of export to neighboring countries like Oman and Saudi Arabia. (It is hard to know whether in the end that was more hope than reality.) Privately owned plantations in the Tihama began to appear, but smaller farmers became well off too. A new agrarian middle-class emerged that could afford a higher standard of living and displayed it by building new houses, buying cars, and so forth.

Expansion in the agricultural sector, of course, required an increase in the overall water supply. Small-scale dams and other water harvesting systems were built by the Ministry of Agriculture and Irrigation. (Though unlike earlier state regimes, scant attention was paid to repairing or restoring existing waterworks, many of which were centuries-old but still practicable.) As the country was in the grips of a long-term drought, these structures turned out to be of limited value, unfortunately. Building a new dam in the end seemed to have more to do with signaling a sheikh's status, not to mention, of course, lining a contractor's pockets, than with sound water management.

The alternative was to tap into groundwater. With low-interest loans from the World Bank, farmers were able to install artesian wells that pumped water from deep below the surface. The problems here, however, lay in the fact that many wells were drilled indiscriminately, with scant attention paid to hydraulics, geology, or long-term viability of the regional water supply. Pumping water out of the ground in one location could leave another one, sometimes quite close to the former, dry. Some of these problems might have been averted had there been a national water law to regulate drilling, but such legislation was not in place until 2002. Even if there had been one, the state would have probably faced the same challenges it does today to enforce it, lacking the political will (especially when up against powerful sheikhs) and sufficient muscle. And there were unforeseen consequences with disastrous effects. In the Sana'a Basin, it was unknown at the time of its largest agricultural expansion that water was being extracted from a large aquifer that contained "fossil" water (meaning water that had been trapped for eons in a geological deposit, encased by nonporous sediments) with the result that it could not be recharged through natural means except over a long period of time (i.e., by surface water slowly draining back into the aquifer).

By the late 1990s, the water table had dropped to 1,000 m or more in some places, making further extraction either uneconomical because of diesel fuel costs for the pump or yielding water quality too saline for use, and farms were left fallow or abandoned. Farm families moved in with relatives where the water situation was less dire or migrated to cities in search of work, which, of course, strained municipality water delivery systems. Eventually, there was not enough water for such water-thirsty crops like citrus fruits, and as these had been the most lucrative, farmers saw their incomes decline precipitously. No wonder many switched to qat cultivation. Though it is the bogeyman of water experts in Yemen, because its cultivation is estimated to take up about 60 percent of irrigation water in the country, it makes sense economically when it brings in many times more money than citrus fruit and other cultigens, and for more or less the same amount of water.

In 1984, oil fields and associated gas were discovered just east of Marib by the Hunt Oil Company. The news made the country euphoric. It was hoped that perhaps now Yemen could join the Gulf countries in reaping the benefits of oil wealth (and some wondered why the discovery had taken so long when oil production had been going on for 40 years on the other side of the peninsula). The elation was perhaps premature. Proven crude oil reserves are about four billion barrels today, and these are small by comparison to other oil-producing countries. Moreover, they are forecast to run out by 2017–2020. On top of relatively small deposits, the other drawback was the "grade" of oil that was less desirable than that of most other oil-producing countries, thus driving down its price. Nevertheless, it is estimated that for at least a decade after the mid-1980s, oil sales accounted for at least 70 percent of Yemeni government revenues. To some extent, the government was able to subsidize the cost of certain food staples and public services with its increased revenues, but it has been charged that much of these were used to pay off regime supporters including the tribes. As a result, the state's patronage system widened, and so did its power. All through the 1990s, the network of military outposts on mountaintops and checkpoints on major highways expanded.

Just as it seemed in the late 1980s that Yemen's economic fortunes were brightening, disaster struck in an unexpected guise. In 1990, Iraq invaded Kuwait (because of a long-disputed land claim near the Shatt al-Arab), and the First Gulf War (1990–1993) began. The U.N. Security Council convened for a vote on a resolution condemning the Iraqi invasion. As it happened, Yemen was the only Arab country on the council that year, and it abstained when every member country voted in favor of the resolution. The political reasons for such a decision on Yemen's part seem unclear. Was Yemen representing not just its own views but also what it presumed to be the views of other Arab countries in the region? Was it intended indirectly as a rebuke less of Saddam Hussein than the monarchial regimes in the Gulf? It may have been courageous, but it was less than wise. The outcry against Yemen from the Gulf countries was deafening. Kuwait, understandably upset because of its generous and steadfast assistance to Yemen, pulled its aid. The Gulf countries including Saudi Arabia retaliated by expelling hundreds of thousands of Yemeni guest workers (estimates vary, but the figures hover near a million). As Yemen depended heavily on remittance payments from these workers, the long-term effect on the economy was devastating (offset only by recent oil revenues). Returning workers might have seemed welcome at a time when the agricultural system was expanding, but it was not yet clear to everybody—as it would be before the decade was over—that agriculture would not be the growth industry everybody had anticipated. Where would these men find work if not in the fields their fathers and grandfathers had tilled for generations?

One hopeful economic sign was the rise to prominence of a few businessmen, whose success signaled the possibility that the economy was expanding and diversifying. The career of one such businessman, Hayil Saeed, is particularly storied. He rose from poverty in Taiz to become Yemen's wealthiest businessman in the 1980s, manufacturing handmade soap, plastics, cookies, and vegetable oil, all of which he also exported to the PDRY, while at the same time importing cigarettes and dates for sale inside the YAR. His business included insurance and heavy construction equipment, at a time when Yemeni cities were undergoing a population boom. He reinvested much of the money he made back into Hayel Saeed enterprises, which became a model of capitalist efficiency. Another, rather different type is al-Royshan, from the famed family of Khawlan tribal sheikhs. Less is known about him than Hayil Saeed, but he is worth mentioning to remind us that tribesmen also participated in the business sector. He became a millionaire by importing motor vehicles and had showrooms in Sana'a and other cities. Though Sheikh Abdullah Hussein al-Ahmar, head sheikh of the Hashid Confederation, became very wealthy, it was his son Hamid who was the entrepreneur and became a multibillionaire, owning Yemen Telnet among other enterprises. Needless to say, networking inside the government (which could lead to lucrative brokering contracts) and greasing the wheels at the customs office were essential to the success of any business venture. (Yemen is the poorest country in the Middle East, but that does not mean that every person in the country is poor.)

Smaller retail businesses proliferated alongside these giants, or when someone figured out how to successfully develop a particular niche, copycats immediately followed suit, until the market became saturated and everyone had to go back to the drawing board. There was no, or very little, business innovation. Nevertheless, it was remarkable how in a relatively short space of time a bustling market economy had emerged. Whole streets were devoted to the sale of computer equipment or kitchen appliances or household and office furniture. A couple of malls were built in Sana'a, ranging in price and product to suit virtually every shopper. These were not the supermalls of the Gulf, of course, but they show that commodities consumption was definitely on the rise. Street signage became ubiquitous and was often sophisticated in design. By the late 1990s, a couple of large, fairly high-end hotels sprang up.

The Sheraton and the Taj were no longer the snazziest hotels in Sana'a, and several major airlines now routed flights to the city. Sana'a had long since displaced Aden as Yemen's international city.

Indeed, the tables had unexpectedly turned between the two countries by the end of the 1980s, and the YAR seemed the more successful of the pair, stronger economically, more powerful militarily, and more stable politically. So when unification loomed in 1990 (as agreed upon 10 years earlier when the YAR was being pressured by its southern neighbor), it was clear who would be on top.

Unification (1990)

Ali Abdullah Saleh was declared president of the newly named Republic of Yemen, and South Yemen's Ali Salim al-Beidh the vice president. In a further show of unity, ministerial posts were divided between the two former countries, though the army (a small one that even at its peak was no more than 60,000 men) remained firmly in the hands of the president and handpicked aides from his tribe, the Sinhan. What would become clearer, if anyone was ever in doubt about it, was that army patronage was all important in the political system, which probably would have been the case even had the south emerged with the upper hand, since the army dominated politics in the PDRY as well.

Democratic institutions began to appear. A political party system came into being, composed mainly of the General People's Congress (GPC), associated with the president's regime, the YSP headed by the vice president, and Islah (meaning reform in Arabic) jointly headed by Sheikh Abdullah Hussein al-Ahmar and Abdul Majeed al-Zindani, the leading Salafi (Wahhabi) sheikh in Yemen. The first two had been in existence before, of course, having been the leading if not sole parties in their respective countries before unification, but Islah (actually the Yemeni Association for Reform) was something comparatively recent and signaled the rise of a conservative religious politics that was not unique to Yemen but part of a larger trend in Muslim countries. Its influence extended deep into the northern part of the country, perhaps not surprisingly given the stature of Sheikh al-Ahmar in that region and its adjacency. It was also attractive not only to voters in the south, mainly among poorer and more disenfranchised people, but also to the likes of Tariq al-Fadhli, a "freedom fighter" in Afghanistan disparaged as a jihadist who came from a prominent southern family. The Islah party in time posed a far greater threat to the regime of Ali Abdullah Saleh than the Socialists. The YSP was the weakest of the three, though it did have significant support and not just in the southern parts of the country where, in fact, it fell victim to some resentment harbored against socialism in the last regime. The GPC was arguably the strongest of the three, employing political tactics to gain followers that some found underhanded though they were not illegal. It would create a GPC subgroup that appeared to imitate some other party in an attempt to weaken the latter by drawing its members into the GPC political fold. As a result of this tactic, it became the most "inclusive" or "pluralistic" of all the parties, though with the least definable platform—other than the president's own agenda. At the end of the day, it was hard to tell how many people in Yemen really cared for or knew anything about these parties and what they stood for. Would they really help to improve their living conditions or their jobs? And as for "democracy," would it offer more uncertainty and instability than the "benign military dictatorship" of the YAR (as one prominent U.S. political scientist described it)?

A free press also began to flourish for the first time in Yemen, not seen even in the heyday of British Aden, and alongside it a lively civil society of nongovernmental organizations (NGOs), many of which were concerned with rights for women and minorities.

Hotly contested parliamentary elections took place in 1993. Irregularities were reported (Hamid al-Ahmar, the son of the powerful northern sheikh, allegedly removed a ballot box illegally), but international monitors declared the elections fair. The GPC gained the most number of seats; Islah and the YSP were a distant second and third, respectively. The results were humiliating for YSP, as they made it difficult for the south to claim power sharing with the north as agreed upon in the unity accord. Ali Salim al-Beidh packed up and left for Hadhramawt even though he could have remained as vice president. The government grew alarmed. Was this the harbinger of a secessionist movement in the south?

It was in fact to be that but not right away and not before a lot of back and forth maneuvering between the president and the YSP. The Islah condemned the YSP and sided with the president.

Fighting broke out in April 1994 at 'Amran, a city to the north of the capital Sana'a. The southern air force bombed Sana'a, including scud missiles that killed and injured many civilians. The northern army in turn bombed Aden. Though the fighting began in the north, most of it took place in the south after the YSP slowly and inexorably lost ground against the northern army that had been augmented by tribal conscripts from the north who suffered the greatest casualties. (This follows a trend in Yemen, where the state attempts to mobilize the tribes as a paramilitary force.) To complicate matters (and politics in Yemen are rarely straightforward), the Saudis supported the YSP vice president, mainly by supplying arms but also with substantial monetary assistance. It may seem paradoxical that the conservative monarchical regime would lend its weight behind the YSP, but Saudi Arabia opposed the unification of Yemen, feeling threatened by its combined strength of about 20 million people who were perched right on its back door. All efforts by the United Nations and the United States to mediate a cease-fire failed.

In May 1994, the YSP leader announced secession, declaring the name of the new country to be the Democratic Republic of Yemen, though apparently it was not what everyone—not even the majority—inside or outside the party wanted. As another example of how complicated Yemeni politics can be, the two-time president of the former PDRY, Ali Nasir Muhammad (see above) sought revenge against YSP leadership for his ousting by siding with President Ali Abdullah Saleh against the secessionist forces. The YSP leader fled into exile. Northern forces, augmented by tribal contingents, now advanced southward, though territory was not always taken in battle; some southern positions like Al-Mukalla surrendered. Finally, Aden was captured in July, and northern forces sacked it. Islah party members destroyed

Aftermath of the scud missile attack on Sana'a in May 1994. (AP Photo/ Santiago Lyon)

or desecrated the tombs of Sufi saints on the grounds of "grave worship." President Saleh only ordered a halt of the looting after his troops had had their fill; one way to repay them for their loyalty and losses.

With the end of the civil war was supposed to come reconciliation between the two sides in the conflict, but the aftermath proved different: it was less a matter of reintegration than of imposition of northern power over the south, or as the latter dubbed it, an "occupation." There is some truth to this accusation.

President Saleh's regime decided that one way to increase northern hegemony was to retribalize the south. Tribalization was something the Socialist regime in the PDRY had tried to suppress, sometimes brutally, justifying this policy on a number of grounds seen in the Middle East more generally. One of these is based on the same Orientalist stereotypes constructed by Western colonial powers (though it inheres deeply in the Islamic tradition as well), which is that tribes are "backward" and "traditionalist," not to mention "feud-addicted," "lawless" and, of course, "ignorant." In other words, they are everything that a supposedly modern and progressive state would want to reform or oppress, and it is no wonder that tribes are seen as fundamentally opposed to modernity (in spite of countless examples, many of which we have already seen in Yemen's most recent history, to the contrary). But there were other grounds for opposing the tribes and that is their independence or autonomy, which made it difficult for a centralized state like the PDRY to stomach them. What Saleh discovered (not for the first or last time) was that the tribes were in fact essential to his survival in power, but they were more than that, as demonstrated by their role in the recent civil war: they were crucial to the north's successful military operations against the south. (The tribes had been the main fighting force for the Imamate.) From his point of view, why not therefore try something different? Why not empower the tribes in the south and make them the linchpin for the unification of the country? One of the main areas of retribalization was Yafi'ah, a mountainous stronghold in Lahaj, north of the city of Aden, and one of the consequences was a resurgence of tribal poetry in that region that was taped and disseminated in stereo stores and markets all over Yemen.

Not only the south, by the way, complained about tribalization. In time, the Yemeni parliament was also dominated by tribal sheikhs who, it was said, were incapable of representing other than their own narrow group interests (which might well be true, but then it is hard to think of nontribal representatives who rose above their parochialism either). Over the years, what really stuck in the craw of southerners was the way in which northerners, many of them sheikhs, claimed ownership over properties that were not rightfully theirs or forced southern businessmen to take them on as "partners" on onerous terms, in the end causing a transfer of wealth from south to north that was ruinous to the southern economy.

SALAFISM

Salafism comes from the Arabic *salafi* meaning "first or original," the idea being to reform Islam by going back to the spiritual principles of the Prophet Muhammad and the first generation of his followers, the founders of Islam. Salafis argue that these principles had become obscured or distorted by "innovations" introduced in the centuries after the Prophet. "Wahhabi" refers to the particular Salafism that was established in 18th-century Saudi Arabia by the religious scholar Muhammad Abdul Wahhab (1703–1792) who allied himself with the Al Saud family in central Najd. The ruler agreed to protect the scholar and help propagate his reformist teachings, based on Hanbali teachings, in exchange for religious acknowledgment of the Saudi House's ruling legitimacy. Salafism is associated with violent jihad in the security studies literature, but this is not necessarily the case when one regards the teachings of Salafis through the lens of theological or religious studies where jihad is seen as a struggle to rid the land of "infidel" influences, with violence seen as the means of last, not first, resort.

Almost working in tandem with tribalization was the "Salafization" of Yemen after the civil war. In return for its help in fighting the southern secessionist movement, the Islah party was granted carte blanche by the regime to set up Yemeni "Islamic institutes" in which a "Wahhabi" Salafi brand of Islam was taught. In the 1990s, the Saudi monarchy encouraged the spread of Salafi beliefs outside the kingdom, a move meant at once to restore its reputation in Muslim eyes—which had been tarnished after the kingdom had allowed a U.S. military base to be built on its soil during the 1990 Gulf War—and to export increasingly more dissident Salafis unhappy with the Saudi regime. These "missionaries" went all over the Muslim world, including, of course, Yemen, where Sheikh al-Zindani worked closely with them. One has to bear in mind that Salafism, though a conservative social and political movement, was not antimodern in principle. Returning to the spiritual principles of the ninth century did not mean shedding modernity as a whole but rather selecting those aspects of it that would be compatible with a fundamentalist vision of religion or help promote religious reform. Thus, modern media like television, video, and the Internet were embraced as were modern institutions such as the university. Al-Zindani founded Iman University (Iman means faith in Arabic) in 1993. Forget the Islamic lesson circles of the past where students sat cross-legged in the mosque to learn about *fiqh* from a learned scholar. Now they go to a campus where they attend classes in modern buildings with thousands of others, taking classes in Arabic linguistics, Qur'an, Hadith, Sharia, and fiqh. They must take written examinations to pass their courses and receive degrees upon completion of their courses of studies. Having thus been certified graduates, they can go out and spread the word in institutes dispersed throughout the country. To appreciate the level of education and sophistication of the Islahi school graduates, an anecdote might prove illuminating. When the author was in a Sana'ani taxi, he struck up a conversation with the driver, a sophisticated young man who spoke beautiful Classical Arabic and was well informed about current events. When asked where he had been educated, he answered, "Iman University."

Needless to say, Saudi Arabia heavily financed the institutes and, arguably, saw them as a way for the kingdom to exercise "soft power" over the Yemenis. These institutes in turn did outreach to the surrounding communities, attempting to recruit them into the Islah party tent, promising to help meet the development needs of the communities if elected to office. To put this movement in perspective, bear in mind that these institutes claimed to have over 300,000 pupils nationwide, nearly 13,000 of whom were training to become teachers. (By comparison, the national government had only about 8,000 pupils training to become teachers, and these graduates often could not find jobs because the government was not building schools and equipping them at nearly the same rate as the Islahis were theirs.)

Eventually, the presence of Salafis in the midst of other Yemeni religious sects became divisive. The desecration of saint tombs in Aden by Salafi activists during the civil war has already been mentioned; these saint tombs are venerated by Sufis. But even relations with Zaydis, arguably the most conservative of Schi'a sects, were tense. And, of course, as the political power base of Islah grew through recruitment of Salafi converts into its fold, the regime of Ali Abdullah Saleh took notice and eventually moved against them. But we are getting ahead of our story, for that did not happen until mid-2000. Incidentally, the conversation with the taxi driver took place then, and the reason he was driving a taxi and not teaching at an institute was that many had been forced to shut down.

On the civil society front, the Sana'a regime clamped down hard on the press, and the open and lively debates of the pre–civil war period evaporated. Newspapers were forced to close. Courageous journalists who spoke up against regime injustices were harassed, arrested, and jailed, or worse. NGOs were also affected, though not always negatively. International "democracy monitoring" NGOs like the National Democratic Institute (the NDI was essentially funded by the U.S. government) were created to "build the capacity" of Yemen and its institutions to be more democratic by promoting citizen participation, openness of the political process, and government accountability. (It was assumed that what is meant by democracy is more or less clear-cut and universal; the ancient Greeks might have invented it, but the Americans perfected it and the rest of the world required instruction in it.) Many of the programs were well meaning—getting Yemeni legislators to read the constitution and learn how to draft legislation, increasing the participation of women in the political process, making political parties more representative, and teaching them how to conduct fair and effective campaigns—though to some it might seem ironic that Americans teach these practices when their own governmental system seems far from adequate (this is being written in 2011 at the height of political battles that have left the U.S. Congress deadlocked). NGOs dedicated to women's issues also were continued or established anew. But there were other NDI initiatives of more dubious value. One of these was to teach tribal sheikhs how to mediate conflict situations using CEO boardroom tactics. The idea that sheikhs should be taught this when they have mastered a centuries-old art of conflict mediation is mind-boggling, and if bloody tribal feuds were on the rise that remained unresolved, they were likely to have other causes such as economic ones (disagreements over water and land) or armaments proliferation (aggravated by the recently concluded civil war). It was the sheikhs who approached the NDI for this assistance, however, which was a little like presenting it with an offer it could not refuse. The sheikhs pocketed their stipends and promised to behave.

NGOs are supposed to be "nongovernmental" so as not to have a conflict of interest when criticizing such institutions as the World Bank or their own governments, but the Yemeni government responded by setting up its own clandestine NGOs as a counterforce to the existing ones. (The law of physics that every action has a reaction could be taken as the modus operandi of the Sana'a regime.) "Not fair!" cries the international order. Indeed, but to ask the Yemeni government to believe, for example, that the NDI had no conflicts of interest when everyone knew it was funded by the U.S. government was to ask it to play the fool. In the end, what did fairness have to do with it?

Another effort on the part of the international community was to support Yemeni feminists and their attempts to introduce and promote academic topics on feminism and gender in the university. In 1996, with aid money from the Dutch government, a Yemeni feminist, Dr. Raufa (the name by which she was popularly known) Hassan, a media specialist, journalist, and human rights activist, founded the first Center for

Women's Studies in Yemen at the University of Sana'a. It was attacked almost immediately by al-Zindani and the Islah party, not because the center promoted women's rights (which the Islah party saw itself already doing, albeit in a highly conservative way) but that it did so under a liberal and basically secular banner. So fierce was the debate and so acrimonious the attack on Raufa Hassan personally that she feared for her life and went temporarily into exile. The center she helped establish and that was so closely associated with her charismatic leadership floundered and never regained its momentum even after her return to Yemen.

The civil war had drained the Yemeni economy, and the country required massive aid to recover: $70 million was pledged by European donor countries and as much from the Arab Monetary Fund. In 1995, Yemen signed an agreement with the IMF and the World Bank to secure aid credits worth a little less than $300 million. Little noticed, perhaps, but in the long run arguably far more consequential than many of the political trends discussed above, was the fact that this loan had a rider on it, known as "structural readjustments." In 1997, the Yemeni government started to implement medium-term economic programs in line with its IMF agreements. These included decreased dependence on oil revenue by increasing the growth rate in the non-oil sectors. To achieve this, the government agreed on a number of SAPs such as freezing government wages or keeping them low, increasing tax revenue collection, and reducing government subsidies on such things as fuel, sugar, and bread by raising the price of these over time. In some respects, these economic reforms were successful. But the Pied Piper was yet to be paid when the loans from the World Bank were due in the mid to late 2000s, and Yemen had to complete its SAPs if it were to get any more aid. The politically most daunting of these was the reduction of subsidies on basic staples; only if the Yemeni economy were doing really well would this be palatable. If not, there would be hell to pay if the price on bread and sugar skyrocketed almost overnight (as in fact it would). But no less sensitive politically were reductions in government wages and pensions, as Yemen (like other Gulf oil-producing countries) has employed many of its citizens in government jobs, paid through oil revenues, as part of its patronage system.

The year 1997 was also when the Republic of Yemen held its second parliamentary elections (the first having been in 1993). Skepticism and cynicism about the democratic process had now set in, and both party and voter participation were sluggish. The YSP boycotted, along with several other more minor parties, leaving mainly the GPC and Islah to battle it out for the seats. It was a landslide victory for the GCP, which gained more than 60 seats over its previous majority in the Parliament. Islah's share slipped even further.

Meanwhile, oil had been discovered outside of Shabwah in the Hadhramawt in 1991. Though it was not as clear at the time as it is today, these oil fields are the most productive in Yemen (well over 30 percent of national production). An oil terminal was built at Al-Shihr on the Arabian Sea coast. Over time, the complaint arose that the northern regime siphoned most of the revenues from oil sales for its own use and that the south was not getting its fair share. This later became a major grievance in the "southern movement" (see below).

Recall that Yemen had signed a loan agreement in 1995 with the IMF on the condition that it successfully implemented certain structural readjustments in its economy. In 2005, the World Bank, which had extended a four-year, $2.3 billion support package, announced that it would reduce this aid by over one-third to punish Yemen for not having gone far enough in implementing its SAPs. Given that the government was dealing with resentment from the population for having to pay higher prices on what were formerly subsidized basic goods, this policy worked against political stability in the country. To offset this, however, the World Bank announced that it would extend $400 million worth of USAID credits to be implemented from 2005 to 2009, and this was followed up by a pledge of $4.7 billion in aid to Yemen from other donor countries from 2007 to 2010. However, little of this aid was spent because of the political situation in the country, and of course the ordinary Yemeni has been the ultimate loser. Ending its government subsidies on basic staples has meant that paying for gas, fuel, and even sugar took up more than half of the average worker's monthly income. Army pensioners demonstrated in the south complaining that with rampant inflation they could no longer survive on their fixed incomes. School teachers rose up in Sana'a for largely the same reasons. Large-scale, but generally peaceful, demonstrations demanding that the government do something to alleviate economic privation had become common long before the Yemeni "Arab Spring"—and perhaps became a training ground for these later and much larger antigovernment protests.

In 1999, the second presidential elections were held. Surprisingly, the president offered to step down and not stand for reelection. Just what motivated this decision is unclear. (He had been in office for 20 years. Had he grown tired of trying to govern a poor and fractious country?) It was no surprise, however, that his party, the GPC, by unanimous acclamation nominated him as their candidate, and it was no surprise, perhaps, that he accepted: noblesse oblige. But it also came as a surprise that the president was also nominated by the Islah party as their candidate (one might have expected Sheikh Abdullah Hussein al-Ahmar or al-Zindani), effectively creating a voting bloc of Yemen's two most powerful parties that assured him a second presidential term. Irregularities again were reported in both the election campaign and the actual voting, but international monitors determined that they were not egregious enough to rule the election unfair. When the final tally was completed, the president had secured about 96 percent of the popular vote. It appeared as though Yemen's strongman—the obscure military man, who had risen to the presidency on the back of the army, led the country to unification and ruthlessly held it together after a bitter civil war—had also managed to win a democratic election, more or less fair and square. While he was a deeply hated man by many in the opposition, he had won the grudging support of the rest of the country. But many also wondered whether he had won on his own strengths or on the weaknesses of the opposition that was in constant disarray, never played the political game as adroitly as the president, and, worse, always seemed to underestimate his strengths.

Terrorist Attacks

In 2000, it looked on the surface as though the country was stable under the leadership of Ali Abdullah Saleh, but even before then, it seemed that Yemen had a problem with terrorist groups. In late 1998, 16 foreign tourists (mostly British) were kidnapped and taken to a place 250 mi south of Sana'a. (Kidnappings of foreign tourists by Yemeni tribesmen were not uncommon in the 1990s, but these were rarely connected to terrorist groups. They had to do with various grievances, economic and political, against the central government, and hostages were used as a bargaining chip in ensuing negotiations. Hostages have attested to the good treatment they received while in captivity, and they were released unharmed in most cases.) Yemeni troops surrounded the kidnappers and hostages, and in the ensuing gun battle, four hostages and two kidnappers were killed and several others severely wounded. The government was later criticized for its handling of the situation, preferring tough confrontation to political negotiation. A group calling itself the Aden-Abyan Islamic Army claimed responsibility, and four of them were put on trial and convicted, three of whom were sentenced to death. Their leader Zayn al-Mihdar was eventually executed.

In January 2000, an al-Qaeda planned attack on a U.S. naval destroyer was attempted and narrowly failed. That should have been a wake-up call. But on October 12, 2000, came another such attack, this one successful. When the U.S. Navy destroyer, the USS *Cole,* was in Aden for refueling, a pair of Yemeni suicides drove a motorized launch carrying explosives alongside the vessel which then blew up, causing massive damage to the hull: 17 sailors were killed and another 39 were injured. The terrorist organization al-Qaeda claimed responsibility. (In fact, these were not the earliest instances of al-Qaeda activity in Yemen. The first known incident occurred in 1992 when bombs struck two hotels in Aden, killing one foreigner and one Yemeni worker, and leaving several other Yemenis severely injured. The attack was meant to frighten Americans who were taking part in the Gulf War and using Yemen as a way station, but it was hardly noticed in the United States.) Then, September 11, 2001 happened, and the revelation that several Yemenis were among the terrorists on board the hijacked airliners that slammed into the World Trade Center Towers in New York City and the Pentagon in Washington, D.C., Bush's "you're either with us or you're against us" polarizing rhetoric created an atmosphere of wariness and even fear among potential U.S. allies like Yemen who could not see the situation in such black-and-white terms. If al-Qaeda was attacking U.S. interests in Yemen, it was because of the Gulf War. Al-Qaeda was seen as America's problem, not Yemen's, but the way the United States framed the issue did not allow for such subtlety. In the immediate aftermath, there was some talk in the Bush White House of attacking Yemen, and rumor has it that Ali Abdullah Saleh was convinced such an attack was imminent.

In any event, Saleh chose to cooperate with the United States in curbing if not eliminating al-Qaeda in Yemen, hoping to balance external pressures with his own internal security needs. In 2002, apparently with Yemeni government approval, the United States launched a predator drone in the desert outside Marib and assassinated Yemeni senior al-Qaeda operative, Qaed Salim Sinan al-Harethi, who was believed to have been the mastermind behind the U.S.S. *Cole* bombing. Five others who died with al-Harethi were also suspected al-Qaeda militants.

It was the first such drone attack in Yemen, but it was not the last. In 2010, the Obama administration, for example, put Anwar al-Awlaki on a U.S. hit list, and he

Aftermath of the U.S.S. Cole *bombing, 2000. (Department of Defense)*

was eventually killed by a drone. In May 2010, another predator drone attack oc-curred in Wadi Abidah, killing other suspected al-Qaeda operatives; however, in the same house, at the time, was deputy governor of Marib, the son of a powerful Marib sheikh, who had been sent by President Saleh to mediate a political withdrawal of al-Qaeda from that part of Yemen. Both men died in the drone attack. The Marib sheikh's tribe militarily engaged government forces, and the president had to pay blood money to the sheikh's tribe and apologize in order to bring hostilities to a close. Poor intelligence information on the ground was blamed for the mistake. One has to bear in mind, however, that the risks of obtaining vague or faulty intelligence in a country like Yemen are high, leading to a greater likelihood of such errors occurring.

Between 2002 and 2005, with military hardware from the United States alongside Special Forces Operations, Yemen security forces appeared to have contained the threat of al-Qaeda inside the country. Many al-Qaeda suspects involved in terrorist attacks on U.S. interests in Yemen were either dead or locked up in Yemeni prisons. Meanwhile, the United States was too preoccupied with its stalled wars in Iraq and Afghanistan to focus on al-Qaeda in Yemen.

In early 2006, however, 23 prisoners from a maximum security prison in Sana'a tunneled their way to freedom, among them al-Qaeda leaders. The circumstances of the escape were highly suspicious, suggesting that the escapees had help from the outside, and even though the president was said to have been furious, some privately wondered whether the government was behind it. The possible motive? The president hoped to leverage the escape to get more military aid from the United States—at a time when the regime was facing rising waves of discontent in the far north, the Houthi Rebellion (which began in 2004)—and could use the weapons against it.

The story of the Houthi Rebellion and the Southern Secessionist Movement that began in roughly the same time are detailed in Chapter 7. In combination with the al-Qaeda attacks in southern Yemen, they represented an unprecedented challenge to the Saleh regime. Then, in January 2011, Yemen underwent what has been called "the Arab Spring," a series of rebellions launched by mainly youthful protestors in countries from Tunisia to Syria that eventually led to President Saleh's peaceful removal from power. In February 2012, Yemen had a presidential election that backed the consensus candidate Abd Rabbuh Mansur al-Hadi, who is now the president of the republic. Whether he can, with the help of his cabinet, face down al-Qaeda and come to terms with two popular rebellions in the country remains to be seen, not to speak of the challenges he faces in reviving the economy. A once united Yemen is now facing the prospect of a federation of semiautonomous regions.

BIBLIOGRAPHY

Burrowes, Robert D. *Historical Dictionary of Yemen.* Lanham, MD: Scarecrow, 1995.

Burrowes, Robert D. *The Yemen Arab Republic: The Politics of Development, 1962–1986.* Boulder, CO: Westview Press, 1987.

Carapico, Sheila. *Civil Society in Yemen: The Political Economy of Activism in Modern Arabia.* Cambridge: Cambridge University Press, 1998.

Dresch, Paul. *A History of Modern Yemen.* Cambridge: Cambridge University Press, 2000.

Peterson, John E. *Yemen: The Search for a Modern State.* Baltimore: Johns Hopkins University Press, 1982.

Phillips, Sarah. *Yemen's Democracy Experiment in Regional Perspective: Patronage and Pluralized Authoritarianism.* New York: Palgrave Macmillan, 2008.

Salmoni, Barak A., Bryce Loidolt, and Madeleine Wells. *Regime and Periphery in Northern Yemen: The Huthi Phenomenon.* Santa Monica, CA: RAND, 2010.

Stookey, Robert W. *Yemen: The Politics of the Yemen Arab Republic.* Boulder, CO: Westview Press, 1978.

Wedeen, Lisa. *Peripheral Visions: Publics, Power, and Performance in Yemen.* Chicago: University of Chicago Press, 2008.

Wenner, Manfred W. *Modern Yemen: 1918–1916.* Baltimore: Johns Hopkins University Press, 1967.

Politics and Government

Stacey Philbrick Yadav and Ali Saif Hassan

TABLE 3.1   Yemen's Government.

Current name	Republic of Yemen
Capital	Sana'a
Government type	Constitutional Republic
Chief of state	President Abd Rabbuh Mansur al-Hadi (since February 2012)
Vice president	Currently vacant
Head of government	Prime Minister Muhammad Salim Basindawa (since November 2011)
Elections	President elected by popular vote for a seven-year term. On February 21, 2012, a special election was held to remove President Ali Abdullah Saleh from power (based on a deal brokered by the Gulf Cooperation Council, guaranteeing immunity from prosecution for corruption or crimes against humanity by the former president and his family). al-Hadi, the only official presidential candidate, was elected president.
Administrative units	20 Governorates: Abyan, Aden, Ad Dhali', Al-Baydha', Al-Hudaydah, Al-Jawf, Al-Mahrah, Al-Mahwit, 'Amran, Dhamar, Hadhramawt, Hajjah, Ibb, Lahaj, Marib, Raymah, Sa'dah, Sana'a, Shabwah, and Taiz
Municipality	Sana'a City

(Continued)

TABLE 3.1 Yemen's Government (*Continued*).

Judicial	Supreme Court
Political parties	The three main parties are General People's Congress party (leader: Abdul Qader Bajamal), Islamic Reform Grouping or Islah party (leader: Abdul Malik al-Makhlafi), and National Arab Socialist Ba'ath Party (leader: Yasin Saeed Numan).

Any analysis of politics in Yemen (or anywhere) that begins and ends with formal political institutions and the rules that are supposed to regulate their function will tell only part of the story, and a small part at that. This chapter defines politics broadly as the struggle over the distribution of power, with power understood as having both material and symbolic dimensions. Efforts to produce and wield power are the messy stuff of politics, are always contested, and must be constantly renegotiated. Struggles for power in Yemen can and have unfolded in parliament, or through elections, but just as often they have been framed through armed conflicts, mosque sermons, editorials in newspapers, nonviolent demonstrations, and the quotidian practices that constitute the everyday experiences of Yemenis across the social and economic spectrum.

Government is something more specific. Analysis of government tends to focus on formal institutions—the rights and responsibilities granted to different branches of government, to citizens, and so forth. But even if the study of government is justifiably narrower than the study of politics, it should never reify those institutions or treat them as though they exist outside of the practices of people who make and re-make them every day. This process of interaction between human beings and institutions (or, as social scientists like to say, between agency and structure) is particularly important in Yemen, where it can help us to understand what sometimes seem like substantial gaps between what is written into law and what is evident reality. Each section of this chapter has something to say about both the government of Yemen and the politics that animate people's interaction with institutions and each other. Readers will encounter themes that overlap with other chapters, especially those that deal with human geography, economics, and tribal dynamics, but the emphasis here is on the ways in which each of these issues intersects with political struggles and the challenges of government.

The chapter is organized into three main sections. The first details political legacies of several different regime types in the decades prior to the establishment of the unified Republic of Yemen (RoY) in 1990. It is here that the chapter explores some of the human and geographic variation of the country, its dominant modes of production, and the various ways in which centralized (and decentralized) forms of political authority were established over time to govern various communities. This section ends with a discussion of the barriers and incentives that leaders of North and South Yemen faced when considering the prospect of unification and the circumstances that ultimately led to the creation of a new state for an old nation.

The second section establishes the basic partisan landscape of post-unification Yemen and discusses each branch of government, with an eye toward the articulation of specific rights and an analysis of how those rights have or have not been realized in practice. In addition to an analysis of the major political parties and three main branches of government, the section also includes a short discussion of Yemen's foreign policy and civil–military relations.

While the second section focuses mainly on the institutions of government in the RoY, the third section delves more deeply into the politics that have complicated the process of governing since 1990. This section includes a discussion of the role of civil society and Yemen's remarkably vibrant associational life, as well as the politics of religion, and the role of women as both objects and subjects of politic struggle.

POLITICAL LEGACIES FROM YEMEN'S HISTORY

Two States, Two Regimes: North and South Yemen

The history of modern Yemen can be periodized in any number of ways, but when thinking of "politics and government," it probably makes most sense to speak of this history in terms of the challenge of political centralization, or state-building. If scholars take a rigid understanding of the state as an entity that can successfully monopolize the legitimate use of force, they are likely to conclude that there has never been a single, coherent Yemeni state. Yet, efforts at political centralization began in earnest in both North and South in the mid-19th century and have consistently deepened the reach of state institutions since then. While the state has never succeeded in supplanting alternative sources of authority, and in many cases has not tried to do so, there has been a steady increase in the bureaucratic mechanisms of government and the coercive capacity of the military.

In the southern and eastern parts of the country that is today the RoY, political centralization was first pursued through British colonial institutions. Yet, British rule itself was a hybrid of direct and indirect rules, with a robust colonial administration (mainly staffed by colonial subjects from India's civil service) centered in the strategically significant port of Aden and a series of suzerainty treaties with local rulers in the peripheral regions outside of Aden and in the desert of Hadhramawt. The British implemented land reform policies that more or less transformed the tribal structure in the south into something that more closely resembled a feudal system and was therefore legible to (and exploitable by) British authorities. The colonial administration also standardized legal practice through the importation of a uniform code of "Anglo-Mohammedan Law" applied by British judges. Through mechanisms familiar throughout the British colonial empire, some local sources of authority were thus uprooted while others were fundamentally transformed or reordered.

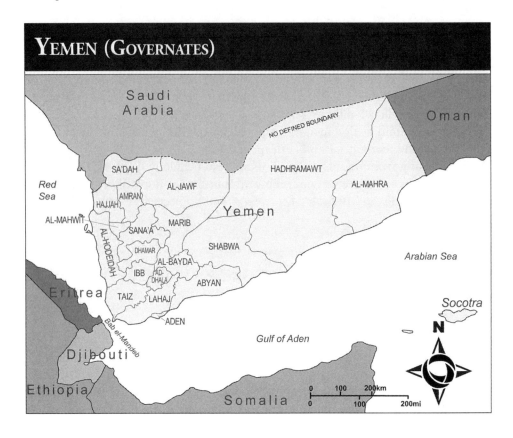

YEMEN (GOVERNATES)

The anticolonial independence movement was centered in Aden, but activists frequently sought refuge over the Northern border, particularly in the midland city of Taiz, where the intellectual culture was itself influenced by the constant commingling of people and ideologies from North and South. It is not surprising that the republican constitutionalism that inspired Northerners in the National Liberation Front (NFL) to struggle to transform the Zaydi Imamate in North Yemen into a constitutional monarchy found its earliest expression among men from Taiz with close contacts with anticolonial leaders in the South. The border was a flexible one, neither geographically fixed nor clearly demarcated in the minds of Yemenis, whose rhetorical and moral appeals were not constrained to the North or South.

In the 1960s, both North and South Yemen experienced cataclysmic political changes brought about through a combination of civic activism and armed struggle. In 1962, the last Zaydi Imam was overthrown by a group of republican-minded military officers, influenced by similar developments in Egypt and elsewhere in the Arab region. In 1967, the South's NFL was ultimately successful in bringing about an end to British colonial rule in South Yemen and established the People's Republic of South Yemen, later renamed the People's Democratic Republic of Yemen (PDRY). After this initial victory, the new Southern leaders set about centralizing the new state and eliminating the rival Front for the Liberation of South Yemen, with which the NLF had fought the British.

While some of the aspirations of earlier NFL leaders in the North were realized when a republic was declared in 1962, it fell far short of the constitutional order that they envisioned, and the new Yemen Arab Republic (YAR) was essentially a military state, owing in part to the civil war that raged in the North from 1962 to 1970. A restorationist movement, based in the city of Sa'dah, sought to reestablish the Imamate and received support from neighboring monarchy, Saudi Arabia, while republican forces were aided by (and to some extent, subservient to) some 40,000 Egyptian troops dispatched by Gamal Abdel Nasser. For its part, the leftist regime in South Yemen offered periodic refuge to Northerners loyal to the republican cause and engaged in cross-border raids on its unsteady northern neighbor.

A cease-fire was reached in the North's civil war in 1970, paving the way for the PDRY and YAR to sign the 1972 Cairo Agreement, establishing the basic framework for their eventual unification. It nonetheless took nearly two decades before unification was a reality, during which time the ruling regimes of both states struggled to consolidate their own power. Coming to power following the assassination of his predecessor, Ali Abdullah Saleh became president of the YAR in 1978, and established the political party known as General People's Congress (GPC) in 1981.

Ali Abdullah Saleh, president of the Yemen Arab Republic (1978–1990) and of the Republic of Yemen (1990–2012). Photo from 1989. (Thomas Hartwell/ Time Life Pictures/Getty Images)

ALI ABDULLAH SALEH

Ali Abdullah Saleh was the president of the Yemen (r. 1978–2012). Born in 1942 into a relatively small (and at the time insignificant) tribe called the Sinhan, he began his career in the army and was promoted to military governor of Taiz in 1977. One year later, he was elected chief of military forces and then appointed president by a rubber-stamp Parliament in 1978 after the previous president, al-Ghashmi, was assassinated. Though the beginnings of his presidency were shaky, over time he consolidated power through a combination of cronyism and cunning tactics, including playing opponents against each other. The fact that oil was discovered in the 1980s helped strengthen his presidency tremendously. Perhaps his single most important achievement was to unify North and South Yemen in 1990, though by 1994 his regime faced rebellion in the south, and he had to lead the republican army (supplemented by northern tribal militias) to a bloody showdown with southern forces that culminated in the bombing and sacking of Aden. He was the only president in the Arab Spring to be removed from office peacefully, through a Gulf Cooperation Council–brokered agreement in which he and his immediate family received immunity for any crimes committed while in power.

The rebellion against the YAR staged by the National Democratic Front, a rebel group backed by the South, was only fully suppressed in 1982. In 1986, major disagreements within the ruling Yemeni Socialist Party (YSP) in the PDRY resulted in a 13-day bloody purge, known as the "Events of January." It was against this tumultuous backdrop in North and South that negotiations for unification developed in earnest.

Road to Unification

While the reality was more difficult to achieve, the basic idea of Yemeni unification was widely popular and predated both the PDRY and the YAR. Indeed, unification was espoused by both Imam Yayha (r. 1904–1948) and his son and successor Imam Ahmed (r. 1948–1962), and since the 1940s by most modern nationalists in both Yemens. While the 1972 Cairo Declaration was probably the most significant written commitment to unification, it would be a mistake to make it foundational in any meaningful sense: historically, between 1972 and1990, there have been many agreements, reports, communiqués, and statements of principle accumulated, some of which contradicted each other. Unfortunately, in addition to these contradictory texts, there was the wrenching political reality of numerous changeovers in government, three internecine wars, three border confrontations between the two states, and several regional uprisings, most of which can be attributed to failed efforts on the part of Northern and Southern leaders to consolidate their own power.

It was only with the decline of Soviet support for South Yemen and the discovery of petroleum along the border between North and South that both sides had an incentive to negotiate a union that fulfilled long-standing public aspirations in both countries.

Discussions of the unification process often focus on the ideological distance between the PDRY and the YAR and on the experiential difference between each of these and the regime against which it rebelled (e.g., the Zaydi Imamate in the North and British colonial rule in the South). But what this obscures is the surprising overlap in the political realities in North and South Yemen, driven by exigencies of economic pressures and the general challenge of centralizing power where multiple sources of authority coexist. In the first case, both the PDRY and the YAR faced the tremendous burden of economic modernization, and both responded with a version of what is called the "developmentalist" model: A system whereby the state is heavily involved in the market, providing necessary infrastructural development and incentives for industrialization. This model was popular throughout the developing world in the 1960s and 1970s, and both Yemens adopted state-led development programs. Despite its Marxist rhetoric (and some central planning), the South never fully eliminated private property, and the North experimented in collectivization through Local Development Associations. In other words, both regimes converged around an economic middle ground between capitalism and communism, in the midst of the Cold War, despite their patronage ties to very different foreign powers.

THE 1994 CIVIL WAR

The war itself was very short and militarily decisive in favor of the North. The more durable legacies, however, came from the social impact of the use of vigilante violence and from the imposition of Northern hegemony in public institutions. Prior to and during the war, Islahi clerics and other conservative salafi figures unaffiliated with the party issued *fatawa*, or religious rulings, that classified Socialists as apostates and the struggle against them—through institutions, or in the streets—as a jihad. These efforts at intimidation had a lasting effect on North–South relations, as many Southerners viewed the clerics' edicts as an informal state policy, a crackdown on freedom of expression and belief. The postwar period in the South was also characterized by Northern political hegemony. Governors were appointed from the North and staffed the civil service with northerners from the General People's Congress (GPC). The electoral law allowed voters to vote in the place where they worked, thus inflating the share of GPC voters in Southern districts and further blunting Southern representation. Streets and other infrastructure damaged during the war remained unrepaired for more than a decade after the civil war, as the GPC administrators engaged in not-so-benign neglect of Southern constituencies.

THE REPUBLIC OF YEMEN

The Unity Constitution

The new constitution not only created the basic institutional structure that contin-ues to obtain in Yemen today, but also set in motion the processes that would lead to civil war and authoritarian consolidation. For this reason, among the many other documents that contributed to unification, it is worth examining in some detail, as are the debates that it inspired and sought to resolve. It was the new constitution (and its drafters) that carried the heavy burden of making two states out of one, of bringing together parties accustomed to sovereignty and compelling them to share power, not simply overtake the other. It is reasonably clear, from the perspective of hindsight, that the senior leaders on both sides lacked genuine commitment to power-sharing and viewed the democratic character of the new constitution largely as a means to an end. But as one member of Yemen's political opposition put it, "Yemen has lots of beautiful laws, like Plato's *Republic*" (personal communication to the author). The challenge has been and continues to be translating these laws into practice.

The 1990 Constitution established the RoY as an Arab and Islamic republic, in which Islam would be "the principle source of legislation" but popular sovereignty— "rule by the will of the people"—would be upheld. This contradiction, between what might be considered a model of judicial sovereignty (whereby Islamic law, and by extension, those who interpret it, is the source of sovereign authority) and the popu-lar sovereignty associated with parliamentary rule, is at the heart of Yemen's most foundational document. A powerful Islamist faction with close ties to the Northern regime, many of whom would ultimately become leaders in Islah, lobbied aggres-sively for language that would make Islamic law paramount. At the same time, secu-larists in the YSP—who had never been particularly democratic in practice when they governed the South—affirmed popular sovereignty as a partial antidote to what they viewed as Islamist domination.

It was easier to accommodate an Islamist–Socialist synthesis in the economic sec-tor, where Islamists and Socialists could converge around the basic language of social justice. The constitution adopted formal commitments: "Islamic social justice," "a developed public sector," "preservation of private ownership," and "comprehensive development" (Republic of Yemen, 1990 Constitution). The details of economic de-velopment were left vague, no doubt in recognition of the fact that foreign donor agendas would steer policy-making.

Pragmatically, in order to facilitate transition from two single-party states to a new democratic republic, Northern and Southern leaders called for the temporary merger of the legislatures of both countries, in effect creating a two-party system on the spot, with the stated aim of passing the legislation needed to enable a more plu-ral, multiparty system in the near term. This merger meant that all elected members of the North's Consultative Assembly and the South's Supreme People's Council would become members of the new RoY lower house, or Chamber of Deputies. It was this parliament that passed the initial legislation regarding political parties and associational life that enabled the vibrant political life of the early 1990s.

Political Parties and Political Pluralism

Article 39 of the constitution maintains that "citizens may organize themselves along political, professional, or union lines," and indeed, immediately following unification, Yemenis formed no fewer than 40 different political parties. Of these, historian Paul Dresch notes that "certain smaller parties were hardly more than a few friends with an office and a telephone, but each had its newspaper, and many had more than one" (Dresch 2000: 190). The vibrancy of the partisan sphere was energizing and is often remembered by political activists today as a period of remarkable political freedom.

That said, Law 66, passed in 1991 by a transitional parliament composed of all deputies from the PDRY and YAR parliaments, established basic redlines that political parties could not cross. These included any platform that would undermine Yemeni unity, the republican system, or Islamic values. Because of this, the platforms of the various political parties have tended to adopt a remarkably similar tone and rhetoric, even when the policies that various parties discuss internally or as part of their campaigns differ more substantially.

The composition of the partisan landscape in the RoY has remained roughly the same over the past two decades, though the balance of power between the different parties has changed considerably. Since unification, the ruling GPC has predominated, with a parliamentary majority beginning in 1993 and a supermajority since 2003 until 2011 (the beginning of the "Arab Spring" in Yemen). The second largest political party is the Yemeni Congregation for Reform, or Islah. It is a loose umbrella party composed of important tribal figures, members of the Muslim Brotherhood, Salafi conservatives, and some business leaders. The YSP, the former ruling party of the PDRY, had a strong showing in the 1993 elections, but suffered a substantial political setback after the 1994 civil war. It boycotted the 1997 elections and has since enjoyed only a small number of seats in parliament. It remains a potent political actor, however, insofar as it is viewed as the clearest representative of the South, and has become an important player in the opposition Joint Meeting Parties (JMP) alliance. Several smaller political parties represent narrower interests and, in some cases, particular families and their allies. For example, the Union of Popular Forces, a Zaydi Nationalist party, is largely a vehicle for the prominent al-Wazir family and members of the al-Mutawakkil family. Nasserist and Ba'athist ideological parties have a small presence, and the Zaydi religious party, al-Haqq, remains a significant part of the opposition despite holding no seats in parliament.

The GPC is what political scientists call a "party of power," or one that is largely devoid of any characteristic ideology. This means that its policies have mainly served to reinforce the power of President Saleh and that the party has often shifted its priorities in keeping with public opinion or the demands of its political allies. From unification until the end of the civil war, for example, the GPC needed help in counterbalancing the threat of the YSP, so it reached out to Islah with important ministry appointments that it knew its Islamist ally would value, giving Islahis oversight over important questions of educational and judicial policy. With the YSP's institutional capacity largely destroyed by the civil war, Islah became less useful to the GPC by the late 1990s and consequently found itself receiving fewer direct benefits from the ruling party.

Gradually, Islahi ministers resigned from government, and Islah's leadership began to explore opportunities for coordinated opposition with the YSP and other parties. While this relationship began in fits and starts—Islah joined the Supreme Council for Coordinating the Opposition, for example, in 1999, but then also endorsed President Saleh's bid for reelection—it gained momentum in the 2000s. As a confidence-building measure, human rights activist and deputy secretary general of the YSP Jarallah Umar was invited to address the Islah party congress at the end of 2003. In an event that shook the foundations of Yemen's partisan system, he was killed in front of a crowd of thousands by an assassin who was later tried and executed for the crime. The killer was a former member of Islah who had left the party, and many Yemeni political analysts allege that he was hired by the Saleh regime to engage in an act that would derail efforts to develop joint opposition. Whether or not there was a conspiracy to divide Islah and the YSP, the assassination of Jarallah Umar prompted an unanticipated recalibration of power within the Islah party that worked to the benefit of the joint opposition. It strengthened the position of a group of reformists—largely under the guidance of Muhammad Qahtan and younger progressives with ties to the media sector—and enabled them to more aggressively pursue a unified alliance with the YSP. For its part, many YSP leaders held Islah indirectly responsible for Umar's death, owing to the fatwas issued against Socialists by Islahi clerics in the 1990s especially, but they recognized the necessity of coordinating their opposition to the authoritarian encroachments of the Saleh regime. The JMP alliance was formally announced in 2005, and in 2006 contested its first election, with Faysal bin Shamlan challenging President Saleh in a direct election (as discussed below).

Since unification, political pluralism has remained vibrant in Yemen, but political freedom and accountability have been on a consistent decline. What this means is that opposition parties continue to exist and ideas continue to be contested in the public sphere, but the ability of any party or organization other than the GPC to translate its ideas into policies by standing for and winning election has been increasingly limited. The GPC's share of seats in parliament has grown with each election, and the scope of real power exercised by that parliament has declined. Because the opposition is cobbled together from ideologically diverse groups with high levels of mutual mistrust, it has also been possible for the ruling regime to engage in a politics of division and cooptation, working to turn member parties against one another. All of this has contributed to the climate of political discontent that has grown more acute over the past five years, driving the conflicts described in later sections of this chapter and in Chapter 7.

THE EXECUTIVE BRANCH

The executive branch, as formerly embodied by President Ali Abdullah Saleh and now by President Abd Rabbuh Mansur al-Hadi, is by far the most significant of Yemen's formal branches of government. This owes less to the specific powers granted to the executive by the constitution than it does to the networks of patronage built over Saleh's 33 years in office and the personalization of politics that has character-ized his governing style.

During the process of unification, Saleh and PDRY President Ali Salim al-Beidh agreed to a transitional power-sharing executive that would distribute power more or less equally between Northern and Southern leaders. In theory, the idea of a collective executive was not unknown in either country, since both revolutionary regimes had for a time used collective "councils" of various sorts to carry out execu-tive functions. The problem with this Presidential Council came from the funda-mental distortions and anxieties of unification itself. From a Northern perspective, this arrangement overrepresented the South, where only a small fraction of Yemenis lived. From a Southern perspective, it helped to offset the loss of sovereignty that formal unification with the North entailed. The Presidential Council was composed of five members, elected by the unified transitional parliament. Saleh and al-Beidh won two of the posts and were in turn chosen as chairman and vice chairman of the council. The agreement, which carefully avoided calling these positions "president and vice president" so as to avoid the appearance of subordination, nonetheless raised concerns among Southern leaders. The other three seats on the council went to Southerner Salim Saleh Muhammad and Northerners Abdul Karim al-Arashi and Abdul Aziz Abdul Ghani, former president and prime minister, respectively. The council itself then appointed former PDRY president Haydar Abu Bakr al-Attas as prime minister, empowering him to form a government of ministers. Following the 1994 civil war, the constitution was amended to stipulate that the president would be a single individual, directly elected to a term of five years. Yemen's system is now formally a "premier-presidential" system, as there is both a president and a prime minister accountable to the parliament; but in practice, the powers of the presidency are so strong and the parliamentary majority enjoyed by Saleh's GPC so large that it has functioned as a presidential system since 1994.

In 1999, President Saleh stood for direct election for the first time under the amended constitution. The election was contested only by a member of his own po-litical party. The only viable opposition party the Yemeni Congregation for Reform (or "Islah") had served as a junior partner in government and pledged to support Saleh in the 1999 elections. Other opposition parties were too small or regionally oriented that they did not field candidates. Electoral competition was thus a façade, and Saleh reportedly won 96.3 percent of the vote. In 2001, the constitution was further amended to lengthen the term of office for the president from five to seven years, further consolidating Saleh's hold on executive power.

The 2006 election, however, was surprisingly competitive, though Saleh once again won the election, and there were reports of electoral manipulation reported by the European Union Electoral Observation Commission. By this point, Islah had joined with the YSP and several other small parties to form the JMP opposition al-liance, and the JMP forwarded its own candidate to contest the election. Faysal bin Shamlan, a Southern technocrat with experience in the petroleum sector, competed on a platform of political and economic reform and won more preelection polls projected. JMP members recall the 2006 election as a "victory," insofar as Saleh was compelled to campaign and engage in public debate of substantive political issues.

In the end, however, Saleh won reelection with 77 percent of the vote and returned promptly to politics as usual. As president, he wielded tremendous power, having reshuffled senior military posts to members of his immediate family, engineered a supermajority in parliament that guaranteed his ability to advance legislation that further entrenched his power, and extended his patronage throughout the judicial system to ensure that prosecutions of his allies were few and his ability to punish his critics through the courts enhanced. This authoritarian encroachment teamed with his efforts to ensure that his son Ahmed Ali Saleh would "inherit" this republican presidency have been major contributors to the crises that have grown more destabilizing over the past decade.

THE LEGISLATIVE BRANCH

The legislative branch, while it exercises little direct power, is the most vibrant and accountable site of political competition within Yemen's formal branches of government. The bicameral legislature is composed of an upper house (the 111-member Shura Council) and a lower house, the 301-member Chamber of Deputies. The upper house's function is largely ceremonial, with appointed members serving in an advisory capacity only. The prestigious, if powerless, appointments serve as a form of political patronage that the regime doles out to secure the loyalty of important families and interest groups. The lower house is what is conventionally referred to as the parliament, and it is here that political parties with competing ideologies, regional affiliations, and personalities vie to shape the national political agenda. Written records of parliamentary debates are not publicly available, but the debates themselves are broadcast live on Yemeni television and make for an often-dramatic form of political spectacle. Perhaps because of the GPC's supermajority, absenteeism has become a major problem in the lower house, further undermining the efficacy of the institution.

The first parliamentary election following unification was a vibrant contest that generated a genuinely unanticipated outcome. The two ruling parties of North and South Yemen were expected to be the largest winners, though the population gap between North and South suggested that the GPC would be the greatest winner. Unexpected, however, was the success of the Yemeni Congregation for Reform, or Islah. This Islamist party, formed only after unification, was a hodgepodge of only loosely aligned groups—Muslim Brothers, businessmen, tribal leaders, and Salafis—united by a common social conservatism and Northern identity, but little else. That said, their ability to mobilize support against the YSP and to make use of existing networks of association, from mosques and study circles to tribal and kinship networks, gave them an organizing advantage over the YSP. Islah came in second to the GPC, which caused some controversy when it came to apportioning portfolios in the new government. The logic of power-sharing that was at the heart of unification was about power-sharing between the GPC and the YSP and did not count on Islah.

In the end, Islah entered the government as a junior partner, but it took powerful ministries through which to extend its struggle against Southern atheism. During

Yemeni parliament members vote, 2011. (AP Photo/Hani Mohammed)

the 1994 civil war, Islahi clerics helped to mobilize irregular forces to attack people and property in the South, famously burning a distillery in Aden, among many other locations. After the YSP leadership was driven into exile or political abeyance, however, Islah was less valuable to the GPC. For their part, Islahis grew increasingly frustrated with GPC corruption and began to resign from cabinet positions and to raise concerns about the issue in parliament.

After the 2003 election, however, in which the GPC secured a 79 percent of seats in parliament, the institution functioned mainly as a rubber stamp. Opposition parties have sometimes been able to embarrass the government in parliamentary debates and have been somewhat successful in building coalitions across the aisle with some GPC members, particularly "technocratic" figures, on issues of a largely uncontroversial nature. Until 2010, the parliament was unable to exercise much oversight over the government budget-making process, but the government has begun to submit year-end reports and preliminary forecasts for government expenditures. These are not likely to be very accurate, but the decision to provide them speaks to growing frustration by MPs from all of the major political parties, including the ruling party, regarding the government's lack of transparency and accountability.

THE JUDICIAL BRANCH

Article 120 of the 1990 Constitution establishes the principle of judicial independence, but judicial practice in Yemen has functioned as an extension of executive power and has been characterized by the dynamics of personalization and patronage that are features of the broader political system. While the law explicitly prohibits interference in the court system by any party, judicial appointments have frequently been made to further secure the Saleh regime.

While judicial appointments ensure that relatively few rulings contradict the prerogatives of the president, there has been increasing public pressure (both domestic and international) to investigate allegations of corruption by public officials. Rather than risk public embarrassment, cases are frequently referred to the public prosecutor, who then faces pressure from the executive not to bring the cases to trial. In 2006, parliament passed a national anticorruption law mandating financial disclosures by public officials and laying the groundwork for the creation of the Supreme National Authority to Combat Corruption (SNACC) the next year. By 2010, SNACC reported that it had received over 10,000 financial disclosures but forwarded only 24 cases to the public prosecutor (International Association for Anti-Corruption Authorities 2000).

Yemen's constitution allows for a judiciary composed of the Courts of First Instance, Court of Appeals, and Supreme Court. It explicitly states in Article 121 that "exceptional courts may not be established under any conditions," yet two such courts have been created by President Saleh. The Specialized Criminal Court was established in 1999 and adjudicates "crimes against national security." This court has been used not only to try suspected militants aligned with terrorist organizations like al-Qaeda in the Arabian Peninsula (AQAP), but also members of the Houthi movement, the Hirak (discussed below), and journalists who have reported on government efforts to put down opposition from both groups through force. In the face of escalating crises throughout the country, the government moved in 2009 to establish a second exceptional court, the Special Press Court, which has been used to prosecute journalists who have investigated corruption, reported on human rights abuses, or published articles that were deemed divisive to national unity or insulting to religion. This strategy has largely backfired: The trials of journalists have made them into public heroes, often attracting far more international attention than they likely would have.

Aside from the corruption of the court system and the extralegal establishment of exceptional courts, personal intercession also regularly undermines the rule of law in Yemen. The president issues pardons by fiat and occasionally declares general amnesties, as in 2010 when he issued an amnesty releasing a large number of journalists—including opposition figure Muhammad al-Maqalih, who had disappeared for a year and was found, tortured, and then charged in the Special Criminal Court and Special Press Court. Consistent with the uncertain nature of personal intercession, al-Maqalih's case has been "discontinued," but not dismissed. This individual case is emblematic of the broader challenge that personal intercession poses for the transparent and equal application of the law, and part of why the political opposition has for many years taken "rule of law" and legal accountability as its central focus. That said, only one day after signing the Gulf Cooperation Council (GCC) agreement that would lead to his transition from power, President Saleh announced a general amnesty for all those who committed violence against protesters during the 2011 Change Revolution (or the Yemini Arab Spring), with a draft of this amnesty law under consideration in the GPC-dominated parliament.

LOCAL GOVERNMENT AND THE DEVOLUTION OF AUTHORITY

The formal powers of local government in Yemen are limited, and the centralizing regime of Ali Abdullah Saleh sought to further curtail local voices and sources of authority in many parts of the country. Yemen has 20 governorates, or administrative governorates, and 1 municipality, but these are not federal units with independent rights vis-à-vis the central government. The existing structure makes the governors accountable to the Cabinet, not to the electorate, though Yemen moved to the direct election of governors in most governorates in 2008. While the constitution affirmed the right of Yemenis to elected local-level government, parliament did not pass a local authorities law outlining an electoral structure for local councils until 1999, and the first election was held in 2001. With more than 27,000 candidates, they were described as a "chaotic affair" in which at least 45 people, several of whom were opposition candidates who appeared to be winning, were killed and with more than 100 documented cases of election-related violence (Whitaker 2001). While they produced democratically elected local councils, these councils had no real authority against the dictates of appointed local governors.

In 2008, however, an intermediate solution was adopted, with local councils indirectly electing provincial governors for the first time. Because the ruling GPC controlled over 70 percent of the local council seats, the JMP viewed this as a kind of "rubber stamp" of the status quo and boycotted the indirect elections. In the end, 17 local councils elected a GPC governor, 3 elected an independent candidate with known ties to the GPC, and 1 province failed to achieve the necessary quorum to hold an election. The JMP opposition has maintained a consistent call for devolution of fiscal power and greater political accountability at the local level, whereas the Hirak has increasingly turned to calls for secession from the Republic.

CIVIL–MILITARY RELATIONS

The 1990 Constitution established a National Defense Council, which was the mechanism through which the two armies of the PDRY and the YAR were to in theory be integrated. At the same time, it stipulated that the chairman of the Presidential Council would be the head of the National Defense Council, which in practice ensured that Saleh, as chairman of the Presidential Council and later president of the Republic, was also the commander of the armed forces. By this time, according to historian Paul Dresch (2000: 180), senior figures in the army "could all be found on the President's family tree." Southern and Northern units were poorly integrated, which meant that when Ali Salim al-Beidh retreated to Aden in 1994, he was able to marshal independent military resources and what might have been a political conflict escalated into warfare." By the end of the civil war, however, there was a wholesale effort by the Northern victors to monopolize military institutions, which continue to be the preserve of Saleh's closest allies. While the constitution prohibits the development of private or personal militias, the Republican Guard, under the supervision

---

MAJOR GENERAL ALI MOHSEN AL-AHMAR

For many years, Yemenis spoke of Ali Mohsen al-Ahmar, the major general in command of the 1st Armored Division responsible for the northwestern military district, with a combination of fear and resignation. The fear stemmed from his close relationship to the president and his seeming indifference to the destruction that he caused to civilian lives and livelihoods, especially when prosecuting the Sa'dah campaign against the al-Houthi family and its loyalists. The resignation came from the assumption voiced by many that Ali Mohsen al-Ahmar was likely to be President Saleh's successor, next in line in a republican regime with its origins in the barracks. This prediction proved false. Reputedly President Saleh's half brother from a different father, Ali Mohsen was instrumental to the success of the military coup that brought Saleh to power in 1978. From that point forward, he served as Saleh's closest military advisor, and when the PRDY and YAR unified in 1990, he retained sufficient autonomy that he was able to lead a successful (if punishing) military campaign against the South in the short 1994 civil war. Despite pledging his support to the Arab Spring protesters in March 2011, he is not a democrat.

---

of Saleh's son and then heir-apparent Ahmed, functions as a private security force for the president.

The relationship between Yemen's military and civilian authorities is made more complicated by the relationship between the state and tribes. There has never been a comprehensive effort to disarm the tribes, with the state preferring to integrate important tribal factions into the military. Beyond this, both the tribes and the military appear to function by a tribal logic that values negotiated settlements of conflicts and views violence as a means toward that end. The loyalties of military and tribal factions, however, are impermanent and constantly renegotiable, and tribal loyalties are only one among many forms of social and political solidarity. This was made evident in March 2011, when prominent tribal allies of President Saleh as well as his closest military advisor Major General Ali Mohsen al-Ahmar joined the opposition, providing critical protection to civilian protesters with the Change Revolution as they faced armed assault by the Republican Guard and other factions of the armed forces.

YEMEN'S FOREIGN POLICY

The foreign policy of the RoY has been largely determined by the dual concerns of development and regime security (often presented as national security). Yemen's sovereignty has been routinely challenged by its complicated relationship to neighboring Saudi Arabia. The border between the two states was only formally demarcated via a negotiated agreement in 2000, and the flow of people and goods through the border region remains somewhat fluid. Political progressives, members of the Left, and leaders of the Zaydi community complain of the influence of Saudi-funded religious institutions in spreading Salafism, a complaint that has been consistent but reached a fever pitch in 2007 and 2008 when Sheikh Abdul Majeed al-Zindani and others endeavored to use their Fadilah group as a kind of public morals council modeled on the Saudi Committee to Protect Virtue and Prevent Vice. The Saudis maintain a "special committee" for Yemeni affairs, through which they have backed many individuals and factions, often at cross-purposes, with the apparent aim of keeping Yemen internally divided. While a long-standing supporter of the Saleh regime—even to the extent that the Saudis coordinated military operations with Saleh's forces in "Operation Scorched Earth," the campaign against the Houthi forces in November 2009—they have also offered financial support directly to those players who have most openly challenged Saleh in 2011, such as Ali Mohsen al-Ahmar, Sadiq al-Ahmar, and Hamid al-Ahmar. Saudi Arabia brokered the GCC agreement for Saleh's departure from office and compelled him to sign it.

Yemen faces numerous challenges stemming from endemic underdevelopment, and these unfortunately reinforce existing social cleavages around regional divisions and gender distinctions. Before the onset of the Change Revolution, Yemen had a per capita income of less than $2,400 and a population that exceeded the total of all the other GCC countries combined, at about 24 million. It also has an unsustainably high population growth rate, nearly a million internally displaced persons, and levels of food insecurity and acute hunger that are approaching the official famine threshold in some parts of the country. This type of endemic need means that Yemen's sovereignty is undermined by dependent relationships on foreign donors and donor agencies, the largest of which are the GCC and the European Union, with Saudi Arabia, Great Britain, and Germany playing particularly significant roles. Under the aegis of the U.K. Foreign and Commonwealth Office, representatives from the foreign ministries and aid agencies of 22 countries formed the Friends of Yemen group in January 2010, with the aim of coordinating development and security assistance while safeguarding human rights. Given that many of the member states themselves have abysmal human rights records, this was largely cosmetic in nature, and meetings of the group have been suspended while individual member states continue to pursue their own bilateral and multilateral programs in Yemen.

Yemen's relationship to the United States has similar clientelistic features, though interactions between the two are much shallower and more recent than the Saudi Arabia–Yemeni relationship. The United States was largely indifferent to Yemen until the bombing of the USS *Cole* in 2000, off the coast of Aden. The attack, carried out by the Abyan Islamic Army, killed 17 U.S. soldiers. After the attacks on the United States on September 11, 2001, U.S. policy in Yemen became attentive to potential interconnections between the Abyan Islamic Army, other Islamist militant groups, and the al-Qaeda network. This concern became the coordinating motif in U.S. donor assistance as well, where U.S. Agency for International Development used development assistance to strategically invest in the most vulnerable communities in Yemen, from which analysts believed terrorists were most likely to be recruited. In Yemeni political circles, this instrumental use of aid—which was only a fraction of what European and GCC donors contributed to development work in Yemen—was viewed with cynicism. In 2009, after the merger of Saudi and Yemeni affiliates of al-Qaeda into AQAP, the United States dramatically increased assistance to Yemen, but the majority was earmarked for military and counterterrorism aids, much of which was in turn channeled into the suppression and surveillance of domestic critics of the Saleh regime. In 2011, the United States backed the GCC-negotiated agreement that granted Saleh legal immunity for crimes committed during the Change Revolution.

STATE–SOCIETY RELATIONS

Civil Society and Associational Life

The vibrancy of Yemen's associational life has been aided by, but should not be reduced to, the freedoms articulated in the 1990 Constitution. In fact, there is a long history of associational sector activism in North and South Yemen that well predates unification, and the existence of alternative sites of authority outside of the state (e.g., tribes, religious leadership, etc.) has meant that few Yemenis expect that the state will be the sole means of organizing public life.

That said, the formal commitment to pluralism in the 1990 Constitution did provide a framework in which civil society could grow and, at least in theory, flourish. Yemenis organized via professional syndicates, labor unions, charitable associations, and myriad nongovernmental organizations (NGOs). Syndicates, while formally state institutions and generally chaired by members of the ruling party, were vibrant sites of public debate and mobilization, and major leadership roles—in the Yemeni Journalists' Syndicate and Lawyers' Syndicate, in particular—were played by members of the opposition. While syndicates were rarely effective in actually changing the laws that regulated their members, they have helped to mobilize public awareness of encroachments by the regime and to publicize violations of their members' rights.

NGOs have been and remain numerous in Yemen, but they are vulnerable to strict licensing requirements that mean that they must resubmit for government permits each year. This gives the government considerable power over NGOs, which nonetheless continue to press for reforms. Some NGOs are politically uncontroversial, and these function largely free from limitation. For example, organizations promoting literacy or providing basic health services to the poor are helping to shoulder the state's burden in the face of extreme need; but organizations that work for political reform, human rights, or gender equality often face much more scrutiny and suppression. In addition to overt efforts to block their work, the government also sponsors parallel organizations, often with confusingly similar names or logos, to "clutter" the public sphere and absorb the organizing energies of the educated middle class.

The greatest defense against such manipulations is public knowledge, which has made the media not only an essential protector of Yemeni citizen rights, but also a routine target of the regime. Aside from official media sponsored directly or indirectly by the regime, Yemen also has a partisan media, composed of papers owned and operated by rival political parties. Unsurprisingly, these are largely a source of editorial comment and not always a reliable source of reporting. But over the past decade, the emergence of a genuinely independent press—both print and online—has promoted investigative journalism. By making space for commentary by members of a wide variety of political parties, this independent press has also made evident the parameters of political consensus among the various parties of the opposition.

The independent media has been a particular target of the regime, especially as crises have escalated throughout the country since 2004 (see below). Reporters have been abducted, disappeared, tortured, and put on trial in extralegal courts. They have had their families threatened, offices ransacked, archives burned, and Web sites hacked. Amazingly, this sector of civil society has remained undaunted, and journalists who have faced such measures have become household names. High rates of illiteracy, however, and low levels of Internet penetration mean that broadcast media remains the greatest source of news for many outside of Yemen's urban centers, and it is in this sector that the government maintains a monopoly over information.

Religion and Politics

There is little separation between religion and politics in Yemen, either formally or in practice. From a constitutional perspective, Islam is recognized as the religion of the state, and the country is viewed as having a distinctive "Islamic heritage." The penal code criminalizes apostasy, and the constitution affirms Sharia as the primary source of legislation. The overwhelming majority of the population is Muslim, but there are sectarian distinctions within this grouping, and individuals or groups who express heterodox interpretations of the faith encounter difficulty accessing their constitutional right to the free exercise of their faith.

While Yemen is hardly an "Islamic state" in the conventional sense insofar as the 'ulama (or clergy) have little institutionalized power, Islam nonetheless provides a potent common vocabulary through which political positions can be strengthened or undermined, a kind of symbolic political economy through which ideas are expressed and power is contested. For example, when the Houthi movement (the northern movement, centered around Zaydi rights, that has waged an ongoing conflict with the Sana'a regime) sought to challenge the legitimacy of the Saleh regime, leaders likened the president to Mu'awiyah, viewed as a usurper of the legitimate authority (in the Shia view) of Imam Ali, the Prophet Muhammad's son-in-law and designated successor. With this simple label, not only did they call into question Saleh's right to govern, but also invoked the specter of rebellion by recalling that it took the partisans of Ali two years to exact their revenge on Mu'awiyah, though they did eventually kill him. On the flip side, Salafi writers often employ a similarly divisive discourse against Zaydis, linking them to schematic groups in early Islam, against whom the Sunni tradition holds it is acceptable to use force. The government itself has often engaged in such rhetorical battles through official media and in public statements.

Sheikh Abdul Majeed al-Zindani, 2010. (AP Photo)

Vigilante groups, sometimes with the support of prominent clerics and clerical associations, seek to police the "vice and virtue" of Yemeni society and inspire vigilante acts of intimidation—often against secularists, members of the political Left, and women who play a visible role in politics. Their tactics can range from verbal harassment to physical force. At the same time, religious organizations like the Islah Charitable Society (which is affiliated with but somewhat autonomous from the Islah party) have played a significant role in advancing progressive and often controversial social causes, from women's literacy to AIDS eradication. The role of religion is therefore a multivalent force in Yemen, but one that certainly cannot be ignored.

SHEIKH ABDUL MAJEED AL-ZINDANI

Born outside of Ibb in 1942, al-Zindani was educated in British colonial Aden and Cairo. While in Cairo, he began to explore what became a lifelong theme in his writing and lecturing: the relationship between faith and science. He spent much of the 1970s in Saudi Arabia, where he developed what has been described by his critics as a "Wahhabi" worldview. He helped to recruit Yemeni and Saudi youth to travel to Afghanistan to fight a jihad against the

Soviets in 1979. He later returned to Yemen, founding with Sheikh Abdullah Hussein al-Ahmar the Islah Party and becoming rector of Iman University in Sana'a. He is a lightning rod in Yemeni domestic politics and foreign policy. Designated a "specially designated global terrorist" by the U.S. Treasury Department in 2004, al-Zindani has also been at the heart of tense diplomatic relations between the United States and Yemen for years. He has launched campaigns of *takfir* (declaring someone an infidel) against any who seek to criticize him, regardless of their partisan affiliations.

The Roles of Women in Politics

Women have been both an object of political debate and important subjects in the shaping of Yemeni politics, before and after unification. It is always important to remember, however, that a woman's experience of the Yemeni political system will depend substantially on where she is from, in terms of her regional background, as well as specific elements of class and family. While many different social, economic, and personal factors influence the way in which women experience the political system, none is likely to be as significant as whether a woman is from the North or the South.

Yemeni woman shows her ink-stained thumb after casting her ballot at a polling station in Sana'a on February 21, 2012. (Mohammed Huwais/AFP/Getty Images)

As a doctrinally Marxist state, the PDRY implemented a progressive personal status law that went some distance in equalizing opportunities for women in education, law, employment, and more. At the same time, it was primarily urban women in Southern cities like Aden and Al-Mukalla who benefitted from this law, while women in rural areas of the South often experienced comparatively fewer gains despite some state programs designed to link the peripheries of the South to the urban core. The General Union of Yemeni Woman was established before the 1967 Revolution, as part of a larger anticolonial political movement, and eventually became an organ of the Marxist state. As such, it was committed to the idea that "the woman should be liberated from the yoke of the patriarchal family" and that her equal moral value should be recognized (Dahlgren 2010: 135). The Women's Union established branches in each of the Southern governorates in the 1970s, with the aim of eradicating illiteracy, promoting education, and facilitating women's integration into the formal labor market. Just prior to Southern independence from British rule, only 15.3 percent of South Yemeni women could read, and only 231 girls attended secondary school. Within the Socialist period's first decade, not only were primary and secondary rates for girls and boys nearly equal, but women outnumbered men in the fields of medicine and education at the university level (Dahlgren 2010: 46 and 51). While the PDRY's formal commitment to Marxism was waning by the mid-1980s, women's gains in education, employment, and mobility should not be underestimated.

The contrast with the experience of Northern women during the same time period could hardly be starker. When the Imamate was dissolved in 1962, there were no government schools for girls in Yemen. A few women from prominent families worked to change this, under the social protection of male relatives who supported their work, but progress was slow and the barriers to women's integration into public life were substantial. This meant that Southern and Northern women experienced unification in very different ways. Northern women have seen a consistent improvement and expansion of gender-based rights since unification, brought about in large part by investments in women's and girls' health and education mandated by foreign-donor agencies. For Southern women, however, the unification period has marked a decline in their political and social equality, through what they see as a kind of Northern hegemony jointly enforced by the GPC and Islah.

But while Islah has complicated the picture for women's rights in Yemen, it has not been as uniform as this account would suggest. On the one hand, it was an Islahi education minister who mandated segregation of boys and girls beginning at the primary level, a change that was interpreted by human rights activists and women's rights activists in the South as part of a wider campaign against women's equality. And student activists and journalists from Islah further lobbied for the closure of the controversial Empirical Research and Women's Studies Center at Sana'a University, a center that funded doctoral research for women researchers. This was a critical turning point for many women activists, who saw limitations on women's equal education access (and all of the other forms of social, economic, and political equality that derive from education) from the primary through the tertiary levels.

At the same time, the Islah party has ironically offered women more opportunities for genuine political leadership than any other political party in Yemen. Though the party does not accept in principle the notion of women's candidacy for national office, it has created a parallel set of institutions through which Islahi women have fulfilled all of the functions of male politicians, campaigning for the party through the Women's Directorate. The success of these skillful female politicians in advancing Islahi objectives is part of why 13 of them were elected to the party's Shura Council in 2007, against the objections of hard-liners in the party.

Despite limited gains for Islahi women within their own party, the authoritarian encroachment of the Saleh regime has meant that opposition parties have become progressively less willing to expend much social capital in support of female candidates who are almost certain to lose. As a result, women have largely found themselves choosing between the "state feminism" of the GPC, with its clear glass ceiling, and activism in the associational sector. The second has been, by far, the more attractive choice and helps to account for the substantial role played by Yemeni women in the Change Revolution of 2011.

CONCLUSION

At present, the prospects for stability and the return to more routine forms of political life in Yemen are decidedly mixed. The popular protests, which have routinely demonstrated the mobilizational capacity of Yemeni society, have produced no real concessions to Yemen's youth, who have been left out of a negotiated settlement. The organized political opposition, the JMP, has made its alienation from the protesters evident through its participation in the National Reconciliation Government (NRG). Saleh has stepped down, and the current government under Abd Rabbuh Mansur al-Hadi has made moves against Saleh's sons and other relatives who have held key military posts, but it is unclear whether the new regime is strong enough to sustain these gains. While the Northern province of Sa'dah has been largely peaceful since spring, the substantive demands of the Houthi movement are unresolved, as are the demands of the Hirak in the South. Fighting continues with Islamist militants (both AQAP and some local groups) and continues to deprive Yemenis of basic human security. Meanwhile, a newly emboldened citizenry has begun a "parallel revolution" to combat corruption in the public sector—storming the offices of government ministries in several cities across the country, shutting down operations, and demanding investigation of corrupt officials.

Elections, while absolutely essential to Yemenis eager to exercise authority over their own political system, are unlikely to do much to consolidate government legitimacy, unless substantial concessions to youth protesters are met and a genuine commitment to inclusive national unity is promoted. In the meantime, the economic and infrastructural damage resulting from nearly a year of warlike conditions in most urban centers has left Yemen in an even more precarious state than at any point since its unification.

BIBLIOGRAPHY

Boucek, Christopher. "War in Sana'a: From Local Insurrection to National Challenge," in *Yemen on the Brink,* edited by Christopher Boucek and Martina Ottaway. Washington, D.C.: Carnegie Endowment for International Peace, 2010.

Burrowes, Robert. "The Republic of Yemen: The Politics of Unification and Civil War, 1989–1995," in *Middle East Dilemma: The Politics and Economics of Arab Integration,* edited by Michael C. Hudson. New York: Columbia University Press, 1999.

Carapico, Sheila. *Civil Society in Yemen: The Political Economy of Activism in Modern Arabia.* New York: Cambridge University Press, 1998.

Carapico, Sheila. "The Economic Dimensions of Yemeni Unity." *Middle East Report* 184 (September–October 1993): 9–14.

Dahlgren, Susanne. *Contested Realities: The Public Sphere and Morality in Southern Yemen.* Syracuse, NY: Syracuse University Press, 2010.

Day, Stephen. "The Political Challenge of Yemen's Southern Movement," in Boucek and Ottaway, *Yemen on the Brink.*

Department for International Development. *Assessment of Humanitarian Situation in Yemen—October/November 2011.* Sana'a: DFID, 2011, pp. 1–3.

Dresch, Paul. *A History of Modern Yemen.* Cambridge: Cambridge University Press, 2000.

European Union Election Observation Mission. *Final Report: Yemen: Presidential and Local Elections, 20 September 2006.* Sana'a: EUEOM, 2006.

Harris, Allistair. "Exploiting Grievances: Al-Qaeda in the Arabian Peninsula," in Boucek and Ottaway, *Yemen on the Brink.*

Haykel, Bernard. "Saudi Arabia's Yemen Dilemma." *Foreign Affairs,* June 14, 2011.

International Association for Anti-Corruption Authorities, April 8, 2000.

Johnsen, Gregory D. "Profile of Sheikh Abd Al-Majid Al-Zindani." *Terrorism Monitor* 4, no. 7 (2006):3–6.

Molyneux, Maxine. "Women's Rights and Political Contingency: The Case of Yemen, 1990–1994." *Middle East Journal* 49, no. 3 (1995): 420.

United Nations Development Programme. *Programme on Governance in the Arab Region (POGAR).* http://www.undp-pogar.org/countries/theme.aspx?cid=22&t=6.

Vom Bruck, Gabriele. *Islam, Memory, and Morality in Yemen.* New York: Palgrave Macmillan, 2005.

Weber, Max. "Politics as a Vocation," in *From Max Weber: Essays in Sociology,* edited by Hans Heinrich Gerth and C. Wright Mills. Oxford: Oxford University Press, 1942.

Wedeen, Lisa. *Peripheral Visions: Publics, Power, and Performance in Yemen.* Chicago: University of Chicago Press, 2008.

Weir, Shelagh. *A Tribal Order: Politics and Law in the Mountains of Yemen.* Austin: University of Texas Press, 2007.

Whitaker, Brian. *The Birth of Modern Yemen.* 2009 (e-book). http://www.al-bab.com/yemen/birthofmodernyemen/default.htm.

Whitaker, Brian. "Elections Marred." *Middle East International.* March 9, 2001. http://www.al-bab.com/yemen/artic/mei74.htm.

The Economy

Charles Schmitz

In a country like Yemen, government ministries and foreign institutions such as the World Bank have compiled reliable statistics on the economy only in the past two decades or so, making it difficult to assess in accurate terms growth rates or declines and other economic variables. A second challenge is assessing what economic conditions are like after Yemen has been through a decade of political turmoil that has caused severe economic deterioration. In short, it is difficult to gain a comprehensive and accurate picture of the economy, and for that reason, this chapter is less a description of its current state than an analysis for putting its economy into some intelligible perspective given what is known about countries similar to it in income levels, natural resources, and so forth.

Here are some general statistics gleaned from the CIA World Factbook for Yemen. All figures are for 2011 (unless otherwise specified).

GDP (gross domestic product; purchasing power parity or PPP): US $58.71 billion

GDP (official change rate): US $33.68 billion

Local currency: Yemeni Rial (YR)

Exchange Rate: 230 YR per US $1

GDP (per capital or PPP): US $2,300

GDP (per sector)

   Agriculture: 7.9 percent

   Industry: 42.2 percent (includes petroleum and natural gas production)

   Services: 49.9 percent

Unemployment: 35 percent (est. 2003)

Poverty: 45.2 percent below the poverty line (est. 2003)

Inflation rate: 20 percent

Main export partners: China, Thailand, India, South Korea, Japan, and the United States

Main import partners: UAE, China, Saudi Arabia, Kuwait, and India

Foreign exchange and gold reserves: US $4.37 billion

External debt: US $6.613 billion

YEMEN'S ECONOMY IN HISTORICAL PERSPECTIVE

The Political Economy of Agriculture

Historically, Yemen's fortunes were tied to agricultural productivity. The famous South Arabian civilizations that emerged in the basin area east of the Yemeni highlands built dams in major wadis and large systems of irrigation to increase agricultural production. Until recently, the mainstay of the Yemeni economy was agriculture and livestock, and these remain very important sectors of the economy today; nevertheless, only 30 percent of Yemenis depend upon agriculture and livestock for a living in 2011. Throughout history, the Yemeni economy was dynamic, changing in response to opportunities and constraints in wider commercial networks, in response to domestic agricultural changes, and particularly in response to changes in power and the relationship of domestic power to the wider world. To say that Yemen was simply a low-productivity economy based upon subsistence agriculture would miss the dynamic change and continual upheaval throughout Yemen's economic and political history.

Yemen's economy in the first half of the twentieth century is often characterized as closed and inward looking. Imam Yahya and his son Ahmed who ruled over the end of the Zaydi dynasty in Yemen tried hard to protect Yemen's sovereignty from the various global and regional powers casting aspirations on Yemen. Power in the Yemeni economy was related to control of agricultural surplus either through ownership of large tracts of land or through taxation, or through control of trade and finance. The Imam controlled large tracts of land that were considered "state" land, though state assets and the personal assets of the Imam were hard to distinguish. People close to the Imam also gained control over land, including a class of merchants tied to the Imam's regime who were able to accumulate large fortunes in agricultural land. Important military/tribal leaders in the regime also had large landholdings. In the rich agricultural regions of Taiz and Ibb, small landholding agriculture dominated, but Yemeni farmers were enmeshed in a set of social relationships that are described as "feudal" in the Yemeni literature. Feudal here is used to indicate that labor was not free; that it was tied to the land, though through debt and lack of alternatives rather than any formal ties; and that the accumulation of wealth was not a result of investment and raising productivity but rather of social control and exploitation. These relations enabled the extraction of wealth from small landholding farmers by the state or state supporters, who came mostly from areas in the northern high plains and mountains. Agriculture was subsistence in the sense that its primary goal was to satisfy the immediate consumption needs of the farmer, but taxes and the need for some exchange required farmers to enter local markets to gain access to cash or manufactured items. Sharecropping was a very widespread form of organizing the relationship between farmer and landowner or farmer and financir or farmer and the state.

Besides land, the second most important sources of revenue were tariffs and commercial taxes, mostly from the coffee trade. There are some very crude estimates that show that tariffs were only about a sixth of the revenue of taxes under the Hamid al-Din family, which is to say that the last Imamate's primary source of income was domestic taxes. Since the overthrow of the Imamate in 1962, the Yemeni state has not been able to organize domestic taxation and has been forced to rely upon tariffs easily collected at the ports and foreign sources of income.

Rural Markets

Throughout rural Yemen, an important part of daily life is going to small, open-air or covered markets, called *souqs,* held on a daily or weekly basis, where people buy and sell their merchandise. With colorful goods on display, pungent aromas wafting from roasting coffee or bags of spice, not to mention the din of traffic, animal noises, and fast-paced conversation, the market is an exciting, sensuously alive place. A market can be found in almost every medium-sized town, and it is understood that people can trade there without fear of violence from blood feuds or other recriminations (though, in fact, fights break out from time to time and have to be instantly mediated by local bystanders).

The weekly markets (named after the day of the week in which they are held—thus, the Wednesday Market, the Thursday Market, etc.) are regional trading hubs servicing many villages in an area. They are the loose equivalent of the weekly "farmer's market" in the United States and Europe, though they tend to specialize in the sale of particular goods (e.g., the "cow" souq, the "sheep and goat" souq, etc.). Far more than agricultural or craft goods are sold in rural markets, however, whose commodities range from clothing to car spare parts. At the end of the day, the sellers put their wares away only to return at the same time the following week.

The smaller, daily markets are the equivalent of the conglomeration of shops found, say, on main street in small towns in the United States, except that the same items are sold together in the same area of the market; in other words, there will be a section for clothing stores, another for kitchen implements and appliances, another for coffee and spices, and so forth. This makes for a different shopping experience than in the United States, so that if one is looking for a particular item, one can

Market in Ar Rubah, a small village in eastern Yemen. (Helena Lovincic/iStockphoto.com)

browse all the likely stores in the same part of the market rather than visiting different stores dispersed throughout a market or even in different towns, as is often the case in the United States. This means that customers can not only compare prices but also merchandise, and if a particular item is out of stock, the salesman will send a hireling to find it from his neighbor rather than sending the customer directly over to the other store. The neighboring store owner obliges because he knows he can count on the same favor when he runs out of an item. It is also the case that merchandise is fairly uniform, so that there is little difference (either in quality or quantity) in the goods sold from one stall to another. Sellers compete not so much on the basis of what they sell or even on pricing, but on how many pieces of goods they sell to an extensive and loyal clientele. Customers tend to go to the same seller either for reasons of kinship or friendship and/or because of credit extended to them. Credit is important in a poor country like Yemen, where people often don't have the cash to pay for items they need on a regular basis. Such an arrangement between buyer and seller only works if the two know and trust each other, a trust built up from kinship or neighbor relations.

Bargaining is a proverbial part of the souq experience, and another reason customers continue to frequent the same stores is that they perceive themselves to be treated "well" there and given a "good deal." (See section on "Etiquette" in Chapter 6.)

The souq in Yemen, as elsewhere in the Middle East, is a place of gossip as well as the exchange of valued, but perhaps hard-to-get, information on economic, social, and political matters. This stands to reason in rural areas where telephones are still scarce, Internet access almost nonexistent, and newspapers intermittent. As meeting points for people from all over a region, markets are important hubs of communication. At times, they can even be hives of clandestine activities of one sort or another. For example, there are three arms markets in Yemen in which smuggled military weapons from all over the world are sold. The sales of weapons are an important part of the local economy. Other contraband goods such as alcohol are a major merchandise in some local markets, especially ones located near coasts or national borders. The souq may also be a place of political intrigue, if the area surrounding the market is embroiled in some conflict or other. Almost all markets have "studios" in which audiotapes (still the preferred technology in Yemen) are sold of music and poetry, the latter of which may be highly critical of the national government and thus have to be sold "under the counter." The phrase "Meet me at the casbah" uttered in conspiratorial tones in countless Hollywood movies may be a laughable stereotype but for all that is not entirely untrue.

Modern Urban Markets

Of course, not all markets, even rural ones, in Yemen fit the above description of being "traditional." The more modern ones—selling industrially manufactured commodities (imported or smuggled), in well-lit, spacious, and clean showrooms, with well-dressed, well-spoken salespeople in attendance on customers—are usually found in the larger towns and all the big cities, and located almost always on commercially developed strips or alongside traffic-clogged highways. Elements of the older markets persist—segregation into districts for sale of particular items, treating the customer to tea, bargaining—but with less prevalence and intensity. Bargains have replaced bargaining per se, the difference being that the former is not a transactionally arrived price between merchant and individual customer (where the customer has an illusion at least of being able to control the price) but a fixed reduced price that any customer can take advantage of who walks in the door. It is perhaps not surprising to find that prices are regulated by an ideal of the "market" (supply and demand) rather than by a host of additional factors such as social relations between kinsmen and neighbors, given that customers circulate through these emporia who are strangers both to themselves and to the merchants. Customers tend to be middle-class "consumers," with different aspirations from their rural counterparts, in the sense that they are buying items that have as much to do with their use-value as they do with class or symbols of modernity. For example, if a customer wants a "traditional" sitting room (where one sits on mats or carpets with thick back bolsters and elbow rests), one goes to the "old" souq and seeks out the section of the *mafraj* makers (mafraj meaning sitting room in Yemeni Arabic); but if one wants a "modern" sitting room (with sofas, chairs, and end and coffee tables), one goes to the "new" commercial strip where such furniture is to be found. Many urban homes that can afford it will have both kinds of spaces: a traditional mafraj in which to entertain in the "older" style and relax with friends while chewing qat, and a more "modern" one for more formal entertainment, especially with non-Yemeni guests unacquainted with traditional Yemeni living. There are also now shopping malls in the largest cities of Yemen, though not anywhere near the size or sumptuousness of their counterparts in the Gulf, a reflection of Yemen's position at the low end of the global commercial ladder (more Chinese flip-flops than Gucci handbags). These upscale urban markets are also social meeting places for youth and for middle-class couples who are discretely "dating" or trying to get to know each other before deciding whether to get engaged.

Republican Government and Economic Transformation

The republican coup in 1962 inaugurated dramatic change in Yemeni society and economy. Yemen became enmeshed and dependent upon regional governments and development agencies. For the first decade of the republican era, the Yemeni civil war preempted any economic planning. In the 1970s, the Yemeni state managed to create a central bank and a central planning agency to channel and direct foreign development assistance. The government was largely dependent upon foreign aid (and remains so even for its current expenditures).

Commercial area in Sana'a. (Davor Lovincic/iStockphoto.com)

Then the OPEC oil embargo in 1973 transformed the Arabian Peninsula and Yemen with it. As Saudi Arabia spent its billions on construction, war-weary Yemenis abandoned their agricultural fields and flocked to the construction projects of Saudi Arabia. Remittances sent home to Yemen fueled a consumer import boom. Inside Yemen, foreign assistance in the form of road projects enabled cars, VCRs, gas stoves, refrigerators, and other consumer durables to pour into the country at the port of Al-Hudaydah and up the mountains to the highlands over the Chinese-built road. Tribesmen who traditionally had detested commerce suddenly opened shops to make their own fortunes in the new markets. Yemen's mountainside farmers became shopkeepers, truck drivers, heavy equipment operators, and local builders, all fueled by remittance sent home by Yemenis in Saudi Arabia.

The Yemeni government had little access to the remittances. It taxed imports at the border, and tariffs became the leading source of government revenue. In an attempt to help increase investment, the government assisted local development associations with matching funds. Local communities invested in a water project, a road project, a school project, or other physical infrastructure project, and the government guaranteed some portion of funds to complete the project. This enabled the government to channel some of the local wealth from remittances into investment in development projects.

In the 1980s, remittances began to decline. The construction boom in Saudi Arabia slowed, and the mid-1980s saw a crash in oil prices, which further reduced the demand for Yemeni labor in Saudi Arabia. As remittances slowed, the Yemeni state imposed import restrictions to prevent large deficits in the nation's trade balance. But just when the Yemeni state began to impose its financial discipline on the country, domestic oil production began in earnest.

LOCAL DEVELOPMENT ASSOCIATIONS (LDAS)

LDAs were common in Yemen in the 1960s and 1970s. These associations were rural-based for the most part and were led by powerful and well-to-do locals who took it upon themselves to develop the countryside at a time when the central government was incapable of doing so. They often acquired the finances to carry out these projects through contributions by locals, receiving remittance payments from migrant workers in the Gulf. The Yemeni government then matched these contributions with additional funds. The LDAs built roads, schools, and clinics, and modernized existing irrigation systems or built new ones from scratch. Development experts were caught off guard by its success, believing that development would work best from the top down. Their skepticism was proven wrong. In the 1980s, when the flow of remittances slowed, the LDA movement was incorporated into the central state and became the basis of the regime's ruling party. It is an irony of Yemen's modern history that development has become decentralized and democratized once again, after two decades of a largely corrupt and failed centralized effort to manage the country's development.

Socialist Government and Economic Transformation

In 1967, Britain withdrew from its colony in Aden and a socialist government, eventually backed by the Soviet Union, came into power, calling itself the People's Democratic Republic of Yemen (PDRY). In the PDRY, the story was similar in many ways to what was happening at the time in the Yemen Arab Republic (YAR), except that the state played a more significant economic role. Whereas in the North, private merchants were benefiting from the commercial explosion and the state only collected tariffs, in the South, it was the state's own marketing corporation that reaped the benefits. Like the Northern economy, the Southern economy saw substantial improvements in income from worker remittances, though the number of labor migrants was smaller in the South. To some extent, the Saudis indirectly mitigated the impact of the poor performance of the socialist economy by employing Yemeni workers from the South. In the 1980s, the Soviets desperately searched for oil in the PDRY in the hopes that they could relieve themselves of the economic burden of their Yemeni socialist comrades, and though the Soviets were able to find oil, they didn't have the capacity to bring it online fast enough to save their socialist comrades.

The economic collapse of the PDRY combined with the infamous bloodletting between socialist comrades in Aden in 1986 led the PDRY's leadership to seek refuge in the very popular idea of uniting North and South Yemen. In the negotiations for unification in 1990, the PDRY's leadership recognized "global realities" and agreed to abandon their socialist economic policies in creating the Republic of Yemen with the YAR.

United Yemen (Republic of Yemen) and Its Economic Challenges

The new Republic faced an immediate crisis, however, when Saddam Hussein invaded Kuwait in August 1990. Yemen was chair of the U.N. Security Council at the time, and according to the U.S. Ambassador at the time, Charles Dunbar, the Iraqis paid a better price than the Americans. Yemen refused to back the American-led coalition, and the Saudis punished the Yemenis by revoking their special status in the kingdom. Yemenis from the YAR did not need a visa or permission to work in the kingdom, but in 1990, the Saudis revoked this agreement and dumped about 800,000 Yemenis across the border in a month's time. For a poor country struggling with growth and employment opportunities, the return of about a third of the workforce to the country was an economic disaster.

The expulsion of the Yemeni workers from Saudi Arabia and the civil war combined to lower per capita income each year in the early 1990s. The political deals between the leaderships of the two states that facilitated the unity agreement broke down in the early 1990s. As often occurs in Yemen, political considerations trumped economic planning in the lead-up to war, and so it was not until after the war that the economy became a priority.

At the conclusion of the war in July 1994, Yemen turned to the International Monetary Fund (IMF) and began a structural adjustment program in return for low-interest loans to fund its development. In keeping with neoliberal policies of the IMF and the World Bank, Yemen liberalized and privatized the economy and received praise from the IMF for their performance. There were three aspects of the implementation of the IMF program that were significant. First, privatization was focused on the former socialist economy in the South, and the program was more privatizing of Southern assets by new rulers from the North than a privatization program. This returned to haunt Yemen in the 2000s as the South rose up in defiance of heavy-handed Northern treatment that the privatization program was a part of. Second, one of the key features of the reform program was the withdrawal of consumer subsidies, particularly fuel subsidies because of the burden they placed on the state's budget. Some of the food subsidies like wheat were removed fairly quickly, and there were attempts to raise the price of domestic fuel closer to world markets, but the fuel subsidies were never eliminated and they strained the state budget throughout the 2000s. Fuel subsidies were benefiting powerful political allies of the regime who were smuggling subsidized oil to neighboring markets where they would reap huge profits. The World Bank estimated that the removal of subsidies without any countervailing measures would increase poverty, but probably the real reason subsidies remained, and remain, is that smuggling is lucrative. Third, the Yemeni economy improved significantly after the IMF structural adjustment, but the improvement was not a result of the reform package; rather, the growth of the economy closely followed the growth of oil income in the 1990s and 2000s. This means that the growth was not tied to sustained improved productivity inside of Yemen but rather to temporary oil rents that will disappear with the decline of oil in Yemen.

CONTEMPORARY ISSUES IN THE YEMENI ECONOMY

The Yemeni economy in the early 21st century faces difficult economic challenges related to the decline of oil. Lack of oil or any other natural resource is not the real issue, though. Economic growth is poorly correlated with natural resource endowments. Sub-Saharan African countries are natural resource rich, yet they are some of the poorest countries in the world. Wealth is created by human labor. The real challenge facing Yemen's economy then is social: How to allow the talent, ingenuity, and hard labor for which Yemenis are famous to flourish? Yemenis are hard working. Through the centuries, Yemenis built their famous agricultural terraces on rocky slopes of the mountainous highlands, they traveled throughout the world to build commercial fortunes, they worked in Detroit in the auto factories and in the California agricultural fields in the mid-20th century, and they created kingdoms in the desert in antiquity. The capacity of Yemenis for hard labor is not in doubt; the question is "How to harness Yemeni efforts in a modern national economy?"

Today, Yemenis shun Yemen. When Yemenis accumulate any capital, the first thing that a Yemeni businessperson will do is invest it outside of the country. Yemeni investors do not trust the government. The former Saleh regime used economic opportunities for political advantage. State contracts were doled out to regime supporters, and state revenues were spent according to political criteria rather than administrative requirements or economic priorities. Worse, the Saleh regime feared institutional stability, preferring to deal with state business through personal relationships rather than institutional processes. Yemen's political and economic institutions are very weak as a result. The Saleh regime also intervened in what Yemeni private sector existed in Yemen. Saleh tried to create personal ties even through marriage to prominent Yemeni private businessmen such that the entire private sector and the public sector were dependent upon the favor of the Saleh clan. Most private Yemeni businessmen preferred to flee Yemen, if they could.

The solution to Yemen's economic woes lies in the Yemeni private sector. When Yemeni investors keep their money in Yemen and when the political economy is geared toward promoting economic development rather than preserving political power, then Yemen will grow. Growth is not dependent upon resource endowments as much as it is the social environment.

Corruption, Politics, and the Economy

Yemenis and foreigners alike often argue that corruption is the culprit for most of Yemen's economic and political ills. But corruption is a notoriously hard concept to pin down, as is its counterpart, good governance. Of course, corruption is bad and good governance is good, but these are moral evaluations, not definitions. As such, claims of corruption in government are often best described as a legitimacy crisis rather than a description of social behavior.

WHAT IS CORRUPTION?

A legal definition of corruption is the use of office for private ends rather than public ones. For example, preference is given to fellow clan members rather than on the basis of some rational criteria developed by the state (such as merit). But this definition ignores the fact that power creates the law; law is not a neutral standard with which we can measure good and bad. Politically, powerful people write laws for their own benefit. In this sense, private gain is expressed through the rule of law. Economic definitions of corruption usually see the state as a monopoly and state officials as rent seekers who "corrupt" efficient market allocation. In fact, the experience of the last half century of development has shown that the state plays essential roles in coordinating and guiding long-term economic development and even creating entire new sectors of the economy. Rather than being the enemy of economic growth, the state in successful development experiences has been a handmaiden of economic growth.

What roles can the Yemeni state play in the economy? The state can play a critical, active role in economic development; it is not a matter of withdrawing it from the economy. What Yemen needs is a regime that cultivates growth through a coherent national investment plan that builds on good social and physical infrastructure as well as coordinates investment toward long-term economic development. The latter depends on a stable society, and the state is usually crucial for keeping social peace, though in the Yemen, this seems to be particularly difficult to achieve. Social peace means that the state makes transfers to the poor, pays off "losers" in economic adjustments, and keeps key power brokers happy, but in such a way that promotes long-term growth as well.

The Yemeni economy will become more diversified than in the past decades when it depended first on worker remittances and then on oil for its income. There is no single resource that will play the central role that those two sources of income played in the past. There are many potential areas of growth in Yemen including greater oil exploration, developing the port of Aden, developing mineral and mining resources, tourism, import substitution manufacturing, and many others. But future growth in Yemen will be more dependent upon the ability of the political regime to cultivate growth in the domestic economy. This will be a difficult task for Yemen, and the current political crises of 2011 are an indicator of the depths of the political challenges facing the country. It is likely that Yemen's economic difficulties will linger because of the seemingly intractable political crises Yemen experiences.

ECONOMICALLY EXPLOITABLE NATURAL RESOURCES

Oil and Gas

Very recently, Yemen developed oil and gas resources. Oil was first developed in the YAR by Hunt Oil in the Marib region in the mid-1980s. Oil contracts with foreign oil companies stipulated that the Yemeni government be given a portion of the production, called "production sharing agreement." The proportion allotted to the government increased over time after companies recouped their initial investment costs. This meant that the Yemeni government bore the risk, and benefits, of the world oil market because they would sell the oil themselves. In the 2000s, this arrangement proved very lucrative to the government.

Oil was certainly one of the motivations for the Unity Agreement implemented in 1990 because the Southerners knew that they had oil, particularly in the border region, and they wanted access to Western oil technology and investment to develop it. In fact, there were large amounts of oil in the Masila block in the Hadhramawt region that was discovered in 1990 and was in production by 1993. Yemeni oil production rapidly expanded in the late 1990s, and by 2001, it peaked at about 450,000 barrels of oil per day. This was a lot of oil for Yemen, but it pales

Oil refinery in Aden. (Karim Sahib/AFP/Getty Images)

in comparison to Yemen's neighbors in the Gulf Cooperation Council (GCC). Saudi Arabia has the capacity to produce 12 million barrels per day. After 2001, oil production began to decline but world oil prices were high, so Yemen's revenues from oil continued to rise until 2008 when oil prices hit a record high of US $140. Oil came to represent a third of Yemen's economy: 95 percent of export revenue and 75 percent of government budget revenue. In 2009, oil prices crashed with the global financial crisis, and Yemen has begun a period of austerity as oil price declines combined with falling production reduced export revenues and government income. Oil production is now about 250,000 barrels per day and will continue to decline rapidly unless new oil is found soon. Only a relatively small portion of Yemen's territory has been explored for oil, and there remains the possibility of new finds. New contracts for exploration have been awarded recently, but nobody expects to find large amounts of oil again.

Yemen has gas in commercial quantities. Gas differs from oil: in that natural gas must be transported in pipelines to the consumer market, whereas oil is a liquid easily transportable in tankers and trucks. Though expensive, liquefied gas enables countries like Yemen to exploit distant markets for gas. Yemen built a liquefied natural gas (LNG) facility at Balhaf on the southern coast that liquefies gas piped from the fields in the Marib region (across the former border of North and South Yemen). Yemen's LNG is expected to produce about US $1 billion for the Yemeni economy and about US $100 million per year for the government for the next 25 years. So while gas revenues will not dominate the Yemeni economy like oil, gas revenues will make a significant contribution to the Yemeni economy in the future.

Mining

As Yemen looks to build a more diversified economy after the decline of oil, one of the resources that Yemen hopes to exploit is mining and quarrying. Assessments of Yemen's potential for mining are encouraging. Yemen shares the geology of Saudi Arabia further north and Ethiopia and Somalia across the Red Sea and Gulf of Aden. Mining operations in both of these areas are encouraging for Yemen because geologists know that the same minerals exist in Yemen. There is currently a new zinc mine in operation, and there is another consortium that is looking to exploit what the World Bank's assessment describes as a "world-class" gold resource. Yemen also possesses enough commercially exploitable marble and granite that there is some interest in developing it. Constraints to the development of Yemeni mineral and stone resources are both physical and human infrastructural. Yemen's rugged physical geography makes road building expensive, and power sources are still unreliable. The regulatory and legal regime in the country is still poor, and Yemen does not have a history of mining, so Yemenis do not yet possess the capabilities to successfully exploit the mining resources available to them. The Yemeni government, international development agencies, and international mining concerns are currently working to develop Yemen's mining sector.

Port of Aden

Aden is a natural deepwater port in the volcanic western portion of Southern Yemen, not far from the Bab al-Mandab. The harbor is formed by the rim of a collapsed volcano that juts into the sea forming a large natural harbor that has been utilized by seafaring traders as long as recorded history. In the 1950s, it was one of the busiest ports in the world, but the Arab–Israeli conflict closed the Suez Canal and the Cold War conflict in the Horn of Africa largely destroyed trade in the port. It figured prominently in the promised renaissance of Yemen after unity in 1990. It was named the "economic capital" of Yemen, and the revival of entrepôt trade in the port as well as the development of an industrial free-trade zone promised a better economic future. Given Yemen's relative resource scarcity, future economic development will need to develop trade opportunities in which the Port of Aden will have a central role. It has seen some development in the last 20 years including the construction of a deepwater container facility, but it has not seen the level of economic growth that was envisioned in 1990. There is significant potential in the port that can be developed in the future, particularly if the country settles into a period of political stability.

Fishing

Yemen has a long coastline, and fishing has always been a part of life in Yemen. New visitors to mountainous capital of Sana'a are always invited to the famous fish restaurants. Fishing only constitutes 1 percent of GDP, though it provides an important source of food and income for a larger proportion of the workforce living

Fishermen gather at the port of Midi, the province of Hajjah, northern Yemen. (Khaled Fazaa/AFP/Getty Images)

on the coasts. Yemen does export fish and fish products. There are canning plants in the south. Most of the fishing industry is small boats. During the socialist era, Soviet industrial fishing ships and Japanese ships scoured Yemen's rich coastline for deepwater fish (and depleted the stocks) that small Yemeni fishermen cannot reach. Fishing is an important but small resource that Yemen can exploit. There is potential to develop the fishing industry, but there are also limits. The fishing industry depends upon the ability to access and manage fisheries. Yemen has not been able to regulate its fishing industry to enforce sustainable harvesting, and thus, Yemeni fishing goes through booms and busts. Yemen also needs to develop domestic infrastructure to better utilize its fish resources.

INDUSTRY

Agriculture

Agriculture still plays a big role in the lives of Yemenis, but its importance to the national economy is decreasing. Yemen's agricultural resources are scarce and limited, so agriculture's role in the economy will only decrease in the future. Yemen is not a country that can base its future growth on agricultural-centered development such as in sub-Saharan Africa. Only about 3 percent of Yemen is arable and less than that amount is usually cultivated each year, depending upon the rains.

Arable land in Yemen is dependent upon water. If there were more water, Yemen has the soils to develop significantly more agricultural regions, particularly on the long alluvial plains in the lowland coastal regions along the Red Sea and the Gulf of Aden. However, Yemen does not currently have the means to develop more

amazon.com

SD714w0Ghk

our order of April 7, 2014 (Order ID 113-4472631-2689817)

ty. Item	Item Price	Total
Yemen (Middle East in Focus) Caton, Steven C. --- Hardcover (** P-3-B33E208 **) 1598849271	$84.55	$84.55

This shipment completes your order.		
	Subtotal	$84.55
Have feedback on how we packaged your order? Tell	Tax Collected	$5.07
us at www.amazon.com/packaging.	Order Total	$89.62
	Paid via credit/debit	$89.62
	Balance due	$0.00

0/D714w0Ghk/-1 of 1-//UPS-PHLPA-3DAY/second/10453552/0407-15:00/0407-10:53   **1A3**

water resources, and so water constitutes the major limiting factor in Yemen's agriculture.

Nevertheless, more Yemenis work in agriculture than in any other occupation. Yemen is urbanizing, but still in 2011, 70 percent of Yemenis live in rural areas and so agriculture predominates. (Not everyone that lives in rural areas works in agriculture, of course, but still about a third of the Yemeni labor force works in agriculture.) Agriculture constitutes about 10 percent of total economic output in Yemen with qat adding about 2–3 percent of GDP, and 30 percent of Yemen's labor produces 10 or 13 percent of total output, so productivity in the agricultural sector is quite low.

Arable Land Scarcity

Productivity gains in agriculture are difficult to achieve because of Yemen's mountainous geography and the smallholding nature of Yemen's land tenure. Yemen's agricultural terraces create a patchwork of small narrow pieces of land that parallel the contours of the mountains. These small mountainous plots of fields make the use of tractors inefficient.

And Yemen's land tenure structure is dominated by small farms. In Yemen, most landholdings are under a hectare (ha; 2.47 acres [ac]) and few farms are larger than 5 ha (17.35 ac). In general, smallholding land tenure is not a block to greater efficiencies in agricultural land if there is a rental market in land. In Yemen though, as in many other poorer countries, small pieces of land are valuable assets to families that they tend to work themselves rather than rent to full-time farmers. Households will pursue a strategy of income diversification in which a small piece of land is still an important source of food for humans or animals, or sometimes for extra income. The small piece of land will provide partial employment for one or two members of the family who will also work in other occupations. Thus, sales or rentals of land are rare, and land sales almost never happen. It is considered a great shame for a family to sell land. Only very desperate families will normally sell land as a last measure. When there are significant full-time income opportunities and households reach full employment, then they will begin to rent their land to full-time farmers.

Land scarcity has also driven Yemenis to seek higher value-added crops to maximize the use of their scare land resources. Yemenis have done this in two ways. The first is to cultivate high value-added crops such as qat, coffee, fruit trees, and vegetables. These crops bring the greatest income in Yemen and where possible, farmers will cultivate them. Qat and coffee are restricted to higher mountainous regions, and qat and vegetables are concentrated around the urban markets they depend upon. The second way that Yemenis maximize the output of their agricultural land is to cultivate fodder for animals rather than food crops. Meat commands a far higher price than grain, and imported grain is relatively cheap, so Yemeni farmers cultivate lots of fodder crops and sorghum is both a grain crop and a fodder crop. Yemen imports the vast majority of grain and all of its rice that are its staple foods.

Food Security

Yemen's dependence on imported grains has become a major concern in the economic crisis of 2011. Food security is not self-sufficiency in food. The United Arab Emirates rarely raises a concern about food security though it produces no agricultural products (when alarms are raised, as recently was the case in Qatar, it had to do with politics in the region and fear of being too dependent upon imports from Saudi Arabia). Food security is about access to food, and in Yemen, people get access to food through the market. This makes economic sense because Yemen's land is scarce, and it is best to use the land for higher value-added commodities. It also makes sense in terms of Yemen's scare water supplies. Grains can be water intense, and so it is best for Yemen to import water intensive crops and use its own water for other more valuable uses, like drinking. But if Yemenis are poor and do not have access to cash, then they cannot buy food on the market and they become food insecure. It is income or access to the market then that determines food insecurity in Yemen.

There is an additional issue related to food security in the Yemeni case, and that is the balance of trade. In order to import things, a country like Yemen must have access to hard currency, a foreign currency used in international markets. In Yemen's case, it must export something or attract foreign investment in order to have the currency to import food. This makes Yemen's food supplies vulnerable to Yemen's balance of payments position. And though the economic crisis of 2011 is greatly exacerbated by the political crisis, in the long run, Yemen's petroleum exports will decline and make Yemen more food insecure as well, unless the economy can recover and find a stable means of earning export revenues.

Crops

Throughout history, Yemenis have adopted crops suited to the various climatic zones in the country. Some crops do well in highland rain-fed agriculture, whereas other crops are better suited to spate irrigation in the hotter climates of the coast and lowland interior. In the past, Yemen's staple crop was sorghum whose drought tolerance is well suited to arid and semi-arid environments and whose leaf and stems are very useful as fodder. Even today, sorghum is the most widely cultivated cereal in Yemen. Most cereals are cultivated in the rain-fed highland terraces and comprise about half of the total area cultivated. Sorghum makes up about 60–70 percent of the land devoted to cereal production, and the majority of land dedicated to fodder and sorghum is cultivated on almost half the agricultural land in Yemen. Other cereals are cultivated in Yemen in lesser quantities: wheat and millet are the most widely cultivated cereals after sorghum, whereas barley and corn are less extensively cultivated.

After cereals, the most widely cultivated crop is fodder due to the high value of animal feed. The dominant fodder crop is again sorghum, followed by nitrogen-fixing berseem clover and grasses. The lowland arid regions of Yemen in the governorates

Sorghum field with traditional water cistern, Mahwit. (Kate B. Dixon)

of Marib, Abyan, Lahaj, Al-Hudaydah, Al-Jawf, Hadhramawt, Shabwah, and Al-Mahrah all have a much higher percentage of their arable land cultivated in fodder because livestock are more important to these regions. In desert regions rains are intermittent and geographically dispersed. Unlike planted crops, livestock are mobile and can go to where the rain has fallen and forage has sprouted. Fodder is cultivated in these regions to supplement foraging. The main livestock in Yemen are goat and sheep, about 8 million heads of each in 2009. Goats are hardy and can handle the heat, so they are more prevalent in the hotter more arid regions. Hadhramawt accounts for almost a quarter of all goats, followed by Shabwah and Abyan. These three governorates produce almost half of all goats in Yemen. Sheep are less hardy and are more vulnerable to heat but are a major food source. Sheep are more predominant in the highlands where it is cooler, but Hadhramawt, Al-Jawf, and Shabwah are still major producers of sheep. Al-Hudaydah is the largest producer of sheep along with Sa'dah and Hajjah.

Qat is almost as widely cultivated as fodder with about 12 percent of total land area. It is a mild stimulant (not a narcotic in medical terms) that most Yemenis chew in the afternoons about once or twice a week, sometimes more. There are occasional everyday chewers. The chewing of qat is a social activity that takes place mostly in homes and during which all politics, business, and other social matters are debated and decided upon. It is chewed fresh, and thus qat production is close to major urban markets in the highlands. It is also a tropical highland crop like coffee and does not grow in the lowlands below about 1,000 meters (3,280 feet) above sea level, so qat in Aden and Al-Hudaydah must come daily from highland areas. There is far less qat in Hadhramawt that is far from qat-producing climes. The Governor-ate of Sana'a surrounding the capital city of Sana'a is by far the largest producer of qat, followed by nearby 'Amran. A quarter of all the land cultivated with qat is in Sana'a governorate and Sana'a and 'Amran together possess 40 percent of all land cultivated with qat.

The other "cash" crops—nonfood items—cultivated in Yemen are coffee, to-bacco, and cotton. As we know from Chapter 2, coffee was at one time a major source of wealth in Yemen. In the 16th and 17th centuries, Yemen was the major source of the world's coffee. But coffee production declined in the 19th and 20th centuries, and now it is cultivated on about a quarter of the land dedicated to qat. Sana'a cultivates almost a third of Yemen's coffee, followed by the Jabal Raymah region. Cotton needs a warmer climate and more water, since it takes a full eight months to mature. Yemen's cotton is cultivated in Al-Hudaydah, Abyan, and to a lesser extent in Lahaj.

Yemen also produces in smaller quantities a variety of fruits, vegetables, and legumes, mostly for the domestic market.

MANUFACTURING

In Yemen, raising per capita income by increasing labor productivity is important, but the country does not have to induce an industrial revolution of the type that Europe, the United States, or Japan experienced. In a globalized world, exports are not an end in itself, but rather a means to imports, and in the developing world, this often means importing intermediate goods that raise the productivity of labor. Yemen does not need a capital goods industry—the Germans are much better at this and the Yemeni can import theirs. Smart development is what Yemen needs,

---

INDUSTRY AND ECONOMIC GROWTH

To most people, industry is synonymous with modernity and development. An agricultural country is backward and an industrialized economy is developed or modern. So the relative size of the industrial sector in an economy is often used as an indicator of its level of development. In the mid-20th century, in-dustry was idealized as the missing ingredient that would bring wealth to the developing economies of the Third World. Newly independent countries of the former colonial world embarked on heavy industrialization plans, and steel was seen as the core of a powerful economy. Recently though, economists have come to recognize that having a heavy steel industry is not necessary and that raising labor's productivity, which is important to increasing per capital wealth, is not so directly tied to industry, at least not in the way that people used to conceive of industrialization strategies. The world is much more inter-dependent now, and countries play more nuanced roles in greater divisions of labor stretched across continents.

and industry could play an important role in a coherent national development policy.

In fact, Yemen's industrial sector is typical of a poor country. Industry produces very little in Yemen except for locally manufactured metal and wood parts for construction and a few import substitution industries in food and beverages and textiles. Industry exhibits what is called dualism; there are a few large, modern, factories that employ large numbers of people with relatively higher levels of productivity and a very large number of family owned and operated small metal assembly shops with very low labor productivity. These are typically rudimentary roadside welding stalls that make water tanks and metal doors. The public sector in Yemen is relatively small and involved mostly in water and electrical utilities and in petroleum refining.

Yemen also displays a great deal of geographic concentration of its industry. Industry is associated with cities and urbanization. Industrialization and urbanization are often synonymous just as industry and modernity are. Industry in Yemen is concentrated foremost in the capital city, Sana'a, then in the main port city on the Red Sea, Al-Hudaydah, and then in Taiz where Yemen's domestic entrepreneurs come from primarily.

Yemen's industrial sector contributes relatively little to the economy. Over the decade of the 2000s, manufacturing's relative contribution to economic output rose slowly from about 5 to about 8 percent of total output. In absolute terms, output grew slowly in the 2000s and contracted in 2010.

Manufacturing employs a small percentage of the workforce, and most of the workforce is in small establishments in the private sector with low levels of productivity. According to official figures manufacturing employs about 5 percent of Yemeni labor. In 2010, private manufacturing employed about 200,000 workers, and about 30,000 additional workers were employed in the public and mixed sectors. So, 50 percent of the manufacturing labor force was employed in small establishments and 30 percent work in large plants, yet workers in large plants made 45 percent of total manufacturing wages. The small establishments only accounted for 37 percent of wages, indicating that labor productivity in the small establishments was low (Central Statistical Office [CSO] 2010). The 2004 industrial survey indicated that 80 percent of the owner-operated or family labor establishments were small, which shows that most manufacturing in Yemen is small scale, of low productivity, and often family owned and operated.

The public and mixed sectors employ about 30,000 employees, two thirds of whom work in the electrical and water companies. The other major public-sector manufacturing companies are the tobacco company and the petroleum refining plants.

LABOR

Sectoral Distribution

Though there are discrepancies in the data, it is clear that the largest portion of Yemen's workforce is involved in agriculture. The 2004 census and the 2006 household budget survey both report that about a little under a third of Yemenis work in agriculture. This is expected given that 70 percent of Yemenis still live in rural areas, though the meaning of rural is becoming unclear. There are many areas where residents are classified as rural, yet they are economically dependent upon urban employment. The large proportion of the labor force in agriculture is typical of an economy at low levels of development. As labor productivity improves, labor will move out of agriculture toward other employment in the processing or service sectors.

The next largest occupation of the Yemeni labor force is wholesale and retail trade with about 15 percent of the labor force. Anyone who has been to Yemen will not be surprised that such a large proportion of the labor force is involved in commerce. Small shops are ubiquitous in urban and rural areas. One of the advantages of shopkeeping is that assets are relatively liquid and mobile, so less vulnerable to social or political instability, than manufacturing with a large physical plant. The Yemeni commercial sector is certainly inefficient in the sense that productivity is low, but it is also clearly playing a social role in distributing small amounts of income among many different small shopkeepers. The Japanese have a similar structure to their retail sector that serves the same redistributive function, though in the Japanese case, of course, there is much more wealth to redistribute.

After agriculture and commerce, construction and government employment each occupy about 10 percent of the Yemeni labor force. Government employment in

Yemeni laborers work at the construction site of a natural gas plant. (Khaled Fazaa/AFP/ Getty Images)

Yemen often serves a political or a social function. It is a means of building political clients for the regime. Tribesmen have taken foreigners hostage in the hopes of gaining government employment. It also serves a redistributive social function. In some areas, government employment of a family member gives households an essential means of survival, without which they would be destitute.

Manufacturing and education are the last two sectors of the economy in which Yemenis are employed in significant numbers. Each occupies about 5 percent of the Yemeni labor force.

Emigration

Resource scarcity in Yemen has always pushed Yemenis to look for opportunities abroad to make income. They have gone overseas in search of business opportunities, in the service of empires, as religious leaders, and in recent history as laborers. For centuries, Hadhramis have migrated to South and Southeast Asia where they are important civic, business, and political leaders. Money from these Yemenis maintained the spectacular palaces of the Wadi Hadhramawt. Hadhramis and Yemenis from other parts of Yemen, particularly the Taiz region, have become important business leaders in other countries as well. In Saudi Arabia, some of the wealthiest business people are Yemeni. The bin Mahfouz family, for example, are extremely influential business leaders in Saudi Arabia and are of Yemeni stock. Yemenis came to the United States in the 1920s and settled in the agricultural fields of California and in the Detroit region to work in the auto industry. Detroit and Dearborn are still centers of Yemeni culture in the United States, and large numbers of Yemenis now reside in Oakland, California, as well. During the oil boom in the Gulf States in the 1970s, Yemenis flocked to the new centers of construction, and the money they sent home transformed the Yemeni economy. Today, remittances sent back by Yemenis abroad are still an important contributor to the economy. Remittances have not only been important contributor to the national economy, but are also an important source of income for households that would otherwise fall into poverty without money sent by relatives abroad. A key to Yemen's current economic transition is the ability of Yemeni workers to migrate in large numbers again to the GCC countries.

In modern history, Yemeni labor migration began with the movement of Yemenis to the British colony of Aden in search of work in the early 20th century. The British tried to create a cosmopolitan, non-Arab city in Aden by isolating Aden from the rest of Yemen and by importing labor from India. Aden was run by the Indian colonial administration until 1937 when it was transferred to London, and the British imported most of the colonial administrative personnel from India. Still today, there is strong South Asian influence in Aden.

With the development of the Port of Aden into a major international hub in the first half of the 20th century, the British were forced to rely upon Yemeni labor coming from the countryside in search of work. Yemenis came from the territory under the Imam and from what was called South Arabia, or the myriad of Emirates and

Sultanates the British had helped create to protect their interests in Aden. Though the British imposed strict regulations to prohibit the immigration of "Arabs" to Aden, eventually many important Yemeni begin to make their economic and political fortunes working in Aden.

At the conclusion of the civil war in the North, the famous period of massive emigration from Yemen to the rich kingdoms of the Arabian Gulf began in earnest. Reliable numbers are unavailable from this period, but it appears that a majority of Yemeni labor left the country in the mid-1970s. Yemeni farmers abandoned their fields and sought work in the construction sites of Saudi Arabia principally. Development specialists became concerned about the erosion of the mountain agricultural terraces that need continual upkeep or they will collapse, causing a chain reaction of erosional destruction down an entire mountainside. The terraces represent hundreds of years of hard work, and in the period of heavy emigration, few were left in Yemen to tend to the maintenance of the terraces.

Remittances transformed the Yemeni economy. Yemenis began importing massive numbers of consumer durables like refrigerators, VCR players, cassette players, cars, trucks, generators, and air conditioning units. They also changed their diet preferring imported rice and wheat to domestic sorghum. Yemen became dependent upon foreign imports for almost everything.

Imports were almost entirely dependent upon remittances, and there was a close correspondence in the 1970s and 1980s between remittances and imports. When remittances fell off, imports declined, and when remittances increased, imports increased. In the early 1980s, when oil prices were highest, more than a quarter of North Yemen's GDP was remittances. Remittances in the early 1980s played as important a role in the economy as oil exports in the 1990s and 2000s.

In the mid-1980s, remittances began to fall off as oil prices slumped and construction slowed in Saudi Arabia and the Gulf. Yemeni appetites for imported goods did not lessen though, and the balance of payments began to run negative. The Yemen governments imposed import restrictions to prevent the balance of payments deficits from running the country into severe debt. The fall in worker remittances left both Yemeni economies facing severe crises. In order to maintain the new higher standards of living in Yemen and support the import consumption, Yemen needed to find an alternative source of income. Fortunately for Northern Yemen, oil was developed in commercial quantities just as the remittance economy collapsed. Southern Yemen was not so lucky; the Soviets were not quick enough to develop Southern Yemeni oil, and so by the late 1980s, when the Soviets withdrew their aid, the PDRY confronted a desperate economic crisis. The economic crisis and the prospect of Western investment in oil was a major stimulus to Yemeni unity in 1990. Southern oil was located close to the border region in Shabwah and, tensions between the North and South prevented development. The PDRY leadership also considered Western oil technology superior to the Soviets, and they were eager to merge with the North in order to have access to Western foreign investment in the oil sector.

Most consider the expulsion of Yemeni workers from Saudi Arabia in 1990 in retaliation for Yemen's stance in support of Saddam Hussein as the end of the remittance economy. However, remittances have consistently played an important, if diminished, role in the Yemeni economy ever since. In the 1990s, remittances in absolute terms actually recovered to amounts similar to the early 1980s boom period. In the 1990s and 2000s, they have consistently contributed about 1.2 billion to 2 billion US dollars to the Yemeni economy. What has changed is the relative importance of these remittances. Whereas a billion dollars was very significant when the total economy only amounted to 4 billion dollars, now a billion dollars or two billion is a much smaller proportion of a 26-billion-dollar economy.

While remittances have declined in importance for the national economy, they remain a very important source of income for households. In the government's Poverty Report of 2007, a quarter of poor households receive remittances from abroad and they estimated that if remittances were to be cut off then poverty would increase by 5 percent. This percentage is actually lower than many other countries in the developing world where even a greater percentage of the poor are dependent upon remittances from abroad. Yemen is unique in that its worker remittances are also an important part of wealthier household's income as well, so the impact of any reduction in remittances is also felt by wealthier households, though they would not enter the ranks of the poor as a result.

Surprisingly, there is labor immigration into Yemen as well. Given the level of poverty in Yemen, the idea that people would immigrate to the country to work seems odd, but Somalis, Ethiopians, and Eritreans, in particular, come to Yemen to work. These are mostly women employed as domestic workers in more well-off Yemeni homes. Yemeni concepts of propriety prevent women from working for a wage in the homes of people unrelated to them by blood. Working in a stranger's home, they would be vulnerable to the unwanted predations of men. As a result, the market for domestic help is highly segregated and women come from abroad to fulfill jobs that Yemenis cannot.

Unions

Labor unions were very important in Aden during the movement for independence against the British. Union activism was a key form of political activity for the nationalist movement. The leadership of the South after independence largely hailed from other regions of the South (and the North as well) though, rather than Aden. The nationalist leadership that fought the British through labor activism was marginalized after independence when tribal fighters and their leadership from rural areas dominated. The four main organizations in the South were the youth union, the women's union, the peasant's union, and the worker's union, and these were organs of the state for mobilization of society by the state, rather than organizations representing the interests of their members.

Yemen's labor structure does not facilitate labor activism. Most Yemenis work for themselves or for a relative. Only a very small proportion of the workforce is in the formal sector of the economy. And most importantly, 70 percent of Yemenis still live in rural areas in isolated villages. Rural society is not conducive to labor organization because class ties are nonexistent and other ties such as clan are much stronger. In urban areas, professional associations are much more common. These organizations are prominent in civil society, and they play very important outlets for political activism for urban professions. The journalist's union, for example, has played a very important role in the resistance to the repression of the Saleh regime in the late 2000s.

Official figures of registered nongovernmental organizations show that the vast majority of nongovernmental organizations are charities followed by a large number of social organizations. Unions account for very few of registered nongovernmental organizations.

TRADE AND FINANCE

Trade Patterns

Yemeni trade patterns are typical of a less developed economy. Yemen's exports are dominated by raw materials, crude oil in the case of Yemen, and imports are more diversified but contain a large proportion of intermediate goods and final finished consumer products. This pattern is indicative of an economy that lacks much of an industrial sector and that sells products with little value in exchange for importing products that contain a large amount of value added. It is indicative of an economy with low labor productivity.

Yemeni exports are almost exclusively petroleum and petroleum-related products from the refineries. In 2006, 88 percent of the value of exports was crude oil. Refined products made up most of the rest with some very small amounts of fish products being the only other commodities exported from Yemen.

Ironically, Yemeni imports are also dominated by petroleum products, though not to the degree that imports depend upon petroleum. In the same year, 2006, about a quarter of Yemeni imports by value were refined fuels. Yemen exports crude oil only to turn around and import again refined petroleum products, because its own refining capacity is limited. In doing so, Yemen loses the value added of the refining process to more wealthy countries with developed refining capacity.

Yemen's trade balance in the 1990s and 2000s has been positive on average, enabling Yemen to build a solid cushion of foreign exchange in the central bank and avoid external debt. Yemen is not highly indebted. Yemen's foreign debt in 2011 was about US $6 billion, which is about a quarter of GDP, quite low by international standards. But the decline of oil exports both because of increasing domestic demand and of declining crude oil production has tilted the Yemen trade balance in the negative in recent years. In 2007, the value of imports exceeded exports by 6 percent of GDP, and in 2009, a year of very low prices for crude oil due to the U.S. financial crisis, the trade deficit reached 10 percent of GDP. In 2010, rising prices reduced the Yemeni trade deficit to 4 percent.

The Yemeni economy trades mostly with the east. Yemen sells its oil and gas to Southeast Asia and East Asia; Yemeni workers are in the Arabian Peninsula; and its imports, though more diversified, are dominated by regional producers in the Arab world.

Finance

Officially, Yemen is not a highly indebted country (as mentioned above) because it has managed to finance imports with worker remittances in the early period of the republic, and since 1990, Yemen has financed its imports with oil exports. Yemen's official external debt is US $6 billion, about half of which is owed to multilateral lenders and the other half to individual countries. Russia and Saudi Arabia are the largest lenders, and thus all of Yemen's debt is public rather than private.

Yemen's financial position is threatened by falling oil revenues. In the last few years, the trade balance has been in deficit and government reserves have declined. These trends are particularly disturbing because Yemen is dependent almost entirely upon imports for its staple foods, rice and wheat. As the trade balance worsens and government reserves fall, Yemen is in an increasingly precarious economic situation that threatens even basic food supplies.

Government revenue is highly dependent upon oil. Since the late 1990s, about 75 percent of government revenue has come from oil. The main source of revenue for the state before oil was tariffs. The government taxed the explosion of consumer durables landing at Aden and Al-Hudaydah for transport inland to Yemeni markets. The high dependence upon oil for state revenue makes Yemen a "rentier" state, a state that is not dependent upon taxing domestic society for its revenue and therefore is independent of domestic political influences, or so the argument goes. Oil gave the Yemeni state an alternative source of revenue that enabled it to avoid entanglements with domestic society; nobody could threaten to withhold taxes or say that taxes were unfairly spent, because there were no taxes, essentially.

Now, as oil declines, the state has been forced to look elsewhere for revenue, particularly domestic taxes. Since 2005, the Yemeni government and the Yemeni private sector have been trying to work out a deal for imposing domestic direct and indirect taxes. Yemen has both personal income tax and a general sales tax, but implementation of both has been problematic. Private sector representatives and the government have been in continual negotiation over the implementation of both the income tax and the sales tax. There were deals reached with private sector representatives in 2010, just prior to the onset of the popular protests in Yemen. ·

The biggest item in the Yemen state on the expenditure side in the 2000s was "transfers" and debt service. Transfers are direct transfers to tribal leaders, a kind of social subsidy for political support. The second largest item was subsidies. This was mostly fuel subsidies. Though the state was able to lift subsidies on basic food items and partially lift the fuel subsidies, the subsidies remained a huge burden on the budget. In 2007 and 2008 when crude oil prices hit record highs, the Yemeni state made a windfall in revenue, but spent even more than they gained importing wheat, rice, and refined fuel products at record prices. Wages follow subsidies and transfers, and these three make up the vast majority of the Yemeni state budget.

MEASURING YEMEN'S POVERTY
AND PLACING IT IN CONTEXT

Yemen is a relatively poor country, but it is not among the poorest countries in the world. In the standard rankings of the international development agencies, Yemen is usually found at the top of the low-income category or at the bottom of the middle-income category. In 2011, the World Bank placed Yemen at the bottom of their new low–middle-income group, but the United Nations Development Programme (UNDP) put Yemen at the top of their low human development group. The World Bank ranked Yemen 173 out of 215 countries in terms of income, using the Atlas method that employs a simple conversion of national currencies to U.S. dollars (and a running average of currency exchange rates to smooth out dramatic fluctuations). In 2011, Yemen's ranking on this scale put it in the company of Vietnam, Pakistan, Lesotho, and Nicaragua. Yemen's gross national income (GNI) per capita was US $1,060, not far from India's GNI per capita of US $1,340.

When Yemen's income was measured against the rest of the world using the parity purchasing power method, which converts currencies according to their relative purchasing power rather than currency exchange rates, Yemen was ranked 167 out of 215 countries, close to Nigeria, Laos, Tajikistan, and a bit higher than Sudan and Mauritania. Employing a broader measure that includes health and education as well as wealth, the UNDP ranked Yemen 133 out of 169 countries on its Human Development Index.

Yemen's relative poverty is sometimes exaggerated because of its inclusion in the Middle East and North Africa region. World regions are sociohistorical divisions of the globe, mostly based upon colonial history. South Asia is the former British India; the Middle East and North Africa are the former Ottoman and Safavid/Qajar empires; and Latin America is Spain and Portugal's former dominions. The Republic of Yemen finds itself in a group of rich countries. The GNI per capita of the Arab world was US $5,250 in 2009 mostly because of the oil-rich countries of the Arabian Peninsula. But if we were to compare Yemen to its neighbors to the west and south, Yemen's economy looks much better. Ethiopia's GNI per capita in 2009 was US $330 and Eritrea's was US $320—these are truly poor countries that are at the bottom of the world's economies. Yemen's GNI per capita of US $1,060 in 2009 is almost twice the average of the United Nations' least developed countries (US $639) and about the same as the average in the South Asian region (US $1,107) as well as in the sub-Saharan African region (US $1,125).

According to the World Bank, in 2011, the proportion of Yemenis living under the upper poverty line of US $2 per day is around 47 percent. This is high by Middle Eastern standards, where only 17 percent of people in the region as a whole live on less than US $2 per day, but both sub-Saharan Africa (72.9 percent) and South Asia (73.9 percent) reportedly have much higher rates of poverty. So Yemen's poverty is high in the Arab world, but not extraordinary by global standards.

In many ways, Yemenis have seen dramatic improvements in their lives over the last 40 years, and conditions have generally improved in spite of very rapid population growth. Life expectancy in Yemen increased from 45 years in the 1970s to 55 years in the early 1990s and to 63 years in 2010. Infant mortality, an important measure of a society's basic health care, is falling steadily in Yemen from around 100 per thousand in the 1980s to 52 per thousand in 2008. Literacy rates have improved dramatically as well. In 1994, adult literacy was around 36 percent and in 2009, it was over 60 percent. Female adult literacy is substantially lower: 18 percent in 1994 though improving to 43 percent in 2009. But the real gains have been made in literacy among the youth. In 1994, literacy among those 15–24 years old was 60 percent and by 2009, it was as high as 84 percent. This is higher than most sub-Saharan countries (65 percent), much higher than Morocco (72 percent) and on a par with Egypt (85 percent) in the Arab world. Female youth literacy in Yemen has shown the fastest improvement. In 1994, among females 15–24 only 36 percent could read and write, whereas in 2009, that figure was 72 percent. In spite of the many complaints about the Yemeni educational system, in some ways, it is making remarkable achievements.

Official figures also show the economy growing, though not fast enough to make substantial increases in Yemen's per capital wealth. Exceptionally high prices for crude oil during Yemen's "oil decade" from 2000 to 2010 gave the economy a windfall in spite of the fact that Yemeni production was actually falling. Population growth was also high during this period, so per capita income growth was slow, but nevertheless rising. In real terms, that is, taking into account annual inflation, World Bank figures show Yemen's per capita income rising slowly throughout 2000–2010, though the improvements have not been transformative. The latest official figures actually show per capita income falling in 2009 and 2010, and the gains have been small enough that a few bad years could reverse it all. Thus, the Yemeni economy can be described as treading water with marginal gains against a strong current of rapid population growth. As noted elsewhere, the population growth rate and fertility rate are falling, indicating that Yemen is entering some form of demographic transition to lower population growth that eventually will ease some of the pressure on the economy.

Improvement in the Yemeni economy is now threatened by structural weaknesses compounded by political crises. Yemen's economic achievements in the 1970s and 1980s were fueled by the remittances of emigrant Yemeni workers in the GCC countries, mostly Saudi Arabia. Then, when worker remittances declined in importance in the late 1980s, oil replaced remittances as the growth sector of the Yemeni economy. Now oil is running out as well, and there is no single sector of the economy that will supply the kind of wealth that the economy enjoyed from remittances and oil over the last 40 years. The future Yemeni economy will have to be more diversified than before and will rely upon wealth created by Yemeni labor inside the territory of Yemen to a greater extent than before.

BIBLIOGRAPHY

Chaudhry, Kiren A. *The Price of Wealth: Economics and Institutions in the Middle East.* Ithaca, NY: Cornell University Press, 1997.

Cohen, John M., Mary Hébert, David B. Lewis, and Jon C. Swanson. "Development from Below: Local Development Associations in the Yemen Arab Republic." *World Development* 9, nos. 11–12 (November–December 1981): 1039–61.

Economic Intelligence Unit (EIU). *Country Profile—Yemen and Oman.* London: EIU, various years.

El Mallakh, Ragei. *The Economic Development of the Yemen Arab Republic.* London: Croom Helm, 1986.

Lackner, Helen. *PDRY: Outpost of Socialist Development in Arabia.* London: Ithaca Press, 1985.

Mahdi, Kamil A., Anna Würth, and Helen Lackner, eds. *Yemen into the Twenty-First Century: Continuity and Change.* London: Ithaca Press, 2007.

Morris, Tim. *The Despairing Developer: Diary of an Air Worker in the Middle East.* New York: I. B. Tauris, 1991.

Pridham, B.R., ed. *Economy, Society and Culture in Contemporary Yemen.* London: Croom Helm, 1985.

Stevenson, Thomas. "Yemeni Workers Come Home: Reabsorbing One Million Migrants." *Middle East Report* 181 (March–April 1993): 15–20.

Swanson, Jon C. *Emigration and Economic Development: The Case of the Yemen Arab Republic.* Boulder, CO: Westview Press, 1979.

Society

Yemen is often stereotyped as a "backward" or "primitive" society, meaning that it has not "evolved" or become "modern," when it would be more accurate to say that it is "poor," with an infrastructure that is underdeveloped by comparison with countries in Europe and North America. A society may be quite poor in a material sense, yet its social organizations and ritual practices are quite complex and sophisticated. The burden of this chapter is to show that this is the case for Yemen. Consider religious life, for example. Yemen is an Islamic country, yet this broad designation hardly does justice to the different varieties of Islam that coexist and their long histories in the country. Yet another supposed sign of its backwardness is that Yemen is a tribal society, by which is usually meant that it is "lawless," "violent," and "chaotic." This chapter hopes to show that the tribes have their own laws and mechanisms for resolving disputes peacefully. Nor are they simply "traditionalists" or "antimodern" in the way they are often portrayed. And, finally, it is the position of women in the country, especially veiling and marriage practices, that is held up as another sign of the society's conservatism, but when one understands women in the myriad contexts in which they are to be found in Yemen, the reality becomes far more complex and fluid.

RELIGION AND THOUGHT

Steven C. Caton

Yemen has had a rich and varied history, starting from the very beginning of Islam. (Yemen was mentioned by the Prophet Muhammad as a most pious land; the name Yemen, according to one legend, meaning "right" or on the Prophet's "right—and therefore preferred—hand.") Yemenis were among the Prophet's most ardent supporters in Medina. His cousin and son-in-law, Ali ibn Talib, is said to have visited the country to spread Islam there.

There are basically four distinct Islamic variants that have been important in Yemen's history: one of which is Sunni (the Shafi'is), two of which are Shia (Zaydi and Ismaili), and the fourth being Sufis (mainly of Sunni persuasion). They share something in common with their fellow adherents in other Muslim countries, but over time they have also developed unique or distinctive characteristics within the Yemeni context. They have not always coexisted peacefully with each other, as a result of which their fortunes have waxed and waned according to circumstances. This appears to be especially true in the last 10 years or so, for reasons to be elucidated below, though the full understanding of which cannot be attained except by examining recent political history (see Chapter 3).

It is impossible to talk about the different varieties of Islam in Yemen without considering their complex and often intertwined histories. Thus, a large part of this section will delve into religious history that is part of the collective memory (and hence thought) of these sects or schools.

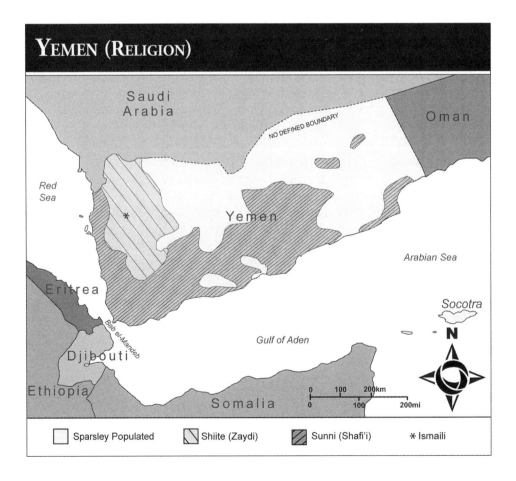

FOUR SCHOOLS OF SUNNI ISLAM: MALIKI, HANAFI, SHAFI'I, AND HANBALI

Sunna refers to the precepts and practices of the Prophet Muhammad, and Sunnis think of themselves as adhering most closely to his original teachings (though there is wide variation on this point within Sunni Islam). Sunnis believe that the four caliphs (leaders of the Muslim community) who succeeded the Prophet were "rightly guided," or that their legal decisions were correct and just. There are four distinct schools of law within Sunni Islam (Hanafi, Maliki, Shafi'i, and Hanbali), each taking its name after the founder of the school. Though there are differences between them in interpretation, they accept each other as legitimate or lawful. For example, where one may see a particular practice as obligatory, the other may consider it optional. The Hanafis are the most populous school in the Muslim world. The Malikis are prominent in Africa and the Gulf. The Shafi'is, who are important in Yemen, take their name after the Sunni jurist Muhammad ibn Idris al-Shafi'i (767–820). This sect can be found also in Southeast Asia, Egypt, and South Asia. Arguably, the most conservative school of law is the Hanbali, which is followed mostly in Saudi Arabia.

Shafi'i (Sunni) Islam

Whereas Zaydism is a homegrown and mostly local affair, virtually unique to Yemen, the Shafi'i school is much more widespread. In Yemen, they constitute a sizeable community in the South, though they are in the minority in comparison with the Zaydis in northern Yemen. The Shafi'is are associated with the highland areas of what is sometimes called "lower Yemen": that is, from the city of Ibb southward to Aden, westward to Zabid (the great center of religious learning in the Tihama), and further east into Hadhramawt. The medieval states of southern Yemen were Sunni for the most part, and only felt threatened by the Zaydis when the northern Imamate, centered around Sa'dah and then Sana'a, spread southward into lower Yemen. This expansionist state was stopped by the Ottoman conquest of Yemen in the 16th century, though this occupation only lasted about 150 years before the Zaydi Imamate reemerged as the hegemonic power in the country. Nevertheless, it was under the Ottomans (who were also Sunni, though of the Hanafi school) that Shafi'is expanded their presence in Yemen (and it is no wonder that Shafi'is saw themselves politically allied to the Ottomans), a trend that continued in the second Ottoman occupation in the last quarter of the 19th century that lasted until the end of World War I, when the Ottoman empire was defeated by the allied powers and collapsed. Thereafter, Zaydi Imamate rule expanded into lower Yemen, though stopped this time by the British and their colonial protectorate, established in Aden and its hinterlands in the 19th century and enduring until the mid-1960s. This, at times turbulent, history between the two sects has led to certain hostile stereotypes each has formed of the other: For example, in Zaydi eyes, the other was a population to be subjugated and ruled; in Shafi'i eyes, the other was a tyrant supported by barbaric tribal populations. But for the most part, these stereotypes kicked in only in times of political tension between the two areas of Yemen and did not inform routine or daily interactions between members of either sect that have been on the whole peaceful.

Both in terms of theological doctrine and pious practice, the differences between the two sects are minor, which may be due to the fact that Zaydis are more conservative than other Shi'is and are in formal terms closest to Sunni philosophy (which, as the term "Sunni"—derived from Sunna or the tradition based on the Qur'an and the Hadith of the Prophet—suggests, adheres to basics or fundamentals). Despite this closeness, there are still some differences between the two that need to be discussed.

First, the Shafi'is (in keeping with the other Sunni schools) prohibit the exercise of private judgment in the creation of legal principles, and from their point of view, the Zaydi doctrine of ijtihad is somewhat suspect. This skepticism is founded on the belief that qualified individuals were lacking the requisite skill to interpret the Sunna (the Qur'an and the Hadith) in a novel but still "correct" way to enact new legislation. For Sunnis, Sharia law was formulated more or less complete with little or no room for "innovation" within the first few generations after the death of the Prophet. Not for nothing is the Classical Arabic term for innovation *bid'ah,* the same as for heresy. The significance of this difference for religious relations within the country has waxed and waned, depending on historical circumstances. Most recently, with Saudi-financed local madrasahs or pedagogical institutes all over the country, not to mention Iman University in Sana'a, a conservative brand of Salafi Islam has been propagated, which has been a source of tension with Zaydis and Sufis (discussed below).

Second, there is a difference in the way the two sects conceive of the head of state. As we have seen, Zaydis were historically ruled by an Imam, among whose qualifications was the requirement that he be a descendant of the Prophet Muhammad through either of his two grandsons, Hasan and Hussein. For Shafi'is (and Sunnis more generally), the head of government did not require such spiritual qualifications and usually did not possess them. Sunni political enclaves in southern Yemen were ruled by sultans. This may seem like a piddling difference, at best, but in actuality, a ruler without this kind of descent could and often did lack legitimacy in the eyes of Zaydis and therefore could in principle be more easily disobeyed or opposed. At the beginning of the 1962 Revolution, for example, Royalists who defended the Imam said of the republican regime that it lacked any legitimacy because it was led by secularists with no kinship ties to the Prophet (it did not help either that the first president, Sallal, was a butcher's son and therefore of low social status). That was 50 years ago, and yet this ideology persists and haunts republican regimes to this day, as in the case of the recent Houthi rebellion in the north of the country (discussed in Chapter 7).

Third, whereas imams have played significant roles as rulers in Shafi'i Islam, where they are also known as *khalifah* or caliphs, they are required only to trace their kinship connection to the Prophet more broadly by being descended from his tribe, the Bani Quraysh, in western Arabia, rather than to the Prophet's family more directly. That said, many of the requirements for Imamate or caliphal rule in Shafi'i doctrine were the same as in Zaydi doctrine: He had to be an adult of sound body and mind, a legal expert, not of slave origins, and courageous. Perhaps, a subtle difference was that the ideal of humility came more from the example of the first caliph of Islam, Abu Bakr, than from the flamboyant or charismatic Ali. This is the doctrine; in historical actuality, however, the religious knowledge ideally required of the ruler became separated from his person and his office, and institutionalized in a cadre of religious scholars known as 'ulama (pl. of *'alim*, scholar). Thus, whereas the Zaydi Imam as head of state was politician, military leader, and religious expert all rolled into one, the sultan or caliph was only expected to be a political head of state and military defender of the nation. The ruler was required to consult the 'ulama to make sure his decisions and laws were in conformity with the Sharia, and in turn the 'ulama would support his rule and give it religious legitimacy; the two institutions thus ideally existing in symbiosis with each other, though in actuality that was not always the case. Also, strong sultans and kings could appoint key clerics to positions of influence as well as dismiss them, so that the executive branch, as it were, and the religious one were rarely independent. Such, for example, is the case of the religious leadership in Egypt and Saudi Arabia.

In spite of these differences between Zaydis and Shafi'is, they share in common the way religious knowledge was learned and propagated even when the specific texts of instruction varied. Religious education began in their respective Qur'anic schools, lasting about four years, where the male child learned not only to recite the Muslim holy book by heart but also basic principles of pious comportment. Teachers in both the Qur'anic school and the later madrasah or lesson circle were "paid" through charitable endowments or *waqfs*. Graduates who wanted to continue with their religious education would join a lesson circle in a local mosque, led by a noted scholar. School started at dawn when pupils joined the Morning Prayer in the mosque, after which the lesson circles in the mosque prayer hall began in earnest.

ORAL RECITATION OF THE QUR'AN

The Prophet was meditating in a cave near Mecca when the Archangel Gabriel came to him and commanded, "Recite!" At first the Prophet demurred, saying he did not know how to read and write, but after the angel repeatedly commanded him, he recited the opening verse. The Prophet then orally transmitted the Qur'an as it was revealed to him, bit by bit over a period of years until near his death. His followers committed the revelation to memory and passed it on by word of mouth to anyone interested in the Prophet's message. Eventually, of course, the Qur'an was written down, but oral modes are still the preferred means by which to learn as well as to transmit the sacred text. Reciting in plain voice is only one of the styles of the oral transmission of the Qur'an; there are several more. The most musically elaborate, widely thought to be the most beautiful, is called *tajwid*. This calls for a beautiful and strong voice, with great breath control, and correct voweling of the text.

Qur'anic school is concerned with the correct memorization of the Qur'an without too much attention paid to meaning and interpretation (particularly challenging, as the language is in Classical Arabic). The lesson circle builds on the practice of memorization to include Hadith and the manuals that are summaries of doctrine and practice, though now the emphasis is on understanding the texts appropriately with the aid of grammar and lexicography, the science of Hadith, and Qur'anic exegesis. The ultimate aim was thorough mastery of Islamic jurisprudence or fiqh. A teacher would recite or read a particular text in question and the pupils would listen to him carefully, endeavoring to repeat verbatim what they had heard. Once they had memorized the text correctly, they would turn to the task of comprehending it. The advanced student would learn exegesis or interpretation from his teacher by engaging with him in a dialogical or Q/A interchange. For example, a student might memorize a particular text and then be given the teacher's interpretation or explanation of it, after which he has the opportunity to ask questions. The next day, the lesson might begin with the teacher asking the students to summarize the interpretation of the day before, to make sure that learning had in fact taken hold in the student's mind. The Q/A was hardly a debate between teacher and pupil, but it did require an active process of learning on the student's part. Supplementary instruction could be sought with other scholars known to have a special mastery of one literature or another. Peer learning was greatly encouraged. And while the mode of learning was oral transmission, students often wrote the lessons down after the class was over, reading and re-reading what they had gleaned. Reading became an important means through which all sorts of ancillary knowledge important to a scholar's overall education was acquired, such as Islamic history, the biographies of the Prophet and other religious figures, in addition to sciences such as astronomy, mathematics, and alchemy. Upon graduating from the madrasah, the student was authorized to become a teacher himself.

It has to be borne in mind that what was described above is a traditional form of religious instruction, little of which exists in that form today, though changes in the system were introduced only recently. When the Ottomans returned to occupy Yemen in the latter part of the 19th century, they introduced reforms that would have a lasting effect, and not only on the Shafi'i system (the Zaydi Imam, Yahya, adapted some of these, realizing that they were useful to his administration and state control over religious education). The Ottomans introduced to Yemen the distinction, derived ultimately from Western models, between religious knowledge and knowledge that was considered secular and "useful" such as modern sciences that the general public ought to know. To impart this new knowledge, the curriculum was systematized and standardized, so that subjects were introduced in sequence corresponding to their levels of difficulty, tests were administered to objectively determine a student's learning, classroom spaces were designed so that students would be cut off from outside distractions, classroom seating was arranged (rows of seats facing a teacher's desk and the blackboard) to insure collective equality among the students if also submission to the teacher's authority, teachers were trained in pedagogical institutes and salaried rather than dependent upon charitable handouts, and instructional texts were printed rather than written or copied and standardized across the country. What may have been lost or attenuated in this zeal to modernize the educational system was the teacher-to-pupil or more dialogical interchange of the older madrasah in favor of a hierarchical and authoritarian mode of instruction. On the other hand, while memorization still played an important role in the learning process, reading and writing came to be dominant over oral transmission that, in turn, required school as well as public libraries to be open to the public (rather than held in the preserve of individual scholars). The reforms instigated by the republic are examined in another section, devoted to modern education.

Zaydi Islam

Zaydi Islam is part of the Shia sect. To understand how this happened, one must delve into the complex history of succession to the caliphate in the early years of Islam. The Shia recognized the Caliph Ali's eldest son Hasan as his rightful successor, but the caliphate was taken over instead by Ali's rival Mu'awiyah bin Abi Sufyan, who founded the Umayyad dynasty in Syria in 661. Hasan became Imam of the Shia community, signing a treaty with Mu'awiyah in which he agreed not to rebel against the latter's rule. His younger brother Hussein became the next Imam, and when Mu'awiyah son Yazid became caliph, he abrogated the treaty signed with his father and rebelled. Hussein along with over 20 of his relatives were killed by Yazid's forces at Karbala on 10 Muharram 61 (or October 10, 680). In the eyes of Shias, this death turned Hussein into a martyr, symbolizing the oppression of the righteous by the forces of ignominy. In many Shia communities in Iran and the Gulf, the event is commemorated each year with rituals of various sorts such as bloody self-flagellation, though they are not performed by the Shias in Yemen. Imam Hussein was succeeded by his son Ali, whose own son Zayd became the fifth Imam of the Shia community, and it is from his teachings that the Zaydiyya religious school stems.

ALI AND THE SHIA

The Shias (meaning "the party of Ali") formed in the first century after the founding of Islam, when they repudiated the claim of the first three caliphs of Islam to being "rightly guided" and insisted that it was the fourth caliph, Ali ibn Abu Talib, who should have been the Prophet's immediate successor. Ali eventually succeeded to the caliphate in 656. However, he encountered considerable opposition in his reign that led to widespread civil strife, and his rule was cut short by an assassin while praying in his mosque in Kufa in 661. Shia claims to Ali's rightful succession to the caliphate immediately after the death of the Prophet in 632 are based in Qur'anic verses and statements of Hadith. For example, in one Hadith, the Prophet returned from his last pilgrimage to Mecca and proclaimed, "He whose lord I am, his lord is Ali." The fact of Ali's close relationship to the Prophet through kinship (as the Prophet's brother's son) and marriage (to the Prophet's daughter, Fatima) as well as his exceptional character and virtues, not least of all being his deep understanding of Islam, legitimated him as a plausible successor to the Prophet.

Zaydi muslims read the Qur'an at the Grand Mosque, Sana'a, on the first day of Ramadan.
(Kamran Jebreili/arabianEye/Corbis)

Zayd's teachings struck a cord at the time in the Caspian Sea region, where the first Zaydi state was formed (in Tabarestan), led by Yahya bin Hussein or Imam al-Hadi (as he is also known). He was eventually invited to Yemen by the tribes of Sa'dah to mediate one of their many conflicts. It was not exactly the case that al-Hadi brought Islam to Yemen (Ali had visited the country during the time of the Prophet), but he certainly revived it. Though he extended his dominion from Sa'dah to Najran in the north and to Sana'a in the south, the most powerful tribes did not entirely submit to his authority. Nevertheless, the second Zaydi state was established in 897 CE, and over the next two centuries, Zaydis from all over the Muslim world emigrated to it, greatly increasing its power and its subsequent hold over the northern tribes.

While believing that the caliph or leader of the Muslim community must be a descendant of the Prophet (i.e., a descendant of either Hasan or Hussein, the sons of Ali and his wife Fatima, daughter of the Prophet), they do not recognize hereditary rule (i.e., succession from father to son) insisting that the Imam be chosen or elected by a body of 'ulama (scholars) and other notables from among qualified saadah (sing. sayyid) on the basis of 14 qualities, the most important among them being religious knowledge, virtue, piety, valor, and wisdom. It is incumbent upon him not only to defend the faith but also to oppose any and all corruption, including corrupt or oppressive rulers, against whom he declares a da'wah and calls for an uprising or jihad. But the imams, unlike the Catholic popes, are not considered infallible and therefore are not above scrutiny and criticism. If an Imam proved to be corrupt or oppressive himself, he could be removed from office. The office of the Imam began to change in the 20th century when Imam Yahya had proclaimed himself "king" of Yemen in

1926, a designation he thought would make dealings with European powers easier. In turn, he wanted to make succession to the Imamate hereditary within his house, the Hamid al-Din, which went against the principle of electing an Imam from the most qualified of all the saadah. These changes were one of the reasons the Imamate began to lose the loyalty of the people, culminating in the 1962 Revolution, though an even more important reason was the policy of keeping Yemen underdeveloped by outside influences that might threaten and erode the Imam's power.

In theological terms, Yemeni Zaydi Islam is distinctive in that it permits ijtihad or the formation of new religious laws based on the Qur'an and the Hadith, whereas in other schools such innovation is considered "closed." In the latter, the law may only be applied or "imitated." This fact has been a source of tension between Zaydis and others in contemporary Yemen who have come under the influence of Wahhabi/Salafi Islam from Saudi Arabia. In the view of these Muslims, Zaydi Islam has permitted all sorts of legal innovations that need to be stripped away because they supposedly run counter to the spirit if not the form of the law as it was originally promulgated by the first generations of Muslims.

It is impossible to get accurate figures on the numbers of Zaydis in Yemen (they range from 25 to 45 percent), though they are confined mainly to the northern portion of the country (from the Saudi border south to central Yemen). There is also a sizeable number in Saudi Arabia. Of all the different sects of Shi'ism, the Zaydis are closest to their Sunni coreligionists.

Ismaili Islam

Ismailism is a variant of Shia Islam, possibly the second largest, even though it is a relatively small minority in Yemen (a rough estimate would be around 60,000). The Zaydis and the Ismailis, though tracing their descent back to the Prophet Muhammad, in time split off from each other over disputes about succession to the Imamate or leadership of the Shia community. The Ismailis claim that after the fourth Imam, Ali ibn Hussein, the rightful successor was not Zayd bin Ali (recognized by the Zaydis) but Muhammad al-Baqir, followed by his son Jafar al-Sadiq, the sixth Imam, and Jafar's son Ismail who actually predeceased his father but "ought" to have been the seventh Imam. Ismail's son Muhammad went into "occultation" (i.e., he disappeared but will return one day as the Mahdi or mankind's savior). All imams of the Shia community after Ismail are considered illegitimate in the eyes of the Ismailis. Because Ismail was the seventh Imam, Ismailis take their name after him and are sometimes called "Seveners" (by the same reckoning, Zaydis might be called "Fivers" because they claim Zayd bin Ali as the last rightly guided Imam, and the Shia community in Iran the "Twelvers" because they believe that Ismail's younger son Musa al-Kazim and the latter's descendants ought to have followed Ismail as "rightly guided," with the 13th going into "occultation").

It is interesting that Imam Jafar al-Sadiq, a great scholar of Islam, taught three of the four future founders of the Sunni schools. Within the Ismailis, the Nizaris and the Dawoodi Bohras distinguish themselves on the basis of yet other narratives about the lines of succession to the Imamate. Originally, the two were united within

TABLE 5.1 Imamic Succession for Different Shia Sects.

Zaydis	Ali ibn Abu Talib (circa 598–661 CE)
	Hasan ibn Ali (625–669 CE)
	Hussein ibn Ali (626–680 CE)
	Ali ibn Hussein (circa 659–712 CE)
	Zayd bin Ali (695–740 CE)
Ismailis	Ali ibn Abu Talib
	Hasan ibn Ali
	Hussein ibn Ali
	Ali ibn Hussein
	Muhammad al-Baqir (676–733 CE)
	Jafar al-Sadiq (702–765 CE)
	Ismail ibn Jafar (721-755 CE)

NOTE: Whereas Zaydis recognize Zayd bin Ali as the successor to Ali ibn al-Hussein, the rest of the Shias recognize Muhammad al-Baqir, Zayd's brother, as Ali ibn al-Hussein's successor.

Tomb of Ahmed Bin Issa, a holy man, Wade Dawan. (Davor Lovincic/iStockphoto.com)

the Fatimid dynasty in Egypt, but then split around 1094 over the succession to the Fatimid Imam, al-Mustansir Billah: those who followed his eldest son Nizar became known as the Naziri Islamilis and those who followed his brother Ahmed al-Musta'li became known as Mustaalis; and it was he whom the Sulayhid Queen Arwa (ruled Yemen from 1084 to 1138), a strong ally of the Fatimids, recognized as Imam of the Yemeni community. Many Mustaalis traveled to India and Pakistan because of the vigorous Indian Ocean trade, where large Ismaili communities in Gujarat and Mumbai thrive today. Eventually, Queen Arwa had the title of the Imam changed to Da'i al-Mutlaq (*Da'i* means "someone who calls [others] to God" and *al-Mutlaq* means "absolute," so a reasonable translation would be "head missionary"), after the Imam al-Tayyib (d. 1130). After him, they were known as Tayyibi Ismailis. With the death of Queen Arwa in 1138, the Ismailis lost a religious patron and protector, and they eventually ran foul of the Zaydi imams who persecuted them. They fled to the Haraz Mountains and the city of Zabid, where they managed to find protection under Ottoman rule in the 16th century. But when Yemen once again came under Zaydi rule, many Ismailis decided to go to India and Pakistan, where their coreligionists had already founded communities.

The Tayyibi Ismailis split in the 16th century into two branches: the Sulaymani and the Dawoodi, named after the successors they followed. In 1640, the Sulaymanis migrated to Najran, a region that is now in southwestern Saudi Arabia (with a population of roughly 400,000 that has its own Da'i), leaving a handful in Wadi Hadhramawt, whereas the Dawoodi that number roughly 700,000 are found all over the world, including Yemen. The Yemeni village of Al-Hutayb in the Haraz Mountains (very near the urban center of Manakhah) is the site of a tomb belonging to one of the Ismaili Da'i, Hatim, and is now a pilgrimage site for both Sulaymanis and Dawoodis (who come from as far as India). The tomb has been renovated and comfortable hotels nearby are reserved for pilgrims, mostly paid for by Ismailis from abroad.

Ismaili faith is based on the Qur'an and the Hadith, and in many respects, its beliefs and rituals are indistinguishable from other Islamic sects and schools. They perform the shahadah (the profession of faith, "There is no god but Allah and Muhammad is His Prophet"), prayer (though not necessarily five times a day and the Imam has the right to amend the prayer times as circumstance requires), *zakat* or charity, fasting during the month of Ramadan (but also a spiritual fasting that "purifies the soul" by avoiding sinful acts and performing good deeds), pilgrimage to Mecca at least once in the believer's lifetime (though "pilgrimage" to the Imam is also important), and jihad meaning "struggle" (though for Ismailis it has more the meaning of struggling against the evils that might tempt the soul rather than warfare against those who threaten the community of believers per se; none but the Imam has the right to declare armed jihad). Like all Shias, they believe that the Imam should be a descendant of the Prophet Muhammad through Ali and his progeny. Commemoration of the martyrdom of Hussein and his family and followers at Karbala, Iraq, on the 10th of Muharram is another of their important rituals.

Yet, certain key elements distinctive of Ismailism are discernable. One of these is the belief that apart from or underneath an official or manifest Islam (*zahir*) is an inner or hidden one (*batin*) that the believer must apprehend. For example, the Qur'an is thought to contain these two layers of meaning, and by studying the writings of the Imam with the help of a spiritual guide, the believer can discern what these hidden meanings are and how to apply them in daily life. Some numbers (not surprisingly, perhaps especially the number seven) have mystical significance. Written poetry can be a guide to hidden religious meanings. Nizari Ismailis, who consider the Aga Khan as their Imam and descendant of the Prophet Muhammad (the Aga Khan being a princely hereditary), believe that he is the "face of God" and is their path to salvation. Like other Shias, Ismailis believe that it is alright to conceal one's religious beliefs to avoid persecution though not otherwise, and it is said to have served them in good stead when they were small minorities in hostile countries.

Until the Mahdi (savior) appears, the Nizari Ismailis believe they are guided on earth by their Imam, the Aga Khan, whereas the Dawoodi Bohras have spiritual "guide" or Da'i who is not an Imam per se but a teacher who guides the believer on the path to God, presumed to be the true desire of every soul. The Dawoodi Bohras are headed by a Da'i al-Mutlaq, who is appointed by his predecessor in office, and serves as the earthly representative of the Imam, believed to be in occultation. He has several helpers or associates who are sent to areas where substantial believers live in order to minister to their congregations. These congregations have a mosque (*masjid*) in which prayers and sermons are held, and adjacent assembly halls (*jama'at khaana*) reserved for various social and economic functions. The origins of the Da'i al-Mutlaq were in Fatimid Egypt, from which the institution was brought to Yemen when the Fatimids, themselves converts to Ismailism, supported the Sulayhid dynasty. Ismailism was greatly expanded under the patronage of Queen Arwa al-Sulayhi (1048–1138).

Though traditionally traders (both in Yemen and abroad), Ismailis are now highly educated professionals and like their Nizari counterparts, engage in many philanthropic projects such as building hospitals, roads, and schools as well as restoring Islamic landmarks. They generally believe that the education of women is as important as that of men (following the Hadith that says, "seeking knowledge is incumbent upon all Muslims, both male and female") and many women also work in a variety

---

HADITH

Hadith refers to a vast collection of texts, which consist of quotations or reported speech of the Prophet as well as descriptions of his behavior that relate to almost every aspect of life and serve as a source of Islamic law. They were compiled by Muslim scholars known for their learning and integrity. Several such collections exist and may vary depending on the sect. The way in which the Hadith were collected is an interesting story. The great majority of them are reports attributed to the earliest companions of the Prophet or to those among his closest and most well-regarded kinsmen and other associates, and various criteria were developed to determine the veracity of the transmission of these reports down through the generations to the compiler. Through these means, the Hadith were authenticated.

of fields, ranging from education to medicine, though not so much in Yemen where such opportunities are more limited.

Sufism

Sufism is often thought to be the mystical or esoteric side of Islam. It originated during the early Umayyad caliphate (661–750 CE) in reaction to what was perceived as its rulers' extravagant lifestyle and decadence. Indeed, one of the etymologies of the term "sufi" is wool, referring to the woolen cloaks Sufi followers wore (though another meaning "he who is pure" is probably more important), representing asceticism, in contrast to the presumably sumptuous garments of the elite at the time. Sufis adhere to many of the same beliefs and practices as other Muslims (e.g., the oneness of God), the difference being that Sufis believe the devout worshipper can achieve a closeness to God on earth that other Muslims say they only achieve after death on the Day of Judgment, when all souls ascend to heaven to be judged by their Lord and Maker.

Like the Ismailis, Sufis distinguish between an outer and an inner Islam, the former being those rules prescribed by the Sunna (the laws derived from the Qur'an and the Hadith) and the latter being the significance or meaning those laws have to man's inner being or heart. The two are supposed to complement each other. For example, there is a prescribed way of performing prayer that must be observed, including a purity of intention that corresponds to an interior state; in addition to such forms, the worshipper should also concentrate on prayer's interior or mystical meaning—the prayer goes to God like Muhammad on his horse ascending the seven layers of the world to Heaven. The aim of inner knowledge is to purify the heart of worldly vices and sins so that the worshipper is fit to come close to God. It is important to emphasize that the great Sufi teachers did not see esoteric knowledge as being in conflict with or in contradiction to the Sunna; rather, as al-Ghazali (one of the greatest of all Sufis) taught, it was meant to complement the latter so as to create a whole or complete knowledge. However, the notion of becoming close to God has been controversial in non-Sufi Islam, seeming to merge man and God into a unity that is considered blasphemous. For that and other reasons listed below, Sufis have often been persecuted in countries where they are a minority group.

To gain this inner or esoteric knowledge, the worshipper had to enter into a hierarchical relationship with a teacher (*murshid* or sheikh), who guided the pupil on the correct devotional path. In the medieval period of Islam, these relationships were organized into orders or *tariqahs,* and almost all the Sufi orders trace their knowledge of esoteric Islam back to the Prophet Muhammad via Ali (the notable exception being the Naqshbandi Sufis who trace it back to the Prophet through the first caliph, Abu Bakr). The dominant Sufi order in Yemen is the Shadhiliyya/Alawiyya, numbering in the thousands, located mainly in the southern parts of the country, especially Wadi Hadhramawt. However, it appears that the Sufi order in Yemen was never of the large and centralized kind prominent in other parts of the Muslim world. The Shadhiliyyas believe that inner knowledge is not just a complement of outward form but is more "real" and thus more important. And, of course, as with other forms of Sufism, the ultimate aim or goal of these practices is understanding God (*ma'rifah*).

AL-GHAZALI

Abu Hamid al-Ghazali (1058–1111 CE), otherwise known as al-Ghazali, was a Persian-born Muslim philosopher, theologian, and mystic, widely considered one of the greatest minds of the medieval age, Muslim or Christian. Some have regarded him as the most important Islamic thinker after the Prophet Muhammad, and he was important, among other things, for having brought the Sharia or legal tradition in closer harmony with Sufi mysticism. In some respects, al-Ghazali holds the same position that St. Thomas Aquinas has in Christian theology (though Aquinas embraced the teachings of Aristotle and pre-Christian philosophy, whereas al-Ghazali taught that they were erroneous and therefore could misguide the believer).

Among the devotional practices Yemeni Sufis carry out is the *dhikr,* a ritual that all Muslims are supposed to perform. The word means remembrance, and all Muslims are enjoined to remember the 99 names of Allah (e.g., the One, the Praiseworthy, the Merciful One, the Compassionate, etc.), often while fingering prayer beads. Sufis take this ritual one step further, in keeping with the esoteric or inner meaning of remembrance. Thus, the Sufi pupil is taught to visualize the Arabic name for God, Allah, as being written on his heart to symbolize that the divine is only a heartbeat away. Sufi practices in Yemen also entail the singing of devotional poetry. Important as well is the celebration of the Prophet's birthday (*mawlid*), something Zaydis observe also, and visitation of the tombs of highly respected scholars (often descendants of the Prophet Muhammad) who because of their knowledge and reputed healing powers are considered especially "blessed" (tomb visitation is something Zaydis frown upon and actively discourage as "idolatry"). To this day in Wadi Hadhramawt, dozens of such pilgrimage sites around the shrine of a "scholar/saint" (usually male but sometimes also female) are still active, drawing hundreds of devotees on the commemoration of the saint's birthday. These shrines usually consist of a square whitewashed room topped by a white copula, in which are to be found the scholar's catafalque or burial chamber alongside some relics such as his books, incense burner (incense was used to clear and sharpen the mind as it embarked on its ritual discipline), coffee-making utensils (coffee was also thought to enhance concentration), and other personal accoutrements. These shrines would be opened to the pilgrims for their inspection, meditation, and devotion. Finally, in some mosques, Sufis sing poetry and perform ritual dances to the accompaniment of drums, something unheard of in Zaydi places of worship.

An important part of the story of Sufis in southern Yemen is that they were among the first proselytizers of Islam in South and Southeast Asia, beginning around the 13th century CE. The Hadhrami saadah were active maritime traders, and when the overland silk route was cut off by the Mongol invasion, they plied the Indian Ocean with their boats, carrying Sufi Islam with them. This accounts for why there are significant Hadhrami populations in India (e.g., Hyderabad), Malaysia, and Indonesia.

The ancestors of these traders in time became wealthy and powerful, sending back money to invest in Hadhramawt and returning with their Asian wives and "mixed" breed children (Arab and Asian)—an immigration that has had a noticeable Malaysian or Indonesian influence on many things in Hadhramawt including food, clothing, and housing style.

Sufism in southern Yemen has seen something of a resurgence since 2000, in large part because of a charismatic preacher by the name of Habib Umar. He has founded a school, Dar al-Mustafa, near the Hadhramawt city of Tarim—long considered the historical heartland of Yemeni Sufism—for the promulgation of Sufi beliefs and practices. With this resurgence has come the elevation of the status of the saadah who had been suppressed and persecuted under the Socialists in the preunification era, and it is not uncommon to see such a personage greeted with the old-style hand kissing, sometimes even the kissing of his robe's hem, in recognition of his standing as a descendant of the Prophet. But roughly at the same time that this was happening, Salafi influences from Saudi Arabia penetrated Yemen and entered into direct conflict with the Sufis in Hadhramawt. (Salafi is the term used for someone who believes in the "basics" of Islam as consisting in the Qur'an and the Hadith, with everything else added on since the first few generations after the Prophet Muhammad as being nothing more than superstition or idolatry.) In Salafi eyes, many Sufi practices such as pilgrimage to saint's tombs are idolatrous. By attempting to destroy these tombs and graves, they have clashed with Sufi adherents, and there is now tension between the different religious sects. It is said that the Salafis are financed by the Saudis and therefore "foreign." Whether the financing is true or not, this does not

Evening prayers at the Sufi school, Dar al-Mustafa, Tarim. (Bryan Denton/Corbis)

entirely account for their success in recruiting adherents. It may not be easy for us to understand that Salafis are considered modern and progressive in the eyes of some who look askance at the social hierarchies that appear to be reinstating themselves in areas under Sufi influence or see "saint worship" as a superstition reminiscent of pre-Islamic Arabia. In turn, Sufis and other Yemenis stereotype Salafis, whether Wahhabi influenced or not, as "intolerant," when in fact different strains exist.

There are Sufis elsewhere in the country (a little less than a hundred in Sana'a) and there are reported to be Sufis also in Zabid, Taiz, and the area south of it, known as the Hojariyyah. Because of tense relations with their Zaydi colleagues (who consider such practices as the dhikr ceremony blasphemous) and the religious conservative political party known as Islah (see "Political Conflicts" in Chapter 7), they have been driven underground, meeting for their dhikr in someone's private home, for example, and though they have not experienced the sort of violence their brethren in Hadhramawt have undergone in recent years, they still try to keep a low profile.

BIBLIOGRAPHY

Boxberger, Linda. *On the Edge of Empire: Hadhramawt, Emigration, and the Indian Ocean, 1880s–1930s.* Albany: State University of New York Press, 2002.

Freitag, Ulrike and William G. Clarence-Smith, eds. *Hadhrami Traders, Scholars, and Statesmen in the Indian Ocean, 1750s–1960s.* Leiden, NY: Brill, 1997.

Haykel, Bernard. *Revival and Reform in Islam: The Legacy of Muhammad al-Shawkani.* Cambridge: Cambridge University Press, 2003.

Ho, Enseng. *Graves of Tarim: Genealogy and Mobility across the Indian Ocean.* Berkeley: University of California Press, 2006.

Messick, Brinkley. *The Calligraphic State: Textual Domination and History in a Muslim Society.* Berkeley: University of California Press, 1993.

Vom Bruck, Gabriele. *Islam, Memory, and Morality in Yemen: Ruling Families in Transition.* New York: Palgrave Macmillan, 2005.

Weir, Shelagh. "A Clash of Fundamentalisms: Wahhabism in Yemen." *Middle East Report* 204 (July–September 1997): 22, 23, 26.

YEMENITE JEWRY

Asher Orkaby

Though only a handful of Yemenite Jews remain in the country, they were at one time a very important ethnic group with a long and complex history and deserve to be included in this chapter. Their heyday in some respects coincided with the medieval Muslim period, and so it is fitting that their story be told here.

Shlomo D. Goitein, a well-known researcher of Yemenite Jewry, once noted that the Yemenite Jews are "the most Jewish of all Jews." Many of their religious and social customs well predated the oral law of European and Sephardic Jewry, transporting Goitein and others back thousands of years in Jewish history. Scholars of

Jewish studies have therefore been fascinated by the Yemenite Jews for decades, producing countless numbers of books on their customs, language, songs, and history. Research and records of the sole minority population on the entire Arabian Peninsula and their well-documented social, economic, and legal interactions within the local Muslim population provide a unique prism into centuries of Yemeni history.

Elaborate Myths of Origin

The origins of people are often a self-characterization of their own imagined historical and social significance. Conversely, myths of origin can also be used by others to justify social stigmas and nationalist movements. According to Arab tradition, the Jews of Yemen are descended from the Muslims of Qatan, the common ancestor of all of South Arabia. Jewish lineage may be traced to the Arabian kingdom of Himyar that supposedly converted to Judaism at some time during the fourth century CE. Yemenis, especially during the rule of the Zaydi imams from 17th through the 20th centuries, utilized this myth of origin to justify coercive conversion efforts as merely returning a cousin to his original faith.

Myths of origin from the Old Testament, on the other hand, took on an added level of importance for a community that saw itself as a transient resident of Arabia, hoping to return to the Land of Israel as part of the Jewish nation. The Queen of Sheba myth traces Yemenite Jewry back to the biblical grand meeting of the Queen of Sheba and King Solomon. Some Jewish traditions claim that a group of Israelites defected from Moses's entourage during their 40-year excursion in the desert and made their way to the Land of Sheba, modern day Yemen. Other modified versions believe that a number of Jews followed the Queen back to Sheba after her meeting with Solomon, several hundred years later.

A later myth harkens back to the prophet Jeremiah's record of a group of 5,000 Jews who heeded his warnings and fled south 42 years before the destruction of the First Temple in 586 BCE. These émigrés are believed to have founded a replica of the Land of Israel on Mount Nuqum in the Sana'a valley. This same group was said to have spurned Ezra the scribe's call for a return to the Land of Israel a century later, for they foresaw the destruction of the Second Temple. Ezra subsequently condemned the community with eternal damnation and banned them from the Land of Israel.

While none of the origin narratives are completely substantiated by historical and archeological evidence, 20th-century Zionists seized the opportunity to propagate these ancient myths when the Jews of Yemen arrived en masse to Israel in 1949. As it was perceived by many, their arrival encapsulated the reunification of a nation torn apart for thousands of years.

Early History as Merchants of the Indian Ocean Trade

Shlomo D. Goitein (1900–1985) lived among Yemenite Jewish immigrants in Jerusalem and traveled to Aden during the 1940s, becoming a well-known expert on Yemenite

Jewry early in his career. He was, however, best known for his work with the Cairo Geniza documents.

From the 13th through the 16th centuries, Aden served as a major port city and transshipment point for goods traveling between the East (India) and the West (Egypt). Living in Diaspora communities across the world, the Jewish merchants were able to traverse the international trade network with greater ease than their Muslim or Christian counterparts, transporting coffee, spices, and other products. Jewish communities opened their doors to traveling co-religionists, welcoming them into their homes and synagogues, and providing them with unrivaled and very lucrative economic connections. The widespread use of Judeo-Arabic dialects, a blend of Arabic, Hebrew, and Aramaic words written in Hebrew script, unified disparate communities that would have otherwise had to overcome multiple language barriers.

The wavering fortunes of the Port of Aden during the 16th century when first Portuguese and then Ottomans vied for dominance in the Indian Ocean have been recounted in Chapter 2. Suffice it to say here that with the decline of the Portuguese commercial empire in the Indian Ocean toward the second half of the 17th century, the Red Sea was reopened to East/West commercial traffic. Aden, however, was no longer the center of maritime trade. As a result, portions of the once thriving Jewish mercantile community of Aden moved to the port city of Mocha or to the Ottoman imperial capital of Sana'a. By doing so, the Jews were able to take advantage of the new opportunities afforded to them by the Ottoman Empire, including a greater level of economic and social autonomy. Many viewed this economic opportunism with enmity, perceiving the Jewish merchants and craftsmen as collaborators with the Ottomans. After several decades, Aden was reduced from a major center of trade to a fishing village of only a few hundred people and fell off the map until "rediscovered" by the British in the 19th century.

THE CAIRO GENIZA

A geniza in Hebrew is a storeroom connected to a Jewish synagogue containing Hebrew language documents with the word God written on them, and for that reason requiring ceremonial burial. The Cairo Geniza is a collection of 280,000 Jewish manuscript fragments found in the storeroom of the Ben Ezra Synagogue in Old Cairo that span a thousand years of Indian Ocean and Mediterranean commerce and correspondence. Now archived at various American and European universities, the documents provide an invaluable source for historical research on Jewish life in the Mediterranean world from the 9th century through the 19th century. The documents tell the story of a vast network of international merchants and contains detailed information on the social practices of Jews, Muslims, and Christians; styles of language; local and regional events; trade practices; architecture; and myriad other topics. Goitein based his monumental six-volume reconstruction of medieval Jewish life, *A Mediterranean Society* (1967), on this material.

Yemeni rabbi with family, Sana'a. (AFP Photo/Ahmad Gharabli/Getty Images)

Transition from Trade to Artisanry

When Ottoman rule in Yemen came to an end in 1636 with the Zaydi revolt, the new Zaydi imams in Yemen viewed the Jews as traitors, regarding them with hostility and readily reversing many of the liberties granted to the community by the Ottoman governors. Jewish clothing and housing were restricted as were various aspects of public behavior such as riding on horses and speaking to Muslims. The notorious orphan decree was an edict, periodically rescinded and reinstated, that sanctioned the kidnapping of Jewish orphans and taking them into Muslim families against the will of their biological family. In an effort to save their orphans, Jewish communities often posed cousins as sons and daughters and married orphaned children off at an early age. A 10-year-old bride was not an unheard of phenomenon.

A combination of factors toward the end of the 17th century irreversibly changed the economic function of Jews within Yemeni society. Advancements in maritime technology allowed ships from Egypt to sail to India without waiting in Aden or Mocha for the ideal sailing conditions. The Dutch East India Company, founded in 1602, took the original Portuguese ventures in Asia to the next level by gaining unprecedented access to Asian raw materials for the European market. The Dutch, along with the British East India Company, assumed the role of Yemen in the global market place. Even the once world-renowned Mocha coffee experienced a sharp decline in comparison with Dutch-imported Sumatran coffee, thus creating the template for the Starbuck's coffee menu.

This overall decline in Yemeni trade during the latter half of the 17th and 18th centuries marked the end of the prominence of Jewish merchants. Their international trade networks of the Middle Ages could no longer compete with the vast Dutch and British colonial networks, forcing many out of the maritime commerce sector. The Jews of Yemen, specifically, retreated inland and concentrated their communal efforts on craftsmanship and artisanry, an economic sector that soon became synonymous with Jewish settlement in the country.

Religious and Social Life

Yemen's transition from an international trade magnate to a more insular and inward looking society was clearly manifested in the centralization of Jewish religious authority. By the end of the 17th century, Sana'a was home to the largest and most influential Jewish community in Yemen. The religious court in Sana'a was headed by the chief rabbi of Yemen, a position first created in 1681. Jews corresponded and traveled from across the country to obtain religious rulings from the chief rabbi and to have their cases heard by the central Jewish court that functioned on the two market days, Monday and Thursday. The chief rabbi's role, however, extended beyond the confines of the Sana'a Jewish court. He would often make cross-country trips stopping by the many local communities to inspect the religious adherence to the laws of ritual baths, kosher meat preparations, and education. Beyond his role as supreme religious authority, the chief rabbi served as the Jewish representative to the Zaydi Imam and the Ottoman authority.

Daily religious matters, however, were not micromanaged by the chief rabbi of Sana'a. Local religious leaders, known as *mori,* functioned as the community's kosher butcher, school teacher, cantor, rabbi, and judge. Similar to the role of the chief rabbi, the mori also served as the Imam's regional representative and tax collector. As these positions were usually voluntary, both the local mori and the chief rabbi continued working in their family trade specialty, particularly in silversmithing, even while serving as community leader.

Yemenite Jewish religious law and customs are often reminiscent of early Talmudic traditions dating around 500 CE. These customs include the weekly reading of a Talmudic era Aramaic translation of the Torah, the early participation of children in the synagogue, and certain customs of family ritual purity. Although dressed in a similar fashion to their Muslim counterparts, the Jews of Yemen could easily be discerned by their signature side curls, also part of an ancient tradition.

Although historians often consider the Imamic period to be one of relative isolation from the rest of the Middle East, the continued interaction between the Jews of Yemen and other Jewish communities is testament to quite the opposite situation. The advent of the printing press made available many published works of religion and philosophy. The Jewish community of Yemen had a particular affinity for works on kabbalah and mysticism.

Within the Jewish community of Yemen, there were three main sects. The Baladi sect was the most traditional, having maintained the original Yemeni customs and religious practices. The Shami sect was particularly influenced by Middle Eastern Jewry, particularly the writings of Rabbi Yosef Karo, a 16th-century Egyptian religious author. The Shamis incorporated Sephardic traditions, producing new prayer books and religious edicts well into the 19th century. The final group known as Dardaim adhered to the 19th-century movement of Dor Deah, founded by Rabbi Yihya Qafih. Following similar models in Europe and the Middle East, the Dardaim made great efforts to combat the influence of kabbalah and mysticism, striving instead for a return to the intellectual origins of Maimonides.

Although the religious sects of the 18th and 19th centuries produced a fair amount of religious writings, the real passion of the average Yemenite was for poetry and song. The *diwan,* an anthology of songs and poetry and a staple in every Jewish household, contains songs commemorating every aspect of life including the Sabbath and Jewish holidays, exile and redemption, biblical references, and mysticism. The majority of the diwan was written by the most famous Yemeni poet Shalom Shabazi (1619–1680), a mystical weaver from Taiz who authored more than 15,000 poems. His poetry—written primarily in Hebrew, Judeo-Arabic, or the local Yemenite Arabic dialect—was popular among Jews and Muslims alike, as he was able to incorporate popular themes in traditional Yemeni poetry form. Excerpts from one of his Judeo-Arabic poems can be found in Mark Wagner's (2009) book on Yemeni poetry.

Shabazi's tomb in Taiz became a mystical place of pilgrimage where Jews and Muslims alike went to seek his divine intervention and to honor his cultural contributions. It is visited to this day. These religious customs and traditional poetry remain in daily practice among Yemenite Jewish communities in America, England, Israel, and Yemen.

A Messianic Community

Private and religious lives of the Jews in Yemen were characterized by a multitude of false messiahs promising to redeem the nation and bring them to the Land of Israel. From the 12th century until the end of the 19th century, multiple messianic movements sparked the hopes of a downtrodden community, only to have them disappointed and punished by the ruling regent. There were often harsh reactions by Yemeni rulers who regarded the false messiahs as threatening alternatives of communal authority.

The first such messiah appeared in 1172 as a Jewish convert to Islam who sought to convert his Yemeni brethren. The community's cry for help reached the famous Rabbi Moses Maimonides, then residing in Egypt, and precipitated one of his most well-known works on religious philosophy, the *Epistle to Yemen.* Maimonides's guidance and encouragement was the beginning of a deep affinity of the Yemenite community for his religious teachings that continues to dominate religious life in Yemenite communities until today.

Why was the Yemenite Jewish community so obsessed with and so readily swept up in cultish messianic movements? Although many more complicated answers exist, it seems likely that the often difficult circumstances of life in a country plagued by famine, poverty, and repressive rulers drove many to follow the false messiahs. Deep down in their hearts, they wanted to believe that the messiah's prophecy of redemption was true. This answer is vindicated by the fact that during the great economic prosperity of the "pax Aden" period from 1200 to 1550, there were no documented messianic movements of consequence. Only after Aden collapsed and the country fell to economic hardship under the Zaydi imams did the next false messiah movement take root. The messiah thereby became a symbol of hope for a community of impoverished Jews.

Beyond the economic hardships, the Jewish community in Yemen was predisposed to messianic movements by nature of their religious philosophy. As is evident from the popular biblical roots of their origin, many believed that settlement in Yemen was only transient and that the true messiah would soon come and carry them all to the Land of Israel. This underlying belief played a major role as a push factor in 1948 when the State of Israel was founded. Indeed, many Yemenite Jews considered David Ben-Gurion to be the modern messiah, carrying them on the prophesized "wings of eagles" to the Land of Israel.

The Jewish Artisan and the Muslim Farmer

After the decline of Yemeni maritime trade in the 18th century, Jews resettled in small communities situated in over 1,050 towns, villages, and hamlets throughout 60 different tribal areas in North Yemen and in the Aden Protectorates. The dispersion of approximately 60,000 Jews reflected their role within the greater Yemeni society. While the Muslim population consisted mainly of landowners and farmers, the Jewish minority assumed a monopoly over the country's craftsmanship, an economic sector spurned by most Muslims in Yemen. Jews, on the other hand, viewed artisanry as a respected profession that kept men near the home and free to partake in the learning of Torah. This economically symbiotic relationship characterized Yemeni society for two centuries. The Muslim farmers and landowners provided fresh produce and grains, while the skilled Jewish artisans produced the textiles, utensils, and manufactured items.

Gold and silversmiths were the most well-known Jewish artisans and the most well-respected professions in the community. In part due to the absence of a formal banking system, most Yemenis wore their bank accounts on their body in the form of elaborate jewelry. Until the 20th century, Jewish artisans produced the *jambiyya,* or the ornate knife and belt worn by most Muslim men. Silver jewelry made by the Jewish Yemeni artisan was coveted by locals and European travelers alike and subsequently became a symbol of Yemeni art and culture. Even today, most Yemeni jewelers who now import gold and silver jewelries from other Gulf countries will speak nostalgically of the quality and beauty of Yemen jewelry in the heyday of the Jewish artisan.

Although lacking the global reputation of the silversmith, Jewish weavers played an important role in Yemeni society. They formed family-run trade operations or even entire villages, such as Al-Gades in the district of Ibb, that monopolized the clothing needs of the surrounding region. As a result, each region in Yemen had a distinct style of embroidery and stitching attributed to the local Jewish weaver family or village.

Beyond goldsmiths, silversmiths, weavers, and embroiders, there were over 60 other crafts dominated by the Jewish population after the 18th century. The more artistic sectors included calligraphy, carpentry, ornate leatherwork, and stonemasonry, and other skilled work included pottery, soap and candle making, bakers, gunsmiths, tobacco manufacturing, and shoemakers. Specific trades were associated with particular families, as were garment and jewelry styles that were passed down from father to son.

Alcohol consumption, strictly prohibited in Yemen, was sanctioned to the Jewish communities of Yemen. Wine and anise-flavored araq were staples of the Sabbath table and at wedding celebrations. Not surprisingly, Muslim tax collectors would often pay social visits to Jewish households and return home visibly intoxicated with the Jewish tax debt magically resolved. Wine cellars were therefore understandably the target of Muslim hostility during times of famine and civil unrest.

With the nearly complete liquidation of the country's craft sector after the Jewish exodus in 1949, consumer manufactured needs and illicit alcohol consumption had no local alternative. The Jews sold off mass amounts of silver and property at fire-sale prices and were forced to pay exit taxes to their Muslim neighbors. The Muslim farmer, once reliant on the Jewish artisan for manufactured goods, used their newly acquired silver and cash to purchase imported substitutes from Aden. These transactions were meticulously recorded by the British customs authority. The Yemeni market remains, to this day, reliant on foreign imports, having since failed to develop a replacement industrial sector.

Exodus of Yemenite Jewry and Operation Magic Carpet

The transitional events of the 19th century affected monumental changes for Yemen in general and for the Yemenite Jews in particular. The incorporation of the Yemeni highlands into the Ottoman Empire in 1872 brought Yemen out of century-long isolation. Consequently, the Yemenite Jews were reintroduced to their regional and European coreligionists.

The 1839 British occupation of Aden established a haven of religious equality unrivaled anywhere on the Arabian Peninsula. Jews in Aden and, by extension, other parts of the British Protectorates to the north and east of the port were given access to new economic and mercantile opportunities and were able to reaffirm centuries-old contacts with the Jews of Egypt, Palestine, and Europe. Additionally, the opening of the Suez Canal in 1869 increased Aden's prominence in Mediterranean and global trade, and created renewed commercial opportunity for the Jews of Yemen.

This global interaction, however, brought not only golden opportunities but also foreign tensions between Jews and Muslims, specifically regarding Jewish settlement in Palestine. As news spread via Arab League propaganda, restive crowds in Aden and Yemen began to ostracize the Jewish minority as subversive foreign collaborators and British agents. Although violence was limited to anti-Jewish riots in Aden in 1947, the reverberations of events in Palestine were felt throughout the country.

What had been a strongly messianic community for generations saw in Palestine a chance for ultimate redemption and salvation. In 1882, the first group of Yemeni migrants arrived in Palestine, preceding by several months the first migration of Russian Jews, traditionally considered the first modern Jewish settlers of Palestine. Yemeni migration continued in a trickle through the end of the 19th century and began to increase in the decades after the 1914 Balfour Declaration of a Jewish homeland in Palestine. The combination of messianic fervor and deteriorating economic conditions in Yemen drove thousands of Yemenis down to horrid conditions in Aden in the hopes of migrating to Palestine. In fact, nearly 18,000 Yemenite Jews made their way to Israel before 1949.

In the years following the 1939 British White Paper restriction on Jewish immigration to Palestine, the declining number of entry visas granted to Yemeni Jews created serious sanitary and logistic concerns for the steady flow of Jewish migrants to Aden. Transit camps around Aden were subject to squalor conditions and many Jews were sent back to Yemen. It was not until after the founding of the State of Israel in May 1948 that concrete plans were put into place for the 1949 Magic Carpet (also called On Eagles' Wings) airlift of over 50,000 Yemenite Jews on 450 flights.

To date, there are still several hundred Jews living in Yemen, remnants of what once was a thriving and widespread Jewish community. Many, in fact, practice the same crafts and artisanry of their ancestors, and all continue to safeguard the religious and cultural traditions of their Yemenite Jewish heritage.

BIBLIOGRAPHY

Ahroni, Reuben. *Yemenite Jewry: Origins, Culture, and Literature.* Bloomington, IN: Indiana University Press, 1986.

Brauer, Erich. "Agriculture and Manufacturing by the Jews of Yemen," in *Shvut Teiman,* edited by Aharon Tsaruk and Yishral Yishavhan. Tel Aviv: Matiman Latsavn, 1944.

Goitein, S. D. *From the Land of Sheba: Tales of the Jews of Yemen.* Translated by Christopher Fremantle. New York: Schocken Books, 1973.

Klorman, Bat-Zion Eraqi. *Yehude Teman: Historyah, Ḥevrah, Tarbut.* Tel Aviv: Universiṭah ha-petuḥah, 2004.

Orkaby, Asher. *Where Have All the Artisans Gone?: A Study of the Economic Impact of the Jewish Exodus from Yemen.* Beer-Sheva: Ben-Gurion University, 2009.

Parfitt, Tudor. *The Road to Redemption: The Jews of the Yemen 1900–1950.* New York: E. J. Brill, 1996.

Saadoun, Haim and Mekhon Ben-Tsevi le-ḥeker ḳehilot Yiśrael ba-Mizraḥ. *Teman.* Yerushalayim: Miśrad ha-ḥinukh, Minhal ḥevrah ve-noar:Makhon Ben-Tsevi le-ḥeker ḳehilot Yiśrael ba-Mizraḥ, 2002.

Wagner, Mark S. *Like Joseph in Beauty: Yemeni Vernacular Poetry and Arab-Jewish Symbiosis.* Boston: Brill, 2009.

SOCIAL GROUPS AND ETHNICITY

Steven C. Caton

Except in the large towns and cities of Yemen, and then only in the last couple of decades, it does not make much sense to speak of social classes per se, if by that we mean groups stratified according to wealth and education. It would be more accurate to speak of status groups that are tinged by ethnic differences.

Historically, there have been four such status groups: Arab tribes, saadah or descendants of the Prophet Muhammad, khaddaam (sing. khaadim) or servants thought to be of Arab ethnicity though low-born, and finally akhdam or servants thought to be of African descent and therefore non-Arab. The ethnicity of the saadah is ambiguous. As descendants of the Prophet, who was himself born into an Arab clan, the Bani Quraysh are Arab, though distinct from the "southern" tribes in Yemen. Others might claim that the Zaydi saadah are of "Persian" ethnicity, having come originally from lands across the Persian Gulf.

This traditional status hierarchy has given way since the 1962 Revolution, when the saadah lost much of their previous privilege and prominence that they enjoyed in the Imamate or Zaydi kingdom. The tribes have also undergone changes, though they remain a powerful—arguably the most powerful—social group in the country. The servant category, both Arab and non-Arab, has also undergone changes, though still socially and economically oppressed.

The Tribes

What Is a Tribe?

As the history of Yemen has repeatedly demonstrated, tribes have been central players—if not the central player—in the politics of the country, since at least the Sabaeans. It is now necessary to say more about their social organization, economy, and everyday ways of life. But what exactly do we mean by a "tribe"? Despite their limitations, definitions can be useful as a point of reference or a way into what is a more complicated question. But it has to be noted that any number of definitions have been offered for tribe.

One of the ways Arab historians as well as anthropologists have talked about tribes is in terms of their livelihoods: the basic divide being between tribes that are nomadic—known in Arabic as badu, Bedouin in English—who depend on camel or sheep pastoralism and those who are settled and are mainly agriculturalists. In Yemen, badu still exist in the eastern part of the country, in and around the city of Marib and the outskirts of the Empty Quarter, the vast and forbidding desert of the Arabian Peninsula, though they are small in number. Settled agriculturalists, the vast majority of the tribal population in Yemen, often do not have a distinct Arabic term attached to them (which is revealing of how tribes tend to be conflated with Bedouins). Badu are contrasted with *hadar* "settled" but with the latter meaning "civilized" and thus implying urban settlement, whereas we are talking for the most part about small-scale settlements in essentially rural settings.

Next to nothing is known about the Bedouin in Yemen because there has been no anthropologist who has done sustained fieldwork among them. There has been no dearth of such studies on similar groups elsewhere, and it is assumed, perhaps wrongly, that the Bedouin of Yemen are no different.

One anthropological definition of tribe is of a social group who conceptualize their identity through notions of genealogical descent from a common ancestor. Thus, the tribes of Yemen claim genealogical descent from an ancient ancestor known as Qahtan, whereas the tribes of northern Arabia acknowledge 'Adnan as their common progeny. They, in turn, are presumed to be descended from Noah, and Noah, of course, from the first man, Bani Adam. But these linkages, if they ever existed, are more often presumed than known beyond the level of say an extended family household (or *bayt* in Arabic), so that if one were to ask an ordinary tribesman who the common ancestor is of all the bayts that make up the clan or subclan, he is more often than not likely to shrug his shoulders and reply, "We know that we are related in blood." He may then point to a sheikh, the head of the tribe, or a learned person and add, "If you want to know the genealogical relationships going back to Adam, consult with him." Thus, this genealogical knowledge is not something vital to his daily everyday life, even if he holds it to be important in certain contexts. Furthermore, it has been suggested by anthropologists that the genealogical model of tribe, particularly in the Arab context where descent is reckoned through males, leaves out females and their importance to the social system that is at least twofold. Females represent marital (or affinal) ties that can be extremely important to the wealth of the lineage in terms of claims to various kinds of wealth, including access to land resources, once the woman inherits these from her father or father's father. Additionally, though it is true for Arab societies that property, status, and authority are passed down through the patrilineage, it has also been pointed out that the actual labor expended in making those resources useable or consumable is done inside the family household, where females (and children) are not only the major laborers but also the organizers of other people's labor, including the labor of males. Thus, a genealogical model to account for tribal groupings not only gets one only so far, but can actually obscure realities that are quite important to the livelihood and continued existence of the tribe.

Another anthropological definition of tribe, which often goes hand in hand with the former one, is a spatial or territorial one: A tribe is a social group that holds a territory in common and splits up to utilize different parts of this territory for purposes of pastoralism and agriculture. The reason that this definition hooks up with the genealogical one is that it is presumed that tribes split up to utilize their common territory according to genealogical units such as clans and lineages: that is, lineage A is supposed to utilize land x, lineage B land y, and lineage C land z, and so forth. Tribes fight wars over boundaries between their territories, and they sometimes have written deeds demarcating those territories, so that there is no question that ownership of land, fiercely contested and just as fiercely defended, is an important identity marker for them. But as with genealogical descent, the territorial organization of tribes is

Yemeni tribesmen attend a tribal meeting in Sana'a to resolve a local dispute in Arhab, 2012.
(Mohammed Huwais/AFP/GettyImages)

more often presumed than known by individual tribesmen and does not figure importantly in their everyday lives. Moreover, marital ties can be just as important for the
utilization of land as genealogical ones. Neither qualification, however, necessarily
weakens the claim that territory is still an important marker for tribal identity, but it
gets trickier when one realizes that a tribe does not necessarily occupy a *contiguous*
territory. That is, lands x, y, and z are not necessarily next to each other but may in
actuality be interspersed with the holdings of other groups, including other tribes,
in a checkerboard pattern, with the result that it is not always that easy or obvious
to draw a circle around a territory and state with certainty, this is the territory of
tribe A. That being the case, territory may be less critical for demarcating tribe from
tribe than lineage from lineage or even household from household. What this discussion suggests is that no one or even two criteria can necessarily denote or identify a
group or a person as tribal, it is more than likely going to be a combination of them
differing somewhat from region to region.

Before we leave the subject of tribe, it is important to note that the above definitions have come under attack, both within and without anthropology. It has been
argued that tribes have never really existed on the ground, so to speak, but are a
"construction" of an anthropology tied to (and compromised by) colonial powers
that needed to identify groups on the ground in order to govern them. "Tribes never
existed," some critics say, "they were an invention of colonial social science." Whatever plausibility there might be to this argument for tribes elsewhere in the world,
it is much harder to substantiate for Yemen or anywhere else in the Arabian

Peninsula for that matter. The Arabic word for tribe is qabilah, and Yemeni literary sources from earliest times (such as the 10th-century Yemeni historian al-Hamdani) refer to them and their power in unequivocal terms. This argument fails for another reason, which is that colonialism made little headway in the Peninsula. Except for the British in Aden and the Gulf, the Peninsula was hardly touched by European colonialism, making it still more difficult to claim that "tribes" are talked about there by Western social science in order for colonial powers to exert their control over them. It may certainly be true that anthropologists and political scientists examining tribal society have had their lenses clouded by Orientalist preconceptions of violence and lawlessness that have not helped our understanding of their nature and role in the Peninsula, but that is another matter. These people do not contest that tribes exist, only how they should be understood.

Another criticism leveled against the anthropological analysis of tribe is that too much has been made of the concept of honor as a guiding or motivating principle of everyday life. That may be so, but this is a far less damaging claim than that honor does not exist or is merely the figment of the anthropologist's fervid imagination. Context and balance are everything, and hopefully they have moderated what is said about tribes in this section.

Who Is a Tribesman?

There is also another way to approach the problem, which is not to ask, "What is a tribe?" but "Who is a tribesman?" (which requires one to think relationally in terms of categories of persons rather than groups). Of course, one answer is for a tribesman to say, "I belong to such-and-such a tribe," and we are back to square one. But if we respond to this by saying, "Yes, I know that, but suppose I want to raise my son or daughter to be a tribesman, what would the little boy or girl have to know?" (This is an actual question the author asked in the field while wrestling with the problem of defining a tribal identity from the perspective of the tribesman.)

As might be expected, knowledge of some genealogical reckoning and tribal territory was expected, but it came as a surprise to find out that they were not foregrounded in the answer. Probably, more important was piety, which came as an even greater surprise, because it is often assumed (mainly by nontribesmen, of course) that tribal peoples are not particularly pious (this is the specialty of the saadah, or descendants of the Prophet Muhammad), or if they are religious, that theirs is presumably a misguided religiosity requiring reeducation and reform.

Next to piety, it was thought important to teach the child how to use a gun properly in case the family or the tribe came under attack, and that meant teaching girls as well (there are many stories of women who turned out to be excellent shots in times of war). This teaching falls in line with some of our own expectations (bordering on stereotypes) of tribesmen, which is that they are prone to conflict and lawlessness and therefore quick to use arms. However, that the gun (and the dagger, jambiyya) is ubiquitous in tribal life does not mean that it is also always used (context is everything here), just as the fact that armed violence exists does not mean that it is the first or preferred means by which tribesmen settle disputes. How to understand tribal violence and how to understand the legal processes through which conflicts are resolved are explained later in this section.

Another surprise was to learn that the ability to compose poetry on the social occasions in which it is required is also what I would have to teach my child, male or female. In fact, this was more than a matter of etiquette, it was a matter of being able to defend oneself and one's tribe when either was under attack, because aggression can come in the form of guns as well as words. Thus, if a tribe accuses another tribe of wrongdoing and hurls its accusations in rhymed and metered verse, the tribe so attacked must be able to defend itself in the same kind of poetry or lose moral ground to the adversary. The same sort of jousting occurs on an interpersonal level, where individuals tease each other in poetic duels. Where tribes accuse each other, it may well be that the defense is best left to reputable poets, but in the case of the interpersonal agon, it is clear that anyone may be vulnerable to attack and has to know how to defend himself or herself. No wonder then that this art is something every child is expected to cultivate.

How to dance is also a mark of a tribesman. Some ethnic groups do not allow dancing (e.g., the saadah), whereas others who allow dancing (the traditional servant group known as the akhdam) do so in an entirely different way, one that tribesmen do not necessarily approve of or would ever dream of emulating. There is less clear justification for knowing the art of dancing, or at least the author was unable to elicit one other than it was something tribesmen "ought" to know how to do, than poetry. That is, one is expected to dance on occasions like weddings and to do so well, and if one sits by the sidelines like some forlorn wallflower, one is apt to lose standing or to be thought less well of.

No doubt other traits might be elicited for the tribal person, such as *'urf* (knowledge of tribal law), though like genealogical descent and territorial demarcations, this is thought to be the preserve of specialists rather than everyday "lay" people. The point or goal is not to come up with a definite or exhaustive list. The point, rather, is to suggest that tribal identity (like any other for that matter) is a question not only of where one is "positioned" within a particular system (in the tribal case, this would be genealogical as well as territorial) but also of how one performs or enacts various practices (religious, martial, and artistic) before others who are discriminating and severe judges.

It is important to understand that these traits are not arbitrary or ad hoc but are connected to an important cultural concept in tribal life, *sharaf* (honor). Central though this concept might be, it is not easy to define. It might be said to be a "dignity" that an individual or a group possesses, partly on the basis of their acquired identity (descent and wealth) and partly on what they have achieved in life through outstanding deeds of one sort or another. It is possible to lose sharaf through the insults and assaults of others, as well as one's own failings or missteps, and that is why it can never be taken for granted but must be achieved. That is why the arts of self-defense, both martial and rhetorical, are emphasized in tribal identity. To be a great marksman means not only that one can defend the tribe's honor in time of attack, but it is also symbolic of one's personal honor or dignity. To be a great poet not only means one can counter the poetic challenge to one's tribe or to one's person, but also means one has achieved greater honor.

Tribal Confederations

Since Sabaean times, tribes have existed in confederations. Historically, there have been four major confederations, including one in the Tihama, but the latter has lost all importance. Today, there are two major confederations: the Hashid roughly in the area to the north and west of the capital, which is the most powerful, and the Bakil roughly to the east and south of the capital.

What does it mean for a tribe to be part of a confederation? It can call on other tribes with which it is affiliated for support in times of need or crisis. Should their tribe be attacked, they can call on another tribe with which they claim genealogical connection for defense. And if the conflict spreads, they can call on still more tribes at higher and higher levels of the confederation for aid.

The issue is not only one of "mutual aggression pacts" (which is the way this model is usually portrayed) but also of "mutual mediation pacts" where high-level sheikhs who have authority over different levels of tribes within the confederation can adjudicate disputes peacefully. For example, should a tribe submit to adjudication by low-level confederation sheikhs but then disagree with the outcome, it can appeal for a hearing to sheikhs at the next higher level of the system and hope for a better outcome. Of course, as in the case of mobilizing more and more people for armed violence by going higher and higher in the confederation that might lead to conflict escalation or spread, the stakes can also become greater in dispute mediations if

---

SEGMENTARY LINEAGE SYSTEM

This is a model developed by anthropologists to describe the social organization of tribes. Above the level of the individual household, tribes will be organized in larger units by lineage descent (i.e., descent from a common male ancestor). These lineage units are differentiated from others, themselves united by common descent from their own ancestor. For various purposes, these lineages may unite into larger segments to form clans, again according to descent, and clans might unite to form a tribe, and so forth, all the way up to tribal confederations that can get to be quite large. This method of "fusion" is counteracted by "fission," where larger units divide into smaller ones (e.g., if tribes need to split up into clans and clans into individual lineages, so that groups can take advantage of dispersed pasturage for their herds). This is an abstract model, and no tribe in reality unites and divides up and down levels of social organization in quite such a clear-cut or mechanical fashion. Nevertheless, the model has been useful in explaining how order exists in societies that may seem "chaotic" or even "lawless" in the absence of a central state.

agreement is not reached. That is, the moral weight and authority of the highest-level sheikhs are such that it is difficult for the recalcitrant party in the dispute to resist their legal decision without alienating them in addition to their enemies. In turn, the honor of the tribe refusing to cooperate is besmirched if the consensus of public opinion is that it ought to comply with the verdict. Usually, these pressures are enough to get the tribe to agree to a peaceful and legally binding settlement.

Tribal Dispute Mediation

It is often assumed that Yemeni tribes, in the absence of a strong state to govern their affairs, will resort to arms in the first instance of conflict to resolve their differences. If that were the case, conflicts would be settled by armed force, and the militarily stronger would be the victor or winner, a situation that would lead to widespread oppression or even chaos. That outcome is rarely the case, however. Why? For one thing, there is the honor code that limits this kind of aggression. For if it does occur, it should do so between power equals, otherwise the aggressor is viewed as a bully. A bully ought not to be tolerated, because he threatens to take away the socially valued autonomy of persons or groups. (Coercion does occur, but in certain contexts only.) But aside from the honor code, what is not sufficiently appreciated by policy people as curtailing violence is the intricate system of ritual and law that has existed in tribal Yemen since time immemorial to handle conflicts.

It is important to understand how deeply embedded in everyday life these conflict–resolution mechanisms are. There is an everyday ritual or social routine called the *da'wah w-ijabah* (challenge-and-response), which is performed to address differences or grievances, large and small, that come up all the time in daily life. Suppose a tribesman believes that someone owes him money. He might approach that person and say, "I challenge you!" meaning they have a problem and need to talk about it. The person so addressed replies, "And I am respectful," meaning that he agrees to submit their dispute to mediation. They may now remove their daggers or jambiyyas from their scabbards, not to lunge at each other in an act of violence but rather the reverse, to signal that the possibility of violence has been postponed by handing them over to a third party. In effect, a truce has been guaranteed by this largely symbolic handing over of personal weapons. The impromptu mediator is often no more than an innocent bystander, but he is morally bound to accept the role impressed upon him. It would be shameful for him to try to excuse himself by saying, "I can't, I am on my way to work," or "But my wife is expecting me at home any moment now!" Why would the disputants submit their conflict for arbitration to such a person? Because it is assumed that every normal tribesman knows enough about tribal law to be able to adjudicate relatively simple disputes fairly and wisely. Such competence is part of what it means to be a tribesman just as shooting a gun, poetry, and dancing are. Having submitted the outcome of the conflict to his decision, the disputants are honor-bound to accept his verdict, unless they have reason to believe that he is biased or is not knowledgeable about legal principles or reasoning. Were they not to, they risk insulting the mediator and having his wrath descend upon them. What is more, the case is usually heard not just by the mediator but also by a crowd of bystanders, curious to know what has happened and eager to offer their two cents' worth regarding the case. The mediator takes in their palaver, evaluates their opinions, and arrives at a decision that inevitably reflects some of their input. In other words, his verdict will reflect something of a social consensus, which makes it even more difficult for the disputants to refuse, for in doing so they risk alienating not only the mediator but also the wider public.

The point of this example, in which disputes are submitted to the court of public opinion, is to show that "being law-abiding" is engrained in everyday behavior and not something alien to a tribal person, and that to be such a person means not only to submit to arbitration but also to be an arbitrator for the sake of maintaining the peace. Far from tribesmen being "lawless" or willful individuals bent on seeking their own ends regardless of the cost even if that means resorting to violent means, we find that they want to adjudicate their differences by a legal or arbitrational process.

The above example of a dispute is not very serious where society as a whole is concerned, but what happens when the boundaries of a tribal territory have been encroached upon (e.g., a piece of land is claimed by one tribe that another says it owns) or sheep have been stolen or women have been abducted or someone has been killed?

The same ritual occurs as the one described above, except that instead of submitting the arbitration to an ordinary citizen, the case now goes to the tribal sheikh or sheikhs and a more formal legal procedure is put in place. Guarantees are sought in accordance with the nature or magnitude of the crime. (Sometimes, it is not enough for the accused to put down a cache of weapons but also hostages). Witnesses may be called. Oaths are taken. Deeds or other documents are consulted. And eventually, the facts of the case will be ascertained and a judgment of guilt rendered. Before the mediators decide what the punishment should be, they consult the tribal code 'urf. In the past, this set of rules was memorized by a specialist who would be able to tell what the exact penalty was for the particular crime, but in recent times, these have been written down and printed, and one can now buy volumes of tribal law for different tribes and districts in bookstores. There appear to be slight differences in these codes even though the basic principles or reasoning behind them are the same.

We hear so much about the violence of tribal peoples (and not just in Yemen) that this picture of conflict arbitration according to legal principles might arouse skepticism. One might ask, "Does violence, then, not play a part in Yemeni tribal society? Why would Yemeni tribesmen wear jambiyyas and carry guns if they did not fear being violently attacked?"

To be sure, violence does enter into the picture of tribal life and it can become a scourge to society as in the case of feud, but it is important to understand its different cultural forms and the contexts in which they occur, as well as the fact—and this is perhaps most important—that violence works hand in hand with arbitration to settle conflict and is not necessarily at odds with it, something harder perhaps for us to comprehend.

One cultural form of tribal violence is as a staging or theater of violence, which is more of a communicative event than it is an exercise of brute force. This is where the plaintiff in the case threatens violence or commits it in such a way as to signal

Jambiyya. (Tim Glaveli Stockphoto.com)

JAMBIYYA

Jambiyya is the name for the curved dagger worn at the waist by Yemeni tribesmen. While it is quite sharp, it has mainly a symbolic significance, a fact that is often misunderstood or ignored by superficial observers of the Yemeni scene. In its most general sense, it stands for the fact that the wearer is of a particular honor group and that he has the right to bear weapons. It is employed in conflicts to signal a problem that requires arbitration and then serves as a token or guarantee of a truce. Conversely, a sheikh might ceremonially break his jambiyya over his knee to indicate that a breach is so serious as to be beyond repair. The jambiyya is also drawn for dramatic purposes in ceremonial dances. It can vary enormously in value, depending on the kind of steel from which the blade is forged, the kind of material from which the handle is fashioned (traditionally, gazelle horn was preferred until the animal became extinct), and the workmanship of the scabbard. The more expensive the material and skilled or elaborate the craftsmanship of the jambiyya, the higher status or power of its owner.

that more is to come, unless the defendant acknowledges that there is a problem that needs to be addressed and submits to arbitration. The author has seen this in a case of tribal abduction where the father of one of the abductees surrounded the village of the abductor, set up marksmen on the mountaintops, and threatened to fire upon the denizens unless admission of wrong was acknowledged. Indeed, shooting did take place, but according even to those fired upon, the plaintiff's tribe was not trying to shoot to kill but at the most frighten them, or as one of them said, "It's a game." Before this explanation, it seemed anything but a game to the author, and he realized that perhaps other witnesses before him of this kind of violence have also mistaken it for being more coercive or at least mortal than it is intended to be. Almost immediately after this show of force and threat, tribal sheikhs came to the village to arrange a truce and begin the arbitration process.

In many cases, the violence ends here, once the parties agree to settle their differences by tribal law and a just settlement is arrived at. In other cases, however, the dispute might become protracted, largely because one of the parties has not agreed to the settlement and will withdraw from the truce, resuming a state of hostilities. This is where violence can become ambiguous, either continuing to be more or less symbolic or tipping into something more coercive and dangerous, a violence intended to force the issue by use of arms. The stakes become higher for the mediating sheikhs too, whose verdicts have been steadfastly refused by the recalcitrant party or parties, and they might now threaten or actually use violence against the latter in order to bring them to heal within the tribal order of law. In other words, they perform a kind of policing function. Thus, it is important to understand that violence and mediation work in tandem to arrive at a *legal* resolution of conflict.

No system is perfect, of course, and the tribal legal system is as susceptible to failure as any other (though the author would argue not more so). The feud is one such example. According to tribal law, a crime such as murder can be redressed in two ways: either by killing the perpetrator after his guilt has been determined or by the perpetrator and his tribe paying blood money. In the eyes of tribal law, the tribe must take responsibility for the actions of one of its members, and so if the perpetrator is not caught to face his punishment, another member of the tribe might be killed in his place. If this happens, and sometimes even when the perpetrator himself is killed, a feud might persist leading to more deaths over time and a state of generalized violence of tribe against tribe. In recent times, this has been acknowledged not only by the critics of the tribes but by many of the tribal sheikhs as well, leading to movements of reform of one sort of another, such as the banning of guns or other assault weapons. But the fact is that historically, the incidents of feud wax and wane, with some tribal areas afflicted by it more than others, and it is not clear what factors, aside from cultural ones, contribute to them. Might it be that feud becomes a pretext under which to act aggressively against another tribe in order to usurp its land, water, or other resources? Might it be that feud is a pretext for largely political dynamics having to do with competition between tribes in a particular region? Unless these causes are not addressed, violence will not go away, whether it is in the guise of feud or some other form.

Before we leave the topic of tribal violence, it is necessary to say something about the relationship of the tribes and state authority in Yemen. The "fact" that tribes are violent (a claim we have sought to contextualize and make more nuanced) is asserted, not just by Orientalist scholars but also by nontribal groups within Yemeni society itself, as the reason that a state is needed to intervene to keep the peace or prevent chaos. There is some truth to this, in the sense that historically, the Muslim state in the form of the Zaydi Imamate sent its representatives, the saadah, to tribal hinterlands where they established settlements known as *hijrahs* (or *hawtahs* in southern Yemen) in which violence was off-limits. Often these settlements were established at tribal boundaries, a potential source of disagreement and conflict. Tribesmen could go there to trade goods or listen to the Friday sermon or have their divorce and other family issues settled according to Sharia law without fear of retaliation because of feud. In exchange for these goods and services, the tribes swore fealty to the hijrah and indirectly to the Imamate. In the author's experience, in one famous hijrah, the saadah were constantly warning him about the supposed lawlessness of the tribes and the chaos that pervades among them, even though they were often consulted in tribal disputes and could see for themselves the mechanisms in place to deal with them, but it was not in their political interests to acknowledge it. One of their ideological justifications for being in the midst of the tribes, for in effect being the long arm of the state in their midst, was that they were the peace-bringers.

Does the state necessarily work to preserve law and order? Perhaps, not surprisingly, the state turns out to have been, and continues to be, as much the problem behind tribal violence as it is the presumed solution for it. Given the power of the tribes in Yemen, the state, in its efforts to extend its hegemony over the tribes, seeks ways to weaken them: one of which is to incite divisions among them, some of which lead to armed conflict. The former president of Yemen, Ali Abdullah Saleh, was often accused of playing this kind of game of rule by sowing the seeds of division among his opponents, though he was only following the historical example of the imams. As has already been pointed out, it is difficult to know what the causes of tribal violence are and how much of it to attribute to the state's machinations; besides which such an explanation turns the tribal sheikhs into incredible dupes and puppets, which is hard to believe.

The modern Yemeni state has resorted to other, more reliable ways to bring the tribes to heal, and that is through a process of incorporation into its central institutions, ranging from the parliament to the army. Two thirds of the parliament is composed of elected tribal sheikhs; almost the entire army is composed of tribesmen. And the economic sector is also marked by tribal entrepreneurs. Of course, this incorporation can be a two-edged sword. For the question is, "Whether institutions dominated by tribal elements can think and act other than in the tribal interest?" And the answer to this would seem to depend in part on whether tribes are changing in their outlook on the world, from a parochial to a national one, and even beyond a national to a transnational perspective. That that change is beginning to happen is argued below.

The Role and Power of Tribal Sheikhs

The question of tribe–state relations also brings up the role and power of sheikhs in tribal society. The power of tribal sheikhs in Yemen differs from that of their counterparts in Afghanistan or Pakistan, where it is not an exaggeration to speak of warlords with almost autocratic authority over their followers. In Yemen, by contrast, sheikhs are voted into office by the elders of the communities they serve (perhaps a dozen or so villages that comprise a fraction of the tribe), though it is true that a son often succeeds his father in the post, if he is deemed qualified. The sheikh has to make decisions through consultation with elders and others of influence, decisions that represent a consensus of opinion if there is one, and rarely independently or against the majority view of his constituents. Were he to do so, objections would be raised; and were he to ignore those, he could face censure and worse (e.g., his followers might depose or desert him). Among the sheikh's duties are to listen to and adjudicate disputes, to lead male tribal fighters in time of war, and to act as a liaison between his constituents and the leaders in the next higher levels of the tribal confederacy, not to mention also representatives of the state or foreign development organizations that might want to work in the area under the sheikh's jurisdiction. In exchange for these services, the sheikh receives a salary of sorts, money, or the equivalent thereof in agricultural goods from his constituents, out of which he is also expected to pay the expenses of hosting people at important political functions and high-profile visitors.

This picture of the sheikh as a "first among equals" might be called into question by changes in Yemeni politics over the last two decades or more. There are some sheikhs who have grown wealthy and politically prominent on the national political scene like Abdullah Hussein al-Ahmar (1933–2007)—the former head sheikh (sheikh of sheikhs) of the Hashid Confederation and leader of the conservative Islah political party—and his sons Ahmed and Hamid. Though their position in the tribal

---

SHEIKH

Sheikh is a term that can be used for both an individual with religious authority as well as a tribal leader. In some Muslim countries, it is used almost exclusively for one or the other. In the Sudan, for example, it is almost always in reference to a religious authority, whereas in Yemen, it is almost always in reference to a tribal one. In the latter as well, the term sheikh of sheikhs can be used to designate a superordinate leader in the tribal system, one who has authority at, say, the confederation level. Occasionally, women may rise to such prominence and influence that they will be called sheikhah (ah being the feminine form), a term of extreme respect if not actual power. To designate a religious authority, the more common term in Yemen is sayyid (if he is in fact a descendant of the Prophet Muhammad), 'alim (scholar), or Imam.

system allowed them access to power and resources from which they benefited greatly, these sheikhs also dispensed much of their gains back to their tribal supporters, in part because this is what sheikhs are expected to do and also because they want to retain the loyalty of their supporters. The other change has to do with the Yemeni state under the former presidency of Ali Abdullah Saleh that tried to bolster the power of certain sheikhs and make them subordinate to central authority as a way of creating a more top-down form of government, but it is questionable whether this strategy has had anything more than limited success. The notion that tribal sheikhs have followers in their pockets, so to speak, and can deliver their votes or their support is delusional, as is the idea that all one needs to do is bribe the "key" sheikh in order to get things done or to guarantee cooperation. Tribal sheikhs cannot force their followers to go along with policies they fundamentally dislike or disagree with.

Given that sheikhs have to lead by persuasion not coercion, it is not surprising to find eloquence and a way with words to be a highly prized leadership attribute. This includes the ability to listen deeply to all sides in a dispute, to extract what would appear to be the consensus of opinions on any particular issue, and to publicly proclaim decisions or judgments in a clear and forceful manner. One can see examples of this kind of eloquence in the subsection "Tribal Oral Poetry" in Chapter 6.

The Saadah

A historically important social status group is the saadah (sing. sayyid), descendants of the Prophet Muhammad. In other countries, the descendants of the Prophet are known as Hashemis (e.g., in Jordan) or *ashraf/shurafa* (sing. *sharif*), and in eastern Yemen, near the city of Marib, one comes across persons who call themselves by that name, explaining that they are descendants from Hasan rather than Hussein in the Alawite line. According to historical sources, they came to Yemen probably no earlier than the ninth century, emigrating from Sunni-dominated lands where as Shia they felt they could no longer practice their religion according to their own lights, and some of them ended up in southwestern Arabia, sometimes at the behest of warring tribes seeking their help in resolving their disputes.

They settled in villages called in northern upland Yemen hijrahs, protected enclaves or sanctuaries in the midst of tribal territory. It was from the ranks of the saadah, or at least of the most learned and accomplished of them, that the ruler of Yemen or Imam was chosen by, as it were, an electoral college of like-status scholars, jurists, and other notables. In other words, within the territories controlled by the Zaydi state, the saadah were the ruling elite.

Because their status was linked to their descent from the Prophet, it is not surprising that genealogies were important, even primary, to the saadah's sense of themselves. It is important to understand that we are not talking about genealogical relations strictly in biological terms or an idiom of blood. True, the reproductive sense of the relation is there—indicated, for example, by such constructions as "so-and-so, son of so-and-so" going all the way back to the Prophet—but lines of descent are traced

HIJRAH

Hijrah in Classical Arabic means migration and refers to the migration of the Prophet Muhammad from Mecca to Medina, an event commemorated by having the Muslim calendar begin at that date (which is why that calendar is called "Hijri" after that year). In northern Yemen, it also means sanctuary or protected place. (In southern Yemen, such enclaves are called hawtahs.) They are not as common nowadays as they were in the past. The saadah inhabitants of these villages were granted protection (*tahjir*), in part because of their status as descendants of the Prophet and also because of their learning and extreme piety. The village's protection was often legalized in a signed document made public in tribal gathering places such as the weekly markets. Because armed aggression within its precincts was strictly forbidden, feuding tribesmen could congregate in it without fear of attack in order to trade in the market or listen to the Friday mosque sermon or seek adjudication of family issues in accordance with Sharia law. Many hijrahs were also centers of religious learning, the most reputable among them attracting students from all over the country.

through males. Even more important is the fact that what flows "through the blood" is a *moral* identity and authority, typified in the character and deeds of the house's apical or founding ancestor, and whose the descendents are obliged to emulate and sustain or even improve upon. These genealogies were important not only for their own identity but also to whom they were connected to in time (history) and space (dispersion through migration). To this day, it is not uncommon to find genealogical trees on display in certain saadah homes, showing their link not only to the Prophet through Ali and Fatima but also to other important figures either in the history of Islam or Yemen. Diasporic or overseas saadah—who left Yemen centuries ago to form successful business enterprises and sometimes also political careers in India, Malaysia, or Indonesia—know their genealogical links to ancestors in Yemen, a land to which they feel connected and visit from time to time. And associated with particular individuals in the genealogical tree may be stories about their personalities and deeds, scholarly or literary works they produced, or various memorabilia such as swords, pens, sayings, and photographs chronicling their histories. Future generations learn about their ancestors through such records and artifacts.

Within this genealogical framework subbranches of saadah will coalesce under a "great" ancestor to form a bayt (house), often with the name of that ancestor attached to it (though other designations are possible such as the hijrah or region in which the house originated). Some of these "houses," which are like vast extended families, are renowned and quite powerful, while others are far less socially consequential. Women maintain their identity and connection with their natal house even when their children are absorbed into their husband's house. Though everyone is equally related to everyone else according to genealogical reckoning, there are differences between branches based on education, wealth, political influence, and profession. Just as in a tribe one is morally obliged to uphold the honor of the larger collective, so in the sayyid house is one supposed to be mindful of its reputation and standing and do nothing to tarnish or diminish it. But unlike the tribe, these houses do not have heads like sheikhs who oversee the house's affairs, at least not in any formal sense. Houses do not own property in common (individuals or families own property), nor do they occupy a common territory, and there are few, if any, ritual or other activities that they perform together. For example, there is no veneration of ancestors (for obvious religious reasons in Zaydi Islam, though in Hadhramawt Sufi pilgrimages to the tombs of sayyid scholars is common and widespread). In other words, they are not quite a "corporation" in the way that kinship units such as tribes have been described.

As for marriage, sayyid women, with few exceptions (e.g., when no sayyid man of eligible age was available), were expected to marry other sayyid men, even though by law they were also allowed to marry notables of equivalent rank; sayyid men on the other hand could either marry within their ranks or below, for the reason that in a partilineal system the offspring would be subsumed into the male line or house. According to the same logic, the children of a sayyid woman to a non-sayyid man would not be considered descendants of the Prophet and therefore would lose the status honor they would have acquired if their mother had married a sayyid man. Yet, while sayyid men may marry "beneath" their position, it is believed that the mother is responsible for teaching children good behavior commensurate with their status in society, and therefore a sayyid mother would be preferable. Marriages were usually arranged by the couple's parents, though in all likelihood the pair knew each other as children playing in the streets and visiting each other's households and were not total strangers. It is important to bear in mind that a sayyid woman's identity and status were determined by her descent (her relations to her natal house) much more, if at all, than by marriage into a particular house, however renowned the latter might be.

Just as with men, sayyid women were expected to demonstrate their nobility through piety as well as proper comportment, such as modesty in public. Many sayyid women were educated to read and write and learned parts of the Qur'an by heart, and the cleverer or more intellectually inclined among them were even encouraged to pursue religious studies in a serious way. As for comportment, it was beneath them to work in the fields, though domestic chores around the house were perfectly acceptable. They had to be especially careful to avoid being heard or seen in public, let alone having contact with strange men, sayyid or not, and to avoid certain kinds of spaces such as the market place. Indeed, high-born sayyid women were more or less housebound, being visited by friends or neighbors rather than stepping out of the house themselves. If they did step outdoors, they would be expected to wear the female garment or *sharshaf* that covered their heads and faces, except the eyes, and their entire bodies, including the arms. Lower-born sayyid women would cover themselves with a large rectangular tie-dyed sheet called the *sitara*. To act indiscriminately or wantonly by violating these everyday norms of behavior would besmirch the honor of these women's houses.

The lives of traditional male (and some female) saadah before the revolution revolved around their education, and not only for the reason that they were morally bound to teach the tenets of Islam and to embody them in their own words and deeds, but also because rule or government was thought to be based on religious knowledge. Many of the great sayyid houses have libraries with hundreds of manuscripts, some of very great age, on different subjects that were consulted by accomplished and novice scholars alike. It would be hard to imagine a family in the United States or Europe whose reputation was based on its library and the learning attendant upon it. Indeed, what has been sometimes called a "manuscript culture" in the academic literature is a distinctive feature of Yemen. Boys were taught by their fathers at an early age to read and write, and then attended a religious school where they learned to recite the Qur'an by heart. At the same time that they became expert in the correct oral transmission of the text, they began their study of grammar, prosody, and rhetoric. Why prosody? Because many scientific and philosophical treatises were written in a rhymed prose (*saj'*), and also because political challenges were often cast in verse to which the individual so addressed would have to reply in kind. Why eloquence? Because rule was not ultimately a matter of coercion or force, but one of persuasion. Though a governor or an Imam might be stern and use force to punish miscreants or to defend the community, his decrees and decisions had ultimately to be based in consensus and arrived at through reason and persuasion, if they were to be considered legitimate and just. The most talented students would go on to study *'ilm* (knowledge such as science, mathematics, history, and literature) and fiqh (jurisprudence), usually with a private tutor or with a celebrated scholar or jurist. They might go on to have distinguished careers as judges, theologians, and scholars.

Aside from his descent from the Prophet and a reputation for religious knowledge, a sayyid acquired his identity through acts of piety and devotion to Allah that put into practice the morality gleaned from his studies. This went beyond performing the five "pillars" of Islam (saying the shahadah or profession of faith, daily prayer, zakat or alms, fasting during the month of Ramadan, and performing the hajj) by steeping himself as much as possible in Islamic theology and history, reciting the Qur'an over and over again by heart, and saying the 99 names of Allah on the *misbahah* (prayer beads), not to mention ordinary or everyday acts of kindness, fairness, honesty, humility, and compassion. Dress was also considered important and marked a man as a sayyid. Fully decked out at a ceremonial such as a wedding or when appearing at the royal court, an adult sayyid would wear a gown, usually white, with wide sleeves tied behind the shoulders (and in cold weather, a long woolen cloak on top of that), a turban consisting of a pillbox hat with a white cloth wound around it called an *'imamah*, a dagger with an ornate silver scabbard, and sometimes a sword.

When the 1962 Revolution overthrew the millennium-old Imamate and instituted a republic in its place, the status of the saadah changed dramatically and irrevocably. The same thing happened to them in southern Yemen when the British Protectorate of Aden ended in 1967 and a Socialist republic was established in its stead with an ideology of egalitarianism that militated against elite-status differences such as the saadah represented. It is not surprising that the ruling royal house of northern Yemen, Bayt Hamid al-Din, was targeted for retribution, its considerable wealth and property confiscated and its members exiled (which was still less Draconian than the measures taken against Royalists in some Arab countries that underwent revolution). Other wealthy sayyid houses were subjected to similar treatment, and there was even talk of sending all the saadah into exile—on the grounds that they were historically "foreign" to Yemen, having migrated there because they had been unwanted in Persia. The republican ideology of egalitarianism that militated against notions of status hierarchy and the privileges that went with them deeply affected the saadah regardless of their connections with the ruling house. In the early revolutionary period, saadah were often treated with derision, their turbans— quintessential symbols of sayyid authority—knocked off their heads, and little boys calling them names or singing ditties ridiculing them. Partly as a result of this harassment and also because of modern tastes and fashions, sayyid men have adopted Western dress with pants and jackets or suits and ties. Even when lounging in casual wear, they will don a *thawb* or white robe that may have originated from Saudi Arabia and the Gulf but has come to signify a generic male dress in Yemen. The custom stipulating that sayyid women ought to marry sayyid men was challenged, though the Islamic principle of *kafa'ah* (equivalence), which entails an implicit notion of status differences, was still clung to. The saadah were marginalized economically as well, partly because of their own attitude that shunned certain forms of manual labor and trade as beneath their dignity or a distraction from their religious studies. (In Zaydi philosophy, it was believed that rulers should not become merchants because it might lead to a conflict of interest, where political power might be corrupted for economic gain.) However, after the revolution, the saadah began to enter into professions considered undesirable or unthinkable before, such as commerce and nonreligious sciences like engineering, medicine, business administration, computer sciences, and government service—with the less prosperous of them cultivating their own agricultural fields; engaging in manual crafts such carpentry, house construction, or embroidering dagger belts; and owning small shops in the souk. It is fair to say that a premium is still put by the saadah on education, though now it is less a route to power than to economic advancement. Nowadays, in fact, few saadah pursue a strictly or primarily religious course of studies, though religious learning and piety are still widely admired. And recently, surviving members of the Hamid al-Din family were allowed to return to Yemen with full immunity, and there has even been talk of returning their personal property to them that was confiscated during the revolution.

That said, the saadah almost always fall under suspicion as a kind of "fifth column" whenever Yemen comes under threat from a foreign and especially religiously conservative power such as Saudi Arabia or Iran, the presumption being that they still harbor a secret hope of restoring the Imamate in which they were dominant. And whether justified or not, they are also accused of harboring attitudes of exclusiveness or privilege because of their descent that get in their way of fully assimilating into a republican society.

The Judges (*Qudhaa'*)

In traditional Yemen, there was a group whose overall social standing was recognized as being quite high, a cadre of jurists (judges) who had no descent from the Prophet Muhammad but nonetheless were considered just below the saadah in status. They are to this day a professional group who have risen to their position of authority because of their training in Islamic law. Many have had careers in the Islamic courts.

Servant Groups

There are two distinct servant groups in Yemen: the khaddaam and the akhdam. These terms are derived from the same triliteral Arabic root kh-d-m, meaning "to serve." Akhdam refers to low-status servants believed to be of African origin, a judgment based on their skin color, whereas khaddaam are servants who are said to be indistinguishable in skin color from their tribal masters. The difference is based on implicit and culturally specific notions of race, hierarchy, and work. For instance, these groups are considered as lacking in honor or social distinction, yet they are not necessarily despised and they certainly possess certain rights such as protection from the tribes (much as the saadah demand protection from the tribes, even though they enjoy far more status and privilege than the servants). Though these groups held a subordinate position to tribesmen and saadah in pre-Republican days, they were not slaves. They were not owned by anyone but were free, being paid or compensated for their services (if perhaps poorly). By contrast, there was a category of slaves known as *'abid* in Arabic, though it is unclear how prevalent they were as a group before the revolution. Slavery was abolished in 1962, though there have been reports of human rights violations in the country from time to time. As with all the status categories in Yemen, that of the servants is changing rapidly, though what is described below is still the case in many parts of the country.

CASTE, CLASS, AND STATUS GROUP

Social scientists debate whether to call the khaddaam or the akhdam a caste, a class, or a status group. While it is true that there are social compunctions on the part of some people about touching them, especially the akhdam, these are not legitimated or prescribed by religion as is the case for the "untouchables" in Hinduism. Islam recognizes the category of slavery, and though akhdam may have originated as slaves in society, they have no religious justification per se and are free according to the Yemeni constitution. Class, on the other hand, has a politico-economic valence within a capitalist system, and though akhdam are definitely constrained politically and economically, it does not help analytically to refer to them as a class. Status group, on the other hand, suggests hierarchical relations (as with caste and class) though one defined according to local concepts of honor or dignity, and it is as a status group that they are perhaps best defined.

Khaddaam

There is an origin story or myth associated with the khaddaam that goes something like this: In ancient times, when the tribes of Yemen were at war with each other, there were always some tribesmen who grew faint at heart and lost courage in battle, a blemish not only to the individual honor of those men but also to their tribe, and in punishment for their cowardice, they were stripped of their tribal descent and either forced to leave or submit to being the tribe's servants. Khaddaam families were not owned by anyone (they were not slaves or indentured servants), and they lived under the protection of a sheikh or other notable. They no longer had the right to bear arms (and some did not even wear the ceremonial dagger), as they now had a protected status. Indeed, for a tribesman to commit armed aggression against such a person was and continues to be considered a grave offense, punishable by tribal law. They no longer had the right to own property, and whatever they built in the way of shelter could always be taken away from them if the owner of the land on which the house was built decided to use it for something else. Nevertheless, they lived in the same villages as their tribal hosts and often as next-door neighbors, and thus were socially integrated into the fabric of the town. A tribesman could marry a khaddam woman, and many did, but hardly ever the other way around, as that would mean the tribal woman's children would take the lower status of her husband. In exchange for their services to the tribe, the khaddaam would receive a fraction of the annual agricultural harvest or payments of a more monetary kind for services rendered to specific individuals. In that way, they were like the Jews of Yemen, though of course Muslims and coreligionists of their tribal protectors.

Among the roles they performed were that of barber or hairdresser and village butcher (a skill that is transferable to village circumciser), ritually slaughtering bulls at important feasts and then cutting up the meat that is handed out to the various households as part of the host's "gift." This person is known as a *muzayyin* and, along with his wife, would act as a master of ceremonies—help families host guests at large gatherings such as weddings (she would tend to the needs of the female guests), help with the cooking and distribution of the food, make sure the sitting room was properly set up for the afternoon qat chew, see to it that the water pipe was functioning properly, and otherwise cater to the comforts of the guests, be it to fetch one man a new packet of cigarettes or another a thermos of freshwater. At some chews, he might even pass around an incense burner for each guest to inhale. During the groom's wedding procession, the muzayyin would lead the groom and his family and friends with vigorous drumming, which he would also do during the dance segments interspersed in the procession. A khaddaam with a fine voice and musical talent might become a *mulahhin,* a singer for the tribal poets, by setting their odes to music and singing them while accompanying himself on a kind of tambourine (without cymbals), a performance for which he would be remunerated by the poet in cash or something equivalent in value. Other khaddaam with strong voices and dramatic flare might also serve as *doshaan,* town crier and praise singer. In olden days, they would memorize proclamations and then publicly declaim them for all to hear, deliver messages from one village to another, or appear with a white flag to carry a message to the enemy (on the presumption that he would not be fired at because of his protected status). When a host had given a feast, the doshaan might appear chanting his praises or those of his guests from the rooftop, and would be reciprocated with food, money, or some trinket or other. So adroit is the doshaan with his words that he can turn praise into parody and the saying goes that "the only way to cut off his tongue is with a gift." In addition to these verbal and ceremonial tasks, khaddaam are also village blacksmiths and carpenters.

There are certain cultural notions underlying this classification of servants, besides that of honor above, that have to do with the nature of work and words. Tribesmen work in the fields, in construction, and in automobile transport, but other kinds of work such as what the servants do are considered beneath their dignity. Sometimes, the distinctions may be hard to define in concrete terms but are nonetheless real in cultural ones, such as the insistence on the part of tribesmen that the words of the praise singer are not poetry, merely doggerel, even though they may contain meter and rhyme, or that the mode of delivery is a "song" (with it being understood that only children, women, and doshaan sing); whereas the performance of poetry is a "chant" (performed only by males of the tribe). Being the issuer or source of a message is one thing, memorizing and delivering it as the dowashaan does carries far less symbolic weight. And servility is encoded not only in the kinds of work performed but also in everyday bodily comportment bordering on the obsequious.

But since the 1962 Revolution, with universal education and the opening of the professions to all kinds of people, the khaddaam have stopped doing work thought to be demeaning and have entered into all kinds of trades, resulting in the breakup though not complete disappearance of the old status categories. Many immigrated to Saudi Arabia and the Gulf countries in the 1960s and 1970s, during the height of the construction boom fueled by oil revenues, and came back with capital to invest in local businesses in which some flourished. The fact that they are phenotypically indistinguishable from tribesmen has also meant that they could blend in or "pass" as a fellow tribesman, if they had to. As a result of all of these changes and mixing, it is almost impossible to say how many people in Yemen would self-identify as khaddaam anymore.

Akhdam

There is an origin myth for the akhdam too, though it is different from that of the khaddaam. According to historical sources, the Abyssinian armies that invaded Yemen in the sixth century CE allied themselves with a slave revolt headed by Najah al-Habashi (Habashi being a term for the Habash or Ethiopians) that led to the foundation of a Najahi state in the central Tihama with its capital in Zabid. When the Abyssinians were defeated and driven out of the Peninsula, the slave state fell with them, and legend has it that the Najahis were condemned to live in the outskirts of the towns and cities and thereafter called akhdam (servants). Needless to say, perhaps, this historical explanation for their origins is not necessarily the same as that given by ordinary Yemenis who will simply say of them that they came from Ethiopia or have African origins. In all likelihood, they came into Yemen over successive centuries as a result of the widespread and lucrative Omani slave trade, though a slave owned by a master might have been better off than the akhdam as we know them today. They are legally free beings in Yemen, even though they have been an impoverished and socially marginalized group in the country for some time.

Population figures for the akhdam group vary between 200,000 and 1,000,000, and though many have immigrated to cities like Sana'a and Taiz in search of work, the densest concentrations of them are to be found in the Tahima, in the Hojariyyah area south of Taiz, and in parts of Hadhramawt. There they live on the outskirts of towns in cardboard hovels with tin roofs, though some who have been servants to the same family (sometimes over several generations) might live in their employer's home or family compound. Many akhdam are itinerants, roaming from town to town in search of work, which is why they squat in makeshift encampments on urban peripheries—often adjacent to refuse areas or sewerage drainage—returning to their home villages to participate in weddings or religious festivals. This would suggest that akhdam villages have their own social organization and no doubt their own leadership structure, but so little ethnographic work has been done on them or is readily accessible that this remains speculative at best. Like the khaddaam, they are not allowed to own property, which makes their arrangements to find shelter precarious. Squatter areas can and are routinely cleared at the order of the state. In nontribal rural areas, the akhdam are often engaged in low-level or marginal agricultural work, such as harvest threshing, and because the work is seasonal, they migrate for that reason as well. Much of the other work they do, however, carries far less dignity or economic worth in the eyes of many Yemenis. In fact, they do what others refuse to do, such as cleaning excrement out of household cesspools and sweeping the streets,

Akhdam woman and her children, Sana'a. (Yahya Arhab/epa/Corbis)

the latter remunerated by a mere pittance. Sometimes, not even this work is to be had and they are reduced to begging.

Men and women of this group need not dress or comport themselves in the same manner as others do, but then again they do not incur the steep symbolic costs to their identities that nonservant individuals suffer for similar behavior. Like the khaddaam who perform their subservience not just in the kinds of work they do but also in forms of daily interactions, the akhdam signal their abjection not only in their work and skin color but also in their everyday dress and comportment. For example, women are not required to cover their heads, let alone veil in public, and men may go around wearing little more than a loincloth in the hot and humid summer months when other males would be expected to keep their chests and legs covered. Women may interact freely with strange men, accosting them in public or haggling aggressively with them in the market—behavior that would cause other women to be embarrassed or lose honor. Such brazenness is "tolerated" because akhdam men and women are in a sense beyond the pale; that is, they exist outside the charmed circle of social honor and therefore have no honor to uphold or protect.

Yemenis and foreigners alike, critical of the treatment of the akhdam in the country, point to racial and not merely social prejudice (as would be the case for the khaddaam) as one of the causes. For example, akhdam qualify for health services like other social groups and individuals in society, but they complain about their treatment at clinics and as a result would rather forego medical treatment except in emergencies or in the most dire cases. And some akhdam internalize the negative stereotypes about them by saying to themselves that an education is useless given an implicit color barrier in economic life. Why does one need to read and write if street cleaning is all one can hope to do?

On the other hand, there have been some efforts by the akhdam to organize themselves and mobilize for their rights, and to improve their lives with the assistance of nongovernment organizations and foreign-donor agencies. The latter have built simple one-story concrete housing clusters in Sana'a and Taiz, consisting of one bedroom leading off to the house entrance, with an adjacent bathroom and kitchen. The Yemeni government purportedly agreed to this not out of humanitarian concerns for the akhdam but in order to remove their slums from the capital where they had become an eyesore. These efforts are in any case largely symbolic, for they do not come close to meeting akhdam housing needs. Akhdam have begun to establish associations to help provide for their needs, such as the Sada Society (Sana'a) and Uqba bin Amer Society, and there has been a gradual increase in their participation in parliamentary elections, but this remains quite limited.

Lastly, it should be noted that Yemen has by now entered the transnational economy of domestic servants who come from Ethiopia, Somalia, the Philippines, and South Asia. Most are female, and most work in the household.

BIBLIOGRAPHY

Caton, Steven C. *"Peaks of Yemen I Summon": Poetry as Cultural Practice in a North Yemeni Tribe.* Berkeley, CA: University of California Press, 1900.

Caton, Steven C. *Yemen Chronicle: An Anthropology of War and Mediation.* New York: Hill & Wang, 2005.

De Regt, Marina. "Preferences and Prejudices: Employers' Views on Domestic Workers in the Republic of Yemen." *Signs* 34 no. 3 (Spring 2009): 559–81.

Dresch, Paul. *Tribes, Government, and History in Yemen.* Oxford: Clarendon Press, 1989.

Meneley, Anne. *Tournaments of Value: Sociability and Hierarchy in a Yemeni Town.* Toronto, ON: University of Toronto Press, 1996.

Vom Bruck, Gabriele. *Islam, Memory, and Morality in Yemen: Ruling Families in Transition.* New York: Palgrave Macmillan, 2005.

Walters, Delores M. "Invisible Survivors: Women and Diversity in the Transitional Economy of Yemen," in *Middle Eastern Women and the Invisible Economy,* edited by Richard A. Lobban, 74–97. Gainesville, FL: University Press of Florida, 1997.

Weir, Shelagh. *A Tribal Order: Politics and Law in the Mountains of Yemen.* Austin, TX: University of Texas Press, 2007.

MARRIAGE, FAMILY LIFE, AND WOMEN

Steven C. Caton

Marriage

It is difficult, if not impossible, for a couple to have a family outside of marriage, which next to the family must be one of the most complex institutions in Arab society. In Yemen, descent is patrilineal, and the "ideal" or preferred marriage partner is with the father's brother's daughter (or son) or *bint 'amm* (the so-called parallel cousin). This may be an actual cousin or a classificatory one, in the sense that she is still within the same patriline, or can trace her descent to the same ancestor as that of the boy. In some societies, the actual cousin is considered too close a kinship tie to permit marriage, and the question arises as to why it is not only permitted but even preferred in many Arab societies. Countless explanations have been given, including that wealth might be more readily retained within the household, if women are entitled to inherit from their families while at the same expected to live with their husbands. That is, if their husbands are their cousins, they will be of the same patriline and whatever wealth either inherits would stay within the line. But if wealth is what marriage is supposed to conserve or enhance through this practice, there are obviously times when it would be more advantageous to marry into a different patriline, and in fact, this kind of interlineal marriage, as it were, happens often enough. What kicks in as the principle regulating such marriages is called kafa'ah or social equivalence (see below). Marriage between close cousins can have medical problems for the offspring, as is well known, though it is expected that deleterious traits would die out over time, leaving a normally healthy population—unless a medically advanced lifestyle can keep people with such traits alive long enough to reproduce—and thus passing these traits back into the population. This is what is happening in the Gulf countries, for example, and now it is a question for the public health system to treat individuals with such ailments and provide them with a social support system to accommodate their infirmities—for example, accommodating people with blindness.

Usually, marriages between young men and women are arranged by their respective families. Though there is a cultural concept of passionate love, it is thought an unreliable basis on which to found a lasting and morally sound relationship between a man and a woman. More important are considerations of personality, presumed compatibility, and above all social status, for it is essential for the man and woman to be of equal or equivalent rank, otherwise it is feared there will be problems in the marriage. If, for example, the wife is socially superior, she might demand more in the way of gifts and favors commensurate with her status than her husband is willing or able to bestow; and if the husband is superior, he might in so many ways, great or small, demean her in public even if he does not intend to do so. And as might be imagined, the ramifications of these slights or ills go well beyond couple and spread to their respective families. It is often said that it is not just individuals who marry but also their families, and that it is to the latter's continuation and well-being that marriage is ultimately all about.

People marry young, sometimes as soon as the onset of adolescence. There have been infamous and shocking cases of "child brides" in Yemen married to much older men, though this practice is hardly common or culturally condoned. Often the young girls come from extremely poor families who can no longer support them; marrying them off to a man whose obligation it is now to take care of them is resorted to as a "solution." To put this practice in perspective, it might be useful to remember that poor families in Europe and the United States as late as the late 19th century used to send their underage daughters to work as domestic servants in wealthier households where their labor, if not their bodies, were exploited and sometimes abused. It is worth repeating that child marriage of this sort is not condoned in Yemen. Indeed, the family is honor-bound to protect its female dependents, not to expose them to dishonor in this way. But there are instances, again rare ones, in which girls and boys (both under 13 years of age) are married to each other, though they are not allowed to consummate the marriage until they are older. The reasoning behind this is that the couple are likely to marry anyway, perhaps on the grounds that they are cousins, and so why not allow the couple a period of adjustment, especially in the case of the girl who is entering into a new household and must learn its routine.

A young man and a young woman are legally married when they sign a contract to do so, which is then validated by a qadi or judge or some other religious authority. It is important to bear in mind that the girl cannot legally be forced to marry someone against her will (though in actual fact she may be coerced to do so against her will), and there have been any number of stories of young women who have refused their parents' choice of their mates. It is also important to know that the woman can insist on certain conditions being placed in the marriage contract, the violation of which constitute grounds for divorce. She may, for example, add a clause stipulating that she be allowed to finish her education (to whatever level she deems necessary), or that the husband may not take a second wife (even though he is legally allowed to do so, under certain conditions, within Islam), or that she be allowed to work outside the marriage household. Finally, it is important to realize that she has certain rights in a marriage she need not insist on in her contract because they come with the Islamic institution, among these being that whatever wealth she inherits is hers to keep (in other words does not automatically revert to her husband upon marriage), and to keep separate from the wealth of the rest of her husband's household. She has the right to expect adequate food and shelter and to be treated with dignity in her domestic relations. She has the right to sexual satisfaction from her husband, the lack of which also constitute grounds for divorce. Conversely, she has the duty of sexually satisfying her husband, of providing for his domestic welfare, and of raising his children (and they are very much "his" because of the patrilineal system of descent). Not living up to these duties constitute grounds for divorce on the part of the husband.

Perhaps, the most important conditions in the marriage contract pertain to what are called "payments" from the groom and his family to the bride and her family, an unfortunate term because it suggests a bride is "bought" in a pecuniary transaction when what is at stake has really to do with family honor. There are two such payments: the one to the bride's family is called *shart* (literally "condition," and arguably the condition or basis for the marriage itself) and the other to the bride is called *mahr* (which has only the specific meaning of a bridal payment). In economic terms (with the old-fashioned meaning of economic as in household economy rather than market commodities), the former acknowledges the fact that young girl's labor power or work is being alienated from her natal household to that of her husband's, and that her natal household should be compensated accordingly. But in theory, this labor power should have the same exchange value no matter the bride, when in fact the shart can vary enormously depending on the bride's family's social rank. This is more a symbolic than an economic value, strictly speaking. As for the mahr, it is a gift (or series of gifts) the groom makes to the bride, symbolizing his love and esteem for her. Jewelry and clothing are usually bestowed. Upon divorce, depending on who is considered at fault (and usually both share responsibility), these payments might be returned in whole or in part.

As in most societies, a wedding is not considered complete without a celebration of some sort or other, and Yemeni weddings are often lavish, colorful, and boisterous affairs that take place mainly in the summer months. They are one of the highlights of village and urban life. One knows a wedding is about to take place by strings of lightbulbs hanging across the street, marking the household of the groom. Men and women gather at separate celebrations: the men's taking place mainly outdoors in what is called a *zaffah* or procession, whereas the women's taking place indoors, including her own procession (she is accompanied by female relatives carrying her floral bouquet into the room in which she will receive guests and be entertained by them, until it is time for her to be taken to her husband). Though weddings differ from region to region (and from tribal to nontribal), there are, besides the procession, some commonalities: dancing (which is quite different in style for men and women), feasting, and often poetry composed especially for the occasion. Special religious hymns might also be chanted.

In addition to raising children and the relentless rounds of meals, house cleaning, and washing that maintaining a household entails, families are also expected to visit each other, a duty that falls especially on the women of the household. They are expected to visit their mothers and sisters as well as neighbors, and, of course, to reciprocate by hosting them in their households, an obligation that is not only time-consuming but also costly. A family's standing in the community is partly determined by the lavishness of its hospitality on such occasions, the cost of which is borne by the male heads but the labor for which falls on its female members and servants.

Though it is true that a Muslim male may divorce his wife by simply uttering the formula, "I divorce thee!" three times, divorce in fact is rarely a simple affair, because a marriage in the end is not solely about a man and a woman but the families their marriage unites as well. There usually is more at stake in a divorce than the couple's own interests, and so they are encouraged by their respective families to work things out. Still, that may not be possible in the end, at which point divorce will be in the offing. A woman has the right to sue for divorce, but this usually requires a male guardian or lawyer to represent her in court, and she may not have the financial means to hire the latter. Some of the grounds for divorce have already been mentioned, to which may be added barrenness, if it can be determined that member of the pair is unable to produce children. Upon divorce, the father usually has custody of the children, largely because it is through his patriline that they inherit and gain their social standing. The mother has visiting rights. If the children are very young, they may stay with her until they are deemed old enough to join their father's household. In principle, the divorced woman returns to her own natal household, whose male heads are responsible for her care and well-being. No shame necessarily falls upon a woman when she is divorced, and many divorced women remarry with the help of their families as long as they wait the requisite number of months after their divorce—the period allotted to determine whether she is pregnant with child in her previous marriage (in which case, her child may be claimed by her husband's family).

The Family Household

Family may well be the most important and treasured social unit in Yemen, more important than lineage or tribe, because obviously not all families identify as tribal or even trace descent back several generations to a foundational "ancestor." But one is referring here to much more than a "biological family," in the sense of a husband and wife and their immediate offspring; household (bayt in Arabic) may be the more precise term, in the sense of a central patriarch with his descendants and their dependents (through descent and marriage) who still live with him under one roof.

The household is the basis not only of an individual's affective and material sustenance but also of his or her social prestige and authority. This is, more or less, in keeping with Western ideals of family life; that they are units in which to bring up and educate children to assume responsible and effective roles as adults, as well as to help them out, if necessary, financially by getting them "started in life" (a college education, a car, a mortgage on a house, etc.). Perhaps, it is less the case now than in years previous that an individual's family "name" was also a source of pride or chagrin, because families do not stay put and are thus do not acquire reputations (except the wealthiest and most famous such as the Rockefellers). In Yemen, however, and in most other traditional societies, families are connected to specific households that, in turn, are invested in real estate or local commercial enterprises that make them known entities to a wider public.

Of course, it is not only a matter of what the family household can do for one of its members. A Yemeni patriarch (male or female) can exert authority over household members to work for the larger family's welfare (ranging from agricultural work to domestic chores). When children in Western society are asked to mow the lawn, rake the leaves, milk the cow, or wash the dishes, it is in the name of learning work and discipline, not of contributing to the household's income. Moreover, what a child earns through babysitting or yard work is theirs to keep and to spend as they see fit. This is a somewhat quaint idea to most Yemenis and in many traditional societies. Children are expected to be part of an economic unit (economic in its ancient meaning of providing for and managing the household) and to contribute to it, according to age and ability. This includes overseeing younger members of the family in the "arts" of household management.

Women and children in Yemen are considered "dependents" in the sense that they are provided for and protected, with males as their providers and protectors. Within that hierarchy of gender and generation are other distinctions that affect the status or position of household members: between older and younger siblings; in-law and lineal descendant; and in the case of polygamous households, one's birth mother versus any other who claims a relationship with the one. Attached to some of the more well-off households might be servants who work for families in return for room and board, and occasionally a modest wage. Because they live in the household, they too are considered "dependents" and are protected, though this relationship may become exploitative and abusive. It is important to bear in mind that the society in no way condones such treatment. In fact, a household that treats its "servants" this way is said to lack honor, because it has failed to protect people who live under its roof and are therefore dependent on it.

It is an ideal, in a sense, of every man and woman in Yemen to establish their own household in order to get out from under such obligations or dependence, while at the same time perpetuating the household institution by reconstituting such relations with children, children's spouses, and their grandchildren. When they do constitute their own households, they (especially women) are expected to visit their natal households where their parents and siblings still reside as a sign of ongoing affection for and loyalty to their families. Upon the return of a family relative who has been away for business or health reasons, the extended family gathers to greet them and welcome them back into the fold, and the relative who is the object of this lavish affection is expected to bring gifts, large and small, to family members as a token of love and gratitude.

The House

Household literally means those who live under a single roof and comprise a family, and it follows that the idea of a house or home is closely associated with it. A home is where one grew up in, in the context of a family. For the same reason, the Arabic bayt means both household in the sense just give and a house or dwelling. There is, in other words, an intimate connection between the idea of a family and a particular kind of dwelling space.

As in any other society, it is hard to speak of a "typical" private residence or house in Yemen, though there are some commonalities. It is often said that family matters are private, or to be conducted in the intimate spaces of the home. In the Gulf, the traditional family dwelling has an interior space, marked by a central courtyard for ventilation (and therefore cooling) as well as light, with covered hallways and rooms immediately adjacent to it that are meant for the intimate side of family life (cooking, eating, sleeping, laundering and relaxing). The spaces adjacent to the "outside" or street are for male gatherings and visitors (reception rooms). To ensure that unwelcome eyes cannot see into the privacy of the courtyard, family houses are usually no more than two stories high and have high walls around them. There are now many Yemenis households that build homes in this form, especially when its members have worked in the Gulf for any length of time. But traditional Yemeni architecture has responded to the needs of family privacy and intimacy in different forms, perhaps because the built environment is for the most part not in a flat and desert landscape but a mountainous and arable one (where land has to be conserved for agricultural purposes). In other words, what the Gulf home has solved through concentric patterns spread out horizontally, the Yemeni one has by building vertically in a layer-cake fashion.

The courtyard (known as *hosh* in Yemeni Arabic) is usually the first thing one walks through in the traditional Yemeni house, like the front garden of a suburban home in the United States though surrounded by a high wall. This is less a space of intimacy than of work, where animals like sheep, chickens, and cows are kept that are later butchered for eating or where laundry is done and other domestic chores. Upon approaching the massive wooden door of the house, which is opened by an old-fashioned wooden or iron key, one raps the brass knocker (and not timidly either). Above the door is a wooden latticed window that projects a foot or so from the wall, which allows the women of the household to scrutinize who is at the door, whether stranger or family member and friend, and if the latter, they can pull a string attached to a wooden bar that unlocks and opens the door. Before that happens, however, a commanding older female voice hollers, "*Man?*" (or "Who?") and waits for the open sesame response (e.g., "Ahmed," your husband). Walking through the door, one is on the first floor of the house (there are no basements or cellars per se), a storage area where the animals are bedded down for the night. Ascending a central stone staircase, the spine of the house, and a feature missing in the Gulf home because of its more horizontal layout, one comes to the second floor, where the kitchen is usually found and other work spaces. A male who is not a member of the household will say, "Allah! Allah!" to alert the females of the house that a stranger is in their midst and they should keep out of sight. The third floor is usually the sleeping quarters and the reception room for female visitors, while above that is the men's sitting room, beautifully appointed with old-fashioned furnishings and the paraphernalia needed for the qat chew and the *shisha* (or *mada'a* in Yemeni Arabic). Finally, what is the equivalent of the interior courtyard in the Gulf home is the rooftop with its high walls, securing privacy for the family when they want to catch a breath of fresh air. The houses are tall but more or less of the same height. Windows have curtains to ensure that people cannot look in and wooden shutters that can be closed in case of violent weather.

But the cultural ideal of maintaining an extended family in the same living quarters under the same roof can sometimes lead to a bit of a squeeze, which is only partly solved by having all the women of the house sleeping on the third floor and all the men in the top reception hall, except for cohabiting couples who might have their own small rooms. The only satisfactory solution is for sons who are beginning their own families to build homes adjacent to that of their patriarch (if such space is available), and over time, this residential pattern produces a neighborhood of kinsmen complexly related to each other through descent and marriage.

The Neighborhood

It is no wonder, then, that next to the bayt or household, the neighborhood or jirah is another important social concept. For Western society, it usually means a collection of individual families who happen to live together for reasons of class, education, ethnicity, or other considerations, but hardly ever for reasons of kinship; while in the Yemeni context (and most Arab ones), it is the reverse: Neighborhood usually means a collection of households that are related to each other through some form of kinship or other social relation such as tribe, and the "stranger" is barely tolerated in their midst. Which is not to say that people unrelated to the households do not live in the neighborhood and over time are not esteemed or respected as much as kinsmen, but it is as if they have become "honorary" kinsmen who can expect the protection of the senior patriarchs and at the same time are expected to contribute to the safety and upkeep of the neighborhood. Protecting the neighbor (*jiran*) is a sacred duty, whether he or she is a kinsman or not. And neighborhoods have physical or spatial correlates as precise as those of Yemeni houses. They are sometimes separated from each other by low walls or other markers such as community gardens or irrigation works, and they may be entered through a gate that can be closed at night (in a sense, the earliest "gated communities"). Within, there are, it is sometimes said, a "labyrinth" of streets and narrow paths, with many thoroughfares that are dead ends or cul-de-sacs (unmarked, of course). Yet, there is a logic to this layout if one bears in mind the need for protection in the neighborhood. Many times a strange male ends up lost or disoriented or comes to a dead end, where he is accosted by playing children and asked who he is and what he wants. If his presence appears legitimate, he is politely escorted by a child to his destination, or otherwise chased out of the neighborhood. In the distant past, when towns and cities were still vulnerable to attack and pillage by tribesmen, this layout served a different purpose, of confusing the attacker and making neighborhood defense easier. By the same token, the staircase in the Yemen house narrows the higher it ascends, with the person having to crouch through a narrow opening that is easily blocked before getting to the rooftop, where presumably household members have taken refuge (and where they also can fire upon their marauders).

Weddings

Weddings are arguably the main ceremonial event of Yemeni society, not excepting even the religious holidays. They are vivid affairs, involving large groups of people out in public, and they usually take place in the summers. Weddings vary between urban and nonurban, sayyid and tribal, modern and traditional, male and female, and northern and southern Yemeni. The wedding ceremony usually consists of the following: a luncheon, a procession of the groom (with a wedding bouquet) filled with song and poetry, a qat chew, a *samrah* or evening of entertainment, gift-giving of the groom's side to the bride's side at the evening's entertainment, the bride's procession where she is taken to the groom's house, and the marriage consummation (with or without a bloodied white sheet to show that the consummation was successful). The festivities usually last several days, ending with the marriage consummation.

The most public part of the wedding is the groom's procession that takes place during the day, usually from the groom's house to the mosque (where he receives advice from the Imam) and back to the place where the afternoon's qat chew is to be held in his honor. The procession is in the form of a line headed by the servants who carry the groom's wedding bouquet. Behind them are the relatives of the groom and the bride, followed at the rear by the groom, dressed in all his finery. It is important for him to wear a somber expression on his face and to maintain a rigid bodily posture. He does not talk to his companions, much less joke with them, keeping his composure throughout. The other public event takes place in the evening when the groom and his relatives congregate in the street, which is decked out with strings

Yemeni groom with relatives in street of Old Sana'a. (Marwan Naamani/AFP/Getty Images)

HENNA

The English word "henna" is derived from the Arabic "hinnaa" and refers to a red dye made from a plant by the same name that is cultivated in Yemen. Its leaves are dried and ground into a powder that is in turn made into a fine paste. This paste is then either rubbed into hair or beards, turning them red, or applied with a stylus or the tip of a feather to women's hands and feet in intricate abstract designs that in Yemen are called *naqsh*. In time, the designs fade and rub off (they are not permanent like tattoos). The Prophet Muhammad is said to have dyed his beard with henna, which is why Muslim men often rub it in their own beards. The use of henna today is widespread in the world (e.g., it is popular in the United States), and there is plenty of archaeological evidence to suggest that it was used in ancient times as far back as the Iron Age.

---

of white lightbulbs. There are musicians who accompany dancers, and eventually a singer leads the congregation in a wedding hymn.

For the bride, there is no public outdoor event, though she has several indoor ceremonies in which she is the center of attention. One of these is having her hand and feet hennaed (a dark-colored dye that is used to make elaborate abstract designs); another is to "sit in state" on a makeshift "throne" all decked out in a beautiful silk dress and dripping in gold jewelry, while she is being admired by her female relatives and friends. Like her counterpart, the groom, she is not supposed to interact but remain quiet and composed. Feasting is a major part of both the male and female ceremonies.

Religious Festivals or 'Ids

The great religious festivals come after the fast of Ramadan (a month-long fast in which food and drink is given up between sunup and sundown) and after the annual hajj pilgrimage to Mecca. Ramadan is observed much as it is in any other Muslim country, but the *'id* coming after it is said to be longer than in other countries. For the 'id that breaks the fast, children, especially girls, dress up and go door-to-door in their neighborhood asking for candy and simple gifts (many receive new clothes from their families). For the 'id after the hajj, households sacrifice sheep or bulls to mark the occasion and then feast on the sacrificial animal's flesh.

Concepts of Gender and Sexuality

Gender is about the cultural conceptions of male and female, and how these conceptions inform each other in a given society. Such constructs usually go far beyond "natural" or "biological" conceptions of sex and reproduction (that men and women have different sexual organs and have different roles to play in the reproductive process) or that men are somehow naturally "stronger" and women for some reason are the "weaker" sex.

Conceptions of gender are hardly ever uniform in a society. For one thing, they change over the life of a girl or a boy, and there is a preadolescent period where adult gender norms do not apply to their behavior. For example, prepubescent girls are not expected to veil, and then not all at once but only gradually as they start to menstruate; the separation expected from their male counterparts as adults is also not in force, girls and boys play fiercely with each other in public. It is also useful to distinguish between a "traditional" and a "modern"—or better yet, a more contemporary—gender system in Yemen. The one has not completely superceded the other. It is the former that will concern us for the most part. To begin with, let us consider traditional notions of sexuality, followed by a discussion of honor and modesty. It goes without saying that these ideas do not go uncontested within Yemeni society, though it is fair to claim that they are powerful and despite changes in the country, quite influential.

Men and women have differing conceptions of each other as sexual beings. Men acknowledge that women are passionate and that they have the right to sexual satisfaction within marriage, but they add that women are unable to control their "urges," which is why controls of various sort need to be imposed upon them. Women do not necessarily agree with male opinions about their sexuality. They do agree that they have strong sexual passions, but they insist on being able to control their "urges" in spite of what men might claim to the contrary. In their view, it is men who are unable to control their sexual impulses, and the reason women submit to restrictions on their movements and dress is to hide themselves from the inquisitive male gaze and protect themselves from men's indiscriminate attentions. Male and female sexuality is defined less by the possession of certain genitalia than performing sexual acts in certain ways. The "proper" sexual act or position for the female is as one who "receives" or is "entered" by the male penis, and for the male, it is to "penetrate" or "enter." Men who have sex with men may not consider themselves homosexual because they take the position of the "penetrator" in the sexual act; the male who is "penetrated," however, is less likely to make that disclaimer.

Honor and Sexual Modesty

Given these conceptions about gender and sexuality, it is perhaps easier to understand (if not necessarily agree with) the regulation of male and female bodies as well as movements in Yemeni society. It is also helpful to consider additional cultural conceptions having to do with honor and modesty.

We know from our discussion of tribe and family that sharaf or honor is a major defining feature of social identity and is applicable to both men and women, though in different ways. Both men and women acquire their honor, which we might otherwise call their dignity or social worth, by reason of their descent, but they can also achieve honor (or lose it) by their deeds in everyday life. For a man, this may mean committing acts of bravery or hospitality or for having reputations for honesty and ethical behavior, and while women may also demonstrate their honor in such ways, it is by remaining sexually "virtuous" that they primarily do so. It is sometimes said that they must protect their *'irdh,* the honor of vulnerable persons like themselves (in other words their chastity), in order for them to maintain their dignity. Though manhood can be violated (by rape or molestation) and thereby a man's honor be-smirched, it is presumed (perhaps falsely) that he is less vulnerable in that regard than a woman. The opposite of honor is shame or *'ayb,* and is commonly used to describe a disgraceful act. As children learn what is right and wrong, they are constantly ad-monished not to do something 'ayb or shameful.

Another important concept for the traditional gender system is modesty or *istihya,* and as in the case of honor, both women and men are affected by it though in different ways. One meaning of modesty is concerned with sexual conduct or comportment, as seen through the prism of the local culture. Thus, women (or girls who have reached puberty) are enjoined to dress modestly in public, and thereby not draw attention to their figures or the beauty of their faces. It is the attention of the male gaze, presumably unwanted by the female, that such dress is supposed to ward off, but not categorically all men; she is not required to veil in private before her father and brothers. How, and how much of, the woman's body should be covered for reasons of modesty varies tremendously in Yemen. While it is often attributed to "Islamic" teachings, there is some disagreement over this contention. (Scholars debate what Qur'anic injunctions about the woman having to be "covered" in fact mean.) Besides dress, conduct or comportment is also subject to modesty regulation. When step-ping out in public, it is rare for a woman to be alone: she either is in the company of other females or at the very least has a male escort to "protect" her—even if it is only her five-year-old brother. Women are supposed to avoid making eye contact with strange men, unless they are conducting business or otherwise engaging with them in conversation. Segregation might be too strong to describe the relations between the

---

VEILING

While we may harbor an image of veiling in Yemen that is stark and uniform (the burka or *niqab* comes to mind), the fact is that veiling practices vary in the population and signal many more meanings than gender. At one end of the spectrum is the black cloak called the sharshaf and the *lithmah,* a rectangular piece of cloth that covers the face or sometimes all but the eyes. Besides piety, this veiling may signal urbanity or class, and possibly both at once. This kind of veiling is also generational. Older and more traditional women may wear a rectangular sheet, with colorful tie-dyed design, to cover their head and backside, with a loose-fitting shirt, skirt, and pants beneath. Women in more remote rural areas, especially while working in the fields, wear little more than a head scarf and a piece of cloth to cover the lower part of their faces. And women who see themselves as modern but still pious may wear a long beige raincoat and a long head scarf to cover their hair but not their faces.

sexes, for many women go to university and work outside the home where they have to come into contact with strange men, yet it is fair to say that the two sexes try to keep themselves separate from each other. Men too are obliged to observe modesty in dress and behavior. Traditionally, men had to cover their torsos even while working out of doors, and to bear the leg above the knee was likewise unthinkable (though boys are seen more and more in shorts). Men should also avoid making direct eye contact with strange women, and touching them except to shake their hand in public would be disgraceful. Of course, women complain all the time of harassment, as they do in our society.

The Female in the Family

Though in some sense a female is considered an adult when she begins her period, she is not really a "woman" until she has married and had a child. The same consideration applies to a man; he is not fully mature until he has married and fathered a child, though it is fair to say that the pressure for a man to marry is not as great. After what has been said about the honor code above, it goes without saying both that the female is expected to be a virgin upon marrying, though whatever sexual experience the groom brings to the consummation is his affair, and that the male be able to penetrate her, though stage fright on his wedding night might prevent him from "doing his duty." How often these presumptions are proven false we will never know, as parents try to keep up appearances for the sake of their family honor or negotiate when such honor seems to be in the balance.

In beginning her own family, a woman's status—and more subtly her power— begins to change, especially if she has a son: a male child assures the husband that his patriline is continued. This is not to say that girls are not valued, quite the contrary. They are productive members of the household and later will represent the family in life, whether in marriage or work. The young mother, however, comes under the watchful eye of her mother-in-law who instructs her in household management, and though the two may become friends, their relationship can be a source of strain and burden for the husband, if his loyalties are divided between his wife and his mother. Making sure that children are raised as proper ethical beings falls on both the father and the mother, though it is the latter who is especially charged with this responsibility while the father has to look after their school education. As the children grow up, it is the mother's responsibility to find them suitable marital partners from among neighbors and acquaintances. Having achieved this, she has fulfilled her last family duty and can, in a sense, relax. Indeed, postmenopausal females are no longer considered a "sexual threat" and may mingle more freely with men than at any other time in their lives since childhood. This means that they can participate in public life—political and economic—if they choose to do so, without jeopardizing the honor of their respective families. At this age, too, they will have inherited whatever wealth from their natal families owed to them, and some women who come into considerable means use it to buy real estate, gold, or their own business enterprises. Women who have gained reputations for being smart and sagacious over a lifetime of household management might be consulted by men on a variety of matters concerning the wider affairs of the community. Ironically, at an age when most women in our society lose their power, many older women in Yemen are at the pinnacle of their authority and influence.

It is important to realize that even in this deeply patriarchal society, there are any number of examples of women who have established themselves as powerful figures outside the confines of their households, though much depends on whether they are helped, or at least not obstructed, by their male guardians such as fathers, brothers, and husbands. For example, one woman from the town of Shibam northwest of the capital Sana'a used her talents as a homemaker and household manager to begin her own business, a restaurant that became famous for its good food, which was then expanded into a hotel much frequented by visitors from all over the country and beyond. She had a forceful personality and prevailed over her husband's reservations about her ambitions. In old age, she acquired the reputation of a "sheikha" (a female sheikh), whom men would consult and borrow money from her for their own businesses—if, that is, she found them to be sound. Throughout her career, not a whisper of scandal was heard about her private life, which would have cost her business and eaten into her profits.

Homosociality

Same-gender relations are very important in the Arab world, for which the term "homosociality" is reserved, and it is not the same as homosexuality. These same-sex relationships and gatherings can be quite passionate and intimate affairs without sex ever being part of the mix. Men and women often hold hands in public as a sign of their close social connection, either as kinsmen or friends, without in the least signaling sexual attraction to each other.

It is in light of such homosociality that friendship or *sadaqah* becomes all important; it is a much stronger practice in Yemeni (and by extension Arab) society than in our own. A friend is not just someone one hangs out with or someone close to oneself because he or she is a neighbor or a school chum, but there is a devotion to that person that goes well beyond what we ordinarily feel or express toward our friends. Close friends are known to spend as much time with each other as they do with their respective spouses, and it is understood that one drops everything to be by the side of a friend in need.

Changes Affecting Women since the 1960s

Since the 1960s, when Yemen became a republic and opened its doors to Western influence, the traditional gender system, like much else in society, has changed. For one thing, women across the social spectrum are more educated (they tend to be the majority in the national university, depending on the subject), and many work outside the home and pursue professional careers in teaching or medicine. Their families encourage such aspirations in part because households cannot be supported on a single income, so both the male and the female heads have to work. National governments such as Yemen's also know that their societies can only develop if the female half of the population is educated and empowered, economically as well as politically. In Yemen, it is legal for women to drive and vote in elections as well as run for public office.

In order for women to pursue their education, they marry later and later in life, postponing the time when they have to raise families until they feel secure in their jobs. Some women have risen in the ranks of their political parties (e.g., see the portrait of Nobel Peace Prize Laureate Tawakkol Karman in Chapter 7) and have gone on to parliament and held ministerial posts in the national government. An example of the latter is Amaat Al-Aleem Asoswa, who was educated partly in Yemen and partly in the United States, became a talk show host and personality on Yemeni national television, and from there went on to serve as the first minister of human rights in the Yemeni cabinet. Until recently, she worked for the United Nations on women's issues and has now become a politician.

But these freedoms and advancements have also posed challenges for women, familiar to their compatriots in other parts of the world. While it is appreciated that they bring money into the household, their responsibilities and work load for running the same have not diminished, though husbands are increasingly willing to share the burden and help out. Another obligation difficult to meet is that of visiting families

Amat al-Alim Alsoswa. UNDP Assistant Administrator and Director of the Regional Bureau for Arab States, 2012. (United Nations Development Programme)

and neighbors, when they have long and tiring work schedules. Husbands sometimes voice the criticism that their wives are more interested in their careers than the welfares of their children and spouses (a familiar complaint elsewhere in the world). Perhaps because of these strains, divorce is not uncommon, though women can and do find other husbands who are more accommodating to their modern point of view.

Governmental as well as nongovernmental organizations have become champions of women's rights and family law, protecting women from the most egregious abuses of a repressive patriarchal system (such as child brides), though it is not always clear that these women have an alternative social and economic network to fall back on for help or support. Civil courts are now learning to interpret new laws pertaining to female rights and enforcing them. Western-style feminism has made some inroads in Yemen, particularly at the university (e.g., Sana'a University's Center for Women); a great champion of which was the late Raufa Hassan (1958–2011). It has to be said, however, that this kind of feminism has been opposed by the religious conservatives in the country like the Salafi Sheikh al-Zindani and others. Countering these Western-style feminists are strong women activists in the religious Islah party, who work for political reform while sticking to a socially conservative agenda.

Exposure to Western media has been all pervasive, though access to the Internet is still a relatively rare phenomenon except in urban areas. The spread of the Internet has facilitated online communications between strange men and women, which would have been impossible before the computer. Sometimes, this has led to clandestine sexual encounters, but for the most part, it has been used as a tool for men and women to get socially acquainted and find out if they might be viable marriage partners. Once they are sure of that decision, they approach their respective parents to announce their engagement. The couple hopes that they will be listened to because traditional views about arranged marriage have started to change. As long as the couple seem evenly matched, in personality and social standing, the parents are likely to go along with their decision.

It is perhaps unfortunate that expressions of homosociality are also changing. Through exposure to modern media, Yemeni men know what Americans think of men holding hands, and so they are less likely to do the same in public and cosmopolitan spaces. Yet, the effect of the media has not always been negative when it comes to affections between men and women in public. Now husband and wife are more likely than they were even a decade ago to hold hands in public (such public display of affection having been considered unseemly, even shameful). Also positively, men and women are more likely to have friendships with each other without this inevitably being construed as sexual, as it would have been in the past. In any case, what we might call the "economy of intimacy" is undergoing profound and rapid changes.

BIBLIOGRAPHY

Colburn, Marta. *Gender and Development in Yemen.* Bonn: Friedrich Ebert Stiftung, 2002.

De Regt, Marina. *Pioneers or Pawns? Women Health Workers and the Politics of Development in Yemen.* Syracuse, NY: Syracuse University Press, 2007.

Dorsky, Susan. *Woman of 'Amran: A Middle Eastern Ethnography.* Salt Lake City, UT: University of Utah Press, 1986.

Meneley, Anne. *Tournaments of Value: Sociability and Hierarchy in a Yemeni Town.* Toronto, ON: University of Toronto Press, 1996.

Mundy, Martha. *Domestic Government: Kinship, Community and Polity in North Yemen.* London: Tauris, 1995.

Obermeyer, Carla Makhlouf. *Changing Veils: Women and Modernization in North Yemen.* Austin, TX: University of Texas Press, 1979.

Sunil, T. S. and Vijayan K. Pillai. *Women's Reproductive Health in Yemen.* Amherst, NY: Cambria Press, 2010.

EDUCATION

Steven C. Caton

It is helpful to distinguish between a traditional educational system in Yemen, which is centuries old but still in existence in many places, and a modern one that was instituted only relatively recently in time, since the 1960s. Because the two coexist, it is important to say something about the older system, as well as to describe how it has undergone modernization.

Traditional Education in Yemen

Traditional education was reserved almost exclusively for males and centered around religious studies. The earliest stage of instruction, from roughly the ages of 4 to 8 or after the child has learned to read and write, was focused on memorization of the Qur'an. The pupil would join a class in the mosque, sitting in a circle around a teacher, who would write the particular passage the student was supposed to learn that day (or week) on a slate tablet or wooden board and then hand it over to the pupil to memorize. The pupil would recite the passage and be corrected until the passage was repeated without mistakes; eventually, the tablet would be taken away and he would be asked to recite the passage from memory without mistakes.

At this stage, no emphasis is placed on understanding the meaning of the passage except in the most basic definitional sense (e.g., "What does wine mean?"); instead, the emphasis is on a phonologically accurate oral transmission. Even that way of putting the challenge is not accurate enough. Transmission may be in a plain-speaking voice but also chanted according to strict rules.

It has to be borne in mind that this oral transmission is not just a pedagogical technique for memorizing the sacred text, but it also reenacts the initial mode of transmission of the Qur'an by the Prophet Muhammad and thus has sacred significance. Once the youngster is able to recite (chant) the entire Qur'an correctly by heart, he graduates from the first stage of Islamic instruction. Many never go beyond it, for they have now gained mastery over a text they will recite privately for the rest of their lives, especially during particular holy times of the year such as Ramadan, or snippets of which they will insert into their daily conversations in order to make a point. The graduate may receive a certificate and along with his peers be honored in a public celebration.

Those pupils wanting to pursue a religious profession (as religious teachers or *muftis* [declarers of fatwas] or lawyers and judges) have to go on to the next stage of instruction, studying with a particular 'alim (scholar) in the mosque. Often this meant living in nearby makeshift dormitories and forming a community of initiates. Although this was partially paid for by religious endowments or waqf set up to maintain the mosque and religious activities within it, in fact parents had to help defray the costs such as school supplies, food, and even the salaries of the scholars. Thus, unless a student received a scholarship, only ones from the more well-to-do families could afford such higher instruction.

Though at this second stage of instruction students continued to memorize sacred texts (the Hadith), the emphasis now was on textual interpretation and explanation. It is important to realize that although the scholar was considered the authority on the correct interpretation of the sacred texts, his interpretations were not simply memorized and repeated verbatim, as in the case of the sacred texts, but arrived at through question-and-answer routines between the pupils and the scholar, the former of whom had to be persuaded through reasoned argument with his teacher. For example, the scholar might repeat from memory a Hadith and ask his pupils to memorize it, and then he would ask them what it means. He might ask one pupil what a particular word or reference means, and then demonstrate through evidence or logic that the answer was either correct or not. He would then ask all the other pupils whether they agreed, and if they didn't, he would take up their objections or questions one by one until they all were in agreement. Mutual agreement would be the basis on which, step by step, an overarching interpretation or explanation was accepted. Sometimes, interpretations given by alternative scholars might be entertained, but then those interpretations would have to be examined in the same reasoned way and eventually shown to be false or lacking in merit of one kind or another. Having learned the Hadith and their interpretation, pupils go on to learn fiqh (the science of religious law), or how Sharia law is constituted from the Qur'an and the Hadith. Two methods are employed by which to formulate new laws: one is called "analogical reasoning" whereby something that was not anticipated in the Qur'an or the Hadith is judged to be permitted or forbidden on analogy with something else that was mentioned and evaluated; or innovation (the creation of a new law on the basis of legal reasoning), though its acceptance or use varies from Zaydi to Shafi'i in Yemen. The best students go on to be deemed religious experts, qualified to pursue careers as judges, and ultimately leading jurisprudents.

While this describes in very general terms a traditional religious education, it should be noted that religious instruction in Yemen was modernized in the 20th century in important ways. Religious institutes were set up, in which curriculum was standardized, teachers certified, and students examined before being passed and allowed to go on to the next grade; and other subjects related to religious learning such as grammar and lexicography, religious history, and Classical Arabic literature were taught in standardized fashion as well. Though congregating in the mosque around a teacher is still a common practice, going to a classroom where the teacher stands in front of a blackboard and the class is seated in rows of chairs in front of him is more the rule. Yemen now has its own religious university, Iman (meaning faith) University, in Sana'a, founded by the Yemeni Salafi cleric and political leader al-Zindani, which is organized and run like a modern university. Its faculty are expected to publish and be promoted on the basis of their writing and teaching, and its students are examined before being allowed to continue with their studies, much less graduate to teach elsewhere in the country or abroad. Curricula are standardized. Of course, these are not the only sites in which students can learn about religion, which has its own department in the national university, but the latter exists alongside others that teach secular subjects such as mathematics, science, and business.

The establishment of specifically Salafi (fundamentalist) schools (or institutes, as they are called) has been on the rise in recent years, most of whose funding comes from Saudi Arabia. They can be found all over the country, and are sometimes sites of bitter political contention between Zaydis on the one hand (as in the north, around Sa'dah) and Sufis on the other (as in Hadhramawt).

Modern Education

Before the 1960s, it was only Aden and the territory immediately adjacent to it under British colonial rule that could be said to have had a modern educational system, whereas the rest of the British Protectorate had limited education and mostly conformed to the religious type described above. As for North Yemen, it was not until the 1962 Revolution abolished the Imamate system and the Republic came into existence that the government committed itself to development, including and perhaps especially in the education field. When the south became independent in 1967, modern education began to take off there, adopting many of the reforms initiated in the north but then diverging from it in some important respects, especially in secondary education. Because of these disparities, when Yemen Arab Republic and the People's Democratic Republic of Yemen united in 1990, it took a while for the government to integrate the two systems. Now, primary education (6–14 years of age) consists of 9 years of basic education, followed by 3 years of secondary education (15–18 years of age, or the equivalent of our high school).

Upon graduation from primary school, students receive an intermediate school certificate and go on to attend secondary school. The latter is usually a feeder for entrance into the national university, Sana'a University, with two large campuses in the capital and branch campuses in Aden, Al-Hudaydah, Taiz, Ibb, Dhamar, and Al-Mukalla (Hadhramawt). The total enrollment for the main and branch campuses is about 175,000. Except for the faculties of engineering and medicine, university education lasts for four years.

There are other secondary schools as well that are more vocational or technical in orientation, including a veterinary training school, a Health Manpower Training Institute, and several agricultural schools, although the numbers in these schools are relatively low. There are also Islamic schools (described above, ordinarily funded by waqf endowments) and private schools, including the International School in Sana'a, a college preparatory school attended by the children of Yemeni elites and expatriate workers in the country.

It is important to bear in mind that academic tracking of students begins after the first year of secondary school, based on interest as well as academic achievement, the two tracks being math and science or literature and history. While in some ways this tracking according to specialization makes sense, one of the problems with it is that once the decision has been made, it is difficult for students to take courses in the other track, which is especially important in the case of math and science for understanding a rapidly changing world. At the end of their final year in secondary school, students take exams, passing of which is necessary for graduation, and receive a general secondary education certificate. Depending on results in the national high-school graduation examination, students may be qualified to attend public university (a little less than roughly 10 percent are admitted).

Only a relatively small number of Yemeni students go abroad annually to study, almost all of whom are dependent upon government scholarships funded for the most part by foreign donors. The complaint is often heard that selection of scholarship students is based less on merit or need than on political connections. Because of difficulties obtaining a visa into the United States and Europe, especially after September 11, the more popular destinations for study abroad are India and Southeast Asia, particularly Malaysia, a predominantly Muslim country.

The management of the public primary and secondary school systems is done by the Ministry of Education. Vocational schools and community colleges are under the Ministry of Technical Education and Vocational Training, and in 2001, the Ministry of Higher Education and Scientific Research was established to manage universities and colleges (public and private) as well as specialized training institutes of various sorts. This step was taken to acknowledge the growth at these levels, and the fact that it was the focus of international aid. This has led to problems of competition and lack of coordination between the various ministries, however, which the government has been attempting to correct.

Problems and Challenges Facing Modern Education

While Yemen's constitution prescribes universal and free education for all children, male and female, through ages six to fifteen, the reality, unfortunately, falls far short of this ideal. Compulsory education is not always enforced, especially in the poorer and more remote areas of the country. Published statistics, which are unreliable in any case, stop around the beginning of the millennium, and they indicate that in 2005 about 81 percent of Yemen's school-age children were enrolled in primary school, with 74 percent of all females enrolled as well (UNESCO's Institute of Statistics database). The percentages declined rapidly for higher levels of education, as might be expected, and are among the lowest, if not the lowest, of any country in the Middle East and North Africa region. It can be said that real strides toward improvement were made in the 1990s, a momentum that continued briefly into the early part of the new millennium, but that it has slowed significantly because of political turmoil inside the country since 2004—the continuing decline of the economy that has meant revenue loss for the government and the pulling back of foreign aid because of instability.

Although education is the second largest item in the annual government budget (after the military), averaging roughly between 14 and 20 percent, this amount is woefully inadequate for the needs of this poverty-stricken country (World Bank 2008: 1). As of 2001, expenditure on education was a little less than 10 percent of the gross domestic product (World Bank 2008, EdStats database). Without significant input from foreign donors such as the World Bank or the Dutch Embassy (the largest donor to the educational sector in Yemen among international embassies that include the Germans, British, French, and Japanese), future progress will be stalled. With recent military conflicts in the north of the country as well as with al-Qaeda in the east and south, it may well be that the military budget has ballooned at the expense of other items such as education, thus further exasperating an already dire situation.

There are certain demographics that partially explain the problem of providing adequate education to Yemenis. With a population growth rate of around 2.575 percent per annum, one of the highest in the world, just keeping up with adequate infrastructure is a daunting task (CIA 2012). Yemen also has one of the lowest adult literary rates in the world, particularly among females: as of 2010, about 46.8 percent females were considered literate (CIA 2012, Literacy). Widespread poverty is also a huge problem. Although education is more or less free (students do not have to pay for textbooks and no tuition or taxes are charged for schooling), poorer rural students often have to trek on foot for long distances to get to school and cannot afford to bring food (nutritious or otherwise) to school, and often forego their main meal, lunch. As educators know, it is difficult for pupils to concentrate or retain information on an empty stomach. In poorer families, too, children are expected to contribute labor to the family household, which means they either are pulled out of school entirely (especially females) or have to work after school, contributing to fatigue and taking time away from their after-school studies. Because of economic necessity, girls are often married at a younger age than their peers in other countries, making it less likely that they will continue with their education. And some parents object sending their girls to mixed gender schools, Yemen not being able to afford the more expensive gender-segregated alternative (more expensive because of the duplication of facilities) that richer Gulf neighbors can.

Although Yemen has made strides in building an educational infrastructure at the primary and secondary levels, it is still inadequate. It is surprising how many empty or only partially utilized school buildings one comes across, especially in the countryside, and only partly for the reasons of low student attendance mentioned above. Schools have not necessarily been matched with need. (Given their symbolic value, it is often a matter of pride or power that local leaders can have them built.) There are many schools that have only a hundred or so regular attendees, the bare minimum needed to keep the schools officially open, and others that are badly overcrowded.

Problems also exist with the provisioning of textbooks and other educational materials. Books arrive late or not at all, or at least not in sufficient quantities. This mismatch is often due to the fact that many schools overreport their need, anticipating future budget cuts that will affect supplies, and as the Ministry of Education runs slow on supplies, it cuts back the delivery to other schools. Once textbooks are used, they are supposed to be returned to the school and redistributed for reuse in the following year, with fees levied on students who fail to return their books. The rate of return varies across the society, relatively high in urban areas but low in rural ones.

Staffing is another problem. Although teachers have to graduate with a certificate from an officially licensed teacher education school or program, they often know their subjects only minimally well or poorly. The qualification requirement for teaching grades 1–6 is a diploma from a teacher training institute (even they are no longer existent!). There is a great need for qualified female teachers, who serve as an inspiring role model for girls in school, but where they are most badly needed—remote rural villages—are precisely where they are least likely to go, among other reasons because of the difficulties of a single female living on her own in these areas. Thus, there is a tendency to hire teachers on the basis of their residence rather than on merit. Financial incentives are provided for teachers willing to relocate to more remote areas, but these are often abused, where teachers who receive such incentives not necessarily teaching in rural schools. Salaries are also inadequate, requiring full-time teachers to supplement their incomes with other jobs, which means they have less time to grade assignments or think about lesson plans. Absenteeism, not surprisingly, becomes a problem in some areas. A qualified substitute teaching staff is almost nonexistent.

Curriculum also has not kept up with the needs of a modern labor force. Instruction in English is particularly weak, but so is teaching of other basic skills such as writing, use of the computer and the Internet, and accounting.

Problems within the Ministry of Education that manages primary and secondary public schooling are also a factor. We have already mentioned the confusion and competition arising from multiple governmental agencies responsible for different levels of the educational system, but there are significant intra-agency problems as well. Increased expenditures do not necessarily translate into better educational results, if the provisioning of education is neither efficient nor equitable or evenly distributed across the society. Budget allocations and expenditures are marked by rigidity (no leeway is given for shifting priorities) as well as lack of predictability and accountability. It is difficult for the Ministry of Education to obtain reliable information on the delivery performance of individual schools. Such procedures lead to overbudgeting of some items, underbudgeting in others, and the possibility of rampant corruption.

Possibilities and Limits of Educational Reform

The Government of Yemen has put in place a basic education strategy (BES; 2003–2015) that it has started to implement (though progress has slowed down significantly because of recent political turmoil in the country, the continuing high birthrate, and decline in international donor support). For one thing, the aim of attaining universal primary education by 2015 seems hopelessly ambitious.

The BES also includes the following goals:

Promoting enrollment of female students, especially in rural areas, and increasing their literacy rates under the Household Incentive Program

Matching new schools with regional needs more accurately and fairly, along with a more effective use and distribution of curricular resources under the Infrastructure and School Facilities Development Program

Strengthening the quality of administration and operation of schools under School Level Management and Community Participation Program

Setting learning achievement targets according to subject and grade and finding better ways to monitor progress on them under the Leaning Achievement and Curriculum Program

Clarifying the qualifications for teachers, enhancing their training, and deploying them to needed schools under the Teacher Development Program

Examining educational materials and whether they are appropriate for achieving learning targets under Learning Materials Development Program

Allocating better and useful resources across bureaucratic ministries and sectors (local administration and civil service) under Sector Management Framework Development Program

Identifying key functions and skills needed for program implementation under Sector Organization and Technical Capacity Program

General emphasis is on improving girls' education and educational delivery to rural areas. Multiple agencies are involved financially and administratively in meeting these goals (besides the Ministry of Education, the Ministry of Finance, local administration, the directorates of all the governorates, local district councils, as well as schools and parental committees). Needless to say, without massive infusions of donor aid, the overhaul of the educational system will ultimately prove ineffective. Levels of donor aid are not encouraging. The total donor aid to Yemen for education amounted to US $237 million in 2010, then declined to US $117 million in 2011, and was at US $61 million in 2012 (www.worldbank.org/en/country/yemen).

BIBLIOGRAPHY

CIA. *The World Factbook: Yemen.* 2012. https://www.cia.gov/library/publications/the-world-factbook/geos/ym.html.

Republic of Yemen, Ministry of Education. "Development of Education in the Republic of Yemen: The National Report." *48th Session of International Conference on Education.*

Geneva, November 25–28, 2008. http://www.ibe.unesco.org/National_Reports/ICE_2008/ yemen_NR08.pdf.

UNICEF. *Assessment of Child Development Project, Yemen: Final Report.* Barcelona: HLSP S. L., September 2005.

World Bank. *Yemen: Secondary Education Development and Girls' Access Project.* Report No.: 41773-YE, February 19, 2008.

Culture

Everywhere on the Arabian Peninsula, countries have undergone tremendously rapid changes since the 1960s due to development and commodity consumption made possible by their oil wealth, whereas in Yemen, the pace—thankfully perhaps—has been much slower. One reason is that the income derived from oil sales has been much less compared to its neighbors, and therefore development and the change that has gone with such wealth have been at a much more moderate speed and a more modest scale. It is not that Yemen isn't changing—it is—but that its traditions retain a vibrancy and a relevance that are rare in the peninsula.

Yemenis justly take pride in their ancient past that, as we saw in Chapter 2, witnessed some of the wealthiest and culturally most sophisticated civilizations to have emerged in the Near East. Over the last three decades, foreign archaeologists in conjunction with their Yemeni counterparts have excavated more and more of this rich heritage, conserving the material remains and recording and studying them so that the rest of the world can appreciate them too. It's fair to say that Yemen is one of the most important sites for archaeological investigation in the entire Near East at the moment (De Maigret 1996). But Yemen's cultural riches extend along the earth's surface as well and almost everywhere one looks. In Chapter 2, we spoke of the 'Ama-riyyah school and mosque complex just outside the city of Rada' in central highland Yemen; it was magnificently restored by a team of art historians and archaeologists led by Selma al-Radi (1997) and her colleague Yahya al-Nasiri, an effort awarded with the 2007 Aga Khan Award for Islamic Architecture. Yet, it is not the only such example. The Old City of Sana'a was restored back in the 1990s and eventually was also awarded an Aga Khan Award for Islamic Architecture (1995). It was declared a UNESCO World Heritage City to help protect its religious and political heritage (UNESCO 2011), as were three other ancient cities in Wadi Hadhramawt: Tarim, Shibam, and Seyoun. In any case, what one rarely hears in Yemen are laments about the loss of language and cultural identity of the sort often invoked in the Gulf. There the effort to maintain a link with the past has been to recreate it in Orientalist theme parks geared to tourism and commodity consumption rather than the restoration of artifactual remains (though to be fair, this too is being attempted now, if somewhat belatedly as most remains have been destroyed by rapid urban development).

Yet, another reason that Yemen's culture is important has to do with its extraordinary cultural and linguistic diversity, something this chapter will try especially to capture. One explanation for this is that Yemen has historically existed at the crossroads of commerce and trade, the movements of people, and international political and religious trends. The same could be said, of course, for the port cities of the Gulf but not of their vast desert interiors. It may come as a surprise to some that Arabic is not the only language (apart from English) spoken in Yemen or that Sunni and Shia are not the only or most interesting religious differences, not to mention the tremendous regional variation between north versus south and coast versus highland versus desert as well as ethnic, racial, and status-group distinctions. One confronts a situation in Yemen today where traditions are changing for sure, but with their continuity with the past remaining vital and compelling.

If archaeological treasures speak to Yemen's great monumental civilizations, what they are harder at capturing is another sort of cultural richness, one based on the word, both spoken and written. As this chapter shows, Yemen produced some of the earliest and most beautiful literature in Classical Arabic. We have learned in Chapter 2 that Yemen was also a center of great Islamic learning in the medieval period, focused not only on Zabid but also on Sana'a and Taiz, and that the administration of the states of that period (especially the Rasulids) depended on literacy and a vast administrative apparatus involved with record keeping. Religious learning in turn fostered both an oral transmission of the Qur'an as well as a reading and mastery of written texts, leading one researcher to refer to this tradition as a book and manuscript culture (Messick 1993). To this day, Yemeni culture places tremendous emphasis on learning, and some of its scholars have amassed private libraries with thousands of centuries-old manuscripts that contain knowledge about dozens of subjects. Yet, this elite, and as it were, scribal culture does not capture the other more spoken or oral form of cultural production (what one might call an oral vernacular culture) that is just as important and just as vibrant. One can find this oral culture almost anywhere in the society, but this chapter focuses on its tribal form, especially its oral poetry, because it is best known and most studied (Caton 1990). Though in some ways jeopardized by universal education and the unfortunate prejudices against the dialect and nonwritten forms of culture that often accompany it, this oral tradition is being kept alive and even encouraged by audiotape recording and the music industry (Miller 2007). Arguably, it may even have a second life on the Net, though this is much less well understood. Finally, this chapter also explores a modern literary art form in which Yemenis are also adept but far less well known than they perhaps deserve to, theater and prose fiction.

REFERENCES

Aga Khan Award for Architecture. *Conservation of Old Sana'a.* 1995. http://www.akdn.org/architecture/project.asp?id=1380.

Aga Khan Award for Architecture. *Restoration of the Amiriya Complex.* 2007. http://www.akdn.org/architecture/project.asp?id=2701.

Al-Radi, Selma. *The Amiriya in Rada': The History and Restoration of a Sixteenth-century Madrasa in the Yemen.* Oxford: Oxford University Press, 1997.

Caton, Steven C. *"Peaks of Yemen I Summon": Poetry as Cultural Practice in a North Yemen Tribe.* Berkeley, CA: University of California Press, 1990.

De Maigret, Alessandro. *Arabia Felix.* Milano: Rusconi, 1996.

Messick, Brinkley M. *The Calligraphic State: Textual Domination and History in a Muslim Society.* Berkeley, CA: University of California Press, 1993.

Miller, Flagg. *The Moral Resonance of Arab Media: Audiocassette Poetry and Culture in Yemen.* Cambridge, MA: Harvard University Press, 2007.

UNESCO. *Old City of Sana'a.* 2011. http://whc.unesco.org/en/list/385.

ARABIC LANGUAGE

Steven C. Caton

The major language spoken in Yemen is Arabic (for exception see "South Arabic" below). Arabic is part of the Semitic family of languages that includes Amharic spoken in Ethiopia, Hebrew spoken in Israel, Tigrinya spoken in Eritrea, and various languages derived from Aramaic (the language spoken by Jesus and used in the liturgy of the Syriac Christian church). Among ancient languages of Semitic origin were Akkadian (Babylonian Empire), Phoenician (empire in ancient Caanan), and South Arabic (see below).

Arabic phonology has a distinctive voiced pharyngeal fricative (though hardly unique in the world's languages), the so-called 'ayn, which has no equivalent in English or other European languages. Its unvoiced breathy equivalent heard at the beginning of the Arabic *habibi* (loved one) sounds like the /h/ in house if pronounced with a very breathy voice. Both sounds require some practice to master. When the author was learning Arabic in the United States, he would practice pronunciation in a language lab, and one day someone tapped him on the shoulder and asked, "What is this beautiful language you are learning?" this said dripping with sarcasm. The reply was, "It *is* a beautiful language, it just takes a while to produce the sounds well."

Even more difficult than the phonology, however, is the word structure, or morphology, which it shares with other Semitic languages, and is based on roots or bases of usually three consonants from which words are derived using a set of fairly regular and highly productive rules. From the root K-T-B, for example, which has a very general meaning of "write," a verb KaTaBa (to write) can be derived as well as KaaTiB (writing), maKTuuB (written), KiTaaB (book), KiTaaBah (writing), maKTaB (office), and so on. In other words, whereas in English, the meanings are conveyed by separate words, which like "writer," "office," and "book" have no structural or systematic connection between them, in Arabic, even if one has not heard the word "kaatib" before but knows the general meaning of the root, it is possible to guess that the word has an active meaning—that is, "writing" or "writer"—because of the morphological rule: "to form the active participle insert a long /a/ vowel after the first root consonant and a short /i/ vowel after the second root consonant." There are other rules for forming the passive participle and various kinds of nouns, including the idea of a place in which an activity takes place such as the Arabic maKTaB (office). Furthermore, from the verb kataba can be derived other verbs simply by altering its form in a rule-governed fashion: for example, by doubling the medial consonant /kattaba/ or by adding the prefix /'a/, a verb with a causative meaning can be produced /'aktaba/ (i.e., to make someone write or dictate). Again, one does not necessarily have to memorize the word's meaning if one knows the morphological rules, and so kattaba is analogous to darrasa (to make someone study or teach), 'al-lama (to make someone learn or teach), and so forth. The system is not airtight. All grammars, as linguists like to say, "leak," but the examples are meant to illustrate the structural "logic," if one may call it that, of the so-called root-pattern system of Arabic.

Given that the morphology does so much of the "work" generating the meanings of sentences (e.g., the English equivalent of kataba in a sentence is "he wrote," which takes two words rather than one), it is perhaps not surprising that the syntax (sentence structure) is relatively less complicated than in English, though it does take some time for the beginner to remember that the verb usually (though by no means always) comes first in the sentence, followed by the subject noun and the object (if there is one), rather than the other way around as in English (Subject–Verb–Object).

Classical Arabic, Modern Standardized Arabic, and Dialect Arabic

Arabic today comes in two registers: Classical Arabic (fusha) and the colloquial ('aamiyah) or dialect (lahjah) Arabic. Classical Arabic refers to the seventh-century CE Arabic spoken by the Prophet Muhammad and his Bedouin tribe, the Bani Quraysh, which was standardized by Arab grammarians relatively soon after his death and in a sense "fixed" or "preserved" as it was spoken at that time. It is the language of the Qur'an, the Muslim holy book, or the Message Allah revealed to His Prophet, and it is therefore considered sacred.

During the Prophet's lifetime and for a while afterward, Arabic remained an oral language, to reflect the recitation of the Qur'an from Allah to the Archangel Gabriel, from the Archangel to the Prophet, from the Prophet to his companions and followers, and from them to the rest of the religious community. It was thought that the spoken word was the preferred means of accessing the sacred text of Allah; and to this day, Qur'anic memorization and recitation is considered a meritorious act, especially during the holy month of fast or on the hajj pilgrimage. But it was not long after the Prophet's death that the caliphs began to worry that oral transmission of the Qur'an might lead to discrepancies and result in discrepant textual interpretations. The danger in the latter was if these formed the bases for religious schisms, and so an effort was made by scholars to write grammars for Arabic as well as to devise an alphabetic script that would become the foundation for a standardized written language. Consonants were represented most prominently (as might be expected, given their morphological importance), and vowels for the most part were added above or below the consonants by special marks. Of most importance was the addition of vowels for case endings that made clear whether a noun was the subject or object of the verb or the object of a preposition. (In Latin, for example, which also has a fairly loose syntactical word order, case is all-important in distinguishing the grammatical function of a word.) Several distinct scripts were devised over time, and Arabic calligraphy became a major Islamic art form. In spite of these different scripts, the structure of the writing was not changed: writing proceeded from right to left, vowels were added by diacritics, and so forth.

It is important to bear in mind that Classical Arabic is not a "native" tongue any longer; that is, no one grows up speaking it but has to be instructed in it, and it takes years to master it. Imagine if Shakespearean English had been standardized as the English to be exactly reproduced for all formal communication, no one would speak it "naturally," as it were, but would have to learn it in school. What the person learns to speak and use at home is an Arabic vernacular or dialect, with tremendous variation from one country of the Arabic-speaking world to another.

Of course, Qur'anic Arabic is not necessarily useful for most modern communication, and so there have been various attempts to modernize it for use in the press, on television, in the schoolroom, for business, and in official or government contexts. This version, sometimes known as Standard Modern (or Literary) Arabic, differs from the Classical mainly in the omission of case endings and in the use of a more modern vocabulary. In this way, Classical Arabic can remain the language of the Prophet and of Allah, unchanged throughout the ages, while another version coexisting with it can be changed and adapted as needed. Despite the creation of this modern variant, however, English has increasingly displaced it as the preferred language in "high-functional" contexts such as secular education, science, and business. Given the difficulty of English and especially the need to learn it soon in school, children find that they are behind in learning how to read and write Classical Arabic. It is not even clear how competent they are in producing Modern Standard Arabic in academic or formal communications, given the strong preference for English. In a country like Yemen, where English has made less inroads than in other places like the Gulf, it is still possible to find many young people with a firm grasp of written Arabic, Classical or Modern Standard, though this might change as Yemen, inevitably, gets pulled more into the orbit of the transnational world in which English is dominant.

That a language like Arabic has two registers—one standardized and written and used mainly for formal situations, the other derived from it and mainly spoken but used in informal situations—is not unique in the world and is sometimes referred to as "diglossia" (two codes or tongues). Other examples of such linguistic communities are Standard French versus Haitian French, Standard German versus Swiss German, and Standard Greek versus Demotic Greek. At one time, British English was more diglossic than it is today, but the differences between regional dialects and the standard language have diminished to the point where they are more like a standard/dialect variation. Diglossia, in fact, resembles more a bilingual situation, given the perception speakers have of switching from one code to another, except that the varieties are understood by native speakers to be "one" language rather than two. To add to the complexity of communication on the ground is that the distinction between a standard language like Arabic and a dialect gets blurred even by speakers who have a firm grasp of the standard language; that is, even in the most formal contexts in which it would be expected that a speaker use standard Arabic, he or she is likely to add colloquialisms, or code-switch, depending on the context. For example, he or she might start out in a high form of the language, but as the interlocutors get used to each other or the topic shifts to nonspecialized areas of knowledge, they will begin to insert dialectal equivalents. The reverse happens as well: a conversation might begin in the dialect but then switch over into more standardized forms perhaps because of a specialized topic or to mark some formality about the situation. We do the same thing in our speech, moving between standard English and some form of the dialect, depending on subtle cues in the situation, but in Arabic the switch is more marked or noticeable.

South Arabic

One last point about Arabic needs to be stressed that is particularly relevant to the history of Arabic in Yemen and the southern part of the Peninsula more generally, and that is that in the pre-Islamic period (before the Arabic of the Prophet Muhammad was spread through conquest and conversion to the rest of the Islamic Empire), distinct Semitic languages called "South Arabian" were spoken and written in what is today Yemen, southern Saudi Arabia, and Oman. It is thought that vestiges of these languages (Sabaean, Himyarite, Qataban, and Mandaean) survive in three languages still spoken in the region: Mahri (approximately 120,000 speakers in the far eastern reaches of Yemen and far western reaches of Oman), Soqotri (about 57,000 speakers on the Indian Ocean island of Soqotra), and Shehri (small numbers in Oman). They share certain features of proto-Semitic (i.e., a language reconstructed from extant Semitic languages), especially those that were once spoken in the Horn of Africa (which has had numerous and deep historical connections with Yemen). It is important to bear in mind that Southern and Northern Arabic were to all intents and purposes distinct languages and were not mutually intelligible. As Northern Arabic spread into the peninsula, Southern Arabic was either obliterated or displaced to the more remote or inaccessible areas of the country where they managed to survive until this day. In the meantime, the remnants of South Arabic continued to change (they did not remain frozen), though because of their relative isolation they did not change in the direction of the dominant Northern Arabic. Speakers of the modern or contemporary languages derived from South Arabic nevertheless must still learn Northern Arabic in the schools and as a way to communicate with people from other parts of the country, and the challenges they face are more akin to bilingualism than diglossia. The existence of modern South Arabian languages in Yemen is greeted with some ambivalence, to say the least, on the part of the Yemeni government and even some Muslim intellectuals. There is a preconception of the Arabian Peninsula as being monolingual (or more accurately, monolithically Arabic), when the truth is far more complicated. Classical Arabic competes with Modern Standard Arabic that competes with English, while forms of historically derived South Arabic hold on at the margins, geographic and social. Organized efforts on the part of these marginalized speech communities to maintain their ethnolinguistic heritage (which entails more than just their language but also their folklore) is greeted differently depending on one's politics: On the one hand, it is seen as showing the cultural diversity of Yemen's people and on the other, challenging the hegemony of Northern Arabic in the country.

The Dialect of Yemeni Arabic

But all of the above does not even begin to capture the richness or diversity within the spoken language or dialect. It is sometimes claimed as a matter of pride by some Yemenis that their dialect is "closer" to Classical Arabic than other dialects of Arabic may be to the sacred language, but this claim is more a matter of perception or expectation on the part of its speakers than based on empirical lexical, phonological, or morphological similarities. Sometimes, the reason is given that Yemen has been more geographically "isolated" or politically "peripheral" in the Islamic world, but if Chapter 2 challenges any perception, it is that one. Historically, Yemen has always been at the crossroads of other civilizations with their own languages (African, Persian, South Asian, and Asian), a situation that would foster linguistic hybridity rather than purity,

Figuring out how many dialects exist in any language community is difficult, no less tricky is demarcating one dialect from another. Much depends on which linguistic differences are thought significant to merit a boundary between them (e.g., differences in kinship terms and names or word pronunciations). This said, generally speaking, there are five dialects based on different regions in the country: Sana'ani (extending from Sa'dah in the north to Sana'a in the central highlands), Taizian (extending from Taiz to Ibb in the north and to outskirts of Aden), Tihami (with Zabid at its center with the coastal Tihama as its region), Adeni (focused on the port city and its immediate environs), and Hadhrami (focused on the Wadi Hadhramawt). There are certain shibboleths or indexes that distinguish one dialect from another. Two sounds are particularly important in distinguishing dialects: the sounds are called in Arabic qaaf and jiim, or phonological /q/ and /j/ respectively. Thus, in Sana'ani Arabic, qaaf, as in the first sound in the word "qaat" (qat), is pronounced with a soft /g/ and sounds like the first consonant in the English "get," whereas in Taizian, it is more likely to be pronounced like the Classical /q/. But the pronunciation of the sound /j/ is the reverse in the two dialects, with Sana'ani retaining the

Classically sounding /j/ as in the English "judge," whereas in Taizian, it is pronounced like the initial sound in the English "get." Thus, the word "university" is pronounced as /jaami'ah/ in Sana'a but /gaami'ah/ in the southern portion of the country. Grammatical differences are noticeable as well (such as distinct forms for the future tense or the continuative aspect of the verb), and there are of course numerous lexical differences as well as idiomatic usages. These notwithstanding, the Yemeni dialects are mutually intelligible to its speakers.

BIBLIOGRAPHY

Caton, Steven C. *"Peaks of Yemen I Summon": Poetry as Cultural Practice in a North Yemen Tribe.* Berkeley, CA: University of California Press, 1990.

Ferguson, Charles. "Diglossia." *Word* 15 (1959): 325–40.

Haeri, Niloofar. *Sacred Language, Ordinary People: Dilemmas of Culture and Politics in Egypt.* New York: Palgrave Macmillan, 2003.

Rossi, Ettore. *L'Arabo Parlato a San(a): Grammatica, Testi, Lessico* [Arabic spoken in Sana'a: grammar, texts, lexicon]. Roma: Istituto per l'Oriente, 1939.

Watson, Janet C.E., Bonnie Glover Stalls, Khalid al-Razihi, and Shelagh Weir. "The Language of Jabal Rāzih: Arabic or Something Else?" *Proceedings of the Seminar for Arabian Studies* 36 (2006): 35–41.

ETIQUETTE

Steven C. Caton

Greetings

In Arab society, there is perhaps no more important ritual of everyday courtesy than the greeting. It is almost impossible to begin a conversation or engage in some other transaction with a person one has not seen that day without uttering a greeting. And not just a perfunctory greeting like ones we tend to utter in our society ("Oh, hi . . .") but elaborate sayings that can sometimes go on for minutes on end. What's more, one may think one is past the greeting that initiates an interchange or transaction of some sort, only to find that one is being greeted again and that one must respond appropriately. The transaction grinds to a halt to give way to this nicety, and only then can the transaction resume. In general, greetings show piety toward Allah and respect for the other.

Partly, this has to do with Islam. The Qur'an is explicit about the kind of greeting devout Muslims ought to give each other:

When those come to thee, who believe in Our Signs, say "Peace be upon you."

(Surah VI, 53)

This greeting serves as a shibboleth for true or devout Muslims, and it may be for this reason that zealous individuals may eschew its use for or by nonbelievers. Thus, the Qur'an also says that for those Muslims who have been saved and gone to Paradise, "their greeting will be 'peace'!" (Surah XIV, 23). Because the expression Salaam 'alaykum (Peace be upon you) is so often heard in everyday interactions, one is not always aware of its Islamic connotations, but these are never far from the surface. Finally, there is no more important injunction mentioned in the Qur'an regarding the greeting than the following:

> If you are greeted courteously, then greet with a better one, or return it (at least) in kind. God takes account of all things.
>
> (Surah IV, 86)

If one returns the greeting "in kind," it is enough to say "And upon you be peace," but if one is returning it with a better one, the riposte may be "And peace be upon you and His mercy and His blessings." The idea being that in replying one heaps or showers greetings upon the interlocutor.

This is not the only greeting pair that can be used in the language, and these others are not necessarily marked for religious piety. Another common greeting is "Ahlan wa Sahlan" (the translation is difficult but has a general meaning of "People and Plain") to which the reply would be "W-Ahlan bik" (roughly, "and the same to you"). Marhaba (welcome) is also heard to which the reply is Marhaba bik or more unusually Maraahib (the plural of welcome). There are also ways of intensifying the response of these ritual greetings.

There are dozens of greetings for nearly every time of day and occasion, as well as tribal region. There is a morning as well as an evening greeting. There is a greeting for a groom, a greeting for the holiday that comes at the end of Ramadan, and a greeting to usher in the New Year. There is a greeting for a collective or group as distinct from an individual.

Greetings are conveyed not just through language, of course. Generally speaking, one shakes with the right hand (though religious individuals might refrain from taking the hand of a member of the opposite sex), and though the handshake is firm, it is not the viselike grip common among some American males. The handshake may also be prolonged, and it is important throughout to look the other person in the eye with a steady glance. To do otherwise is to suggest insincerity or even worse. A person who is particularly close to one, either through kinship or friendship, may be greeted by pulling the other's hand toward one in the handshake and then exchanging light kisses on each other's cheeks. Sometimes, a person will offer their wrist rather than the hand because the hand is dirty or wet, and the proper thing to do is to shake the wrist. In the past, extreme respect was shown to a patriarch or matriarch by dropping to one's knees and kissing the hem of their garment before standing to greet them, and sons and daughters can still be seen doing this to their parents, especially if they have been away from home for a long time.

Upon entering a room, it is usual to greet everyone with a loud Salaam 'alaykum or good morning or some other equivalent, after which everyone in the room in unison utters the appropriate paired response. At this point, one has a choice, either to stop the greeting and get to the point of the transaction or conversation, or to initiate a greeting with every individual in the room before joining the conversation. The latter might be desirable given the nature of the occasion (e.g., one has not seen the people in the room in a long time or the personages are of some status and importance). When greeting more than one person, one begins on one's right-hand side and works one's way around the room, stopping to linger with someone one knows well and inquiring about common acquaintances or family, before continuing on down the line. If people are sitting down and are being greeted individually, they must stand for the person and shake their hand (remaining seated would be an affront). Greetings are just as elaborate and heartfelt between women as they are between men. If no transaction can get started without a suitable greeting of a person one has not seen previously that day, no transaction can be complete without some show of hospitality by the person in whose "space" one temporarily finds oneself—be it their home, their office, their qat chew, or their store or place of business. Usually something to drink (water, tea, coffee, or a soft drink) is offered, with perhaps a token biscuit or fresh fruit or candy. These cannot be refused, unless one is feeling ill (an acceptable excuse might sound like this: "I'm very sorry but my stomach is upset and I don't think I can have any. But thank you very much."). The danger of the latter, however, is that this will elicit elaborate concern over one's health and lengthy inquiries into what one has eaten or where one has been that might have caused such health problems, thereby complicating the situation and delaying the transaction. Better to be polite and simply take a sip from the

---

MAFRAJ

Mafraj is the common Yemeni word for sitting room (diwan or majlis in Standard Arabic). It is the public space in the house where guests are received, where qat chews occur, and where large meals are served (and when guests are not around, it is where the family may congregate in the evening). It comes from the root F-R-J, which has the general meaning of furnishing and may be translated as the place that is furnished for comfort. The basic furnishings are almost always the same, geared toward sitting on the floor, and differing only in the sumptuousness of the fabric and other decorative materials: a carpet to make walking more comfortable, thickly padded seat cushions lined against the walls, back bolsters, and elbow rests. There will be spittoons in which to expectorate qat, thermoses to keep water cold or tea hot, and the so-called water pipe known in many parts of the world as the shisha but in Yemen as the mada'a. Not least is the location of most mafrajes in highland Yemen at the top of the house, with breathtaking views of the scenery.

drink and nibble the food in order not to offend the host's hospitality. Having cleared this hurdle, expect now to answer inquiries about the health and well-being of family members before proceeding to the transaction.

It should be borne in mind that these are not simply formalities one has to go through before the "real business" at hand can transpire. For a transaction to occur, mutual respect has to be demonstrated, otherwise the transaction might not be trusted. Furthermore, it always helps if people like each other or learn to like each other, at least from first impressions, for the transaction to work smoothly. And, above all, people like these displays of respect and affection, as much for what they express toward the other as for what they signal about themselves; that is, that they are honorable and God-fearing persons.

As elaborate as greetings are, farewells or good-byes tend to be brief. It is perhaps just the opposite with us, for we linger on our farewells and find it awkward to finally take our leave. In Yemen, it is more common to say good-bye once, individually or collectively, and then depart without further ado. It is important to bear in mind, though, that if one is a host and saying good-bye to the guest, it is perhaps impolite to close the door on them until they have turned their back and walked away. As with other things in the world, timing is everything.

Conversation

Most conversation takes place in a sitting position, and often on the floor of a sitting room called a mafraj in Yemeni Arabic. The host has to make the guest feel comfortable by providing a comfortable chair (or vacating his own for the guest), and in the sitting room, by providing comfortable elbow rests and back cushions. Of course, the guest has certain obligations as well. When entering a house, it is usual to take off one's street shoes and leave them in the vestibule or immediately outside the sitting room (which is located near the door of the house). If the sitting room is located on the top floor of the house (usually the case in the older style "tower" houses), the guest will walk up the stairs with his or her shoes on, and if he is a male, he may utter "Allah, Allah!" to alert the females of the house that a stranger is in their midst. Arriving at the door of the sitting room, he or she takes off their shoes and leaves them outside the door. Entering the room, one utters whatever greetings one thinks appropriate, after which the host will indicate one's "seat of honor" in the room (usually on either side of the host at the head of the room, furthest away from the door). Sitting cross-legged or with one knee bent and the other leg extended requires its own etiquette. Never extend the foot so that the sole is exhibited directly at anyone. And if wearing a wrap that looks like a sarong (to be recommended when one is sitting on the floor), the male must make sure he is not exposing his crotch.

Conversation is a highly valued art form in Yemen. A high premium is put on wit and eloquence. It is not enough to provide information, it has to be done with a certain style or attitude that amuses or entertains. A stranger is often asked what to Westerners may seem like startlingly personal or irrelevant questions, such as how much money they make or whether their parents are dead or alive (a sign of concern and respect), but this is not thought to be rude. It has sometimes been explained as an attempt to place the stranger in a wider social network so that one knows what level of respect or hospitality is appropriate to show them. It sometimes happens that in the course of such conversation something comes to light about the stranger's status or prominence that requires the host to ratchet up the hospitality.

Hospitality toward the Stranger and Guest

It is understood that strangers who do not threaten the safety of the group can expect to be received hospitably. That includes the protection of the group as well as food and water. There is an expression in Yemen that if one has broken "bread and salt" with the stranger, the latter cannot be harmed. However, the traditional period of this hospitality is three days, after which time the stranger may be asked to leave.

Hospitality is a key cultural value among all Arabs, but especially so among tribal people. Honor largely hinges on how hospitably one has been received and how hospitable one has been toward the guest. In other words, if one has an acknowledged social status, one may expect to be treated with a certain amount of respect, including hospitality; conversely, enjoying a certain amount of respect means that it is incumbent upon one to exert every effort to be hospitable toward guests.

Meals

If invited to a meal (lunches are the equivalent of our dinner, eaten usually after the midday prayer, between 12 and 1 P.M.), it is not customary to bring anything (and though needless to say, it bears emphasizing that bringing a bottle of wine or any alcohol would be a terrible gaff). Bringing salad or dessert, now fairly common among guests in our culture, would send the wrong signal: that the host doesn't have the means or the skill to prepare a decent meal. In even quite modern and cosmopolitan households, it is common for dinner to be served on the floor, with a tablecloth underneath the dishes to keep everything clean. And though a Westerner might be given silverware as a courtesy, one must be prepared to eat with one's hands, or to be more precise with one's right hand only. One reaches for or accepts things only with one's right hand. In recognition of the fact that one eats with the hand, before the meal begins, the host passes around a bowl of clean water in which one can dip one's fingers and then dry them on a towel, or indicates where the washroom is. Not all dishes are eaten with the hand; soups are sipped, and custards and other kinds of desserts might require a spoon. When dinner is over, one has the chance to wash one's hands again, and depending on the formality of the occasion, the host might also insist on sprinkling rosewater on one's clothes or some other kind of perfume.

Men gather to eat for a special occasion in a rural mountain village. (Dirk Panier/ arabianEye/Corbis)

Dining is a gender-segregated affair, though a Western woman often has the choice of whether to eat with the women or the men. She does not lose respect by deciding to eat with the men, but she may lose the affection of the women (and possibly even their help or support) if she does so. Of course, men have no choice in that regard; they can only eat with the other men. There is another reason why the woman may chose to eat with the men; it is they who get first stab at the food, women and children eat the leftovers.

Meals are also usually silent affairs. One eats fairly rapidly, though sparingly of each dish, because there are several courses leading up to the pièce de résistance, usually a meat dish, and one has to reserve one's appetite for the grand finale. Of course, the host worries that one is not getting enough to eat and is constantly urging one to "Eat! Eat!" and placing choice cuts of meat on one's plate that one cannot refuse. In the meantime, chitchat is kept to a bare minimum. Conversation is reserved for the afternoon chew. After everyone has had their fill, the food is cleared and tea or coffee is served. But this too is rapidly drunk, sometimes with a loud slurping sound that we might consider unmannerly but is a sign of appreciation. Guests do not compliment the women of the household for a job well done in preparing the food and cooking it, though if female guests decide to eat with the women of the house they may want to. It is appropriate, however, to compliment the host for his generosity, and there are formulaic expressions for doing so.

QAT

The shrub *Catha edulis,* or qat as it is known in Yemen, is banned by the U.S. government because it contains a monoamine alkaloid called cathinone, an amphetamine-like stimulant (though it should be noted that it is legal in many countries, including Great Britain, whose court rulings are based upon the same scientific evidence). Certain negative physiological effects are associated with its use: short-term ones include insomnia, acid buildup in the stomach and esophagus, mild constipation, temporary impotence, and suppression of appetite; longer-term effects may include increased blood pressure, liver damage, and oral and esophageal cancers (though not enough longitudinal studies have been carried out to fully substantiate these claims). Far more exaggerated and harder to verify are the assertions that qat chewing can induce trancelike or even mildly psychotic states such as a high degree of emotionalism, agitation, and even trembling in the hands and limbs in people who are presumed to be "normal" otherwise. The side effects of withdrawal are more severe for coffee drinking or tobacco smoking. It does not produce the same level of addiction or dependence as either of these substances that are legal in the United States and other countries, and has arguably less deleterious side effects.

The Qat Chew

There is perhaps no more important social event in the everyday lives of most Yemenis than the qat chew. This is where Yemenis, men and women, will get together in someone's sitting room and chew the succulent leaves of the qat bush (in the larger cities, men who are away from home may congregate in public halls set aside for that purpose and pay a little money for a water pipe). It takes several hours of an afternoon to attend a chew. Many Yemenis chew every day, while others chew only once a week (on Friday, the holy day of the week in the Muslim calendar).

Though often fun, it is a mistake to think of the qat chew as merely a leisure-time activity. This is also an occasion for exchanging news, conducting business, and networking. It is best to go to a qat chew with the intention of chewing qat, of course, but if for health or other reasons one does not chew, one may still attend these events for the sake of sociability and conversation. Not only foreigners eschew the chew (though some foreigners are habitués), but there are also Yemenis who refrain from chewing it for economic, health, or religious reasons (stimulants of any kind, even coffee, might be considered unlawful). In some circles, it is even seen as "politically incorrect," because of the drain on water resources that qat cultivation is presumed to represent (though this issue is more complicated than such views capture).

Before one even arrives at a chew, there is an elaborate process of buying qat and cleaning it that is at once practical and ritual in import. It is not strictly speaking legal to sell it anywhere in a city; designated areas are set aside for that purpose in which

Men chew qat in a Sana'a street. (Jack Malipan/Dreamstime.com)

producers display their wares in stalls or in the back of pickup trucks. A customer heads toward those areas just after work and before lunchtime in order to secure the best grades of qat. Not all qat is deemed of equal value: that cultivated in the tribal area to the northeast of the capital, Sana'a, known as Hamdani, is widely considered the best, though it has close competitors from other areas of northern Yemen. Generally speaking, the best quality is grown in the highland regions rather than in the coastal plains or southern wadis of the country, where air temperature, soil content, and aridity are not conducive to optimal cultivation.

Unless they are first-time buyers at a particular qat market, customers will go to a preferred seller first to check out his supplies because they know they will get a price closer to the market value. Buyers will find it prepared in different ways. Often the most expensive is the qat that appears in the form of branches (*oudi,* in Yemeni Arabic) cut off whole from the shrub or tree (some stand well over six feet) that are then loosely tied together at the base of the branches. Another form, called *ghutbah,* is a bundle made up of the leaves and their stems that are wrapped in banana leaves to retain their moisture. The buyer inspects both the tips of the leaves and the base of the stems or branches, and might even sniff them, as though inhaling the aroma of a bouquet of flowers, to determine their freshness. He may then inspect the leaves more carefully for evidence of insecticide spray and be assured by the seller that only dust was used to keep the bugs off (whether only natural fertilizer was used is not usually asked, at least in this writer's experience, which would make it truly "organic").

Satisfied that the buyer is offering quality qat, the customer now begins the bargaining process:

"How much?" the customer asks. The seller responds with a price.

"No, brother, that's way too high."

He inspects it and makes criticisms of it here and there, building a case for why he thinks the asking price is inflated. After a while, he puts in a low bid, and it is now the seller's turn to rebuke the buyer for an unrealistic price. Back and forth they go—the buyer's price inching upward, the sellers inching downward—until both parties are in agreement or one of the two decides to back out of the transaction, moving on to the next stall or the next customer. When the bargaining has been successfully concluded, the seller wraps the qat in a sheet of cellophane (in the case of the branches) or puts the bundle in a plastic bag and hands the merchandise over to the customer, reassuring him that he won't be disappointed and admonishing him to return for more. It is often said that foreigners get the raw end of the deal, but the more seasoned ones bargain as hard and as successfully as any Yemeni.

At home, the buyer usually washes the qat to remove dirt and possible chemical contaminants. Some people do this by soaking it in a small plastic tub, perhaps adding a bit of salt as an astringent. Draining the water, they then dry it, a more delicate process than might be imagined. Each branch is whisked in the air to remove drops of water and then placed inside a headcloth or shawl to soak up excess moisture. In the case of the smaller qat bundles, the individual stems are placed inside a plastic bag, which has been perforated with small holes, and the bag then rotated by the outstretched arm several times in wide circles or arcs, sprinkling water drops on the floor and walls. The leaves are then removed and placed inside a dry bag or in a headcloth or shawl. It is now ready to be chewed.

It is thought important to have a full lunch before chewing qat, presumably because food in the stomach soaks up acid buildup and prevents heartburn. The preferred meal is *saltah,* a tasty vegetable stew cooked at intense heat in a special soapstone pot with whipped fenugreek folded into it at the end and chunks of boiled beef added as well. This is eaten with delicious flat breads of various kinds.

Though individuals do chew qat by themselves (especially when doing physical labor), it is more usual for them to get together in sitting rooms, because a chew or *takhzin* is widely considered a social occasion. Indeed, some of its culturally understood side effects are sociability and, above all, talkativeness. Most chews involve close kinsmen and friends, but there are also specialized chews according to professional networks or the political and artistic interests of its participants.

The qat chew has an elaborate etiquette. The host is responsible for providing a clean and comfortable room that is well appointed with carpets, bolsters, and elbow rests to accommodate the anticipated number of guests, along with such accoutrements as spittoons, water thermoses or extra bottles of cold water and sodas, ashtrays, and sometimes also the water pipe or mada'a. Guests are expected to bring their own qat (unless they are being hosted at a special event), along with at least one bottle of water. Upon arrival, he or she (for women have their own chews and female qat consumption is almost as high as that of males) is welcomed by the host and ushered into a seat near to him according to a social status subtly calibrated on the spot. The guest is expected not only to greet the host but also the rest of the assembly with formulaic and flowery expressions. Making himself or herself comfortable in his or her seat, he or she may now begin chewing qat.

The qat session goes through roughly two phases. In the first, people get settled in (it is important to sit comfortably) and begin stripping the leaves from the branches to chew. It is important not to swallow the masticated leaves but to push them with the tongue into one or the other cheek, a bolus or wad of qat building up there. Indeed, a chew is known as a takhzin, which literally translates as the storing (of qat). If the bolus becomes too big, the chewer has the option of expectorating some of it into a spittoon. Meanwhile, the juice released from the leaves is swallowed, eventually producing a physiological effect of heightened attention. Another can be profuse sweating (acerbated by the close atmosphere of the sitting room, considered beneficial to the chew). Water is drunk regularly to rehydrate as well as to keep the throat from becoming too dry. Should one suddenly choke, a swig of soda or a spoonful of sugar, kept at hand specifically for such an eventuality, can provide relief. Conversation in this phase is animated and often very witty, but in the second, climactic phase—somewhat enigmatically known as (the Prophet) Solomon's hour—the room grows quieter and the mood is more introspective. At some point, the chewer will decide it is time to go home (usually before the sundown or evening prayer): He will expectorate the last of his qat, pack up his things, and take his leave with a brief goodbye. If he or she stays after the chew is over, it is often considered proper etiquette to provide a light refreshment of flat bread and cheese with tea, not to feed the guest (for qat usually kills the appetite) but to help settle the stomach and ease the digestion. Because qat can cause insomnia, milk can also help (though sometimes stronger drinks are imbibed even though they are forbidden).

The importance of the qat chew in Yemeni society cannot be overestimated. It is not about getting high on a drug but about getting into a mood, enabled by a substance that acts as a stimulus, in order to socialize and eloquently discuss important topics. The political scientist Lisa Wedeen, for example, has argued that the chew is fundamental to the practice of a critical discourse in the Yemeni public sphere and hence is part and parcel of a democratic process, though one, to be sure, that most political analysts who think in conventional Western analytical categories would not recognize as such (Wedeen 2008). My own experience bolsters this view. Chews can be freewheeling and profound discussions of current events, national and international, though they need not be. Often they are just a lot of fun. And for those who see Yemenis chewing qat on the streets or doing some work and think that this is a sign of laziness or tuning-out, think again: qat can provide bursts of energy and concentration for limited periods of time; and because it assuages hunger, it can be a way of getting through a day without hunger pangs.

Gift Giving

Gifts may be given all the time, but there are ritual occasions at which they are prescribed such as the end of certain holidays like the one celebrating the end of the fast of Ramadan (though these are usually gifts to children) and by the returning hajj pilgrim to his family and relatives. If someone has been traveling abroad, it is expected that they return with gifts for friends and relatives (one reason that bags on many flights to the Middle East from destinations abroad are bulging with gift items).

Bargaining

Bargaining, of course, is a famous aspect of Arab society, and though it is becoming less common in modern urban areas, it is still an important practice in the older or traditional markets. It occurs when there are no "fixed" prices for commodities, the final price being set through a process of sometimes protracted negotiation between buyer and seller. Though there is no fixed price, there is an unstated or implicit price range that both need to know, and this varies depending on a number of circumstances not all of which are necessarily clear to either party. There is, of course, supply and demand set according to how things seem to be selling in the market or how dearly or cheaply they are bought from the outside to be sold in the market, but this is almost never the exclusive factor. From the seller's point of view, it might be advantageous to secure a customer's long-term loyalty, for which he is ready to sell at a discount. If the customer is a kinsman or friend, he will probably ask a steeply reduced or minimal price. On the other hand, he may decide that the buyer is rich and can afford to pay slightly more than the "going" price for a certain good (a presumption often made of foreigners). The buyer, in turn, wants to offer as little as possible for the commodity in question, but he cannot start his bid at too low a price without a certain risk of either insulting the seller (and thus terminating the transaction) or revealing his own ignorance about the "going" price and showing himself inept or unsophisticated. In other words, bargaining is an elaborate dance, and one might as well enjoy it.

It's unnecessary for the buyer to agree to a price and conclude the sale in the first bargaining attempt. In fact, bargaining often takes place over several sessions, particularly for expensive items. It is good for both seller and buyer to see what the acceptable range is, and then over successive tries to narrow it to a point where an agreed price is reached. When it is, the seller often celebrates the sale with the customer by sharing some tea (offered at the beginning of the transaction in any case). As for payment, sellers often accept credit and will write the amount of the debt in their account book. Indeed, accepting credit is not only a sign of trust in the buyer but also a sign of social contentment with the seller. To pay a debt too quickly or to insist on paying for an item in cash when the seller offers to extend credit risks insulting the seller; of course, waiting too long to pay an outstanding debt risks the seller's ire and jeopardizes the relationship with him. As with bargaining itself, payment has its own delicate etiquette.

Friendship and Hand-Holding in Public

Arguably, there is no more important social relationship than friendship, though parental and sibling relations are deeply prized. One is expected to do more for a friend than one would for the equivalent person in our own society. If a friend comes to call, drop whatever you are doing and welcome them for a chat. If they are in trouble, do everything to help. One can count on friends, and they in turn can count on you.

The affection friends display toward each other often exceeds what, for example, married couples might feel comfortable showing toward each other in public. Same-sex friends are far more likely to hold hands than would a married couple. The first time it happens to a Westerner that his or her hand is held by a friend, it can be a bit disconcerting, simply because we are not used to holding the hands of our friends in public, which usually means that the relationship is sexual. Just the opposite is assumed when two friends hold hands in public in Yemen. The emotional passion or intensity is there but not the sex.

Of course, that does not mean sex is impossible or unheard of in friendships, though this is not publicly condoned as "natural" or "acceptable." When this happens, the sexual behavior is understood within the frame of friendship rather than of sexuality—as something that has happened within a certain context of intimacy between two persons of the same sex rather than as something one "prefers" or "desires" for his or her own sake. As people learn more about Western concepts of sexuality, however, this way of looking at things is changing.

Challenging Someone in Public

In Yemen, the preferred way to resolve a conflict or dispute between people is to resort to mediation rather than to call in the police or a lawyer. The latter is a recourse of last resort. There is an everyday ritual for initiating such mediation that is useful to know even if one never has to resort to it. If someone owes one money or has perpetrated a slight or some other offense, it is common for him to confront that person and say something like, "I challenge you!" and then to pull a neighbor or mutual friend aside and give them something of value (it can be a wallet or a watch or even a dagger) as a guarantee of a truce between oneself and the person so challenged. If that latter is respectful, he will do the same thing by handing over some personal item of value to the impromptu mediator. By the way, it is difficult, if not impossible, for the mediator to refuse; it is considered a social obligation to intervene in disputes and help resolve them peacefully and justly. The plaintiff and the defendant will now give their sides of the story, the mediator will ask them questions for further clarification or information, if necessary. Hardly ever does this process go unnoticed and unremarked by passersby, who listen to the arguments and offer their own judgment of the case, particularly as they are likely to know both parties in the dispute. Satisfied that he has heard enough and that a consensus seems to emerging from the crowd as to what to do about the case, he issues his verdict and suggests ways of reconciliation through payments and other forms of reconciliation. Unless the verdict has been blatantly biased or founded on bad evidence or unsound judgment, it is difficult for the two parties in the dispute to refuse reconciliation without angering the mediator and making the matter worse.

BIBLIOGRAPHY

Caton, Steven C. "Salam Tahiyyah: Greetings from the Highlands of Yemen." *American Ethnologist* 3, no. 2 (1986): 290–308.

Caton, Steven C. *Yemen Chronicle: An Anthropology of War and Mediation.* New York: Hill & Wang, 2005.

Chelhod, Joseph. *Culture et Institutions du Yemen [Culture and Institutions of Yemen].* Paris: G.-P. Maisonneuve et Larose, 1985.

Gerholm, Tomas. *Market, Mosque and Mafraj: Social Inequality in a Yemeni Town.* Stockholm: Department of Anthropology, University of Stockholm, 1977.

Wedeen, Lisa. *Peripheral Visions: Publics, Power, and Performance in Yemen.* Chicago, IL: University of Chicago Press, 2008.

LITERATURE

Classical Poetry and Prose: From Ancient Times until the Present

Mohammed Sharafuddin

Classical Poetry

The eighth-century Arab critic and poet Amr ibn al-Alaa once remarked, "Yemen almost took [Arabic] poetry all for itself." He meant by this that the best of Arabic poetry either came from poets who were Yemeni or whose place of origin was Yemen. His statement reflects the importance of Yemenis in the history of Arabic poetry. Given that Arabic poetry is often about important personages and events, it also reflects the important role Yemenis have played in Arab history, both as actors in and witnesses of those events.

Yemeni poetry—and here is meant poetry written in Classical Arabic—can be divided into three major periods:

- *The Early Period, 500–750 CE:* This covers the pre-Islamic and early Islamic period up to the end of the Umayyad caliphate (681–750 CE), the second of four major caliphates that succeeded the Prophet Muhammad.

- *The Middle Period, 751–1837:* This covers the Abbasid caliphate (750–1519 CE) and the first Ottoman occupation of Yemen up until the British established their colony in southern Yemen.

- *The Modern Period, 1838 until the Present:* This covers the so-called Arabic Renaissance or Nahda, which began in Egypt and then spread to Lebanon, Syria, and other Ottoman lands, as well as the colonial regimes set up by the British and French in the Near East and the postcolonial modern period that began after World War II until the present.

Yemeni literature connects and intertwines with political events in each of these periods. Arabic literature is very much about art being engaged with the social world rather than being a retreat or haven from it. Poetry in particular is seen as a vehicle by which men may persuade each other to analyze what is happening around them and to offer solutions.

Especially in the last two periods, Yemen witnessed the succession of some 15 polities or states (from the medieval kingdoms to the current republic), all of which vied for control of Southern Arabia. The events connected with this turbulent and complex history produced a massive literature, one reflecting the religious and political strife of the times. While other Arab countries experienced religious strife, Yemen may well have been unique in this respect because of multiple Shia and Sunni sects that competed for power.

First Period: 500–750 CE

It is important to note that history as a form of collective memory (passed down from generation to generation) is embedded in poetry. To some, Yemen or Southern Arabia is more generally considered the source of early Arabism, the origin of great pre-Islamic civilizations such as the Sabaeans, a land blessed with fertility and industrious people. It earned the sobriquet "Arabia Felix" or "Happy Arabia." The Qur'an mentions the Queen of Sheba, Bilquis, which Yemenis regard as a sacred recognition of their special heritage. The story of her encounter with the Israelite King Solomon in Palestine is told with some elaboration. It describes how the hoopoe, a favorite bird at King Solomon's court, tells his liege the strange news of flying to the land of Sheba and finding "a woman ruling them" (Qur'an XXVII, 23). Yemenis have always felt proud of this story, and poets since early times have celebrated the queen's fairness and wisdom.

But when she makes an appearance in verse, it is not only to commemorate her and Yemen's greatness. Within the story of Bilquis is a parable for many Yemenis of the importance of being open to that which is foreign, even if it entails arduous travel over long distances. Bilquis's journey set an example for future generations to do likewise, and indeed, Yemenis are now found in nearly every corner of the globe. For those modern critics skeptical as to why a female monarch should make such a long journey, there is historical evidence of other Sabaean monarchs having journeyed outside the confines of Southern Arabia, such as the founder of the Sabaean dynasty itself, King Saba Ben Yashjub, who made conquests outside Yemen all the way to the precincts of Babylon. One can also read in the poetic texts of this period a moral justification for the Queen's trip. She journeyed in search of the truth, and what the pre-Islamic monarch found was the idea of monotheism that later became a major precept in the teaching of the founder of Islam, the Prophet Muhammad.

But in many respects, these stories of Queen Bilquis and the Kingdom of Saba were a nostalgic backward glance to a glorious period in Yemen's history that, by the beginning of the sixth century, was in marked decline. The destruction of Marib Dam, also related in the Qur'an and often figuring as an allegory of punishment for arrogance and impiety in subsequent literature, occurred around this time and was a major reason for the collapse of Yemeni civilization. Another factor was the invasion and occupation of Yemen by Christian forces from Ethiopia (the infamous

Abraha mentioned in the Qur'an, who invaded Mecca with elephants with the intention of destroying the pre-Islamic site of the Kaaba, only to be defeated miraculously by birds carrying stones in their beaks that they dropped like missiles on the invaders), whose empire in Yemen was driven out by the hero Sayf bin Dhi Yazan with the help of Persian forces. The exploits of this Yemeni hero became the source of a great oral saga, *The Story of Sayf bin Dhi Yazan,* though it was probably first composed in Egypt rather than in Yemen, where it is less well known or popular.

During this period, too, Yemenis interacted with northern tribes in the peninsula, and theirs is the lion's share of the poetry composed at that time. One of the greatest of Yemeni poets was Amr ibn Baraqah, a pioneer in writing the earliest form of the Arabic *qasida* (epic poem). In one of his poems, he describes how he took revenge on some local invaders who stole his cattle. Ignoring the warnings of a local prophetess, he decided to go after the thieves and eventually recovered his property. This is how he celebrated his victory:

Whenever you gather a clever heart
With a strong sword
Along with a generous face,
All injustices shall vanish from thee.[1]

THE SAGA OF SAYF BIN DHI YAZAN, YEMENI FOLK HERO

The legend of Sayf bin Dhi Yazan, who is considered a folk hero in Yemen, is due to a great oral poetic saga called the *Life of Sayf bin Dhi Yazan.* On a par with the *Song of Roland* and comparable to other 'Arabic poetic sagas as the *Chronicle of the Bani Hilal* and the *Story of 'Antara ibn Shadad,* the *Life of Sayf bin Dhi Yazan* starts out in a mythical time and place, filled with jinni, sorcerers, and enchanters of various kinds, who are fighting each other for control of the universe. The forces of good, representing the monotheistic tradition of Abraham from which the Semites stem, are badly outnumbered by the forces of evil who worship false gods. Sayf's mother, herself a great sorceress on the side of evil, attempts to usurp her husband's throne through magic. Her son would have perished by her own hands had he not been rescued by a king, whose beautiful daughter he falls in love with. A heroic journey follows in which Sayf confronts a powerful Abyssinian (i.e., Aksumite) emperor along with two wizards, over whom our hero eventually triumphs and founds a new kingdom that follows the Abrahamic way.

---

[1] Translations of this and all other poetry in this section are by the author, Mohammed Sharafuddin.

He attributed his success not only to his physical strength but also to his moral righteousness.

Although there is not enough space here to do justice to the complexity and richness of the Arabic qasida that originated in the pre-Islamic period (known as the Age of Ignorance in the Qur'an), brief comments about its esthetic form and content or meaning are still necessary. It is usually around 50 lines long (though there are much longer poems as well), and each poem is composed in a uniform meter, there having been many complex metrical patterns in use. Indeed, meter is one of the great esthetic accomplishments of this genre. Every line has the same rhyme. And every poem is composed with a singular idea or purpose in mind (the term "qasida" derives from the word "intention" in Arabic). Some of the greatest poetry of that era was lyrical or love poetry, in which the beloved comes across the ashes of his beloved's encampment in the desert and then follows her footsteps, recounting her charms as he does. Panegyric or praise of important personages was also a popular verse form, as was too its opposite, the searing satire.

The qasida poets dating from the early period are considered the greatest in Arabic literature. (It is rumored that seven odes from this period were chosen to be suspended in the Kaaba in Mecca, the large black cubical structure in the middle of the Haram Mosque that is circumambulated by pilgrims, and for that reason came to be known as the "Suspended Odes," though this has not been substantiated.) Among these early poets were Yemenis like Malik ibn Ka'b and Amr ibn Ma'di Karib al-Zubaydi (some Yemenis claim Imru al-Qays as one of their own, though he was likely born in Najd, in present-day Saudi Arabia). While all three poets lived in the pre-Islamic period, Amr ibn Ma'di Karib al-Zubaydi, lived till after the founding of Islam, and he witnessed the famous Qadisiyyah Battle (636 CE) against the Persians. The following is an excerpt from one of his poems, a perfect example of a pre-Islamic qasida full of martial pride:

> Beauty is not a cloth, so get to know that
> Even if you have donned a gown, Beauty is minerals and traits begetting glory
> I have prepared for calamities, [with] good arms and a strong steed,
> A stout horse, a sword with two edges that cleave a helmet,
> And weapons well-built.
> Since then, I have come to know that I was going to spar with Kaab and Nahda
> These are warriors when they put on the iron
> They turn into tigers, with bracelets and with armor.
> Every man runs thus to the Day of Turmoil
> With what he is prepared.

When Islam spread from Arabia across the Levant and North Africa, Yemenis fought in the armies and ended up scattered throughout the empire. Their pride in their Yemeni origins never faltered, however. Some of the big names in Yemeni poetry after the advent of Islam were Amr ibn Zayd al-Ghalibi, A'sha of Hamdan, Wadah of Yemen, and Ilqimah ibn Thiljadan. Wadah wrote love poems to celebrate important female personages renowned for their beauty. These women took pride in his verses because they knew they would be circulated throughout Arabia. Ilqimah ibn Thiljadan is famous for having written poetry lamenting the passing away of the culture and power of ancient Yemen. He wrote abundant poetry on this subject, and for this reason earned the nickname "the Lamenter of Yemen."

Second Period: 751–1837 CE

In this period, prose writing emerged with poetry as an important form of literature. Often manuscripts on academic or scientific subjects were written in a kind of rhymed prose called saj' that required a fair amount of artistic skill.

The Islamic world, Yemen included, was under the influence of the Abbasids (751–1284 CE). Their capital, Baghdad, was a center of learning and political power that they extended to other parts of the Islamic empire. Yemen followed suit but not without resistance. Rebellions were widespread, which the Abbasids put down cruelly. For example, a rebellion in the coastal Tihama in 819 was quelled by the caliph's general, Muhammad ibn Ziyad, who was known for his notoriously severe treatment of the rebel forces. After accomplishing his task, he decided to stay in Yemen, founding his own dynasty and establishing the city of Zabid, which became a great center of Islamic learning during this period.

The children of Ibn Ziyad had to share the rule of Yemen with other dynasties like the Yafurites (840–1003 CE), who came to power after they staged their own rebellion in 834 CE. Poetry was a rhetorical weapon in the struggle for power between rival dynasties. The Yafurites, for example, had support from such great poets as Abu Nasr al-Hanbasi and Ibn Mannounah.

For the first time, prose became practiced as an art, especially by writers in the city of Sana'a. Names like Bishr al-Balwi and Muhammad ibn Ibban al-Khanfari left an indelible impact on the literary scene of that time. Bishr al-Balwi was renowned for his rhetoric. For his accomplishments, al-Balwi was appointed to a very prestigious position as clerk in the "House of Discourse" in Sana'a. Hamdani, a great 10th-century Yemeni geographer and historian, quoted 11 letters in his book to prove al-Balwi's superb command of Arabic rhetoric. Al-Balwi was a contemporary of al-Shafi'i and Ibn Hanbal, two prominent jurists who founded their own "schools" of Islamic thought that have large religious followings to this day. Both jurists knew al-Balwi through their correspondence with him. Not only great personages appear in his prose writings, but in one of his letters, he also speaks of events taking place in remote parts of the Islamic empire. He refers to the rebellion of Abu Muslim (died in 685 CE) of Khorasan (an historic region that covered parts of modern-day Afghanistan and Iran), who was otherwise known as al-Muqanna' (meaning "The Veiled One"), after the fact that he donned a veil to hide his beautiful face.

After the Ziyadis and Yafurites, Yemen became the stage for a power struggle between various religious schools of thought that also used poetry as a vehicle to advance their ideological causes. The authors came from outside Yemen in most cases, fleeing persecution in Baghdad and other cities of the Islamic empire by seeking refuge in Yemen where they successfully propagated their causes. Yemenis, who were ever open to outside ideas, proved to be excellent listeners and receptive audiences.

In 835 CE, Ali ibn al-Fadhl and his colleague Mansur Hasan ibn Hawshab arrived in Yemen from Iraq with one important mission: the spread of Kurmuti (or Carmathean, as it is more commonly known in English) thoughts. The Kurmuti movement first started in Iraq as a clandestine opposition to the Abbasid caliphate. It advocated Ismaili ideas that, mixed with a militant form of religious socialism, were soon to attract a large following in Yemen.

Zaydism was yet another persecuted religious movement in the northern lands of the empire that sought refuge in Yemen during this period, establishing a stronghold in the northern Yemeni city of Sa'dah in 894 by the Zaydi Imam, al-Hadi Yahya ibn al-Hussein. Tensions erupted between the Zaydis and the Ismaili Kurmutis in the South, as well as with their Shafi'i Sunni rivals in central and southern Yemen. The conflict took different forms—polemical, religious, and military—and inspired great amounts of literature. The period was the most productive so far as poetry was concerned. To this day, some of the greatest poets of that period are still celebrated in religious and cultural events. Among these was al-Hasan ibn Ahmed al-Hamdani, who, in addition to his geographical and historical works, was a prolific poet and took a strong pride in Yemeni history. On the Zaydi side, Imam al-Hadi Yahya, the founder of Zaydism in Yemen, was also a renowned poet.

Not all poets took sides, however; some tried to stay neutral. Such was true of one of the greatest of Yemen's poets of any era, Umarah, a Yemenite. He was always seeking the truth, and though born and raised as a Sunni, he came to know some Ismailis who initiated him into their theology and urged him to try his hand at poetry. Within a short period of time, he became the favorite poet of the Ismaili court, visiting the Ismaili sultan in Cairo after he made the pilgrimage to Mecca. But when Salahuddin took control of the government, Umarah was suspected of being part of a political conspiracy and was hanged in public.

Another outstanding poet of this period was Nashwan al-Himyari (d. 1163 CE). As his name suggests, he was descended from the Himyarite kings of Yemen, and not surprisingly was an ardent supporter of Yemen's ancient heritage. Though he is the

---

ABU MUHAMMAD AL-HASAN SULAYMAN AL-HAMDANI

Al-Hamdani was a ninth-century geographer (circa 893–945 CE) of Yemen. He was well educated and traveled extensively in Arabia. He compiled his description of his travels in *Geography of Arabia*, one of the most famous texts of the period. But his most important work was titled *The Crown* (*Al-Iklil*), an original collection of tribal genealogies and oral histories, most of them from Yemen, dating from the pre-Islamic period until the time he lived. There were supposedly ten volumes, but unfortunately only four are known to exist. They are a priceless source of historical information on the Yemeni tribes.

author of an eight-volume encyclopedia of Arabic language and literature, he is best known for his classical epic poem, *Al-Hour al-Ayn,* a paean to ancient Yemeni history. It begins with a moral contemplation on the passing of time and the frailty of life:

> The issue is serious and no jest.
> So, do good yourself, O friend.
> How is existence possible with such variance in dispositions
> And the succession of night and morn?
> Fate is the best preacher for the youth.
> It adds to the advisor's words.

The poem goes on for another 132 verses in which Nashwan narrates with outstanding accuracy the names and records of the ancient kings who not only ruled Yemen but also conquered lands outside the country as far as China.

The civilizational highpoint of the medieval period came with the Rasulid dynasty (1228–1454). Famous for their luxurious lifestyle, their monarchs encouraged literature and the spread of learning. In keeping with their royal sponsors, court poets were lavish in their outpouring of feelings in their verse, deemed excessive and even libertarian by some. Such a poet was Ibn Falitah whose love of wine was a commonplace expression in his poetry:

> Turn it on, lo, with the left or right,
> And heal the heart from the disease of the vinery.
> A deer is roaming in it,
> His cheek in redness resembles it [the wine].

Another feature of this period's poetry is the use of the gazelle as a symbol, especially for beautiful women. Even Sufi poets like Abdul Raheem al-Bura'i employed this style in their otherwise religious poetry:

> Golden in her parts, wonderful in her youth
> When she gazes, even the slender deer envies her.

The gazelle is noted, among other things, for its beautiful eyes.

Third Period: 1838 until the Present

The colonial age began in Yemen when the British entered Aden in 1839. Despite its painful consequences for the Yemeni people, the British presence prompted an interesting cultural exchange between the traditionalist Zaydi in the North and the acculturated Shafi'is in the South on the question of political reform and revolution. The 20th century in Yemen saw the country's exposure to Arabic and international literature despite the cultural isolation the northern regime tried to impose on its people.

Literature during this period could be divided into two phases. The first extends from 1911 (the founding of the Mutawakkilite Kingdom in the North) until Imam Yahya's assassination in 1948, followed by the constitutional revolution in that same year (which was put down by Yahya's successor Imam Ahmed). The second starts in 1949 and continues until the present.

Most men of letters in the first phase called for reforms and change in politics and culture. Poetry was still dominant despite the appearance of new forms of literature such as drama, the short story, and novel (see below). For example, the author has been doing research on an encounter between Yemen's most important modern poet Muhammad al-Zubayri and Imam Yahya in 1947. The only written record of this important meeting is available in a poem by the late Ahmed al-Shami, who was also a friend of al-Zubayri and whose poem espouses al-Zubayri's revolutionary ideals against the despotism of Imam Yahya. A northern group of sayyid men of letters who had opposed Imam Yahya for not pursuing badly needed development in the country became implicated in the plot to assassinate him in 1948. They were imprisoned in Hajjah, where they passed the time writing poetry—an incident recounted by one of his inmates, Ahmed al-Shami (1975). They plead their cause with the next Imam, Ahmed, by writing poems to him, and the story goes that he was so moved by their verse that he became lenient toward them.

In the beginning of the first phase from 1911 to 1948, poets followed the more traditional classical style, as was the case with Ahmed al-Wareeth, who was to become editor-in-chief of the influential literary magazine *Al-Hikmah*. But thanks to his publication of new Arabic poetry in his magazine as well as to books imported by Arab expatriates working in Yemen, Yemeni authors were able to keep abreast of literary developments in other Arab countries, which had been deeply influenced by trends in European literature since the 19th century. Meter became "freer" and verse structure less rigid. A new spirit or "renaissance" swept the literary classes of the country that inspired a whole new generation of writers, among them Muhammad al-Zubayri, arguably the chief poet of the period leading up to the 1962 Revolution, along with his compatriots al-Moushki and Ahmed al-Shami.

Much of their influence continued to be felt in the second phase of this period, from 1948 until the present. Al-Zubayri, for instance, who had called on Imam Ahmed to reform the government and stop acting like a tyrant in the mold of the pharaohs, deeply influenced a whole new post-1962 generation of poets, sometimes called the New Poets, among whom were the blind poet Abdullah al-Baradouni (d. 1999), often called the Conscience of Yemen because of his frank and unsparingly critical poetry, and Abd al-Aziz al-Maqalih (b. 1937), a poet who writes in free verse and is also a prolific literary critic. Other New Poets were Hasan al-Lawzi, Ismail al-Wareeth, and Abdul Wadoud Sayf.

Modernist tendencies gained momentum over the years. Most poets after the unification of North and South Yemen in 1990 employed a modernist style in their writings to address mostly social as well as personal concerns. Modernist tendencies have also played a role in the development of other literary genres such as drama, the short story, and the novel.

BIBLIOGRAPHY

Al-Baraduni, Abdullah. *A Journey through Yemen's Poetry* [in Arabic]. Damascus: Dar al-'Ilmi lit-taba'ah w-an-nashr, 1977.

Al-Maqalih, Abd al-Aziz. *The Book of Sana'a*. Translated by Bob Holman and Sam Liebhaber. Ardmore, PA: American Institute for Yemeni Studies, 2004.

Al-Maqalih, Abd al-Aziz. *Contemporary Poetry in Yemen* [in Arabic]. Beirut: Dar al-'Awdah, 1979.

Al-Shami, Ahmed Muhammad. *On Yemeni Literature* [in Arabic]. Beirut: Dar al-Shuruq, 1974.

Al-Shami, Ahmed Muhammad. "Yemeni Literature in Hajjah Prisons: 1367/1948–1374/1955." *Arabian Studies* 2 (1975): 43–59.

Humayni Dialect Poetry

Steven C. Caton

Humayni poetry is a term first associated with the works of the Yemeni writer Ibn Falitah (d. circa 1332), a courtier in the Rasulid Kingdom (see "The Rasulid Dynasty (1228–1454)" in Chapter 2) who lived in Zabid. But he was not its inventor, and the origin of the poetry itself remains obscure. A modern Yemeni historian, Ahmed al-Shami, argues that it may have emerged out of the Muslim conquest of Spain in which Yemenis participated, and from which came a classical form of poetry called the Andalusian al-Muwashshahaat. This genre the invading Arabs, including Yemenis, supposedly took back to their countries, the difference being that Yemeni poets wrote this verse in their "dialect" (*lahn*) while continuing to produce poetry in the classical language, whereas their colleagues elsewhere in the Arab world produced the muwashshahaat only in the elevated register (see "Arabic Languages" in this chapter). Another explanation for Humayni's origin lies in Sufism as practiced in the Rasulid era, specifically the ecstatic poetry sung in the dhikr ceremony (see "Sufism" in Chapter 5). But Sufism was highly controversial in Zaydi thought, and when several Zaydi imams became enamored of this poetry, its Sufi roots were obscured if not obliterated.

In addition to imams, many of the great Humayni poets were *qadhis* (judges) like Ali al-Anasi and scribes, in other words members of the ruling class or their servants, who hailed from the great urban centers such as Sana'a, Taiz, and Zabid. This is not surprising, given the emphasis on knowledge or education as the basis of rule in both the Rasulid and Zaydi courts, and the role poetry played as an instrument to learning. But this would not necessarily account for the fact that they composed in a nonclassical language. They were often assigned administrative posts in the Imamate court distant from their birthplaces or family homes. Thus, it was not uncommon for a highly educated member of this scribal cadre to be born and raised in Sana'a but to spend many years in outlying provinces of the country or even abroad in the Islamic empire's administrative system. According to one theory, these men grew homesick for their *bilad* (home turf) and wrote nostalgic poetry in its dialect. Not surprisingly, chewing qat is a common theme, and one of the most beautiful of all Humayni poems is an ode to the coffee bean by Ahmed al-Anasi; the consumption of both substances have been a hallmark of Yemeni social gatherings. A lot of the poetry was also composed to praise imams and other important personages to whom the elite were beholden in one way or another, reflecting their position (and vulnerability) in a royal court. But there need not have been a specific occasion or reason for composing such poetry, for as they do today in Yemen, men of learning gathered together to chew qat in the afternoons and to exchange poetry with each other for their own amusement.

What was meant by a dialect in Humayni poetry is not always clear. Yemeni poets and their educated audiences were well aware that vocalic case endings, a marked feature of Classical Arabic, were dropped and that much of the poetry's flavor was due to its colloquial ingredients. One term might index a colloquial from one region of the country, another from the colloquial of a different one. This language was deemed "ungrammatical" by the educated elite (and hence ideologically inferior to classical verse) even though in a strictly linguistic sense this was not true (any naturally spoken language is grammatical, in the sense that it has consistent rules for producing meaningful sentences and dialectal equivalents of the Classical Arabic future tense or the continuous aspect were used, for example). The language of this poetry is best described neither as classical nor dialectal but a combination of the two, a hybrid that often arises in diglossic language situations (see "Arabic Languages"); but in the poetry of some of the greatest exponents of the Humayni tradition, the admixture becomes even more extreme and complex, involving different regional dialects of Arabic, different professional argots (e.g., street calls), and influences even from other languages such as Turkish.

The verse was cast in classical poetic meters (the *basit* and *rajz* being the most popular), with each line divided into two and sometimes three hemistichs, the ends of the first hemistich rhyming with each other and the ends of the second hemistich rhyming with each other. Lines constituted higher-order blocks of verse that varied in size and in function (roughly, introduction, development, and close). Humayni poetry is also riddled with puns, the mainstream of its humor and one of its supreme listening pleasures, and is classifiable according to different subject matters (love poetry or *ghazal,* religious poetry, political satire, elegy, panegyric, parodies of various sorts, etc.). Much of the poetry is licentious and filled with homoerotic references as well as the occult (the poet Ali al-'Ansi was said to have had a jinni familiar) and other kinds of mystical experiences such as ecstatic union with Allah (the latter of which would have been in keeping with its alleged Sufi roots).

To focus on the text, as important as this is to the poetic tradition, is to miss much about its performance, however, which was done in the complex Sana'ani musical style. A singer, who is usually also an *oud* (lute) player, sang the verses, accompanied by percussionists of various sorts. Musical performances of Humayni poetry took place in weddings or at private qat chews held by notable personages.

The heyday of Humayni poetry extended from roughly the mid-17th century until the mid-19th century CE. The poems of great Humayni poets were collected and printed in diwans, the most famous of which are by Ali al-Khafanji, Yahya Ahmed al-Anasi, Ali al-ʿAnsi, Muhammad bin Abdullah Sharif al-Din, and many others, and these can be purchased in any decent bookstore in Sana'a. In the post-1962 republican period, the composition of Humayni poetry (though not its sung performance that was taped on audiocassettes and sold in music stores) went into a brief decline for reasons not altogether clear—perhaps because of its associations with the elite of the ancient regime or perhaps because of the dominance of standard Arabic in the modern school curriculum—and poet after poet as well as critic after critic said that composition now was in Classical Arabic only, not the colloquial. However, some investigators have found something of a reinvention of the tradition in recent years, this time in a nationalistic frame. Whether its comeback is assured or not, what is clear is that Humayni poetry represents one of the greatest outpourings of colloquial poetry in any language or society.

Tribal Oral Poetry

Steven C. Caton

Poetry

Although the tribes of Yemen have been mostly illiterate until quite recently in their long history, they have nonetheless produced great oral poetry. This poetry is cast in Yemeni tribal Arabic that is understandable to most people with the exception perhaps of a few words or phrases that have specific or local references. It is important to bear in mind that tribesmen in the past, when education had not yet become universal, did not consider their spoken language as a "dialect" of Arabic in contrast to a "standardized" written language learned in school, rather they thought of their spoken Arabic as a direct descendant of ancient Arabic spoken by the tribes of Yemen in the days of the Sabaeans and the Himyarites. This is to ignore the fact, of course, that those tribes spoke South Arabic, a different language from the North Arabic spoken today by most people in Yemen (with the exception of the Mahris and Soqotris), but we are speaking about the linguistic ideology by which tribesmen interpreted their ways of speaking and not necessarily historical fact. Thus, to tribesmen, their language is not somehow nonstandard or "ungrammatical" in the way a dialect is ideologized by educated people almost everywhere in the world today, including Yemen. Ask an educated townsman in Yemen what he thinks of Yemeni tribal Arabic, he is likely to say that it's not even a language but doggerel and illiterate, and the same prejudice often extends to tribal poetry as not being worth the time to listen to because it's not composed in a standard or Classical Arabic, such as the educated poetry of today. The argument here is that analysts must get past these and other prejudices or preconceptions about what poetry is if the art of tribal poetry is to be understood and appreciated.

It is poetry, for the most part, that is composed in the act of performance—that is, "spontaneously" rather than recited from memory—and therefore a high artistic premium is placed on improvisation or the ability to come up with novel lines of verse on the spur of the moment. The performance involves both music and dance and therefore is a multimedia artistic act. Our English tradition used to produce poetry of this kind, in royal court poetry dating as far back at least to late medieval and early renaissance times, but then these arts developed separately from each other, coming together only in certain genres or forms such as opera, for example.

Tribal poetry is also "occasional" and "situational," in the sense that it is composed for either a specific ritual occasion such as a wedding ceremony, a religious festival, or a dispute mediation, and is situational in the sense that it may also be composed in reference to an event that has occurred in the tribal region, nation, or world-at-large. Indeed, the same poem is usually both simultaneously, that is, composed for an occasion like a wedding but perhaps addressing something important that has recently occurred like a dispute or a policy announcement by the state, and so forth. In this sense, too, tribal poetry is unlike most poetry we are familiar with in the west (though similar to rap and certain forms of Caribbean poetry of today). Though poets in our tradition do draw on their biographical or everyday experiences for expressive purposes, the presumed intention is to say something of "universal" significance; in the tradition under examination here, it is safer to assume that what is being expressed has significance for a specific person, group, or situation and does not necessarily reflect more generally on the human condition. It is not that tribesmen are not interested in the latter, but it is presumed that Islam already serves that purpose.

Some tribal poetry has been written down or collected and printed in anthologies, but it is important to bear in mind that improvisational poetry of this sort, especially when it involves music and dance also, does not lend itself well to this kind of transcription. Writing fixes the poem's text and passes it down through the ages in this form, but this is to capture one moment in an iterative process of composition and not the process itself, which is what the tradition esteems. For example, when asked to produce the text of a particular kind of poem, a tribesman will respond that such texts are not memorized but produced anew in each performance, but that one has to wait for it to emerge in that artistic context. The English novelist and poet D. H. Lawrence captured this idea when he said of poetry he admired most that it should be produced "on the wind," otherwise it becomes like blooms pressed between the pages of a book, dry and lifeless.

However, some oral poetry—in fact, the long ode known as the qasida in both the tribal and the Classical Arabic tradition—is only rarely composed for a ritual occasion, though it is most certainly situational in the sense that it treats of a particular event in recent memory. This ode may be composed orally or in writing, though the act of creation is not a public one (as is the case for the others), and the poet can take as much time as he or she needs to compose it. Once the text is complete, the poet or a professional memorizer may commit the text to memory and recite it before an audience, or it may be written down and disseminated through writing; in either case, the sense of the text is of something more or less "fixed" or "established" and of aesthetic interest in its own right. When passing the text on to listeners or readers, it is important to mention the name of the poet (which is less important for the other performative genres that are collectively composed and performed) and the situation for which it was composed, thus linking the text to an event of some sort that it is to be interpreted. In the days before the 1962 Revolution when most tribal poets were illiterate, the ode was memorized by a khaddaam who then composed a melody for it on which it could be sung (usually accompanying himself on a tambourine-like instrument called the *tabal*) and he would travel from village to village, being paid to perform the ode for the amusement of the assemblies. Whereas today this ode is written and printed with greater frequency, the art of its musical performance has had its life extended through audiocassette tape recording, which is then sold in markets all over the country. Arguably, this is the preferred way for tribesmen to hear new odes, even for tribesmen who are completely literate, because it captures the multidimensionality of the performance rather than leaving him only with the text.

Before we enter into the details of this poetry, three questions need to be briefly considered. The first has to do with the ancientness of this poetic tradition. The qasida is indeed ancient, dating to pre-Islamic times, for it bears many resemblances to the odes that have been preserved from earliest times in Arabic literature, and there is no reason not to assume that the contemporary tribal ode is continuous with that earlier one. But the question is a lot harder, and may be impossible, to answer for the other performative genres of verse that coexist with this ode in the tribal tradition, for—as I have argued above—these do not lend themselves to writing and thus are not likely to be preserved before the invention of sound-recording. Another question is whether the performative genres described in this section are unique to Yemen or may be found elsewhere among tribal groups on the Arabian Peninsula. This question is easier to answer because we are fortunate in having ethnographies of Arabian tribes dating back to the end of the 19th century, and these reveal the existence of such genres, even though they are not analyzed in depth. In other words, we are talking about a poetic system that is peninsula-wide. The final question has to do with tribal females, and whether they also compose poetry and what its features are. Indeed, women poets of the ode do exist, and some of them were so good that they became the poetic "spokespersons" for their tribes when a male of equal talent could not be found. They also compose poetry for female wedding celebrations that has a lot in common with their male counterparts. In some tribes, males and females used to compose poetry in public together, though because of the influence of conservative Islam in the country, this custom has started to die out. But to date, no full-fledged ethnography of the female poetic tradition has been produced (largely because it would require a female ethnographer and none so far has done the fieldwork), so little can be said about the women's side in the poetic performances.

No more will be said in this section on the qasida, a topic covered in the other sections on written Arabic literature. The emphasis here is on two oral genres of poetry, most often known as the *balah* and the *zamil*. (These are not the only such genres in the tribal poetic tradition, only arguable the most famous, and they are not all recognized or performed by every tribe in Yemen, one or the other being composed but not necessarily both.)

It is easiest to begin with the zamil, largely because it resembles some of the aphoristic poetry familiar to us from other traditions such as the Japanese haiku. Here is a famous one composed by a poet who was also one of Yemen's greatest sheikhs, Ali Nasir al-Qarda'i, head of the al-Murad tribe in the far eastern part of the country. Because he was such an important historical personage, the poem was pre-served and handed down to posterity, though the version here is one of several variants that have been passed down (such variation being common in an oral tradition). He composed the poem in 1948, upon arriving at his natal village after having escaped from prison in Sana'a. He had assassinated Imam Yahya, the then ruler of Yemen, because he would not initiate badly needed reforms that the sheikh and many other like-minded progressives thought were important for the development of the country and the welfare of its people. Assassinating an Imam, under any circumstances, was a very serious matter indeed, and so al-Qarda'i had to justify his action before his people, which he did with this zamil poem:

> O these fortress towers that loom before me // there is no blame on the fugitive
> Say to Yahya bin Muhammad, // "We will meet on Judgment Day."[2]

The "fortress towers" refers to the multistoried tower houses that are characteristic of Yemeni architecture (see "Yemeni Architecture"). Yahya bin Muhammad is the Imam whom the sheikh had just killed, and "Judgment Day" refers to the day when all souls will be called to Heaven to be judged for their sins by Allah. The implication of the poem is that al-Qarda'i refuses to be judged by anyone on earth for what he did, claiming that it will be between his conscience and God.

A poem like this one conforms to rather strict textual rules of composition. It is usually only two lines in length, each line divided by one and sometimes two hemistichs. There are rhymes, always at the end of each line (bayt) and sometimes at the ends of each hemistichs, and the line conforms to a distinctive meter, in this case made up of a foot with two long syllables followed by a short and long syllable, or /__ __ u __/ (though different metrical patterns are possible). If the poem does not conform to these rules, it is evaluated as inferior and usually forgotten.

Though we cannot know for sure, al-Qarda'i in all likelihood would have composed the poem on the spot, rather than ahead of time, and then recited it from memory. The performance would have entailed a traditional tune (one of several extant in the tradition) on which the words of the poem can be chanted (i.e., requiring a meshing of verse and musical structures as any lyrics set to music) and is performed in a high tenor (almost a falsetto) tone of voice. This voice production is called a chant (*sayhah*) rather than a song (*ghina'*), because it is thought to resemble war cries (song being what women, children, and the low-status muzayyin do). It is hard on the larynx and meant to be so, for the performance is supposed to be a demonstration of endurance. The chanting of the poetry is done by a "chorus," consisting of two groups of men, one chanting the first line on the first half of the tune, the other the second, and they alternate in this fashion until it is decided in an impromptu fashion to stop and produce a new poem.

So far we have elucidated the verse and musical aspects of the performance, but we have yet to discuss the dance component. This involves a simple dance step

---

[2.] Translations of this text and all others in this section are by the author, Steven C. Caton.

done while holding the hands of one's companions on either side and proceeding down a wadi or riverbed toward a village where the addressees of the poem presumably are to be found. The men have to move in rows and keep in step with each other, with their rifles slung over their shoulders.

Zamil poems often provoke a rejoinder, the challenge poem and its response linked together by their common rhyme and meter. Al-Qarda'i's poem did not provoke such a response or at least not one that has been collected. But here's an example of a pair of poems dating from the civil war (1962–1972). The first was composed by one of the great sheikhs, Naji al-Ghadir, from Khawlan al-Tiyal, who had first been a supporter of the Republic but when the Egyptians came in to fight on its side, he balked, considering tantamount to an invasion and occupation by a foreign power. He expressed his displeasure in the following zamil:

> Mt. al-Tiyal he declared and to all the peaks of Yemen // We will never join the Republic even if we are snuffed out for ever
> Even if yesterday were to return today or the sun were to rise from the west // Even if earth were to turn to fire // and the clouds rain bullets.

Mt. al-Tiyal is the tallest peak in the region, which is named after it. The sheikh is announcing his poem to the entire region. He says that his group will never join the Republic even if a series of counterfactuals were to turn out to be true, such as "yesterday were to return today" or the "clouds rain bullets."

This is considered one of the great poems to have come out of the period, but there was a response to it by Republican Sheikh al-Royshan, which is considered even greater. It imitates the earlier poem in rhyme and meter but intensifies some of its sound patterns as a kind of one-upmanship. For example, the challenge poem has an internal rhyme (-an) in the first hemistich ("Mt. al-Tiyal he declared (-an) and every peak in Yam (-an)") that the response poem "tops," as it were, like this: "Beg pardon (-an) of someone who has wended (-an) a devious course (-an)." In addition, the phrase "wended a devious course" is a beautiful chiasmus made on a consonantal pattern t-l-w (-an) / w-l-t (-an), which subtly suggests the sheikh's turning round on his original position in the war:

> Beg pardon of someone who has wended a devious course // the Mig, the Yushin, and the black fighter plane
> These planes will not be stopped by the bandolier and the M-1 rifle // Say to Hasan and al-Badr, O Naji, "Silver has turned to brass!"

The meaning of the poem is that the Republicans have planes that are superior to the old-fashioned weapons like the M-1 rifle of the Royalists. Sheikh Naji is enjoined to tell Hasan (one of the Royalists generals) and Imam al-Badr (the deposed king) that the monarchy is finished (silver having been the symbol of monarchial rule).

The three examples of zamil poems illustrate the use of poetry as a form of political rhetoric, something no longer common in our tradition. Imagine one of our presidential candidates casting his or her platform in rhymed and metered verse, or for that matter, chanting it with a sprightly dance step. The cultural explanation for this is the belief that politics should operate through persuasion and consensus more than through coercion, and that eloquence—especially the beauty of poetry—is key to such power. It follows, therefore, that the above poetry is composed by sheikhs though not all poets or even the majority of them are tribal leaders. Ideally, any man should be a poet, for he never knows when he might be challenged by a poem and have to reply in kind or better, or else lose face.

Turning now to the other great performative genre, the balah, we see some of the same forms though elaborated or developed many times over. This ode (for it can be as long as the text of a qasida) is composed at one occasion, the night spent entertaining the groom before he is to consummate his marriage. One of the ways its text is spoken of in the poem is as a "gift" (to the groom) or a "game" created by three or more poets at the same time (one poet composes one line, another composes the next, the third the line following that, and so forth until the conclusion). The first poet sets the rhyme and meter that the other contestants have to replicate exactly or their contributions will be disqualified. The line is chanted on one of the traditional balah tunes by a chorus, made up of a half-dozen men who form a circle and move in a simple dance-step, the poet having broken through their ranks to chant the poem with his hand cupped to his mouth (much like the *mu'adhdhin* calling the people to prayer) and moving in a counterclockwise direction. One half of the course chants the first half of the line, the other half the second part of the line, and they alternate this way until the next poet breaks through their ranks and chants his contribution.

The poem's content consists mainly of a series of conventional speech acts that carry cultural meaning in tribal society. Thus, the poem begins with religious speech acts that invoke Allah and His names, followed by a blessing for the Prophet and his family; this act is performed by each poet who competes in the performance. This signals the piety of the tribal poet. Following these religious speech acts, poets will greet individual members in the audience, which again has religious significance in so far as the Muslim is enjoined to greet people and return a greeting in kind or better intensify its feeling. A line might begin with a standard greeting such as "good evening" or "welcome," but then the intensity of the greeting is conveyed by a following clause such "as many times as the rain drops fall in the wadi" or "as loudly as the winds blow in the storm." Sometimes the metaphor can be quite fanciful and even amusing, as in the example, "Welcome as many times as the wheel of the car bumps on the unpaved road." As the analysis of these examples suggest, the lines of poetry are composed using set phrases or formulae that can be repeated from poem to poem, being modified only slightly to fit the meter.

But as the performance warms up, a new routine begins, called a "challenge-and-retort," in which only the most gifted and wittiest dare to participate. Now a poet may challenge anyone in the audience, be he the host of the evening's festivities or a fellow guest, and it could be on any topic imaginable. Perhaps the person challenged has a long-standing quarrel with the poet and the challenge is an allusion to it, cast in rhyme and meter and chanted on a traditional tune. The person so challenged must come up with a response, and preferably one that tops the challenge in wit or imagination; and so the two go back and forth, with the audience following their joust throughout the poem and possibly in subsequent performances during the evening. And that is not all, for there are usually several such challenge-and-retort routines carried out simultaneously between different pairs of poets performing in the same balah. It is like listening to a piece of contrapuntal Western music such as a Bach fugue where one has to listen to four voices at the same time. One of the joys of the balah is to hear dueling poets carrying on in the same poem and tracing their encounter throughout the evening. Given what has been said about the oral tradition, it may not be surprising to learn that these challenge-and-response routines are often on political themes or current events such as a dispute, and that poets use the occasion to analyze the event from different angles and moral perspectives.

The larger point is that politics is debated through poetry (though, of course, not only poetry), and that any of the genres—and usually all three—are used for that purpose. For a sheikh to be able to participate in and influence this larger discourse, he will have to be able to compose zamil and balah poetry, not to mention also the qasida. Another way to look at this is to say that the entire poetry system is mobilized for the discussion of political topics.

Tribal Poetry in the 2011 Yemeni "Arab Spring"

Like other Arab countries in spring of 2011, Yemen underwent a revolution to overthrow its ruler of the past three decades and a half, President Ali Abdullah Saleh. And though these other revolutions in Tunisia, Egypt, Libya, and Syria produced their own poetry, perhaps none was as rich in that regard as Yemen's and for the reason that it could draw on not just the standard or Classical Arabic literary tradition but also the tribal one. Indeed, of the millions of people who turned out in the streets, a very large percentage were tribesmen led by their tribal sheikhs. They left their weapons behind and joined the peaceful protests in the streets, preferring poems over bullets with which to wage their political battles. Even the president's supporters cast their support and their replies to the protesters in verse.

All three genres of poetry were represented, and it will take a while to collect these and translate them. The poems would have been performed in the streets as described above, at least for the zamil: that is, while marching with thousands of others along the massive boulevards in the modern parts of the capital, Sana'a, and the southern city of Taiz. While these poems are available on the Net, they are not performed in the traditional manner but are often jazzed up with orchestral accompaniment or chanted in a full-throated baritone without choral alternation of zamil lines. To the purist, this may be disturbing, but we have to understand that the poetry is being melded to fit the Internet age and to reach out to audiences unfamiliar with these ancient tribal forms but responsive to more modern artistic genres. An oral tradition is a dynamic one, and the oral poetry from tribal Yemen is no exception. We welcome this transformation.

BIBLIOGRAPHY

Caton, Steven C. *"Peaks of Yemen I Summon"*: *Poetry as Cultural Practice in a North Yemeni Tribe*. Berkeley, CA: University of California Press, 1990.

Ghanem, Muhammad Abduh. *Sung Poetry of Sana'a* [in Arabic]. Sana'a: Center for Yemeni Studies and Research/Beirut: Dar al-Kitab al-'Arabi, n.d.

Lambert, Jean. *The Medicine of the Soul: Music and Musicians among Urban Dwellers in Sana'a (Republic of Yemen)* [in French]. Lille: A.N.R.T. Université de Lille, III, 1990.

Miller, Flagg. *The Moral Resonance of Arab Media: Audiocassette Poetry and Culture in Yemen.* Cambridge, MA: Harvard University Press, 2007.

Serjeant, Robert W. *South Arabian Poetry, 1: Prose and Poetry from Hadhramawt.* London: Taylor's Foreign Press, 1951.

Wagner, Mark S. *Like Joseph in Beauty: Yemeni Vernacular Poetry and Arab-Jewish Symbiosis.* Boston: Brill, 2009.

Non-Arabic Poetry

Steven C. Caton

It was mentioned earlier in this chapter that there are languages derived from old South Arabic that have survived in Yemen, among them Mahri (spoken for the most part in an area between Yemen and Oman) and Soqotri (spoken on the island of Soqotra). We know far less about their literatures and cultures than we do about Arabic, though the scholarship on them has intensified in recent years. There are also emerging nativist ethnolinguistic movements on their behalf in the face of opposition from some Islamists and defenders of mainland Yemen language and culture. Not only do these language groups have their own literatures, the Soqotrans, at least, but also have their own "Arab Spring."

REFERENCES

Liebhaber, Samuel. *The Diiwaan of Hajj Daakoon: A Collection of Mahri Poetry.* Ardmore, PA: American Institute for Yemeni Studies, 2011.

Peutz, Nathalie M. " 'Shall I Tell You What Soqotra Once Was?' World Heritage and Sovereign Nostalgia in Yemen's Soqotra Archipelago," *Revue des mondes musulmans et de la Méditerranée* 121–122 (April 2008): 163–82.

Peutz, Nathalie M. "Bedouin 'Abjection': World Heritage, Worldliness, and Worthiness at the Margins of Arabia." *American Ethnologist* 38, no. 2 (2011): 338–60.

Peutz, Nathalie M. "Revolution in Socotra: A Perspective from Yemen's Periphery," *Middle East Report* 42, no. 263 (Fall 2012): 14–21. www.merip.org/mer/mer263/revolution-socotra.

Yemeni Fiction and Theater

Katherine Hennessey

Yemeni Fiction

Though Yemen has a reputation throughout the Arab world for the beauty and wit of her citizens' oral and extemporaneous poetry and storytelling, the nation's contributions to written literature are less extensive and less well known. The

Yemeni populace is hampered by poor education and by abysmally low literacy rates; recent surveys suggest that 55 percent of the nation's female population lacks basic reading skills, with illiterate males at a slightly less appalling figure of 20 percent (UNESCO 2012).

Given that such numbers, especially in the northern part of the country, actually represent a significant *improvement* from the situation that prevailed until the September revolution in 1962, it will come as no surprise that the Yemeni novel is a rare beast, with fewer than one published per year, on average, between 1939 and 2004 (al-Mutawakel 2005: 82).

Yet for all this, Yemeni fiction is a surprisingly vibrant genre. For decades, newspapers and magazines have provided a readily available means of publication for short stories and serialized novellas. The literary merits of numerous Yemeni authors have attracted international interest and acclaim, and since 2005, there has been a remarkable resurgence in both the quantity and quality of the Yemeni novel. There are, in fact, too many significant Yemeni authors and works to mention here; what follows is a chronological outline of certain important figures and events in Yemeni literary history rather than an exhaustive list.

Yemeni fiction begins in 1939 with the appearance of two short stories, Yahya al-Nahari's "How Palestinians Defend Their Country" and Ahmed al-Bareq's "I'm Happy" in the Yemeni journal *Al-Hikmah,* and with the publication of Muhammad Ali Luqman's novel *Sa'eed.* These are straightforward narratives, composed primarily to convince readers of the authors' particular views on moral and social issues. In 1940, Luqman founded the literary magazine *Fatat al-Jazira* in Aden, which provided additional opportunities for publishing original writing (Ibrahim 1977).

The years from 1945 through 1970 saw the proliferation of Yemeni short stories. Generally speaking, Yemeni authors of this period strive for a realistic portrayal of characters, their surroundings, and their dilemmas, and attend to character development and psychology, with these techniques increasing in sophistication over time. Mohammed Abdul-Wali is, deservedly, the best-known Yemeni author of this period. Born in Ethiopia to a Yemeni father, educated in Cairo and Moscow, Abdul-Wali returned to Yemen after the 1962 Revolution; he died at only 33 years old in a plane crash, having penned some of Yemen's finest short stories.

His "Abu Rubbiya" focuses, as do many of his works, on the plight of Yemenis living abroad in Addis Ababa; the title character laments the lost beauties and past glories of Yemen, and the corruption and cowardice that drive Yemenis from their homeland. An artist who draws clever cartoons depicting people as animals, "Abu Rubbiya" is eventually deemed crazy and deported. The narrator sees him five years later, eking out a miserable existence in the homeland he spoke of with such longing (Jayyusi 1990).

In Abdul-Wali's "Brother, Are You Going to Fight Them All," the harried protagonist's hopes for a peaceful morning are shattered by the arrival of a policeman who drags him to the station, refusing to explain the charges against him. At the station, he is roughed up and put in chains. Eventually, they discover he has been confused with a swindling butcher of the same name—but the protagonist is still forced to pay the arresting officer's "fee" for unlocking his chains (Abdul-Wali 2001).

The ordinary Yemeni's lack of recourse in the face of endemic corruption and incompetence, and Yemeni society's resistance to change, is a theme that pervades the stories of other authors of this period as well. Saeed Aulaqi, a writer and dramatist from Aden who has been called "one of the finest authors of Yemen," takes up this theme in "The Succession," pitting the illiterate peasant Fadeel against "emperor of the market" Hajj Fari'. Having incited a crowd of peasants to revolt against their oppressor, Fadeel takes Hajj Fari''s place—and soon becomes just like him. Through "fits of sexual frenzy" with his beautiful new wife (the Hajj's daughter), Fadeel attempts to drive away the anxiety of maintaining his new status, until another peasant, Mansur, arrives to begin the cycle of succession anew (Jayyusi 1990: 533, 315).

"The Final Ring" by Abdul Majeed al-Qadi, a short story writer and dramatist from Taiz, distinguishes itself by its sympathetic portrayal of a female narrator and the toll taken by her repeated pregnancies: She loves her two children but has multiple abortions because her husband's extravagance and laziness renders her unable to leave her job. A botched operation leads to the story's harrowing conclusion: The mother imagines her baby daughter "drowning in her morning excrement," while she herself slowly drowns in blood, too exhausted to get up from the bed (Jayyusi 1990: 422).

Other important writers of this period are Salih Saeed Ba-Amer, who sets short stories in his native Hadhramawt; F. Ahmed, pseudonym of the first female Yemeni author, who in *Dhalem, ya Mujtama'* (Injustice, o society; 1961) describes a self-fulfilling prophecy that a daughter will become just like the mother who deserted her family; and Shafiqh al-Zuqeri, whose *Armalat Shahid* (A martyr's widow; 1970) illustrates the varied roles women played during the revolution (Abdullah 1992).

This same period (1945–1970) is not as fruitful for the Yemeni novel: only four appear after Luqman's *Sa'eed,* of which the most interesting is *Massat Wag al-Wag* (The tragedy of Wag al-Wag; 1960), a sarcastic exposé of Yemeni politics by Muhammad Mahmoud al-Zubayri, Yemen's revolutionary poet and martyr. But the 1970s are a different story: 14 Yemeni novels are published, including Abdul-Wali's *Ymotoon Ghuraba'a* (They die as strangers), Ahmed Muhammad al-Alimi's *Ghurba'a fi Otanhim* (Strangers in their own country), and the first Yemeni novel by a female author, Ramziyya al-Iryani's *Dhahiyat al-Jash`e* (The martyr of greed), about a young woman forced to marry an old man for his money, and her eventual suicide (al-Mutawakel 2005).

One of the seven Yemeni novels published in the 1980s, *The Hostage* (1984) is a brilliant portrayal of the authoritarian nature of the Imamate, as seen through the eyes of its young narrator, imprisoned in the governor's palace to guarantee his family's obedience to the Imam's dictates. This is the best-known work of Zayd Mutee' Dammaj, also a master of the Yemeni short story (Dammaj 1994).

Publication of novels and short stories declined somewhat in the 1990s, though the decade did close with a strong contribution from Yemeni women novelists: three novels by Aziza Abdullah (*Ahlam . . . Nabilah* in 1997, *Arkenha al-Faqeeh* [Rely on a priest] in 1998, and *Taeef Walayya* [The image of Walayya] in 1998) and Ramziyya al-Iryani's *Dar al-Sultanah: Riwayya Tarikhiyya* (The palace of the sultan: a historical novel; 1998), a historical novel about the reign of Queen Arwa. This was followed by Nabilah al-Zubayr *Inho Jassadi* (It's my body; 2000), narrated by a comatose protagonist from her hospital bed (al-Mutawakel 2005).

The first decade of the 21st century has been perhaps the best ever for Yemeni fiction, with the publication of imaginative short-story collections such as Bassam Shamseldin's *A Fight to the Finish* (2009) and Yasir Abdel Baqi's *The Black Cat* (2008), and a number of fascinating and provocative novels. Habib Abdulrab Sarori's *The Bird of Destruction* (2005) narrates in the second person the return of an expat to his home in Aden, now rendered unrecognizable by squalor and misery; this harsh reality parallels the inhibition and frigidity of his beloved Ilham, from which he tries to escape through orgasmic fantasies. *The Tale of Mr. M* (2007) by Samir Abdulfattah explores the narrator's recurring nightmare of a ghost arriving to drag him off to "the world of the dead." Ali al-Muqri's *Taste Black . . . Smell Black* (2008) portrays life in an akhdam settlement outside of Taiz, through the eyes of outsiders: a couple eloping from a tiny Yemeni village. And *A Land without Jasmine* (2008), by novelist and short story writer Wajdi al-Ahdal, is a novel with multiple narrators, including a young university student named Jasmine, who suddenly disappears, and the thoughtful police inspector charged with the investigation (Obank 2009).

As varied and interesting as it is, however, this list of novels merely scratches the surface of Yemen's intriguing and increasing contemporary literary production.

Theater in Yemen

Though little known outside the country, Yemeni drama has a rich history that spans the 20th century and continues to flourish in the 21st. Though poetry remains the literary medium of greatest prestige, a surprising number of Yemeni authors have written works of drama, just as they have translated and adapted scripts by Western playwrights like Shakespeare, Brecht, Shaw, and Pirandello. In fact, according to Yahya Muhammad Sayf, a Yemeni theater scholar, at last count, Yemen had produced 65 theater troupes, 125 dramatists, and 500 scripts presented by 43 directors (Gamal 2009).

The seminal work on the history of Yemeni theater is *Saba'un 'Aaman Min al-Masrah fi al-Yaman* (Seventy years of theatre in Yemen) by Saeed Aulaqi, whose short stories we examined in the previous section. His history of theater in Yemen, the source of much of the information presented in this section, begins in 1904 with the arrival of an Indian acting troupe in the southern city of Aden, at the behest of the city's community of Indian expatriates. The amazement on the part of the audience at the wondrous world evoked by their theatrical performance soon inspired the formation of indigenous Yemeni acting troupes. In 1910, a student group at a British government school gave the first public performance by Yemeni actors: Shakespeare's *Julius Caesar* in Arabic. This was followed in 1914 by *Martyrs for Love,* an Arabic adaptation of *Romeo and Juliet.*

Given British colonial domination in the South, Shakespeare was a logical choice for Yemen's first plays. Furthermore, since local social strictures encouraged the segregation of men and women in public, these plays were performed as they were in Shakespeare's day, with male actors playing women's roles. But some Yemenis soon realized theater's potential as a means to criticize the colonial administration; they wrote political satires and dramatizations of triumphant moments in Arab and Yemeni history, which served the burgeoning anticolonial movement.

These political plays coexisted with romantic comedies and tales of action and adventure, and soon gained a devoted local following. There were no buildings dedicated solely to theater; performances took place in schools, public squares, and later in cinemas. Plays drew audiences from miles around, at a time when people's modes of transport were limited to animals or their own two feet. The crowds and the content gave rise to censorship; performances would be shut down if suspected of inflaming the populace.

Ali Muhammad Luqman (son of Muhammad Ali Luqman, the founder of *Fatat al-Jazeerah*) authored a version of George Bernard Shaw's *Pygmalion* (1944), and performances of Shakespeare continued. *Othello* proved too tragic for Yemeni audiences' taste, however; director Muhammad Abduh al-Duqmi bowed to popular pressure and rewrote the play's final scene, reconciling Othello and Desdemona and condemning Iago to be beheaded. This new version, performed under the title *The Punishment of Treachery* (1948), met with fervent acclaim.

Drama began to take root in other parts of South Yemen, like the Hadhramawt and Lahaj, in the 1940s and early 1950s. The "pan-Arab acting troupe" from Al Hawtah performed Masrour Mabrook's *Tarfisha and Shorban* (1941), the first full-length comedy performed in Yemeni dialect, about two lovers entangled in a power struggle between rival princes. There are other linguistic experiments—bilingual (English and Arabic) plays and plays performed by Yemeni students entirely in English. A girls' school in Aden performed plays with all-female casts.

In 1956, the first Yemeni actress, Nabiha Azeem, appeared in a public performance, and in 1962, *Queen Bilqis* became the first production to feature a Yemeni actress in a starring role. The early 1960s saw Yemeni productions of plays by the great Egyptian playwright Tawfiq al-Hakim and by Yemen's most prolific playwright Ali Ahmed Bakatheer in Aden and other southern cities.

In North Yemen, the evolution of theater followed a different path. Despite the Imamate's suspicion of foreign influence and cultural innovation, performances did occur during the reign of Imam Yahya: generally in schools, for didactic purposes, focusing on significant events in Islamic history. Theater for public performance did not occur in Sana'a, Taiz, and Al-Hudaydah until the 1940s; the preference for plots drawn from Islamic history remained, with Yemeni legends and the Arabian Nights occasionally providing dramatic material.

Between 1947 and 1957, plays were inspired by Cleopatra, the *Kalila wa Dimna* animal fables, and the stories of Juha. Some theatrical activity took place in northern villages as well. But theater sparks controversy: An influential group of religious leaders condemned even Islamic history plays, for making actors wear "infidel" costumes—as Crusaders, for example, in a play about Saladin.

With the fall of the Imamate as a result of the 26 September revolution, many barriers to public performance were lifted. Both the president and the prime minister of the newly established Yemen Arab Republic attended a performance of Ibrahim

Sadiq's *Playing with Fire,* a play that portrays the corruption of the Imamate, produced as part of the celebrations of the first anniversary of the revolution in 1963.

Up till this point, theatrical productions, both North and South, had possessed certain unique charms: witty improvisation, elaborate costumes, and the incorporation of Yemeni songs and poetry into the plays. But performances suffered from actors' lack of training and technique, from rudimentary lighting and sound effects and a lack of attention to set design, and from a tendency to prioritize narrative at the expense of dramatic action.

This changed with the advent of the first Yemeni television station, which began broadcasting in Aden in 1964. Whereas in many countries, television and theater are seen as rivals, in the south of Yemen, the advent of television provided theater practitioners with a previously unimaginable access to material and technical resources, as well as a huge potential audience, through the *Masrah al-Televisiun* (Television theatre) program. Every week for four years, *Masrah al-Televisiun* broadcast a live performance of a new script, in genres from satiric comedy to melodrama to murder mystery. The quality of these television productions greatly exceeded that of the typical Yemeni performance, and the program strongly encouraged female participation and new Yemeni writing.

Off the screen, theater in the postrevolutionary periods, both North and South, was often employed as pro-revolution propaganda. One particular plot repeated in numerous plays of the period features a corrupt, despotic sheikh-landowner who exploits his naïve peasant tenants, until the peasants band together and revolt against him, afterward forming a just and autonomous government (if the play was performed in the North) or a just and autonomous commune (if in the South). Part of the reason that this type of plot recurred was that, on both sides of the border, newly formed Ministries of Culture were providing state support for dramatic productions. There are some notable exceptions to the rule, however: A play called *Madrasah al-Maghafaleen* (The school for suckers), for example, performed in Sana'a in 1972, criticized the contempt with which the recently appointed officers of the new northern government treated the common people in their charge.

The 1970s witnessed some significant milestones in the South: the first conference of Yemeni theater practitioners in Aden in 1973, the first-ever large-scale Yemeni theater festival in 1974, the establishment of a theater department at the Institute of Fine Arts in Aden, and the formation of a national theater troupe. The North likewise founded a national troupe (1974), which benefited from the talents of provocative poet-playwrights like Muhammad al-Sharafi and Palestinian director Hussein al-Asmar, a driving force behind many of North Yemen's best productions. Zahara Talib made history in 1976 as the first northern Yemeni woman to appear on stage in a starring role, in al-Sharafi's *Tariq ila Maarib* (The road to Marib), about Yemeni women's lack of access to education.

Also produced in North Yemen in the 1970s are *The Mouse in the Dock* by Abdul Kafi Muhammad Saeed, a courtroom trial of the mouse that destroyed the Marib Dam, featuring prominent figures from Yemeni history; al-Asmar's adaptation of Luigi Pirandello's *La Giara,* rewritten in Yemeni dialect and set in a Yemeni village; and Jean Racine's only comedy, *Les Plaideurs* (The litigants), performed as *al-Mutaqaadun,* a pointed critique of the Yemeni judicial system. There were also numerous northern plays about the 1948 and 1955 revolts against the Imamate, the 1962 revolution, the issue of Yemeni emigration, and even a pioneering attempt to dramatize Abd al-Aziz al-Maqalih's poem "Letter to Sayf bin Dhi Yazan."

But the flourishing of Yemeni theater in the 1970s was fueled in part by the economic boom and by remittances sent home by expatriate Yemeni workers working in oil and construction in the Gulf. The drop in oil prices in the early 1980s decimated remittances; the economic deterioration resulting from the 1979 war between North and South Yemen and the 1986 civil war in the South occurred in tandem with the rise of Islamist groups and ideologies in northern Yemen. The ideological impetus of the Socialist South foundered with the crumbling of the Soviet Union beginning in 1989; the euphoria of Yemeni unification in 1990 was tempered by the Gulf War and the expulsion of Yemeni workers from Saudi Arabia; and civil war broke out in 1994.

This economic, political, and intellectual uncertainty had a suffocating effect on Yemeni theater in the 1990s. Massive public spectacles were organized to showcase the ruling regime, but politically provocative performances risked heavy reprisals. In the widening gap between rich and poor, theater became increasingly associated with wealth, power, and leisure, rather than with popular culture.

Fortunately, the first decade of the 21th century has seen a resurgence of theater in Yemen. Basic difficulties, like finding appropriate rehearsal and performance spaces, remain, but so do dedicated directors and performers. Adeni director Amr Jamal and his troupe, *Khaleej Aden,* have won national and international acclaims for their productions, especially for *Mak Nazl* (I'm coming with you): In this Yemeni adaptation of a German musical, catchy tunes and humorous dialogue intermingle with sharp criticism of the corruption and exploitation that characterizes current Yemeni society. Other troupes have bravely taken on the challenges of public performance. Yemeni women, especially, are finding in the theater opportunities for expressing their aspirations for and dissatisfactions with contemporary Yemen.

The long history of Yemeni theater is thus a tale of determined struggle against a series of unrelenting economic, social, and political obstacles, and of a staunch and courageous refusal to allow those obstacles to stifle creative expression.

REFERENCES

Abdul-Wali, Mohammed. "Abu Rubbiya," in *The Literature of Modern Arabia: An Anthology,* edited by Salma Khadra Jayyusi, 275–79. Translated by Lena Jayyusi and Naomi Shihab Nye. Austin, TX: University of Texas Press, 1990.

Abdul-Wali, Mohammed. "Brother, Are You Going to Fight Them All," in *They Die Strangers: A Novella and Stories from Yemen.* Translated by Abubaker Bagader and Deborah Akers. Introduction by Shelagh Weir, 75–78. Austin, TX: University of Texas Press, 2001.

Abdul-Wali, Mohammed. Ymotoon Ghuraba'a [They die strangers], 84. Quoted in al-Mutawakel, Gender and the Writing of Yemeni Women Writers.

Abdulfattah, Samir. "An Excerpt from the Novel *The Tale of Mr. M,* translated by Ali Azeriah," *Banipal Magazine of Modern Arab Literature* 36 (Autumn/Winter 2009): 158–72. http://www.banipal.co.uk/back_issues/73/issue_36/.

Abdullah, Aziza. *Ahlam . . . Nabilah.* Cairo: al-Madni, 1997, 169. Quoted in al-Mutawakel, *Gender and the Writing of Yemeni Women Writers.*

Abdullah, Aziza. *Arkenha al-Faqeeh* [Rely on a priest]. Cairo: al-'Alamiyya, 1998, 169. Quoted in al-Mutawakel, *Gender and the Writing of Yemeni Women Writers.*

Abdullah, Aziza. *Taeef Walayya* [Walayya's Image]. Sana'a: Dar al-Tawjeeh al-M'anwi, 1998, 169. Quoted in al-Mutawakel, *Gender and the Writing of Yemeni Women Writers.*

Abdullah, Nahila, ed. *Aswat Nisa'iyya fi al-Qissa al-Yamaniyya* [Female voices in the Yemeni short story]. Aden: Abdullah Ba Dhib National Library, 1992.

Ahmed, F. *Dhalem, Ya Mujtama'* [Injustice, o society]. 1961, 15–24. Cited in Abdullah, *Aswat Nisa'iyya fi al-Qissa al-Yamaniyya.*

al-Ahdal, Wajdi. "A Chapter from the Novel *A Land without Jasmine,* translated by William M. Hutchins," *Banipal Magazine of Modern Arab Literature* 36 (Autumn/Winter 2009): 178–99. http://www.banipal.co.uk/back_issues/73/issue_36/.

al-Alimi, Ahmed Muhammad. *Ghurba'a fi Otanhim* [Strangers in their own country], 84. Quoted in al-Mutawakel, *Gender and the Writing of Yemeni Women Writers.*

al-Bareq, Ahmed. "I'm Happy." *Al-Hikmah* (1939). Quoted in Ibrahim, *Al-Qissa al-Yamaniyya al-Mu'asira.*

al-Iryani, Ramziyya. *Dhahiyat al-Jash`e* [The martyr of greed], 82. Quoted in al-Mutawakel, *Gender and the Writing of Yemeni Women Writers.*

al-Iryani, Ramziyya. *Dar al-Sultanah: Riwayya Tarikhiyya* [The palace of the sultan: a historical novel]. 1998, 104. Quoted in al-Mutawakel, *Gender and the Writing of Yemeni Women Writers.*

al-Muqri, Ali. "Excerpt from the Novel *Taste Black . . . Smell Black,* translated by Tony Calderbank," *Banipal Magazine of Modern Arab Literature* 36 (Autumn/Winter 2009): 78–91. http://www.banipal.co.uk/back_issues/73/issue_36/.

al-Mutawakel, Antelak. *Gender and the Writing of Yemeni Women Writers.* Amsterdam: Dutch University Press, 2005. http://arno.uvt.nl/show.cgi?fid=90383.

al-Nahari, Yahya. "How Palestinians Defend Their Country." *Al-Hikmah* (1939). Quoted in Ibrahim, *Al-Qissa al-Yamaniyya al-Mu'asira.*

al-Qadi, Abdul Majeed. "The Final Ring," in *The Literature of Modern Arabia: An Anthology,* edited by Salma Khadra Jayyusi, 419–22. Translated by May Jayyusi and Elizabeth Fernea. Austin, TX: University of Texas Press, 1990.

al-Zubayr, Nabilah. *Inho Jassadi* [It's my body]. 2000. Quoted in al-Mutawakel, *Gender and the Writing of Yemeni Women Writers.*

al-Zubayri, Muhammad Mahmoud. *Massat Wag al-Wag* [The tragedy of Wag al-Wag]. 1960, 84. Quoted in al-Mutawakel, *Gender and the Writing of Yemeni Women Writers.*

al-Zuqeri, Shafiqh. *Armalat Shahid* [The martyr's widow]. 1968, 57–86. Quoted in Abdullah, *Aswat Nisa'iyya fi al-Qissa al-Yamaniyya.*

Aulaqi, Saeed. *Saba'un 'Aaman Min al-Masrah fi al-Yemen* [Seventy years of theatre in Yemen]. Aden: Ministry of Culture and Tourism, 1983.

Aulaqi, Saeed. "The Succession," in *The Literature of Modern Arabia: An Anthology,* edited by Salma Khadra Jayyusi, 310–17. Translated by Lena Jayyusi and Naomi Shihab Nye. Austin, TX: University of Texas Press, 1990.

Baqi, Yasir Abdel. "A Short Story *The Black Cat,* translated by Ali Azeriah," *Banipal Magazine of Modern Arab Literature* 36 (Autumn/Winter 2009): 126–33. http://www.banipal.co.uk/back_issues/73/issue_36/.

Dammaj, Zayd Mutee'. *The Hostage.* Translated by May Jayyusi and Christopher Tingley. Introductions by Robert Burrowes and Abdul 'Aziz al-Maqalih. New York: Interlink, 1994.

Gamal, Raghda. "Yemeni Theatre Needs More Attention from Culture Ministry." *Yemen Observer,* March 21, 2009. http://www.yobserver.com/culture-and-society/10016018.html.

Ibrahim, Abdul Hamid. *Al-Qissa al-Yamaniyya al-Mu'asira* [The contemporary Yemeni short story]. Beirut: Dar al-Awda, 1977, Chapter 1, 21–36.

Jayyusi, Salma Khadra, ed. *The Literature of Modern Arabia: An Anthology.* Austin, TX: University of Texas Press, 1990.

Luqman, Muhammad Ali. *Sa'eed.* 1939. Quoted in Ibrahim, *Al-Qissa al-Yamaniyya al-Mu'asira.*

Obank, Margaret, ed. "Literature in Yemen Today," *Banipal Magazine of Modern Arab Literature* 36 (Autumn/Winter 2009). http://www.banipal.co.uk/back_issues/73/issue_36/.

Sarori, Habib Abdulrab. "Excerpts from the Novel *The Bird of Destruction,* translated by William M. Hutchins," *Banipal Magazine of Modern Arab Literature* 36 (Autumn/Winter 2009): 54–71. http://www.banipal.co.uk/back_issues/73/issue_36/.

Shamseldin, Bassam. "A Short Story *A Fight to the Finish,* translated by Michael Scott," *Banipal Magazine of Modern Arab Literature* 36 (Autumn/Winter 2009): 42–50. http://www.banipal.co.uk/back_issues/73/issue_36/.

UNESCO. *UIS Statistics in Brief: Education (All Levels) Profile—Yemen.* http://stats.uis.unesco.org/unesco/TableViewer/document.aspx?ReportId=121&IF_Language=eng&BR_Country=8850&BR_Region=40525.

DANCE

Steven C. Caton

Just as saltah might be said to be the national dish, so *bara'* may be said to be the national dance. Images of this dance are often shown on national television, and it is also performed at certain tourist sites. It is, however, a quintessentially *tribal* performance and not everyone in Yemen identifies with it as *their* dance. Furthermore, women are excluded from it; they have their own form of dancing in the privacy of their homes that nonrelated men are ordinarily not allowed to see.

The *bara'* is usually performed on only certain occasions—weddings are the most common ones, religious holidays and national commemorations are others. Though every adult male is expected to be able to do the dance, it is not something men spontaneously perform when they feel like it. The dance is accompanied by two kinds of drums or percussion instruments, struck by servants who have learned the art. One drum is round and open at one end, with the head covered by a hard leather backing that is struck with rods. The other is shaped like a bowl with a leather cover and is struck by a wooden stick or mallet with its head covered in leather. The beat is usually slow and stately to start but then shifts rhythm and gathers speed as the dance reaches its climax.

It requires more than two dancers, and usually half a dozen or more participate. To begin with, the dancers form a line, their rifles slung at their shoulders, their daggers held aloft in their right hands, stepping in unison but simple fashion as they get used to the beat and to each other. Ordinarily, there is a leader of the dance— an older, more experienced man—from whom the other dancers take their cue as to when to change their steps or the group formation. But his guidance is subtle, given by the way he exaggerates a step or steers another's body with his hands. More inexperienced dancers are at the ends of the line, and they may drop out as the speed accelerates and they find themselves unable to keep up. Around halfway into the dance, the performers form a circle, periodically whirling around each other with their daggers drawn and held close to their faces. By the end, only a couple of dancers are left facing off against each other in an agonistic way, lunging with their daggers or dodging them as the case might be, until it is clear that one has more skill and dexterity and is the last one "standing," as it were. Not surprisingly, many observers, including Yemeni ones, say this dance has a decidedly martial aspect.

Different tribes have different variations on this basic description; the most important being whether in the final stage of the dance, the leader has a woolen shawl, which he holds in his hand and taunts his opponent with, who of course tries to snatch it away from him. Smaller differences have to do with the particular dance steps themselves.

As for women's dancing, it tends to be more solitary or individualistic rather than strongly interactive among the dancers, though because it has not been studied as fully as the *bara'*, not much can be said about it that is not impressionistic or anecdotal.

BIBLIOGRAPHY

Adra, Najwa. "Dance and Glance: Visualizing Tribal Identity in Highland Yemen." *Visual Anthropology* 11 (1998): 55–102.

Adra, Najwa. "Dance in the Arabian Peninsula," in *The Garland Encyclopedia of World Music,* edited by Virginia Danielson, Scott Lloyd Marcus, and Dwight Reynolds. Vol. 6, *The Middle East,* 703–12. New York: Garland Publications, 2002.

FOOD

Steven C. Caton

Yemen cannot be said to have a cuisine like some other countries in the Middle East such as Iran, Turkey, or Morocco, if by cuisine is meant a distinctive style, often associated with a national culture, of preparing and cooking food. Nevertheless, it has some delicious dishes and is justly prized for some of its food and beverages.

Bees and honey were beloved by the Prophet Muhammad. According to one of the Hadiths, one is enjoined "To make use of two remedies, the Qur'an and honey." Yemen is justly famous for its honey (*'asl* in Arabic), of which the kind called *sidr* made in Hadhramawt (specifically Wadi Dawan) is one of the best and most expensive in the world. Honey is ingested not only for its taste but also for its medicinal effects. It is presumed that honey is good for curing any number of ailments, from coughs and soar throats to indigestion and kidney problems. So prized is honey that whole stores are dedicated to the sale of its different varieties in all of the major souks of Yemen.

Less well known is the fact that Yemen produces superb grapes, of which different varieties exist from red to yellow (or green). Grapes are not converted into wine, of course, but are eaten as a delicious fruit or dried and turned into raisins. Almonds are also considered a delicacy, and are often served along with grapes as a snack. Palm trees do not thrive in Yemen except in the coastal region, and so its dates are not as renowned as they are in the Gulf (from which Yemen imports many of its own).

Coffee, for which Yemen was once world famous, is less often consumed in the form we know it in the West, that is, with the roasting of the bean that is then ground into a powder and brewed. Rather, the shell of the coffee bean is ground into a powder and then placed like an infusion into a cup of hot water, flavored with cloves, sugar, and possibly cinnamon. This drink is called *qishr,* and it not only has a delicate flavor but is also thought to have medicinal advantages, among them aiding digestion.

Lamb and chicken are ubiquitous meat dishes (beef being more expensive), and in the eastern and southern areas of the country, tender camel meat may also be served on special occasions. Not surprisingly, fish (bass, halibut, shark, and shrimp being common varieties) is commonly served in the coastal areas (though fresh fish is often available in the markets of the main highland cities such as Sana'a and Taiz).

Yemen is justly famous for its many varieties of flat bread. What is more commonly known as pita bread in the Levant (and is available at most urban supermarkets) is baked fresh at local bakeries, along with a foot-long narrow loaf of white bread called roti. The special ovens made for baking these breads are called tanours. For special occasions, there are traditional unleavened breads such as *lakhoukh* (a soft spongy bread the size of a large pizza, usually made from sorghum) and *malouj* (a harder, crisper bread with a crust). A simple multigrained loaf, the size of a fist, often called "army bread" for reasons requiring no explanation, is quite wholesome though thought of as the equivalent of our "street food."

If there is one national dish in Yemen, it is saltah, a meat stew of Turkish origin, combined with a rich mixture of chilies, tomatoes, garlic, and herbs (this spice mixture is known as *hawa'ij* and is found as a base in other dishes as well), with the addition of potatoes, scrambled eggs, and other vegetables, as desired. Once the stew has been thoroughly cooked, a dollop of whipped fenugreek is added at the last minute and folded into the mixture to give it a distinctive flavor. Flat bread is used to scoop up the stew and place it into the mouth. This dish is considered ideal, if not required, just before a qat chew.

Two traditional northern Yemeni dishes, saltah *(left) and* fahsa *(right). (AP Photo/ Nasser Nasser)*

Other popular dishes are *shafut* and *bint al-sahn.* Shafut is made from the spongy bread known as malouj that has been soaked in sour milk, with chopped lettuce, onions, and tomatoes sprinkled on top, and is usually served as an appetizer or side dish. Bint al-sahn is more like a dessert, made from a cake drizzled with delicious Ye-meni honey on top and sprinkled with a spice called *habbah sowdah* (black caraway seeds, botanical name *Nigella sativa*), much appreciated by the Prophet Muhammad for its medicinal properties. In tribal Yemen, another common dish is called *'asiid wa zoam.* This is like a soup and dumpling combination, though it is in fact a mound of sorghum dough that has been boiled in water like a dumpling and placed at the bottom of a large bowl, surrounded by a heavy chicken broth. One scoops a chunk of the dough with one's fingers, drops it into the molten-hot broth for flavor, and then pops it into one's mouth. Today, these traditional dishes might be supple-mented by rice and pasta dishes (both of which are imported ingredients).

Liquids are usually not served with meals, except for water or coke sola. Besides qishr, black tea might be served with milk, spices, and heaping teaspoons of sugar. In the last couple of decades, various fruit juices made from limes, mangos, strawber-ries, and other flavors have become a popular refreshment, and can be acquired at "juice bars" in every major city. Street foods are shawarma (meats that have been roasted on a spit and then thinly sliced to be served in a sandwich) and a version of a crêpe sometimes called *murtabaqiyyah* (a thin flour, milk, and egg mixture cooked on a hot skillet, with minced meat and vegetables added and the dough folded over them).

What we consider lunch is the main meal of the Yemeni day. Breakfasts tend to be simple, with beans (*fasuliyyah*) eaten with unleavened bread and served with black tea being the most common. Lunch (which is the equivalent of our dinner) is served with one or more of the main dishes described above. Since many Yemenis chew qat, which tends to dampen or quell the appetite, there is only a light snack for dinner, usually milk along with some cheese and bread.

BIBLIOGRAPHY

Purdyk, Grace. *The Honey Trail: In Pursuit of Liquid Gold and Vanishing Bees.* New York: St. Martin's Press, 2008.

Robinson, John Brian D. *Coffee in Yemen: A Practical Guide.* Berlin: Klaus Schwarz, 1993.

YEMENI ARCHITECTURE

Steven C. Caton

Traditional or vernacular Yemeni architecture is one of the most distinctive and beautiful in the world. Though many regional varieties exist in Yemen, architecture, broadly speaking, is of three kinds: the multistoried buildings of stone and mud-brick characteristic of highland architecture and most dramatically exemplified in the Old City of Sana'a; the adobe and white plaster domestic architecture of the Tihama, of which Zabid is distinctive, along with conical thatch houses and circular reed villages along the coast; and the mud-brick tower houses densely clustered into urban centers found in southern Yemen, particularly the cities of Siyoun, Shibam, and Tarim in the Wadi Hadhramawt. Within these styles, there is some historical variation as well (e.g., the Rasulids versus other dynasties). Of these styles, only the northern and southern ones have received extensive study. What is interesting from a preservationist standpoint is that these quite ancient cities are still inhabited and vibrant (being designated as "living" heritage sites by UNESCO) and not just empty tourist attractions.

Highland buildings have foundations made mainly of stone (usually basalt, which is plentiful), hewn into square blocks with chiseled-smooth façades. These are fitted closely together with a locally made, cement-like binding material in the spaces in between. On top of the foundation rise several stories (three or more) of reddish adobe brick with walls that are quite thick at the bottom and taper toward the top (to reduce the weight). The adobe construction also has an ecological function, re-taining heat in the winter and keeping it out in the summer. The foundation houses the domestic animals like mules and chickens and serves as a general storage area. Immediately above it are the kitchen, bathrooms, and bedrooms. And above them are to be found additional sleeping rooms as well the women's quarters, and on the top floor, the men's sitting room or mafraj.

The brickwork on the house front may be more or less patterned or ornate (e.g., a decorative band or girdle extending around the top of each story), depending on the owner's wealth. Ceilings are made from the trunk or branches of the tough acacia tree, interspersed with a thick wattle of mud and small stones, which are then cov-ered in white plaster, as are also the interior walls. Floors and interior stairwells are also often made of stone. It narrows toward the top of the stairwell, requiring one to

Traditional house in Sana'a.
(Vladimir Melnik/
Dreamstime.com)

crouch low to get onto the roof. It is said that this design was for defensive purposes, at a time when—until the 1960s in fact—Sana'a was vulnerable to being sacked by tribal armies. The house occupants would take refuge at the top and seal off the rest of the house by making it difficult for an intruder to get past this narrow gap. The rooftop is surrounded by a high wall to protect the privacy of household women who go up there to hang laundry and occasionally seek respite from the summer heat. Sometimes, the corners and sides of the roof wall are topped with crenellations (a design that is perhaps another survival of a more volatile past), giving the housetop the majestic or noble aspect of a crown.

But these are not even the most distinctive or beautiful aspects of the domestic house, they undoubtedly are the windows and doors. Windows come in four types, though not all are necessarily found in the same house. There are plain-glass windows fitted into a wooden frame, and they have wooden shutters on either side of them. They are the principle source of daylight, which can be quite strong in Arabia. Above them are large semicircular windows, made of a hard white plaster with colored glass arranged in intricate abstract patterns or occasional symbols such as the "Star of David" (Jews were the master masons of Yemen before they immigrated to Israel in 1949) or the "Eagle of the Republic." These designs obviously temper the light, and the colored patterns splashing across the whitewashed walls add to the beauty of the interiors, though they are also beautiful to behold from the outside when they are brightly lit up at night. Next to these ornate windows might be smaller circular ones, resembling in size and shape a ship's porthole, covered in a thick sheet of amber. This much-prized, translucent stone is mined in the highlands and is thus readily at hand. For purposes of ventilation, narrow window slits are inserted high up in the walls.

As for the doors, as one might imagine of a house that resembles a fortress, the front door is made of thick, solid wood with an enormous brass knocker and an old-fashioned lock that can only be operated with a large, custom-made metal key (in other words, each key fits only a particular lock). Above the house door is a large wooden structure, known locally as *mashrabiyyah,* a kind of window covered by intricately carved latticework that lets one to look out into the street without being

Old wooden door (house entrance). (Helena Lovincic/ iStockphoto.com)

clearly seen within. This is to allow the women of the house to see who is at the door and decide whether to allow admittance, something to be accomplished by a simple pull-string attached to the door latch. Each room can be closed by wooden doors, and the male mafraj often has an elaborately carved and ornate one. Another distinctive feature of the traditional highland house is a semienclosed shelf, jutting out from the wall exterior. Because this cubicle is porous, drafts of air can circulate in and around it, acting as a coolant and an ideal space in which to keep jars of water.

There are specialists who build these houses (stone masons, brick layers, and window makers), but the art of building a house was one that was passed down from father to son and was part of everyday knowledge. Most houses had walled courtyards attached to them that could only be entered through a massive gate. The courtyard may have shade trees and is usually also a farmyard for the domestic animals or in modern times, a place in which to park the car. As with all premodern Arabian cities, houses tended to be built close together along narrow streets, thereby maximizing shade. Sometimes, these streets would lead out to a central square that might also have a small shaded area of trees. These clusters in turn form neighborhoods made up of kinsmen and their extended clans. Each neighborhood also has its own mosque and small shops, including a local bakery, with the town market or souq not far away for larger or more important items.

In Sana'a today, there are well over 100 mosques, each with a high minaret, ornamented in patterned brickwork and with whitewash on its dome. Attached to the larger local mosques is usually a "community" garden, in which vegetables and fruit trees are cultivated by neighbors and irrigated by water channeled from the ablution tanks. This is considered waqf land or land donated to the mosque for its own use.

The Great Mosque (al-Jami' al-Kabir) is the most important one, and according to tradition was built on the order of the Prophet Muhammad. Its location is near the site of the ancient Ghumdan Palace, a huge edifice purportedly built by the Himyarites whose stones are said to have been used for building the Great Mosque (though this cannot be substantiated). Of greater certainty are the many Sabaean limestone columns and Himyarite capitals decorated with acanthus leaves and other plant motifs that have been incorporated into the Great Mosque's construction, including sheet metal–covered doors engraved with pre-Islamic inscriptions and Byzantine arches. Architecturally, it is a large rectangle with high stone walls and two high minarets on its eastern and western sides; the stonework of which was laid in early Islamic times and is rather different from what is in style today, with the outer face of each stone leaning slightly outward to create a tiny step-like projection. The Great Mosque is also distinctive for having arcades rather than columns to support the roof.

There are many splendid medieval monuments in Yemen, but almost all were built in the central region of the country. One of the most beautiful and certainly the best documented, because of a meticulous reconstruction of it that took place between 1982 and 2000, is the 'Amariyyah madrasah or school in Rada', built by the Tahirid Sultan Amir ibn al-Wahhab.

The madrasah is multistoried, a feature that is shared by other such Tahirid buildings though it was not common before its time. It is likely that the idea for this design came from abroad, probably Egypt, though it is also to be found in Iran, Central Asia, and India. Mughal mosques in Delhi, for example, were often built on large platforms, supporting a multistoried structure. When Indian Muslims passed through Yemen on their pilgrimage to Mecca and Medina, it is likely that they passed on their ideas about architecture to the Yemenis. They might have even temporarily stopped in Yemen to work on the buildings, as some of them would have been highly skilled craftsmen and laborers.

The ground floor consists of a narrow passageway on either side of which branch out narrow rectangular rooms, with square ones lining the northern end of the building. The walls are thick, as they had to bear the weight of the rest of the building. The ceilings are vaulted, with the exception of the *hammam* or bathhouse that is flat. It is located opposite to the ground-floor entrance and consists of 14 shower stalls with head-high walls to insure modesty for the bather. Entrances into the stalls had to be done obliquely, further guaranteeing privacy. Hot water from a natural hot spring was ingeniously conducted into the stalls from a channel at head height, with 14 spouts in the channel carefully spaced so as to allow the water to drip into each individual stall. Another channel on the floor of the hammam collected the used water and conducted it outside for reuse in the adjacent fields.

The walls are plastered in a local material called *qudad,* similar to our cement though far more durable. The lower half is plain, but the upper half is carved in elaborate and quite beautiful floral and geometric designs. Aside from the hammam, scholars are not absolutely certain about the exact function of the ground floor, though a good guess is that the rooms were rented out to visitors or to pupils who boarded at the school, the income from which went toward the upkeep of the building.

At the southern end of the building, just outside the hammam, a doorway leads to an outside platform and to steps on either side of it, which lead down to a large rectangular cistern and to toilets and ablution areas beside it. Because these structures are not aligned precisely with the rest of the structure and the workmanship on them is crude by comparison, it is assumed that they were a later addition.

Massive building entrances are another important feature of Islamic architecture, and the 'Amariyyah madrasah is no exception. The door to the building is reached by an impressive staircase that rises from street or ground level to the first floor and is topped by a horseshoe-shaped arch, another characteristic of Indian mosque architecture. Once through the arched doorway, one enters a porch with a massive wooden carved door on the right that leads into a large, square, and open-air court. On all four sides of it are arcaded galleries or shaded walkways. Off these walkways, to the east and west, are two large rectangular classrooms in which students received their instruction. There are many small niches in the walls in which to put books, paper, manuscripts, and writing implements. The large windows admit plenty of daylight.

To the north of the courtyard is the square prayer hall, or mosque, which can be entered by nine different doorways and is surrounded by arcades on all sides with arched openings facing out toward the town. The ceilings are flat except in the four corners where they lift into magnificent domes that from the outside look ribbed, a little like a lemon squeezer. The walls of the prayer hall are higher than that of the arcades and extend upward onto the roof, and are capped by six soaring domes that are magnificently carved and brilliantly painted. Qur'anic inscriptions are inscribed in the stucco everywhere. The *mihrab* or niche that indicates the direction of prayer is no less elaborately ornate, the overall effect being both intricate and sumptuous. Although no minaret is left standing, 19th-century photographs show there to have been one on the roof but that it collapsed when that part of the roof caved in. Two pavilions grace the roof, similar in design to those that are found on Indian monuments, and provide views of the town.

The 'Amariyyah was on the verge of collapse when a team of experts, headed by the archaeologist Salma al-Radi and funded jointly by the Dutch and Yemeni governments, undertook the long and arduous task of its restoration, which began in 1982 and took 15 years to complete. One of the innovations of this project was to resurrect the process in which qudad was made, using trial and error until the right combination of substances and their treatment was arrived at. This guaranteed that the building material would resemble, if not be identical to, the original. Another innovation was to hire local Yemeni artisans to do much of the skilled finish work. This was possible because Yemenis still practice the art of building in the traditional style and have master craftsmen for that purpose. In 2007, the 'Amariyyah Restoration Project received the Aga Khan Award for Excellence in Islamic Architecture.

Al-'Amariyyah School and Mosque in the town of Rada'. (Mohammed Huwais/AFP/Getty Images)

REFERENCES

Al-Radi, Selma M. S. *The 'Amiriya in Rada': The History of Restoration of a Sixteenth-Century Madrasa in the Yemen.* Oxford: Oxford University Press, 1997.

Borelli, Caterina and Pamela Jerome. *The Architecture of Mud.* Waterbury, MA: Documentary Educational Resources, 2007.

Marchand, Trevor Hugh James. *Minaret Building and Apprenticeship in Yemen.* Richmond: Curzon, 2001.

Serjeant, R. B. and Ronald Lewcock, eds. *Sana'a: An Arabian Islamic City.* London: World of Islam Festival Trust, 1983.

Um, Nancy. *The Merchant Houses of Mocha: Trade and Architecture in an Indian Ocean Port.* Seattle, WA: University of Washington Press, 2009.

POPULAR CULTURE

Steven C. Caton

Yemeni youth enjoy listening to music, whether their own based on Humayni sung poetry or more modern forms of Arab song that have developed in the 20th century in Egypt, Beirut, and most recently in the Gulf, where Western orchestration is combined with traditional Arabic harmonics and rhythms to produce a hybrid sound. In the Gulf, some great pop stars have originally come from the Yemeni song tradition, especially as represented in the South. One of the greatest of these is Abu Bakr Salem, but some fresh young talents from Yemen have also burst upon the pop music scene. Foad Abdulwahed (from Taiz) became the Star of the Gulf in 2010, an annual singing contest held in Dubai. And Bilquis, daughter of another renowned Yemeni singer, Ahmed Fathi, is said to be the hottest young star as of 2012. Rap artists have also been produced in Yemen or in the Yemeni diaspora in the United States and the United Kingdom who have learned this art form while growing up abroad, adapting its contents to local themes. Given the structural similarities between rap and Yemeni tribal poetry, it is perhaps not surprising that this competitive oral poetic form would catch on, though no crossover poets from these traditions have become famous. There is little consumption of comics or other illustrated art forms, though political cartoons are a favorite feature of many newspapers. Television and especially radio are important media in Yemen; the latter of which broadcasts some popular comedic programs that are heard by millions.

Though there are three strong and quite unique film industries in the Middle East (Egyptian, Iranian, and Turkish), few nations in that region actively produce films, and Yemen is certainly no exception. But whereas in other countries such as Tunisia and Lebanon, one might speak of a cinema-going public (even if the cinema that is consumed is mainly from Bollywood), the same may not be said of Yemen. In the Gulf generally, movie exhibition for national audiences is frowned upon (presumably because of the moral dangers of having young people sitting together in darkened theaters). But the difficulties of making feature films in Yemen may stem in part from some of the work of Paolo Passolini, the avant-garde Italian director, especially his film *Arabian Nights* (1974), which might be described as soft-core pornography and was shot in Sana'a and Zabid. (To this day, tour guides of Zabid will point out the house in which it is claimed some of the film's interior scenes were shot.) So mortified were Yemeni authorities by the film's sexual depictions, it has been claimed that no filmmaker after Passolini was able to gain access to the place: that is, its extraordinarily compelling visual appeal—created in part by its light, in part by its breathtaking scenery, but above all by its charismatic people—would have attracted other filmmakers as well, but not until the next 30 years was a feature film made in Yemen. That film was *A New Day in Old Sana'a* (2005), which was produced, written, and directed by the British Yemeni filmmaker Ben Hirsi, in collaboration with al-Abdali. Other than its gorgeous cinematography of the Old City, the film was not very distinguished though it is well worth watching for its almost ethnographic examination of gender and status. It is a story of an ill-starred romance between a low-status young woman (played by a Lebanese actress), who paints the florid henna designs known as naqsh on women's hands, and a handsome qadhi's son (played by a Yemeni nonprofessional), slated to be married to a tribal sheikh's daughter who is a beautiful but haughty girl, as told through the eyes of an Italian photographer, Federico, who is on a quest to penetrate the "mystery" of the veil in Arabia. And in part *A New Day in Old Sana'a*—which is a fairy tale, comedy, and romance rolled into one—succeeds in giving us an unusual and powerful glimpse into the woman's world: The story's developments hinge on the actions of women who are by far the most powerful characters.

The film was made under difficult circumstances for the director, actors, and crew. The original actor intended for the role of Federico was stabbed in Sana'a by a fanatic who wanted the production stopped, and it took a while to find an intrepid replacement. Some of the leading roles were taken by Yemeni women who were criticized in the press, and parliament demanded that the script be vetted by a special committee to determine that it was not scandalizing Yemeni women or insulting Islam. It also insisted that the footage be seen by the committee before it was taken out of the country for editing. Ben Hirsi, in fact, smuggled the footage out of the country, fearing that he would never see it again otherwise, thus breaking the agreement, and that fact stood in the way of it being shown in Yemen after its release in 2005. It took a presidential pardon, of sorts, for this to be overcome, and the film has been exhibited in several venues in Yemen in the intervening years. It went on to win the Best Arab Film Award at the 2005 Cairo International Film Festival. Neither Ben Hirsi nor any other director has attempted to go back to Yemen to make a feature film. There are a number of documentary films about the situation of women in Yemen, including the oppressed akhdam, though these are made mainly for Western audiences.

Finally, it is safe to say that Yemeni male youth's favorite pastime is soccer, a sport that was cultivated in both North and South Yemen and has only become more popular since the country's unification in 1990. Sports clubs catering to soccer fans are found throughout the country. Matches are played on Thursdays and Fridays, and stadiums are usually well attended. Though Yemen has a national soccer team, it is not on a par with teams in other countries in the Arabian Peninsula, not to speak of the Middle East. As in other countries where football is popular, soccer games in Yemen are about more than just sport, they are about performing a certain kind of nationalism.

BIBLIOGRAPHY

Ben Hirsi, Bader, director. *A New Day in Old Sana'a.* Sana'a: Felix Films Entertainment Ltd., 2005.

Ciecko, Anne. "Cinema of Yemen and Saudi Arabia: Narrative Strategies, Cultural Challenges, Contemporary Features," *Wide Screen* 3, no. 1 (June 2011): 1–16.

Passolini, Paolo, director. *Arabian Nights*, 1974.

Stevenson, Thomas B. and Abdul Karim Alaug. "Sports Diplomacy and Emergent Nationalism: Football Links between the Two Yemen, 1970–1990," *Anthropology of the Middle East* 3, no. 2 (Winter 2008): 1–19.

Contemporary Issues

Yemen faces a number of crises that challenge the political stability and economic viability of its future. At the moment, the most pressing ones are political: the Houthi conflict in northern Yemen, which has quieted down in recent months but is still not resolved, an ongoing Southern Secessionist Movement that is even more serious and seems more intractable still, and an ongoing problem with al-Qaeda. If the Houthi rebellion and Southern Movement are not resolved, the fear is that the military response to them by the previous regime may make peaceful arbitration impossible, leading to the possibility of a federal state composed of a northern, southern, and central portion and thus dissolving the union that was created in 1990. The country has also only recently gotten over its "Arab Spring" (dubbed "Change Revolution" in Yemen) with the withdrawal from power of former President Ali Abdullah Saleh and the election of his former Vice President Abd Rabbuh Mansur al-Hadi as his successor, but the new regime is still shaky in its hold over power and it remains to be seen how long it can survive or how well it will respond to protestors' demands for political reform. Meanwhile, there are a host of economic problems the country faces: a staggeringly high unemployment rate, increasing inflation, growing poverty, and a looming water crisis. Of these, the water crisis is perhaps the most urgent and daunting of the issues the country faces in the long run. Finally, included in this chapter on contemporary issues is a section on Yemeni incarceration at Guantanamo Bay, Cuba, though Schmitz's individual analysis is more on the legal and political implications of the case for both the United States and Yemen than on the lives of the prisoners and their various fates.

POLITICAL CONFLICTS

Stacey Philbrick Yadav

The Houthi Conflict (2004–Present)

Houthis (alternatively Huthis) are a family whose members are saadah (i.e., descendants of the Prophet Muhammad) who have long been ensconced in the northern Yemeni highlands around the city of Saʻdah. Like some other saadah elsewhere in the country, they have complained about their treatment at the hands of the republican government in Sana'a, charging economic neglect and political marginalization. In 2004, they began an armed insurgency against the regime after alleging that their complaints went unaddressed. Exact figures are always hard to come by, but the Houthis have claimed upward of 3,000 tribal fighters and many times more that number of loyal followers or supporters calling themselves the "Believing Youth" and sympathizers among the general population as well ("al-Shabab al-Mum'en/ Shabab al-Moumineen (Believing Youth)," GlobalSecurity.org). The conflict has waxed and waned over the years, with sometimes the rebels gaining the upper hand, sometimes the government (for details, see Salmoni et al. 2010), but this chapter will deal less with the chronicle of events than an analysis of their import, especially for Yemen's future.

Violence associated with clashes between the Yemeni armed forces and irregular militias loyal to the house of Houthi has contributed significantly to declining human security in the Saʻdah region and political polarization throughout the country since 2004. The violence has been cyclical, with a series of truces and cease-fires routinely collapsing. In this regard, the Houthi rebellion, while the earliest of the major crises threatening stability in Yemen, is like the others insofar as political accommodation probably could have resolved—but perhaps no longer can resolve— the movement's primary demands.

From the perspective of the regime, the Houthi rebellion, which began when the government brought charges against (and ultimately killed) former MP Hussein Badr al-Din al-Houthi in 2004 (whose brothers have since led an eight-year campaign against government forces), constitutes a challenge to the very heart of the Republic. The republican regime created by the 1962 revolution in North Yemen unseated a form of religious authority, a Zaydi Imamate, that was the staple of governance in North Yemen for over 1,000 years. This system, which was itself quite variable over time and across the space, was built on two pillars: a social hierarchy that assumed that only members of the Prophet Muhammad's family, or saadah, could legitimately govern, and a belief that among those descendents of the Prophet, the Imam should be the man who could wisely apply Islamic law. Thus, the dominant political ideology of North Yemen was for many generations one that was simultaneously meritorious and egalitarian (in selection among Hashemites) and exclusive and discriminatory (by restricting eligibility to the Hashemites). Republican ideology, by contrast, was built on the rhetoric (if not reality) of equality among citizens and meritorious advancement.

The governorate of Sa'dah, in the far north of Yemen, and the city of the same name that serves as its capital, are Zaydi-predominant areas and were the center of Royalist opposition to the republican forces during the civil war that followed the 1962 revolution. In recent years, however, the region has seen a substantial growth in the number of Muslims professing a Salafi faith and a decline in Zaydi predominance, both demographically and socially. While most attribute the growth of Salafism to Saudi financing of religious schools and the government's acquiescence to Islah in the 1990s, others point to the underlying hierarchies that have ordered Zaydi society for generations and the appeal of a more egalitarian Salafi tradition to low-status Zaydis in the 1970s and 1980s. The saadah have attempted to reconstitute themselves as republican citizens and many have become widely respected technocrats, but a republican ideology that disavowed the idea of hereditary status has left them in a more vulnerable social position, within and outside of Zaydi circles.

While Hussein al-Houthi was accused by the government of trying to restore the Imamate, the Houthi rebels have mainly articulated their political aims less as a restoration of Zaydi (and saadah) supremacy than as a bid for political inclusion and equality. They have called, for example, for the establishment of a Zaydi university, revision of the public school curriculum to remove anti-Zaydi passages, and the ability to organize a political party under the Houthi banner. By contrast, ruling party members have been quick to frame the Houthi movement as antirepublican fanatics seeking to restore an anachronistic form of political rule, with one official maintaining that "inside the heart of every Hashemite there is a tiny Imam waiting to hop out" (personal communication to the author).

The formal opposition adopted a mid-range approach, neither endorsing the use of force by Houthi militants nor accepting the government's scorched-earth response, which has displaced hundreds of thousands of civilians. In March 2011, the Houthi militias took full control of the territory north of Sana'a when Major General Ali Mohsen al-Ahmar and the 1st Armored Division, previously responsible for prosecuting the military campaign against them, joined with the opposition in calling for President Saleh's departure from office. Since then, they have continued to stand with the opposition, but there have been increasing reports of skirmishes between an Islah-backed militia and Houthi forces, whose sectarian tension is now exacerbated by their differing positions on the Gulf Cooperation Council (GCC)-backed agreement signed by the opposition (and opposed by the Houthi leaders, among others). Meanwhile, the Houthis continued to widen their power over areas in the northern part of the country that were once under government control. In November 2011, Houthis were reported to have control of the majority of the governorates of Sa'dah, Hajjah, and Al-Jawf and were erecting barricades on roads leading northward from the capital Sana'a, ostensibly in anticipation of ongoing conflicts with the government (*Yemen Post* 2011). So far, armed clashes have not been severe.

Any future government will have to take account of the Houthi's legitimate political demands, while working to disarm or otherwise diffuse the power of their militias.

The Southern Movement (2007–Present)

The Southern Movement, known as the Hirak, is a more recent development than the Houthi rebellion, but probably more realistically threatening to the integrity of the Republic. Like their counterparts in Sa'dah, leaders of the Hirak began with legitimate political demands that could be (or at least could have been) accommodated peacefully by a central government willing to deal more equitably with its citizens. They were frustrated by the punishingly slow pace of reconstruction in the South, where some areas continued to be hobbled by the 1994 war, and by efforts to route all development aid and foreign investment through Sana'a, diluting their share of government revenue. They chafed under an electoral law that diminished Southern votes and wanted more accountable local government with greater decision-making authority. Like the Joint Meeting Parties (JMP), a coalition in opposition to President Saleh, which was preoccupied by politics in Sana'a, the Hirak sought reduced corruption and procedural reforms that would strengthen Yemeni democracy. Unlike the JMP, however, the Hirak had widespread grassroots support and could mobilize large nonviolent protests.

It is not incidental that the sit-ins and strikes that constituted the beginning stages of Hirak mobilization in 2005 were staged by former military officers from the South. President Saleh's decision to largely ignore Southern political demands and to put down nonviolent protests through force confirmed what many already believed about Northern hegemony, and was skillfully crafted into evocative analogies between Northern and British colonial rules, still surprisingly alive in daily discussions in the South, by linking the killings of Yemeni citizens in specific locations in 2007 to killings by British colonial forces nearly 50 years earlier. By 2009, the protests had taken on a decidedly secessionist tone, and flags from the former People's Democratic Republic of Yemen were (and remain) a regular feature of political protests and marches. When Southern Sheikh Tariq al-Fadhli, a former "Afghan Arab" and brother-in-law of Ali Mohsen al-Ahmar, joined with the Hirak in April 2009, followed shortly by a declaration of support from AQAP (al-Qaeda in the Arabian Peninsula) leader Nasir al-Wuhayshi, former President Saleh was able to more effectively generate support for his anti-Hirak policies in Sana'a and, importantly, in Washington. While the international community may have been shocked by the brutality with which Saleh's forces turned on civilian protesters in Sana'a in March 2011, they might have been less surprised if they had been following developments in the South over the preceding two years.

Hirak also posed a challenge to the integrity of the JMP alliance, which was divided over how much or what kind of support to offer the movement. On the one hand, the substantive political demands of the movement aligned well with the existing aims of the JMP. On the other hand, overt support for the movement carried two risks. First, the Hirak was a grassroots movement, and its rapid and largely unexpected rise constituted a kind of critique of the inefficacy of the JMP that some leaders found embarrassing. This probably could have been overcome, and some JMP leaders made well-publicized trips to major Hirak rallies in an effort to capitalize on the movement's momentum. But others, especially senior leaders in the

AQAP (AL-QAEDA IN THE ARABIAN PENINSULA)

Named after the organization al-Qaeda, led by Osama bin Laden (deceased), AQAP has been active in both Saudi Arabia and Yemen where it has claimed responsibility for the bombing of at least two foreign ships in Aden harbor plus any number of bombings on Yemeni governmental installations, including a suicide bombing on May 21, 2012 (Yemen Unity Day) at a military rehearsal that killed over 90 people. It is said to be a training ground for foreign-born terrorists like Umar Farouk, the "Christmas Day" bomber who failed to ignite an explosive device concealed in his underwear aboard a jet airliner headed for Detroit. Despite being considered a top security threat, it is thought to have only a few hundred active members, though the number of sympathizers is much greater. It has managed to gain tribal supporters, which is why, perhaps, its influence is far greater than these numbers suggest. Some claim that al-Qaeda members have intermarried with Yemeni tribes, while others dispute this, arguing that adherence is more ideological than kinship-based, especially in a country where many men are poor and unemployed. AQAP's leader is Nasir al-Wuhayshi.

Yemeni Socialist Party, were wary of being associated with the growing secessionist tone of the Hirak, given their own political vulnerabilities. For the most part, then, the JMP avoided much overt support for the movement, though individual figures, Southerners from Islah (which was never quite as exclusively Northern as its critics might allege), and from the Leftist parties alike did offer statements of support as private citizens.

As with the Houthi movement, any genuine resolution to the current crisis in Yemen will have to take seriously those demands of the Hirak that fall short of outright secession. Robust decentralization and fiscal federalism may be able to restore Yemeni unity, but there is no guarantee of this. Southern citizens have borne the brunt of government neglect and state-sponsored violence for two decades, and face deteriorating human security as they are increasingly caught between AQAP and other Islamist militants and government forces. They are unlikely to be easily placated by cosmetic reforms.

The Rise of AQAP (2009–Present)

Yemeni concerns over the growth of AQAP and other Islamist militant groups are real and deeply felt. They are also amplified by the regime, which has deftly exploited the anxieties of the United States, in particular, to secure military resources to continue fighting its many domestic challengers. While it is tempting to view AQAP largely as a local cell in a global organization, this risks missing the key reasons for its success in Yemen, in particular. In the Southern hinterland of Abyan and Lahaj, AQAP has found refuge among those who have been largely neglected by the state for generations. But government efforts to combat AQAP have in many ways worsened the situation by fueling the grievances that have driven the organization's recruitment of members and sympathizers.

The use of unmanned aerial drones to assassinate suspected AQAP operatives has been a controversial policy. Such attacks, first launched by the United States in Yemen in 2002, were dramatically expanded under the Obama administration following a failed attack by Umar Farouk Abdul Mutallab in December 2009. These unmanned aircraft operate over Yemeni airspace with the consent of the Yemeni government and rely on human intelligence provided by Yemeni security forces. As revealed by the *Wall Street Journal* in late 2011 (Entous et al. 2011), U.S. government sources now report that in at least one significant case, they believe this intelligence was used misleadingly by the Saleh regime to direct air strikes at a domestic challenger with no ties to AQAP.

Even in those instances where the attacks do, in fact, strike AQAP targets, they also frequently cause large numbers of civilian casualties and contribute to growing numbers of internally displaced persons (IDPs) living in emergency camps in Aden and elsewhere. By June 2011, the United Nations estimated that the fighting between AQAP and Yemeni and U.S. forces in Abyan had created at least 40,000 new IDPs, almost entirely reliant on emergency humanitarian relief (UNOCHA 2011). The coordination between the U.S. military and intelligence services and the Yemeni regime has "simply given credence to the narrative of extremists like AQAP that the West is using the Sana'a regime proxy to kill innocent Muslims" (Harris 2010). While there is no question that Yemeni communities are imperiled by the unchecked operation of AQAP, whose affiliates often use intimidating methods against local residents, it

---

DRONE ATTACKS

Drone is the common name for "unmanned aerial vehicle" that is remote-controlled either by a computer or by a pilot on the ground. Since 2000, "predator" drones have been employed most famously and notoriously by the U.S. military in its continued "War on Terror." Drones have become the preferred means for taking out high-value targets such as al-Qaeda operatives, because they involve far less loss of U.S. military personnel than otherwise would be the case in ground combat. But drone attacks have been problematic and controversial. They have killed innocent bystanders due to faulty intelligence. They violate national sovereignty when leaders are not aware of the impending attacks, presumably to insure secrecy. And legal questions arise when U.S. citizens are targeted for assassination by their own government without due legal process. Anwar al-Awlaki, an AQAP operative, was a U.S. citizen killed in a drone attack, and his father is suing the U.S. government, charging that his son was illegally executed because he was never proven guilty in a court of law. Finally, security analysts worry that drone technology will proliferate to other countries, creating greater instability.

Yemeni army soldiers celebrating the retaking of the southern city of Zinjibar from al-Qaeda militants, 2012. (AP Photo/Hani Mohammed)

is also clear that government responses have been insufficiently sensitive to the needs and rights of civilians and have further contributed to AQAP's recruitment potential.

Meanwhile, though the Hadi government in conjunction with U.S. assistance has made some inroads in rooting out terrorist strongholds in the southern part of the country (McEvers 2012), AQAP continues suicide attacks in Aden and Sana'a, mainly on government targets. The most devastating recent attack occurred in May 2012 at a military parade rehearsal that killed over 90 people (Curran et al. 2012). It is clear that AQAP is changing its tactics, remaining adaptable in the face of determined government military attacks, and continues to pose a serious security threat in the country.

BIBLIOGRAPHY

"Al-Houthi Expansion Plan in Yemen Revealed." *Yemen Post,* Wednesday, November 9, 2011.

Al-Wesabi, Sadeq. "Tension in Change Square." *Yemen Times,* December 27, 2011.

Boucek, Christopher. "War in Saada: From Local Insurrection to National Challenge," in *Yemen on the Brink,* edited by Christopher Boucek and Marina Ottaway. Washington, D.C.: Carnegie Endowment for International Peace, 2010.

Curran, Cody, James Gallagher, Courtney Hughes, Paul Jarvis, Adam Kahan, Patrick Knapp, Matthew Lu, and Jared Sorhaindo. "AQAP and Suspected AQAP Attacks in Yemen Tracker 2010, 2011, and 2012." *AEI Critical Threats,* May 21, 2012. http://www.criticalthreats.org/yemen/aqap-and-suspected-aqap-attacks-yemen-tracker-2010.

Day, Stephen. "The Political Challenge of Yemen's Southern Movement," in *Yemen on the Brink,* edited by Christopher Boucek and Marina Ottaway. Washington, D.C.: Carnegie Endowment for International Peace, 2010.

Entous, Adam, Julian E. Barnes, and Margaret Coker. "US Doubts Intelligence that Led to Yemen Strike." *Wall Street Journal,* December 29, 2011.

Harris, Alastair. "Exploiting Grievances: Al-Qaedah in the Arabian Peninsula," in *Yemen on the Brink,* edited by Christopher Boucek and Marina Ottaway. Washington, D.C.: Carnegie Endowment for International Peace, 2010.

Haykel, Bernard. "Saudi Arabia's Yemen Dilemma." *Foreign Affairs,* June 14, 2011.

International Crisis Group. "Breaking Point? Yemen's Southern Question." *Middle East Report* 114 (October 20, 2011).

International Crisis Group. "Yemen: Enduring Conflicts, Threatened Transition." *Middle East Report* 125 (July 3, 2012).

Johnsen, Gregory D. "Profile of Sheikh Abd al-Majid al-Zindani." *Terrorism Monitor* 4, no. 7 (April 6, 2006). http://www.jamestown.org/single/?no_cache=1&tx_ttnews%5Bs words%5D=8fd5893941d69d0be3f378576261ae3e&tx_ttnews%5Bany_of_the_words% 5D=Gregory%20Johnsen&tx_ttnews%5Bpointer%5D=1&tx_ttnews%5Btt_news%5D= 726&tx_ttnews%5BbackPid%5D=7&cHash=ca6328647d.

McEvers, Kelly. "Al-Qaida Takes to the Hills of Yemen's Badlands." *NPR,* June 21, 2012. http://www.npr.org/2012/06/21/155515909/in-yemens-badlands-al-qaida-takes-to-the-hills.

Salmoni, Barak A., Bryce Loidolt, and Madelaine Wells. *Regime and Periphery in Northern Yemen: The Houthi Phenomenon.* Santa Monica, CA: Rand Corporation, 2010.

Terrill, Andrew. *The Conflicts in Yemen and U.S. National Security.* Carlisle, PA: Strategic Studies Institute, U.S. Army War College, 2001.

United Nations Office for the Coordination of Humanitarian Affairs (UNOCHA). "Yemen: Increasing Displacement Challenges Humanitarian Agencies." *UNOCHA,* June 22, 2011. http://www.unocha.org/top-stories/all-stories/yemen-increasing-displacement-challenges-humanitarian-agencies.

Weir, Shelagh. "A Class of Fundamentalisms: Wahhabism in Yemen." *Middle East Report* 204 (Fall 1997). http://www.merip.org/mer/mer204/clash-fundamentalisms.

THE "CHANGE REVOLUTION" (2011–PRESENT)

Stacey Philbrick Yadav

The "Change Revolution" (otherwise known as the "Arab Spring" to refer to events that swept the region more generally), which began in January 2011, can be understood as both a cause and a consequence of deteriorating political, economic, and security conditions throughout Yemen. On the one hand, increasing limitations on practical opportunities to influence political decision-making or hold elected officials accountable contributed to a climate of discontent, fueling existing opposition in the South and the North and escalating reform-oriented protests by the organized JMP-led political opposition. At the same time, the focus on procedural reform and negotiations with the regime at that time were viewed by many as a failure, and the broader revolutionary fervor of the regional "Arab Spring" contributed to the rapid escalation of nonviolent protest in major urban centers in January and February of 2011. The JMP made some effort to align itself with this protest movement but was widely characterized as "behind the curve," which echoed sentiments throughout the region. In Sana'a, the movement was centered in newly dubbed Change Square (formerly Tahrir Square) outside of Sana'a University, and quickly developed into a tent encampment of permanent protest. Nonviolent marches and sit-ins were staged in most urban centers.

A major turning point in the movement came on March 18, 2011, when government agents fired live ammunition on protesters in Change Square, reportedly killing 52 unarmed civilians and wounding hundreds more. Dozens of Yemeni government officials—including many ambassadors, parliamentarians, and senior figures in the civil service—resigned over the incident. This was followed by commitments of both General Ali Mohsen al-Ahmar and Sheikh Sadiq al-Ahmar, the head of the Hashid tribal confederation (the largest in Yemen), to support the civilian protestors, by force if necessary. Continuing attacks by military units and republican guards loyal to President Ali Abdullah Saleh escalated the conflict at the same time that a negotiated settlement was sought. This led to the key distinguishing feature of the revolutionary movement: the continuation of nonviolent demonstrations by hundreds of thousands of unarmed civilians (many of them tribesmen), paired with a protective belt of armed actors engaged in ongoing exchange of fire with

Yemeni activist and 2011 Nobel Peace Prize Laureate, Tawakkol Karman, leading a peaceful demonstration in Sana'a, June 27, 2011. (AP Photo/Hani Mohammed)

TAWAKKOL KARMAN

In 2011, Tawakkol Karman was named corecipient of the Nobel Peace Prize. Originally from Taiz, she was raised in a politically active family and became active in university campus politics, while rising quickly through the leadership ranks of the Islah party. Against the objections of Sheikh Abdul Majeed al-Zindani and other hard-liners, she was elected to the party's highest council when she was only 27 years of age. She practiced journalism and founded a nongovernmental organization, Women Journalists without Chains, to pursue government corruption, to press for more governmental transparency and accountability, to advocate for democratic reforms, and she lobbied successfully to have the minimum marriage age for girls raised to 17. Karman began staging weekly demonstrations in front of the Ministry of Justice, calling for investigations into government corruption and for greater press freedoms. When she was arrested in January 2011, hundreds of thousands of Yemenis rallied in Sana'a demanding her release, and she became an iconic figure in Yemen's "Change Revolution." In spite of government intimidation, Karman and her supporters stood their ground vowing a revolution through peaceful means, and they succeeded.

elements of the army loyal to the president. After Saleh refused on three occasions to sign a GCC-brokered agreement to leave office, the fighting continued until an assassination attempt on the president on June 3, 2011, led to his departure to Saudi Arabia for medical treatment.

In his absence, the violence escalated precipitously under the command of Saleh's son and nephews. The city of Taiz, outside the media spotlight, bore the brunt of much of the violence and deployed "People Protector" tribal militias of its own. Saleh returned from Saudi Arabia on September 23, 2011, at which point unconfirmed reports attributed to his own deputy information minister put the death toll for the uprising at 1,480. Facing a growing stalemate, Saleh signed the GCC agreement on November 23, 2011.

President Saleh's immunity from prosecution was a key guarantee contained within the GCC agreement (and the main source of opposition to the agreement among protesters in Yemen). From December 20th–24th, 2011, tens of thousands of Yemenis marched from the city of Taiz to the capital in Sana'a, in protest against this immunity provision. Designated the "Life March," the event was widely covered via social media but received little attention in international and regional media (Al-Harazi 2011). The marchers were met by force as they entered Sana'a, and at least 13 protesters were killed. Undeterred, a similar "Dignity March" was organized from Al-Hudaydah to Sana'a in January 2012. Protests notwithstanding a wide-reaching amnesty law granting Saleh complete immunity was unanimously approved on January 21, 2012, by the national parliament composed of deputies elected in 2003. The United States, which defended the controversial amnesty bill, then granted Saleh a visa that enabled him to seek medical treatment in New York City.

As Saleh's departure was being managed, the transitional government was also moving forward in preparation for the scheduled February 21, 2012, presidential election outlined in the GCC agreement. Members of the former ruling regime and Yemen's partisan opposition collectively endorsed Vice President Abd Rabbuh Mansur al-Hadi as the sole "candidate of consensus." Public attitudes toward the February 21 election were mixed. Some activists who opposed the GCC agreement or questioned the value of an uncontested electoral process advocated boycott. On the whole, however, Yemenis were eager to participate in the election as a means of moving forward in the national reconciliation process, and some prominent figures within the opposition, like 2011 Nobel Laureate Tawakkol Karman, urged Yemenis to participate as a means of advancing the transitional process. Despite the lack of a challenger, then-Vice President al-Hadi undertook a national electoral campaign in which he repeatedly pledged that the hard work of national reconciliation would begin as soon as the election was complete.

Election day, however, was marred by significant violence, especially in the South, where there were reports of voters being prevented from going to the polls. In total, at least 10 people died in election related violence on February 21, 2012 (Al-Harazi 2011). Escalating instability has continued to plague the postelection period, with hundreds dying in violence that has ranged from suicide attacks on government and military installations to civilian kidnappings and executions.

A process of National Dialogue was slated to begin by summer 2012 but did not begin until February 2013 while the government claimed to prepare for it in the intervening months (International Crisis Group 2012), in which the government would seek to incorporate many of the individuals and groups who were alienated by the GCC process. Whether this National Dialogue will succeed—or, indeed, even the full scope of its aims—is not yet clear. What is more certain at this stage is that the National Dialogue is being patterned on established groups that predate the revolutionary movement (e.g., the JMP, the Houthis, and the Southern Movement), but planners do not yet seem clear on the scope of inclusion beyond this.

The transitional period has included the establishment of new parties (often, but not always, breaking off of existing parties), such as the Zaydi Shia Umma Party or the Salafi Rashad Union. Further complicating this terrain has been the emergence of Ansar al-Sharia, an organization linked to AQAP, with ambitions regarding territorial governance in at least some regions of Yemen. While there is little willingness on the part of the transitional government to include Ansar al-Sharia in the National Dialogue process, there is no clear rationale for its exclusion—when other armed groups, like the Houthis and some elements within the Southern Movement, expect to be included. How such dilemmas are resolved will likely have considerable impact on both the agenda and the success of the National Dialogue process.

Finally, the Hadi government has begun to move on stalwarts of the old regime, especially in the military, and has been attempting to replace them. Hadi successfully removed the former president's half-brother as air force chief, along with four governors and more than a dozen military officers, but the former president's son Ahmed and nephew remain in charge of two of the most important military posts (*Voice of America,* 2012).

BIBLIOGRAPHY

Al-Harazi, Shatha. "Protests Continue Over 'Life March' Killings." *Yemen Times,* December 26, 2011.

International Crisis Group. "Middle East/North Africa: Gulf, Yemen." *Crisis Watch* 108 (August 2012): 11. http://www.crisisgroup.org/~/media/Files/CrisisWatch/2012/cw108.pdf.

"Yemen Fires Former President's Half-Brother in Military Shake-up." *Voice of America,* April 6, 2012.

YEMENIS IN GUANTANAMO BAY

Charles Schmitz

This section focuses on the legal implications for Yemenis detained in Guantanamo and for the U.S. government's detention and prosecution of alleged terrorist suspects in its continuing "War on Terror." It is very much the opinion of someone with a long history of involvement with the defense of Yemeni detainees in the prison. It is not about the lives of individual Yemeni detainees in the prison (reports on conditions and accusations of abuse are well documented), nor what has happened to the few who have been released back to their home countries. For a glimpse of what life was like for one Yemeni who was Bin Laden's driver and living in Yemen, see the film by Loira Poitras, *The Oath* (2010).

Nothing is more emblematic of America's "War on Terror" than Guantanamo Bay, Cuba. There the U.S. government tried to create a legal black hole where the only law was that of the president of the United States. Casting aside traditions of American justice and post–World War II principles of international law did not go unchallenged, of course, and detainees held by Joint Task Force GTMO have won significant legal victories, but after more than a decade little has really changed. In 2011, President Obama determined that he had the legal right to hold someone forever in Guantanamo Bay without any judicial review simply because he determined they were a threat to national security. The Yemenis play a central role in this drama because their cases raised the most difficulties for the U.S. government, mostly because the Yemeni government refused to collude with the American government's attempts to evade international standards of law and conduct, at least publically.

About 800 prisoners have passed through Guantanamo since 2002 (Masters 2011). The largest populations by nationality were the Afghanis, the Saudis, and the Yemenis, in that order. Over 100 Yemenis were brought to Guantanamo but very few have been released, and as a result, the Yemenis now constitute the bulk of the prisoners at Guantanamo. Many have been ordered released by Federal judges, most have been cleared for release by the U.S. military in Guantanamo, and a small number are designated either for trial in the Military Commissions or indefinite detention under the new laws passed by Congress in 2011. (In 2011, a defense bill was passed by Congress containing a security provision that extended the definition of the battlefield in the "War on Terror" to the United States including the proviso that alleged terrorists, among them Guantanamo Bay detainees, could be subject to indefinite military detention. President Obama could have vetoed the bill but decided not to, supposedly reluctantly so.)

The reason Yemenis are still there is that unlike the rest of the home governments of the Guantanamo prisoners, the Yemeni government and the U.S. government could not come to an understanding about how to treat the Yemeni prisoners. The U.S. government wanted the Yemenis held indefinitely in Yemen, but they did not trust the Yemeni government to contain them. So the U.S. government offered to build a prison in Yemen like they built in Morocco for the same reason. But the Yemeni government refused to become America's jailors and demanded that Yemeni prisoners be afforded Yemeni laws. If the Yemeni nationals had committed some crime by Yemeni law, then they would be afforded Yemeni justice, argued the Yemeni government. The United States wanted the men held simply at the request of the U.S. government, without legal justification. In essence, the U.S. government wanted to export their legal problems onto their "allies" in the "War on Terror".

Then in 2008 when the branch of al-Qaeda in Yemen became very active, it simply became politically too difficult for the Obama administration to return anyone from Guantanamo to Yemen. Congress passed laws making it virtually impossible to release anyone from Guantanamo, so now Yemenis who are deemed not a danger to the United States are stuck in the legal and political black hole that is Guantanamo.

Following the attacks of al-Qaeda in New York and Washington, the Bush administration went to Congress to get an Authorization for the Use of Military Force (AUMF), a declaration of war from Congress as stipulated in the constitution. But this declaration of war was unusual, in that the enemy was not another state as is usually the case. Terror is not a military objective but a tactic. Because the enemy in the War on Terror had to be defined, so in the AUMF, Congress defined the enemy as al-Qaeda, the Taliban, and its affiliated organizations.

On basis of the declaration of war, the White House argued that people affiliated with al-Qaeda or Taliban could be detained by the military as enemy soldiers. Under the international laws of war, captured soldiers can be held for the duration of the war; no one expects a military to release enemy fighters back into the battlefield. But the White House argued that that the enemy in this new "War on Terror" were not regular members of a military and thus were not subject to the laws of war. The "War on Terror" was not a conflict between states but a conflict with a transnational organization, and therefore the prisoners were "illegal combatants" or "unprivileged belligerents," terms created by the White House to skirt international law.

The White House wanted to exempt the prisoners in the "War on Terror" from international laws of war for two reasons. First, it wanted to use interrogation methods outlawed in U.S. domestic law and international law. Second, it wanted to collapse the traditional division between military intelligence and law enforcement.

When enemy soldiers are captured, military intelligence interrogates them for strategic information about the enemy forces. The military intelligence officers do not care about the actions of the captured soldier, except as they relate to the development of intelligence. In law enforcement, interrogations focus on revealing a crime and getting a conviction in court. The person under interrogation can be a suspect. The nature of interrogation is quite different because the information given can harm the suspect. The concept of due process attempts to safeguard the suspect against abuses of law enforcement in such situations.

The White House wanted to do away with this traditional division between military intelligence and law enforcement so that those captured could be interrogated without the normal safeguards and protections of due process in law enforcement. They could then be prosecuted based upon the information they provided in their interrogations.

In order to carry out this plan out, a place had to be found outside the jurisdiction of international law and U.S. domestic law. Guantanamo Bay was chosen because its Cuban territory is in the control of the U.S. military, but not subject to Cuban courts. On most U.S. bases overseas, there is a Status of Forces Agreement (SOFA) that details the jurisdictions of local host country courts and U.S. military courts. There is no SOFA with Cuba because Cuba contests the U.S. Naval base there. So the White House argued that Guantanamo Bay was outside the jurisdiction of U.S. courts and international courts as well. This idea was overturned by the Supreme Court in the summer of 2004, but most intelligence gathering (including abusive interrogations) had already occurred by that time. American forces used illegal interrogation techniques in the "black sites" where prisoners were held without registering them with the International Committee of the Red Cross as required by international law, and "enhanced" techniques were also used in Guantanamo Bay.

By international and domestic standards, information gathered in interrogations conducted in this manner is not admissible in court. So the White House had to create a new set of courts that would allow prosecutions using coerced interrogations. In addition, the White House wanted to allow hearsay evidence not admissible in normal courts, military or civilian, and they wanted to allow secret evidence that the accused could not see. These practices go far beyond international standards of justice, let alone U.S. domestic law.

The Secretary of Defense was initially tasked with creating a set of courts and procedures. The White House argued that the Pentagon had authorization under the AUMF to create a new system of justice. The new courts were called military tribunals, but while these courts were run by the military, it is important to recognize that they were not regular military courts. The military has a system of military courts that are governed by the Uniform Code of Military Justice, which closely follows due process laws applicable to U.S. civilian courts. Thus, the new courts created by the Pentagon, though run by the military, are not in accordance with "military justice," rather they are a new system of courts that do not implement military laws or civilian laws but a new set of laws.

Lawyers contested the legality of these courts and the detentions in Guantanamo Bay, and this new system of justice did not stand up to judicial review. The Supreme Court rejected many of the arguments made by the White House. In 2006, after a particularly damaging ruling for the White House in the Yemeni Hamdan case, the Bush administration went to Congress and pushed through a new set of laws called the Military Commissions Act (MCA). The current courts in Guantanamo are governed by an updated version of the MCA under the Obama administration. The MCA does away with some of the more pernicious aspects of the original military tribunals, but it still does not compare to standards of civilian or military courts.

Under attack from lawyers in the United States, the White House backed off its original plan of making Guantanamo the focus of the new methods used in the "War on Terror". As U.S. courts gained jurisdiction and began reviewing practices at the base, the White House devised a new strategy for dealing with people captured in the "War on Terror". Rather than holding people in Guantanamo, the United States began transferring those captured back to the security apparatuses of their home governments. This strategy was beneficial from the perspective of the White House. Home countries such as Saudi Arabia did not have due process laws and they could hold prisoners solely at the request of the United States, without legal justification. The United States got what they wanted without the domestic legal problems that Guantanamo had created.

Thus, the real effect of Guantanamo Bay was to create a system of repatriation of foreign nationals back to their home governments, but one that achieved many of the goals of the White House of irregular detention and interrogation of terrorism suspects. Guantanamo has been exported to places where civil rights and the rule of law are weaker, but the Yemenis have maintained a stubborn resistance to this abuse. The 2011 upwelling of popular support for civil rights in the Middle East will also complicate America's plan to export its abuse of law onto compliant regimes there.

BIBLIOGRAPHY

Claeys, Noah M. ed. *Closing Guantanamo: Issues and Legal Matters Surrounding the Detention Center's End.* New York: Nova Science Publishers (e-book), 2012.

Garcia, Michael John, Jennifer K. Elsea, Chuck Mason, and Edward C. Liu. "Closing the Guantanamo Detention Center: Legal Issues." *CRS Report to Congress,* July 6, 2011.

Masters, Jonathan. "Closing Guantanamo?" *Council on Foreign Relations,* November 9, 2011. http://www.cfr.org/terrorism-and-the-law/closing-guantanamo/p18525.

Poitras, Laura, director. *The Oath.* New York: Zeitgeist Films, 2010.

Wilber, Del Quentin. "Legal, Diplomatic Issues Stall Guantanamo Detainees' Confinement Challenges." *Washington Post,* July 31, 2009.

Wittes, Robert. *Detention and Denial: The Case for Candor after Guantánamo.* Washington, D.C.: Brookings Institution Press, 2010.

Wittes, Benjamin and Robert Chesney. "The Emerging Law of Detention 2.0: The Guantánamo Habeas Cases as Lawmaking." *Brookings,* May 11, 2012. http://www.brookings.edu/research/reports/2011/05/guantanamo-wittes.

Wittes, Benjamin, Matthew Waxman, and Robert Chesney. "Transfers of Guantánamo Detainees to Yemen: Policy Continuity between Administrations." *Brookings,* June 15, 2011. http://www.brookings.edu/research/papers/2011/06/15-yemen-wittes.

WATER CRISIS

Steven C. Caton

If no country in the Middle East seems immune from water problems and their attendant political conflicts (not even the Gulf countries that can afford, at great expense, the process of desalinization), it could be argued that no other country has been more deeply hurt by water shortages than the Republic of Yemen (Alkaff 2000). As we saw in Chapter 2, since ancient times Yemen has been an intensely agricultural country, when it was known as Arabia Felix. Because of its terraced valleys that have produced abundant crops ranging from cereals to coffee, it has even been considered at one time a "bread basket" of the Arabian Peninsula.

History of Sustainable Water Use in Yemen

The crisis that has struck Yemen is thus a relatively recent phenomenon. But throughout its history it has been a semiarid country, with no internal rivers and thus heavily dependent upon rainwater for its irrigation (230 millimeters average annual rainfall in Sana'a Basin), as well as surface springs and hand-dug wells whose depth hardly ever exceeded 50 meters (m). Indeed, it has been claimed that until the 1970s, most of the country practiced a subsistence form of agriculture (Varisco 1982, Mundy 1995) in which agricultural production was in careful balance with available water supplies.

But from that time onward, the picture has begun to change as a number of perspicacious observers have noted (see especially Kohler 2000, Lichtenthaler and Turton 1999, Tutweiler 1980, Ward 2000, Varisco 1991). A drought that began in the 1980s and has not really abated until this day (despite intermittent years of rainfall) has made reliance on rainwater extremely precarious. But there are even more profound disturbances at work. One of the engines of change has been demographic, a combination of an explosive birthrate and the forced return of well over a million migrant laborers from Saudi Arabia after the Gulf War. Once their savings had run out, they had nowhere to turn as soon as it was clear that the agricultural sector could not absorb them. Another factor has been politico-economic. Since the 1980s, the Yemeni state, spurred on by loans from a host of international development agencies including the World Bank eager to see the country "develop" and "modernize," pursued an ambitious scheme that included capitalization and aggressive expansion of the agricultural sector. Besides the cultivation of traditional crops such as cereals and grains or valuable cash crops such as grapes and of course the ubiquitous qat, which has been chewed in nearly every household in the country since the 1960s, fruits such as lemons, oranges, plums, apples, and melons as well as vegetables such as potatoes, onions, lettuce, and zucchini were cultivated—and not just for household use but also for countrywide consumption. Such agricultural production cannot be a bad thing, one might conclude, when it appears to free up the country from importing foods from places like Egypt or Lebanon, except for the fact that what made it all possible was the almost indiscriminate use of artesian or borehole (sometimes also called tube) wells, which in turn have lowered the water table by over 300 m or more in many places. Only the rich can afford drilling at such depths and, as a result, less well-off farmers have had either to abandon their farms entirely or supplement their incomes with off-farm work, usually in the larger cities where they compete with other low-skilled laborers driving taxis, hawking goods in the streets, serving as guards to the wealthy, and so forth.

The Impacts

As a result of declining water tables, whole areas of the country have been affected. In the North, around the city of Sa'dah (DHV 1993b), in the northwest region known as Hajjah (DHV 1993c), and in the central valleys of 'Amran (DHV 1993a), whole wadis that were once fertile and green have now become desiccated. Those who can afford to buy their water from adjacent areas have it transported to their farms, while women travel greater and greater distances from well heads to their homes lugging potable water on their heads. Otherwise, people simply give up farming for a while and migrate to relatives in other regions of the country or go to the cities to find work. But it is not just the rural areas that have been affected. A few years ago, during the time known as "the crisis," the municipal water system of the southern city of Taiz ran out of water for 45 consecutive days (Ward 1998c). And in the summer of 2004, the coastal city of Al-Hudaydah had no water for 10 days. Out of desperation, people began to tap into known contaminated sources, thus risking the spread of contagious diseases such as cholera and typhoid. According to some predictions, the capital Sana'a is to run out of water soon, spurring some lawmakers to advocate that the capital be moved to Aden (though whether this is realistic in the wake of a Southern Secessionist Movement is another question).

New or Additional Water Sources?

As for finding new sources of underground water, one major aquifer was recently discovered north of Al-Mukalla, which is said to have enough water in it to sustain the water needs of that city and its environs for the next 50 years or so. But this find is a rarity, and there is no reason to expect additional underground water resources to be discovered. Desalination plants already exist on the coast (and date from British days), but these are still relatively expensive for a poor country like Yemen, and they pose risks to the coastal ecology as well.

Internal Migration?

Populations will migrate from water-stressed areas to other areas in the country where water is less a problem, and in Yemen, the latter would be the Tihama (which might become economically viable through commercial fishing and canning) and the Hadhramawt (which has abundant underground water that can be used for agriculture). But while the Tihama remains a viable future option for northern highland Yemenis, the Hadhramawt may be far less so, given the political tensions between

Farmers irrigate fields with a rubber hose from a water truck, Wadi Dhahr, 2010. (Helena Lovincic/iStockphoto.com)

the North and the South these days. An influx of northerners in Hadhramawt may be perceived by southerners as yet another instance of northerners trying to take over their region.

Rural–Urban Transfers

Municipalities have tried to augment supplies by entering into exchange relationships with groups outside the city, drawing on their water supply in exchange for goods such as badly needed roads, schools, and clinics or services such as education and health, but the complaint is often heard that these groups are not adequately compensated for the arrangement, citing broken promises as evidence of bad faith on the part of the local government. Tensions have ensued, at times boiling over into armed conflict such as happened in Taiz in the mid-1990s.

Water Markets

If one is an ordinary citizen and well-off, one can hire a water truck or *haayit,* owned usually by a tribesman who has more water than he needs and can earn money selling it on demand; in the meantime, however, he may be depleting his own family's future water supply. Water trucks are also sold to other farmers, which is one reason that agriculture can survive even in areas with a low water table. In the wealthier districts such as al-Hadda in Sana'a, families might combine their resources to drill a well in their neighborhood to supply water for their needs, but that will only work if the water table beneath them is shallow enough; otherwise they too must rely on the water truck. Wealthy and middle-class people buy bottled water for drinking purposes, reserving tap water for cleaning and cooking. The urban poor either haul their water from a municipal or communal water tap, spending as much as 30 percent of their household income on water, or rely on certain water-purification units in the city (some that give water free of charge to the neediest) and the *ibn al-sabil* (a water tap for the "wayfarer" or "sojourner," usually located outside mosques or well-to-do person's houses).

Shifting Crop Production

Another response has been for farmers to shift away from citrus and other water-thirsty crops that they had been encouraged to produce in the 1990s by the government and international donor agencies. But this has had a dire impact on farming household incomes, to which farmers have responded by shifting to increased qat production, which according to some estimates accounts for as much as 60 percent of water consumption in the agricultural sector (which itself consumes about 90 percent of the total water supply).

Yemenis gather by a water source to fill their jerry cans in Sana'a, 2011. (Ahmad Gharabli/ AFP/Getty Images)

It has been claimed that qat cultivation requires more water than other cultigens, though this is debatable. Qat requires a lot of water at certain times of year and practically none at others when the plant lies dormant; furthermore, the watering is fairly concentrated on the individual plants or rows of plants, and the field is not flooded as in the case of, say, rice cultivation, which can lead to evaporation and other water loss. From an economic standpoint, qat production makes sense when compared to other kinds of less-lucrative cash crops. According to some estimates, qat is worth twice as much as other cash crops per cost of water (Lichtenthaeler 2010). A similar case can be found in Jordan where banana cultivation is extremely water thirsty but also quite lucrative. Of course, in terms of nutritional value and global market demand, bananas and qat are hardly equivalent commodities, but the economic rationale is the same (see Zeitoun et al 2011). Get rid of banana cultivation and what does one replace it with so that farmers continue to make a decent living?

National Administrative Reform

As for the Yemeni government's responses to the emerging water crisis, these have been largely administrative or organizational and legalistic, but shying away (perhaps understandably) from the hard political decisions that have to be made.

Since the 1970s and 1980s, various governmental agencies existed to manage Yemen's water. Certainly the most powerful of these (which it arguably still is) is the Ministry of Agriculture and Irrigation (MAI), but there were agencies in charge of urban and rural supplies as well (though these were only the official bodies, for other ministries that might not have any obvious connection to water might have their own water-exploration or water-management offices). Realizing that these efforts to manage the country's water supplies required more coordination, the government, apparently at the strong recommendation of the World Bank, created in 1996 the National Water Resource Agency (NWRA), a largely technical unit of civil engineers and water experts, which was supposed to coordinate what was being done in all the different agencies in regard to water management. Unfortunately, the first director of NWRA was not active or very effective, though to be fair, water reforms faced enormous political opposition, especially from the Ministry of Agriculture and Irrigation, widely acknowledged to be an arm of the farm lobby. Frustrated, the world donor community (primarily under the direction of the Dutch and the World Bank) pressured the government to create another agency to replace NWRA's function of general oversight and coordination. Apparently, there was some debate as to whether this agency should be an office in the president's or prime minister's office, thus giving it at least cabinet-level power, or whether it should be a ministry on a par with the MAI, making it symbolically equivalent to the latter and requiring it to compete with the latter for power. In the opinion of some, it was unfortunate that the latter was the choice, and it is now known as the Ministry of Water and the Environment (MWE). The two ministries, MWE and MAI, have been on a collision course ever since the former's inception, primarily because of their competing visions of how to respond to the water-scarcity problem in Yemen.

For MAI and its supporters (mainly the powerful farm lobby), the problem is to be solved by increasing the water supply either through desalinization, by increasing water harvesting through small dams, or by finding new aquifers. This approach has had mixed success. Building additional desalinization plants on the Red Sea would undoubtedly increase the water supply for people living in the Tihama, but that is not the majority in the country that lives in the highlands, and transporting water to those urban centers 5,000–7,000 feet above sea level (presumably by trucks) would not be economically feasible. As for building more small dams, already far more exist than are needed or are useful, these structures often having built at the whim of a sheikh (as a sign of his prestige or authority). And from an engineering standpoint, they are not necessarily in a location best suited for their purposes though perhaps of political benefit to the local leader.

For the MWE and its supporters (mainly the international donor community), the response to the emerging crisis in water sustainability is to manage existing water supplies in a more "holistic" or "integrative" fashion, as well as promoting water conservation techniques such as drip irrigation, and increasing public awareness about water wastage in the home and in the city more generally. The integrative approach, sometimes called IWRM (for Integrated Resource Water Management), is pushed by the international community, and is a philosophy that emerged out of the World Bank and various development organizations in the 1990s. Integrative in this context means that the water needs of various societal sectors—be they agriculture, manufacturing, and tourism, public (i.e., the army and government) or private (the domestic realm), urban or rural—have to be coordinated, with everyone getting their "fair share" (though how this is determined is not at all clear). Furthermore, in line with an international democratization and decentralization discourse, the stakeholders in water basins have to be identified and brought into the efficient and equitable management of water resources through what are called "water user associations" (WUAs); in other words, management is no longer top-down but bottom-up. These are supposed to have representatives from the government (or local government administration), from NWRA, and from the farmers and nonagricultural entrepreneurs who use water for their own economic purposes, and collectively they are supposed to determine what sorts of water projects to pursue and how to pursue them. The difficulty with this arrangement, besides that of democratic representation is funding, for these WUAs are supposed to be self-financing after a certain period of time (i.e., the international donor community will stop its loans to these development projects), but presumably that in time would favor the larger, wealthier farmers who possess the investment capital. But all these well-meaning if also perhaps politically naïve endeavors may be doomed to failure at the very outset because of the fact that irrigation, which accounts for 90 percent of the country's water supply, is under the control of the MAI, so no matter how efficacious the integrative management approach might be, it will only affect less than 10 percent of the total water consumption.

Efforts have been underway since at least 2005 to change the power dynamic between the MAI and MWE, primarily through an accountability scheme whereby a five-year national water plan (reflecting an integrative management approach) would be funded by international donors (primarily the Dutch and the Germans) but on an incremental basis and only if the planning goals of each sector (including agriculture) were met; otherwise, the sector that fell below its targeted water management plan would only be partially funded, if at all. In 2005, this five-year plan under the daunting acronym NWSSIP (National Water Sector Strategy and Investment Program, 2005–2009) was produced by the MWE. At the end of each year of the program, the international donors got together with the various Yemen agencies in charge of water management (MAI, MWE, Rural and Urban Water Supply and Sanitation, and a number of other smaller entities) to discuss the latter's progress reports to date. The first review was disastrous in the sense that the MWE was not thought to take it seriously and thus did not plan for it adequately, and that the MAI never even bothered to show up. Presumably, after the donor community read the riot act to the Yemeni water managers, the latter got their act together for the second review and did much better. The political tension between the MAI and the MWE was still very great, and likely to continue for some time. However, it was also clear that the MAI was at least making a show of cooperating with NWSSIP in order to receive investment funding for some of its approved initiatives. MAI may have been "ordered" to do this by the "higher ups" in the government, but it is also fair to assume that as agriculture becomes less attractive for private investment, the MAI will need more not less development money to finance its own schemes, and these latter will have to be brought into some kind of alignment with the plans and objectives of NWSSIP.

National Water Law

Besides administrative initiatives, there have also been legislative ones on the part of the national government. In 2002, the Yemen parliament passed its first national water law, and quite a good one too (the few loop holes in that law have since been plugged by legislative amendments passed by parliament). In principle, for example, one has to get a permit or license to drill a well, which has to be obtained from NWRA, after a visit to the proposed well site has been made along with a survey study. But as one might imagine, the difficulty has been the implementation of the law, both from a juridical and a law-enforcement perspective. It is not so much that court judges are corrupt but that they are still not knowledgeable enough about the context of the new law, modern agriculture and how it works, to adjudicate cases properly or well. This, one assumes, can be fixed easily enough through reeducation programs tailored for law judges. More difficult is enforcing the law. Consider a case in which someone has drilled a well without going through the necessary procedure stipulated in the water law. Technically speaking, NWRA, the branch of MWE in charge of making sure that water is managed "correctly" in Yemen, has neither the authority nor the means to investigate alleged violations of the law and bringing offenders to court. This they would have to do in cooperation with some law enforcement agency, either the police or the army. But given that many offenders are powerful sheikhs (who want to drill on their own lands regardless), it is difficult for low-level officers to challenge them and bring them to the authorities unless they have the full backing of the president's or prime minister's office. This is an instance, perhaps, of why the planners of what came to be the MWE initially wanted its authority to be placed within the offices of the top members of government. But the political dilemma may well be this: Will any president or prime minister of Yemen get involved in individual cases of water law violations that could potentially alienate a powerful political constituency and also encumber them in cases that might take up all their time and squander much of their political capital? If the carrot does not always work (in the form, say, of international donor monies to sectors managing water according to NWSSIP's integrative approach), then the stick may have to be applied to noncompliant parties. But who is to wield that stick and in what form? The donor community has been somewhat schizophrenic here, on the one hand claiming that governments like Yemen's have mismanaged their water resources, thus requiring their intervention by working with grassroots WUAs, and on the other hand complaining when these governments do not intervene politically to enforce the laws and management approaches the international community has insisted upon.

Reeducating Yemen's Civil Engineers

There is one last thing to mention about the response to the emerging water crisis in Yemen, which is more of a scientific and academic sort. Sana'a University has a civil engineering program as well as several colleges and departments devoted to agriculture, and they have served the infrastructural needs of the country fairly well. But a critique has emerged of the training these engineers have received (mainly in Iraq, Egypt, and Jordan) that emphasizes technology and engineering as ends in themselves, without sufficient consideration of the complex socioeconomic and political contexts in which they are to be deployed. A former deputy minister of MWE once said to the author, "We have to learn to become *social* engineers, not just technical engineers," pointing to another meaning of IWRM. This critique is not unique to the situation in Yemen. It has emerged at certain engineering schools in Europe since the 1970s, and especially in Holland. In this view, technology is always a social product, and if this is not understood, many infrastructural designs—though seemingly rational and efficient from a purely scientific standpoint—will fail in the contexts in which they are installed. To retrain Yemeni engineers in the new water resource management, the Dutch government funded a program designed by the Water Irrigation Group at Wageningen University to be carried out jointly with the Center for Water and the Environment at Sana'a University. The program began in 2005 and ended in 2010. To what degree this program has had an impact on the way Yemeni engineers think about water issues is another matter and remains to be seen.

BIBLIOGRAPHY

Alkaff, Huda F. 2000 "Water Scarcity Problem." Bulletin of the American Institute for Yemeni Studies 42: 51–54.

DHV. *Groundwater Resources and Use in the Amran Valley: Final Report of Northern Agricultural Development Project.* Report No. YEM 87015, 1993.

DHV. *Groundwater Resources and Use in the Northern Tihama Region (Hajjah): Final Report of Northern Agricultural Development Project.* Report No. YEM 87015, 1993.

DHV. *Groundwater Resources and Use in the Sa'dah Plain: Final Report of Northern Agricultural Development Project.* Report No. YEM 87015, 1993.

Handley, C. D. *Household Water Use Survey.* Taiz: UNDP, 1999.

Kohler, Stefan. 2000 "Customary Water Rights and Modern Technology." *Etudes rurales* 155–56 (July-December): 167–78.

Lichtenthaeler, Gerhard. *Political Ecology and the Role of Water, Environment, Society, and Economy in Northern Yemen.* Ashgate: Aldershot, 2002.

Lichtenthaeler, Gerhard. "Water Conflict and Cooperation in Yemen." *Middle East Report* 40, no. 254 (2010): 30–35.

Lichtenthaeler, Gerhard and Turton, Anthony R. *Water Demand Management, Natural Resource Reconstruction and Traditional Value Systems: A Case Study from Yemen.* Occasional Paper No. 14. London: School of Oriental and African Studies, University of London, 1999.

Maktari, Abdulla M. A. *Water Rights and Irrigation Practices in Lahj.* Cambridge: Cambridge University Press, 1971.

Moench, Marcus. *Local Water Management: Options and Opportunities in Yemen.* Occasional Paper No. 5. Sana'a: World Bank, 1997.

Mundy, Martha. *Domestic Government: Kinship, Community and Polity in North Yemen.* London: I. B. Tauris, 1995.

Schmitz, Charles. "Politics and Economy in Yemen: Lessons from the Past," in *Yemen: Into the Twenty-First Century,* edited by Kamil A. Mahdi, Anna Würth, and Helen Lackner, 31–52. Reading: Ithaca Press, 2007.

Tutwiler, Richard N. "Research Agenda for Sustainable Agricultural Growth and Natural Resource Management in Yemen," in *Yemen: Into the Twenty-First Century,* edited by Kamil A. Mahdi, Anna Würth, and Helen Lackner, 221–46. Reading: Ithaca Press, 2007.

Tutweiler, Richard (with Christine Ansell). *Social Aspects of Water Distribution and Consumption in a Subdistrict of Mahweit Province.* Applied Research Report No. 1. Sana'a: American Save the Children Fund, 1980.

Varisco, Daniel M. *The Adaptive Dynamics of Water Allocation in Al-Ahjur, Yemen Arab Republic.* Ann Arbor, MI: University Microfilms International, 1982.

Varisco, Daniel M. "The Future of Terrace Farming in Yemen: A Development Dilemma." *Agriculture and Human Values* 8, nos. 1 and 2 (December 1991): 166–72.

Ward, Chris. "The Political Economy of Irrigation Water Pricing in Yemen," in *The Political Economy of Water Pricing Reforms,* edited by Ariel Dinar, 381–94. Oxford: Oxford University Press, 2000.

Ward, Chris. *The Political Economy of Irrigation Water Pricing in Yemen.* Occasional Paper No. 3. Sana'a: World Bank, 1998a.

Ward, Chris. *Practical Responses to Extreme Groundwater Overdraft in Yemen.* Occasional Paper No. 2. Sana'a: World Bank, 1998b.

Ward, Chris. *Yemen: Local Water Management in Rural Areas—A Case Study.* Occasional Paper No. 5. Sana'a: World Bank, 1998c.

Ward, Chris et al. *Yemen's Water Sector Reform Program: A Poverty and Social Impact Analysis.* Washington, D.C.: GTZ and World Bank, 2007.

Zeitoun, Mark, Tony Allan, Nasser al-Aulaqi, Amer Jabarin, and Hammou Laamrani. "Water Demand Management in Yemen and Jordan: Addressing Power and Interests." *The Geographical Journal* 178, no. 1 (March 2012): 54–66.

Glossary

Aden—It is one of the great natural harbors in the world, strategically located near the entrance to the Red Sea (the straight known as the Bab al-Mandab) and shipping lanes to the Indian Ocean. The British occupied it from 1839 until independence in 1967, during which time it became one of the busiest shipping ports in the world. It has gone into slow decline since then.

Aden Protectorate—The British turned the port city of Aden into a crown colony in 1937, the lands east and west in South Yemen were termed the eastern and western protectorates, held together by a series of treaties between local leaders and the British.

Al-Ahmar, Sheikh Abdullah Hussein (1933–2007)—He was the paramount sheikh of the Hashid confederation of tribes in northern Yemen and cofounder with al-Zindani of the Islah party. He also became speaker of the parliament. He was one of the most powerful men in post–civil war Yemen. He is the father of Sadiq al-Ahmar, who succeeded his father as paramount sheikh of the Hashid and of Hamid al-Ahmar, a prominent Yemeni businessman.

Al-Hamdi, Ibrahim (1943–1977)—He was a charismatic military leader who led a coup d'etat that overthrew President Abdul Rahman al-Iryani of the YAR and who then became head of the Yemeni state from 1974 to 1977. He was assassinated in 1977. The killers were never found as the assassination was never fully investigated. Despite his short presidency (in some respects, he resembles another charismatic president of that era, John F. Kennedy, Jr.), he is considered by many Yemenis as one of the most energetic and important of Yemen's Republican heads of state.

Al-Hudaydah—It is an important port city on the Red Sea coast of Yemen.

Al-Mahrah—It is the name of a governorate located in the extreme southeastern corner of Yemen, abutting the border with Oman (with Mahris located on the other side of the border as well), and of a people who live there who call themselves Mahris. They speak a language (Mahri) that is distinct from Arabic and is derived from South Arabian languages spoken by the great incense kingdoms of Yemen's past. The Mahri are presumed to be descendants of the ancient people of 'Ad. (See "Qabr Huud.")

Al-Qaeda (also AQAP)—It is the name of the international terrorist organization most closely associated with Osama bin Laden, though it has its own leaders in Yemen (the most famous of whom was Sheikh Anwar al-Awlaki, a Yemeni American preacher who was killed by a drone in Yemen in 2011). Various affiliates united to form al-Qaeda in the Arabian Peninsula or AQAP. The organization in Yemen is credited with several failed terrorist attacks in the United Kingdom and the United States. Its propaganda arm has been more successful, recruiting young men to its organization. No reliable figures exist, but it is thought that the number of members is in the range of 500–600.

Al-Sallal, Abdullah (1917–1994)—He was the first president of Yemen (1962–1967). He rose from being a butcher's son to become the highest-ranking officer in the Imam's army. He led the coup d'etat against the Mutawakkilite king, Imam Badr, in 1962 and founded the Yemen Arab Republic, with heavy military and economic assistance from the Egyptian government of Gamal Abdel Nasser.

Al-Zindani, Sheikh Abdul Majeed—A militant Islamist, he is one of the most powerful religious and political figures in Yemen. He is cofounder with Sheikh Abdullah al-Ahmar of the Islah party and founder of Iman University in Sana'a, Yemen. His name is on the U.N. 1267 Committee's list of individuals associated with al-Qaeda and has been banned from entry into the United States.

'Amariyyah Mosque Complex—It is a beautiful 16th-century mosque-and-school complex built by the last Tahirid ruler of Yemen, a stunning example of Yemeni medieval architecture. It was restored in the 1980s by a team of archaeologists and restorers headed by Selma al-Radi and was awarded an Aga Khan Award for Islamic Architecture.

Ansar al-Sharia (Followers of Islamic Law)—It is an amalgam of local militants and al-Qaeda fighters. It was active in the Governorate of Abyan in 2011.

AQAP (Al-Qaeda on the Arabian Peninsula)—It was composed out of al-Qaeda in Yemen and Saudi Arabian affiliates in 2009. It has been staging attacks in the governorates of Abyan, Shabwah, and Hadhramawt.

Arab ('Arab in Arabic)—It can be used to refer to any person whose native language is Arabic, though when used in contrast with Arabic badu, refers to a person who is settled rather than nomadic.

Artesian well (or tube well)—It is a tube that is drilled deep into the earth for the purpose of extracting groundwater by a diesel-powered pump.

'Ayb—It is the Arabic term for shame or disgrace.

Ayyudbids—it is a dynasty of the 12th to the middle of the 13th centuries, founded by the famous general who led Muslim forces in the Crusades, Salah al-Din Ayyub (or as he is known in the West, Saladin). His brother conquered Yemen and the Ayyubids ruled the country from 1174 to 1228 CE.

Badu (Bedouin)—It is the ethnic term for nomadic, camel-herding groups who live on the eastern part of Yemen, near the outskirts of the Empty Quarter, the great interior desert of central Arabia.

Balah—It is the term for a genre in tribal poetry, composed at weddings, in which men (and in the past women) get together to compose a poem collectively. The lines are composed on the spot by individual poets, not recited from memory, and are carried by a chorus on a set melody. During the course of the performance, poets break out into verbal duals (or provocation and response), on any theme imaginable, and poets who are not up to the challenge must cede their turn at versification and lost face.

Bayt—It is the term for house, but also with the meaning of extended household or clan.

Bronze Age (2500–1100 BCE)—The term "Bronze Age" is used in archaeology to refer to a period of prehistory when peoples first learned to smelt ore and produce metal tools and weapons, especially from copper and its alloy, bronze. In Yemen, Bronze Age sites correspond to a period of long-term climactic changes, with the atmosphere becoming drier and the soil more eroded, prompting a greater reliance on herding animals such as the camel. Agriculture is practiced, and pottery also makes its appearance at this time.

Cairo Agreement (1972)—It is an agreement between North Yemen (YAR) and South Yemen (PDRY) for unification of the two countries.

Change Revolution—It is the name given by Yemenis to the protests that erupted in February 2010 against the regime of Ali Abdullah Saleh, which led to his removal from office eventually. It was coincident with protests against other autocratic regimes in the Middle East known as the "Arab Spring."

Civil society—It is a term used to describe a level of society between the state and its organs on the one hand and social groups such as families and tribes on the other, in which issues are publicly debated and policies are advocated for. Media such as newspapers, television, and radio are usually thought to be part of civil society as are such organizations as nongovernmental organizations.

Classical Arabic (fusha in Arabic)—It refers to the language of the Qur'an and today to the standard language taught in school. Because the Message of Allah is believed to be revealed in this Arabic, it has a near sacred status. Grammatically, it can differ greatly from the spoken dialect, especially in its use of case endings.

Coffee (qahwah in Arabic)—It is an important cash crop in highland Yemen. As a drink, coffee probably originated in Yemen (for Sufi ritual) and from there spread to Egypt and Turkey. From the 16th until the mid-19th centuries, Yemen held a near monopoly in the international coffee market and became rich on its export. That monopoly was broken by the Portuguese in Brazil and the Dutch in the East Indies who managed to grow a variety of coffee not quite as delicate in taste but much cheaper to produce.

Colloquial Arabic ('aamiyah or lahjah in Arabic)—It refers to the spoken dialect. What makes a spoken language a distinct dialect is determined less by the number of linguistic features that holds them apart than the sense its users have that they are distinct, a matter of perception and cultural categorization. In Yemen, it is widely believed that there are many distinct dialects, and that some of these retain features that historically are associated with South Arabian languages, especially Himyarite.

Developmentalist Model—It is a system whereby the state is heavily involved in the market as well as providing infrastructural assistance to areas dependent upon it. This model was popular throughout the developing world in the 1960s and 1970s, and was adopted by both North and South Yemen. Structural adjustment programs were instituted by the International Monetary Fund and World Bank to decentralize or privatize Yemen and move it away from this developmentalist model.

Diglossia—It is the existence of two registers of the same language (a standardized or formal register and an informal or colloquial one) that is characteristic of most Arabic-speaking communities in the world.

Drone—It is an unmanned plane used for intelligence gathering, but when armed also capable of striking targets with pinpoint accuracy. The difficulty is that that accuracy is still dependent upon reliable intelligence on the ground, and that lack has resulted in some tragic mistakes in Yemen. The use of drones raises serious ethical questions, not to mention questions about state sovereignty that their use violates, and there is the question of whether the push-back from local populations on their use, leading to anti-American sentiments, might ultimately undermine whatever military advantages drone attacks bring to the fight against terrorism.

Frankincense (Boswellia sacra)—Known as lubaan dhakr in Arabic, it is an ancient incense much coveted by the Romans for their funerary rituals. It is still in use in Yemen and can be purchased in most traditional markets.

Friends of Yemen Group—It consists of aid agencies from 22 countries. This organization, formed in January 2010, aims to coordinate development within Yemen while safeguarding security and human rights. However, the group has temporarily suspended its meetings, while member nations pursue their own programs in Yemen.

General People's Congress (GPC)—It was founded by former President Ali Abdullah Saleh. It was the ruling party of Yemen since its inception in 1981, though its future power is uncertain since the uprising that removed the president in 2012.

Ghumdan Palace—It is a legendary palace presumably built by the Sabaeans whose foundations are believed still to exist in Sana'a. (Indeed, according to one story, the stones for the Great Mosque in the capital were taken from the ruins of this great building, said to have been many stories tall, and alike Marib Dam one of the architectural marvels of the ancient world.)

Greater Yemen—This is the term used by some Yemeni geographers to refer to what in essence is southwestern Arabia, a far greater territory than the present-day country (everything from Mecca and Medina down the Red Sea coast to Aden and along the southern coast up to and including the region of Dhofar, now claimed by Oman, and from the Red Sea coast across the highlands to the outskirts of the great interior desert of Arabia, known as the Empty Quarter).

Gulf Cooperation Council (GCC)—Created in 1981, it is composed of Saudi Arabia, Kuwait, Bahrain, Qatar, the United Arab Emirates, and Oman. Jordan and Morocco have been invited to join the council but not Yemen. The aims of this organization are economic and political cooperation to further the joint interests of member states.

Hadhamawt—It is the name of a great wadi in southwestern Arabia, as well as the name of a kingdom (500 BCE–350CE) that rose to prominence, with Shabwah as its capital.

Hawtah—It is the name in southern Yemen for a sanctuary, placed under the protection of a "saint" or deceased pious scholar whose tomb is visited and venerated on a certain day of the year. The precinct of the hawtah is off-limits to fighting, and pilgrims can go there without fear of being harmed. (See also "Hijrah.")

Hijrah—It is the name in northern Yemen for a sanctuary, inhabited by descendants of the Prophet Muhammad, in which fighting is off-limits and where local tribesmen can go to trade their wares in the market and where they can visit the local mosque on Fridays to pray and listen to the Imam's sermon with impunity from attack by other tribesmen for reasons of feud. (See also "Hawtah.")

Himyarites—They are one of the ancient "incense and spice" kingdoms of Yemen, competitor with and then successor of the Sabaeans. They had their seat of power in the central highlands of Yemen. In addition to their military prowess, they are famous for their unique writing.

Hirak—It is a southern movement that began in 2007 as a popular protest movement, calling for political and economic reforms in southern Yemen (or what formerly made up the PDRY).

Honey ('asl in Arabic)—It is a great delicacy in Yemen, produced mainly in southern Yemen, especially Hadhramawt.

Houthi (Houthi Rebellion)—Houthi is the name taken by a family whose members are saadah (and thus descendants of the Prophet Muhammad). Since 2004, they have spearheaded an armed conflict with the Yemeni central state, arguing for more rights and regional autonomy. Despite fierce government counterinsurgency, the Houthi rebellion has persevered, though its future is in doubt in a post-Saleh Yemen.

Humayni Poetry—It is a colloquial poetry highly prized for its dialectisms. It was originated by Yemeni elite in the medieval period and was usually sung with 'ud and percussion instruments.

Imam Yahya (1869–1948)—He was a Zaydi Imam (appointed Imam in 1904) who, after the Turks left Yemen in 1918, declared himself king of the Mutawakkilite Kingdom of Yemen, which he ruled until his assassination in 1948. Possessed of a brilliant mind and determined character, he was a strong ruler of Yemen, although despite his learning, not a particularly enlightened one. He resisted modernization and remained highly suspicious of foreign assistance (which was not unfounded), fearing that Yemen would lose its cultural and political autonomy to the West. Others suspected that his foot-dragging had more to do with his fear of losing his grip on power should Yemenis learn about Western democracy. He was assassinated by a tribal sheikh of the Murad in 1948.

Iron Age (1100 BCE–650CE)—It was the period in which competing city states and kingdoms grew rich on trade of frankincense and myrrh in southwestern Arabia (must of them hugging the Western edge of the great interior desert of the Peninsula), starting with the Sabaeans and ending with the Himyarites. Besides monumental temple architecture and large-scale engineered irrigation works of the sort found at Marib and Sirwah, this period is also characterized by the use of an alphabetic script and mortuary art.

Islah—It is the name of the religious party founded in the 1980s by Sheikh Abdullah Hussein al-Ahmar, paramount sheikh of the Hashid tribal confederation. After the GPC, it is arguably the most important political party in Yemen.

Ismailis—They are a branch of Shia Islam. Though the second largest branch after the Twelvers in Iran, they are scattered all over the world and are to be found also in Yemen, where they were once widespread and powerful but are now a small minority.

Jambiyya—It is a curved dagger, whose handle was made in the past from gazelle horns but is now made from wood, with often an elaborately decorated metal hilt. It is largely a ceremonial and symbolic weapon worn by nearly all traditional Yemeni males.

Joint Meeting Parties (JMP)—It is an alliance of disparate groups formed in opposition to the GPC (the once dominant or ruling party).

Karman, Tawakkol—She is one of the recipients of the 2011 Nobel Peace Price, granted in acknowledgment of her peaceful protests against the regime of Ali Abdullah Saleh during the Change Revolution. Before then, she was a practicing journalist and pro-media activist who rose to prominence within the Islah party.

Local Development Association (LDA)—This term was used in Yemen from mid-20th century until roughly the end of the 1980s to refer to local self-help groups that developed their villages and regions by building roads, schools, clinics, and water systems, largely by remittance payments from overseas Yemeni workers.

Madrasah—It is the Arabic term for school. In the premodern period, it was used for a religious school, usually connected to a mosque. Nowadays, any elementary or secondary school may be referred to as a madrasah.

Mafraj—It is a Yemeni sitting room, often used for qat chews.

Malas—It is the architectural term for a lime-plaster coating applied usually to interior house walls and then brought to a high or glazy finish that resembles ceramic tile.

Marib—It is the name of a town in eastern Yemen that was the capital of the Sabaean Kingdom. It is also the name of a large dam built in its vicinity, which is considered one of the engineering feats of the ancient world. This dam was completed around the late sixth century BCE, and it irrigated a large area. It is mentioned in the Qur'an and legend has it that it was destroyed by a rat burrowing through its foundations. In fact, neglect on the part of the Sabaean state to maintain it in sound working order probably contributed to its ultimate destruction, shortly before the rise of Islam. Remains of the dam are still visible, and a 1986 reconstruction of the dam was paid for by Sheikh Zayid of Abu Dhabi whose tribe was supposed to have migrated from Yemen centuries ago.

Mocha—It is the name of a port on the Red Sea that was built in the 16th century by the Qasimi Zaydi imams, from which Yemeni coffee was shipped to Egypt, Turkey, and ultimately Europe. In its heyday from the 16th until the mid-19th centuries, it was one of the major cosmopolitan ports in the region, though when Yemen lost its near monopoly of the coffee trade to Sumatra and Brazil (which managed to grow cheaper varieties), it went into rapid decline. Almost nothing of its once great architecture remains in the city today.

Mukarrib (federator)—It is the term mentioned in Sabaean inscriptions to refer to a ruler who probably ruled over a federation of tribes, possibly appointed through the consensus of the various tribes.

Mutawakkilite Kingdom—This is the name the Zaydi Imamate took, from 1918 until 1962, when it was overthrown in a revolution.

Myrrh (Commiphora myrrha)—It is known as *murr* in Arabic. Along with frankincense, this incense was the main item traded in the ancient caravans that went from southern Yemen to the Mediterranean world.

Neolithic—It is a term used in archaeology to refer to a time in prehistory when humans were manufacturing stone tools and experiencing a transition from hunting–gathering to pastoral nomadism as well as settlement and agriculture. In Yemen, the earliest Neolithic sites found to date are from the period 8,000 to 7,000 years before the present. The Neolithic came to an end in Yemen between 2,000 and 1,500 years BCE.

Nurah—It is the term for a lime plaster applied to houses for waterproofing.

Operation Magic Carpet (also called On Eagles' Wings)—It is the term given by the Israeli government for its massive airlift of Jews from Yemen between 1948 and 1952.

Paleolithic—This is the term used in archaeology to refer to a time in prehistory when humans first learned to manufacture stone tools and practiced some form of hunting and gathering. The beginning of the Paleolithic in Yemen is difficult to date, but probably coincides with the migration of *Homo erectus* from Africa into the Peninsula (as a likely entry route was the Straight of Mandab, linking southwestern Yemen with eastern Africa when the two were much closer together than they are today).

PDRY—It is the People's Democratic Republic of Yemen (1970–1990), the name taken by South Yemen after it achieved independence from Great Britain in 1967.

Qabr Hud (the Grave of Hud)—Hud was an ancient prophet mentioned in the Qur'an as the prophet of the people of 'Ad (presumed to be the ancestors of the present-day Mahri people) who ignored his warnings to repent of their sins and change their ways, and whom Allah thus punished by destroying their great city, which in some sources is called Ubar. Hud's grave (*qabr* in Arabic) is found in extreme southeastern Yemen (at one end of the Wadi Hadhramawt), and for centuries has been an important annual pilgrimage site (and remains so to this day).

Qasida—It is the term for an Arabic ode that can be dozens of lines long, following a strict meter and rhyme, and usually composed by an individual poet. This ode is ancient, and to this day is regarded the pinnacle of Arabic literature. It is today part of both the Classical Arabic and the tribal Arabic traditions.

Qat (Catha edulis)—The succulent leaves of this plant, which is grown widely in Yemen, is chewed at afternoon gatherings by men and women. It has a mildly euphoric affect (being amphetamine-based).

Qudad—It is the term used to refer to a lime plaster applied to the walls of mosques and irrigation structures for waterproofing and to lend them added strength.

Queen Arwa—One of the greatest rulers of Yemen, this long-lived queen ruled Yemen, either in the name of her invalid husband or later outright in her own name, for about 70 years in the 11th and 12th centuries CE. Under her rule, Yemen became unified for only the second time in its long history and prospered, becoming one the wealthiest medieval kingdoms in the Islamic empire. She was the last ruler of the Sulayhid dynasty. To this day, her crypt inside her own mosque in Jibla, the town in central Yemen she made her capital, is a pilgrimage destination for devout Ismailis.

Queen of Sheba (Hebrew for Sabaa, known in Yemen as Bilquis)—One of the greatest rulers of Yemen, this Sabaean queen is one of the most legendary rulers of all time. Despite her fame, however, little is known about her historically apart from what is mentioned in the Old Testament and the Qur'an. She is supposed to have met the Jewish King Solomon (a prophet in the eyes of Muslims) and visited his kingdom in Palestine.

Ramlat al-Sab'atayn (also known as Sayhad desert)—It is a region of sand dunes that stretches north to south on the eastern flank of Yemen, located within the Sayhad desert extending from Wadi al-Jawf (northwest of Marib) south to Wadi Hadhramawt. This corridor is where many of the great incense kingdoms established themselves, and through which caravans carrying frankincense and myrrh from ports on the Arabian Sea passed on their way to Najran and the interior of Arabia.

Rasulids (1228–1454 CE)—They are the greatest and most powerful of Yemen's medieval dynasties, whose kingdom extended from Sana'a to Aden and well into Hadhramawt. Their capital was Taiz, and it is thought that Zabid in the Tihama was their winter home.

Republic of Yemen—It is the name taken by unified Yemen in 1990. It is both an Arab and an Islamic Republic. That means it respects Islam in its legislation and at the same time upholds the will of the people.

Saadah (singular Sayyid)—They are the descendants of the Prophet Muhammad. They are considered to be the religious elite of Yemen who ruled the country during the time of the Imamate but now possessing mainly spiritual authority.

Sabaeans—They are who founded the Sabaean Kingdom (circa 1100 BCE) in eastern Yemen, the most powerful and richest "incense" kingdoms of ancient southwestern Arabia.

Sa'dah—It is a city in northern Yemen, near the border of present-day Saudi Arabia, that was anciently the seat or stronghold of the early Zaydi Imamate. It is important to this day as the stronghold of the Houthi rebels and their supporters.

Salafism—It is the religious movement that calls for a return to the fundamentals of Islam as exemplified in the Qur'an and the Hadith. Followers of this movement are known as Salafis (or sometimes Wahhabis, followers of the Saudi Salafi reformer Muhammad ibn Abdul Wahhab).

Saleh, Ali Abdullah (1942–)—He was the president of Yemen (1979–2012), the longest serving. He rose to power through the army and was then elected twice to the presidency of Yemen before being forced out of office in 2012. Though a highly controversial leader, he may well be remembered for having unified the two Yemens under his presidency.

Sana'a—It is the capital of the Republic of Yemen, and one of the fastest growing cities in the world today. It is an ancient city, and according to Yemeni legend was founded by Noah's son, Shem (or Sam). The Old City, still densely populated, has been declared a UNESCO World Heritage City.

SAP—This is the acronym for Structural Adjustment Program, a condition often placed on loans from the International Monetary Fund and the World Bank to developing countries like Yemen, requiring the latter to restructure their economies more in line with competitive, market-driven principles.

Servant (khaddaam and akhdam in Yemeni Arabic)—Khaddaam refer to low-status individuals who do menial work often considered too low or "shameful" for tribesmen to perform (in light of their perceived honor). Akhdam are also a servant group, though believed to originate from slaves or of African ancestry from Ethiopia (or Abyssinia) that once ruled Yemen.

Shafi'i—It is a branch of Sunni Islam practiced by the majority of people in southern Yemen (from Ibb southward to Aden and across the Hadhramawt).

Sharaf—This is a key cultural term, meaning honor or social dignity.

Sharia—It is an Islamic law based on the Qur'an and the Hadith, or Sayings of the Prophet Muhammad.

Sharshaf—It is a female garment that covers the body from head to toe, except for the eyes. It has all but replaced an older covering known as the sitara.

Sheikh (plural mashaayikh)—This term can be used in two different ways. The most common in Yemen is to refer to the head of a tribe. However, in Islam, the term can also be used to refer to a spiritual guide or leader (especially in Sufi Islam).

Soqotra (also spelled Socotra)—It is an island that belongs to Yemen, located several hundred miles off its coast in the Arabian Sea. It is also the term used for a denizen of that island or the language, distinct from Arabic, that is related to South Arabian languages of the past.

South Arabian (or South Arabian Epigraphic)—This is the term used to designate South Arabian inscriptions, thought to be comprised of four dialects: Sabaean, Minaean, Qatabanian, and Hadhramatic.

Southern Secessionist Movement (also known as Hirak)—This protest movement began peacefully enough in 2006 in the form of mass urban demonstrations by military pensioners and underpaid civil servants like teachers, but then has grown as it was joined by other groups disgruntled with the Sana'a regime and its handling of southern affairs. By 2009, the protests took on a secessionist line of argument, and it remains a real possibility that the region known formally as South Yemen might form an independent state or at least an autonomous region within Yemen.

Sufism—The equivalent of Islamic mysticism, it has had a long history in Yemen, though it has had to be practiced in secret in conservative Zaydi areas. There are significant numbers of Sufi shrines throughout the southern parts of the country, however, particularly in Hadhramawt.

Sulayhids (1047–1138 CE)—They were a great early medieval dynasty of Yemen that had their roots in the region of Manakhah (to the northwest of Sana'a) and whose greatest monarch was a queen, known as Arwa.

Tahirids (1454–1517 CE)—They were a local tribal dynasty of southern Yemen who replaced the Rasulids as the commercial and political powerhouse in the Tihama and in the South. Their competitors were the Zaydi imams who controlled the northern part of the country. Their power effectively came to an end when the Mamluks and the Ottomans took Sana'a in 1517, and the Portuguese began to threaten their trade routes in the Indian Ocean in the early 16th century.

Taiz—It is the largest city in central Yemen.

TAJ—It is the Democratic Forum for South Yemen. Located in the United Kingdom, the United States, and a number of other countries outside Yemen, it advocates for independence for southern Yemen.

Tawila Aquifer—It is an aquifer that runs for some distance under the Sana'a watershed. It contains fossil water (meaning that the aquifer is encased in nonporous sediment and therefore has not been added to for hundreds of thousands of years). Water has been withdrawn from the aquifer through artesian wells, and because it is not recharged, it is now almost dry.

Tihama—It is the name for the Yemeni coast, both on the Red Sea and on the Arabian Sea.

Tribal Poetry—It is an important literary tradition in Yemen, and very likely a most ancient one, genres of which are attested in the earliest known scripts. Composed for many different social occasions and on a vast array of topics, it is an important medium of political rhetoric in tribal society.

Tribe (qabilah in Arabic)—Arguably, it is the most important or powerful social group in Yemen. The tribes of Yemen trace their ancestry to a mythical figure known as Qahtan (Joktan in the Bible).

'Ulama—This term is used to refer to an Islamic clergy who decide on Islamic legal issues and also advise civilian governments in religious matters, and generally act as a religious intelligentsia.

'Urf—This term is used to refer to customary or tribal law in Yemen.

Wahhabis (or Salafis)—They are the followers of what, in the context of Arabia, may be described as a reform movement in Islam, founded by Muhammad Abdul Wahhab. He is an 18th-century preacher of Najd (located in present-day Saudi Arabia) who described pilgrimages to saint's tombs as "grave worship," which he criticized as polytheism (and thus threatening the fundamental tenet of Islam, the "Oneness of Allah"). His brand of Islam took hold in central Arabia, thanks in large part to the military campaigns of the House of Saud to which Wahhab was allied. Followers of Wahhab are sometimes called Wahhabis, but this is not a term they condone, preferring instead to be called Salafis with the meaning of returning to the basics or fundamentals of Islam as found in the Qur'an, the Hadith of the Prophet Muhammad, and the rulings of the first generation of Muslims after the Prophet's death.

Waqf—It is a plot of land that once was privately owned but has been donated or bequeathed to a mosque, to be used for the upkeep of the mosque or for other charitable purposes.

Yemen Arab Republic (YAR)—It is the name taken by Yemen after its 1962 revolution and until 1990, when it was renamed the Republic of Yemen.

Yemeni Civil Wars (1962–1970 and 1994–1995)—The first civil war overthrew the 1,000-year-old Zaydi Imamate in 1962 that led to the creation of the first Yemeni republic. The second civil war occurred in 1994, when the southern half of the country, which had been united with the North in 1990, seceded, leading to a bloody confrontation that the South lost.

Yemeni Socialist Party (YSP)—It was the former ruling party of the PDRY. It suffered substantial setbacks after the 1994 Civil War and has since enjoyed only a small number of seats in parliament. Nonetheless, it remains a potent political player.

Yemenite Jews—They were an important economic group in Yemen as craftsmen and merchants, possibly since Sabaean times. Most left Yemen between 1948 and 1952 to migrate to Israel.

Zabid—It is a town in the central Tihama of Yemen, once famous as one of the most important centers of learning in medieval Islam. It was built up as the winter capital of the Rasulid dynasty.

Zamil—It is the name for a certain genre of tribal poetry that is formally intricate but also terse (usually no more than two lines) and pithy (with many meanings condensed into a few words). It has some qualities of the Japanese haiku.

Zaydis—They belong to a Shia branch in northern Yemen that is conservative in its views (and to be distinguished from another Shia branch, the Ismailis). Like other Shias, they believe that the political leader of the community must also be a spiritual one, represented in the office of the Imam. Accordingly, the head of the Zaydi state in Yemen (founded at the end of the ninth century and ending in 1962) was an Imam. That state, unsurprisingly, was called an Imamate.

Facts and Figures*

Table A1   Country Information

Location	On the southernmost portion of the Arabian Peninsula, bordering on Oman to the east, Saudi Arabia to the north, the Arabian Sea and Gulf of Aden to the south, and the Red Sea to the west
Official name	The Republic of Yemen
Local name	Al-Jumhuriyah al-Yamaniyah
Government	Republic
Capital	Sana'a
Weights and measures	Local weights and measures are in force and vary with location
Time zone	8 hours ahead of U.S. eastern standard time
Currency	Yemeni rial
Head of state	President Abd Rabbuh Mansur al-Hadi
Head of government	Prime Minister Muhammad Salim Basindawa

(*continued*)

* Created with the assistance of Ramyar Rossoukh and Shenandoah Hage.

307

TABLE A1 Country Information (*continued*)

Legislature	Shura Council (appointed by president) and House of Representatives (elected by popular vote)
Major political parties	General People's Congress (GPC), Yemeni Alliance for Reform (al-Islah), Yemen Socialist Party (YSP), Nasserite Unionist Party, and National Arab Socialist Ba'ath Party

Sources: ABC-CLIO World Geography database, *CIA World Factbook* (https://www.cia.gov/ library/publications/the-world-factbook), and UNESCO.

TABLE A2 Demographics

Population	24,771,809 (2012 estimates)
Population by age (2011 estimates):	
0–14	43.0%
15–64	54.4%
65+	2.6%
Median age (2012 estimates):	
Total	18.3 years
Males	18.3 years
Females	18.4 years
Population growth rate	2.575% (2012 estimates)
Population density	122 people per square mile (2012 estimates)
Infant mortality rate	53.5 deaths per 1,000 live births (2012 estimates)
Ethnic groups	Predominantly Arab, with some Afro-Arab, South Asians, and Europeans
Religions	Overwhelmingly Muslim (Sunnis dominant in the south and Shias in the north)
Majority language	Arabic (official)
Other languages	Regional dialects of standard Arabic; Somali and Hindi are among immigrant languages
Life expectancy (average)	64.1 years (2012 estimates)
Fertility rate	4.45 children per woman (2012 estimates)

Sources: ABC-CLIO World Geography database, *CIA World Factbook* (https://www.cia.gov/ library/publications/the-world-factbook), and UNESCO.

TABLE A3 Geography

Land area	203,850 square miles
Arable land	2.9%
Irrigated land	2,625 square miles (2003)
Coastline	587 miles

(*continued*)

TABLE A3   Geography (*continued*)

Natural hazards	Sandstorms and dust storms in summer, and limited volcanic activity
Environmental problems	Limited natural freshwater resources, overgrazing, soil erosion, and desertification
Major agricultural products	Grain, fruits, vegetables, qat, coffee, cotton, dairy products, livestock (sheep, goats, cattle, and camels), poultry, and fish
Natural resources	Petroleum, fish, rock salt, marble, small deposits of coal, gold, lead, nickel, and copper
Land use	Arable land, 2.9%; permanent crops, 0.25%; and other 96.84%
Climate	Mostly desert; hot and humid along west coast; temperate in western mountains; and hot, dry, harsh desert in the east

Sources: ABC-CLIO World Geography database, *CIA World Factbook* (https://www.cia.gov/library/publications/the-world-factbook), and UNESCO.

TABLE A4   Economy

Gross domestic product (GDP)	US $33.68 billion (2011 estimates)
GDP per capita	US $1,360 (2011 estimates)
GDP by sector	Agriculture, 7.9%; industry, 42.2%; and services, 49.9% (2011 estimates)
Exchange rate	229.8 Yemeni rials = US $1 (2011)
Labor force	More than 75% of Yemenis are employed in agriculture and herding; less than 25% are employed in industry and services
Unemployment	35% (2003 estimates)
Major industries	Crude oil production, petroleum refining, cotton textiles, leather goods, food processing, handicrafts, cement, and natural gas production
Leading companies	Yemen Mobile and Yemen Petroleum Company
Electricity production	6.153 billion kWh (2008 estimates)
Electricity consumption	4.646 billion kWh (2008 estimates)
Exports	US $7.127 billion (2011 estimates)
Export goods	Crude oil, coffee, dried and salted fish, and liquefied natural gas
Imports	US $9.183 billion (2011 estimates)
Import goods	Food and live animals, machinery and equipment, and chemicals
Current account balance	US $3.1 billion (2011 estimates)

Sources: ABC-CLIO World Geography database, *CIA World Factbook* (https://www.cia.gov/library/publications/the-world-factbook), and UNESCO.

TABLE A5   Communication and Transportation

Telephone lines	1.046 million (2009 estimates)
Mobile phones	11.085 million (2009 estimates)
Internet users	2.349 million (2009 estimates)
Roads	44,303 miles (2005 estimates)
Railroads	None
Airports	57 (2012 estimates)

Sources: ABC-CLIO World Geography database, *CIA World Factbook* (https://www.cia.gov/ library/publications/the-world-factbook), and UNESCO.

TABLE A6   Military

Defense spending	6.6% of gross domestic product (2006 estimates)
Active armed forces	66,700 (2010 estimates)
Manpower fit for military service	4,058,944 males and 4,116,895 females (2010 estimates)
Military service	Conscription system, with terms lasting two years

Sources: ABC-CLIO World Geography database, *CIA World Factbook* (https://www.cia. gov/library/publications/the-world-factbook), and UNESCO.

TABLE A7   Education

School system	Students in Yemen attend nine years of primary school, beginning at the age of six. They may then continue to three years of academic or vocational secondary school
Education expenditures	5.2% of gross domestic product (2008 estimates)
Average years spent in school	9 (2005 estimates)
Students per teacher, primary school	NA
Primary school-age children enrolled in primary school	3,426,991 (2010 estimates)
Enrollment in tertiary education	236,972 (2007 estimates)
Literacy	50.2% (2003 estimates)

Sources: ABC-CLIO World Geography database, *CIA World Factbook* (https://www.cia. gov/library/publications/the-world-factbook), and UNESCO.

TABLE **B1**   Additional Population Statistics

Population sex ratio	1.03 males per female (2011 estimates)
Birthrate	32.6 per 1,000 (2012 estimates)
Death rate	6.8 per 1,000 (2012 estimates)
Urban population	32% (2010)
Rate of urbanization	4.6% (2010–2015 estimates)
Sana'a (capital)	2,229,000 (2009)
Maternal mortality rate	200 deaths per 100,000 births (2010)
Infant mortality rate	53.5 deaths per 1,000 births (2012 estimates)
Adult mortality rate	209 deaths per 1,000 births (2009)

Sources: CIA World Factbook (https://www.cia.gov/library/publications/the-world-factbook) and *World Health Organization 2011* and *United States Agency for International Development 2010.*

TABLE **B2**   Life Expectancy (2012 Estimates)

Country	Male	Female	Average
Yemen	62.05	66.27	64.16
United States	76.05	81.05	78.55

Source: CIA World Factbook (https://www.cia.gov/library/publications/the-world-factbook).

TABLE **C**   Geographic Features

Borders	Oman (288 km) and Saudi Arabia (1,458 km)
Elevation	Highest: 3,760 m (Jabal an Nabi Shu'ayb); Lowest: 0 m (Arabian Sea)
Regions/Geographical Divisions	
Mountains	Major mountain range: Al-Sarawat; Major mountains: Ataq, Bayhan, Bukairas, Al Dhali', Yafi'ah, Sabra, Hadhour Alsheikh, Miswar, and Prophet Shu'ayb
Highlands	In Sana'a, Al-Jawf, Shabwah, Hadhramawt, and Al-Mahrah
Coasts	Overlook the Red Sea, Gulf of Aden, and Arabian Sea
Empty Quarter	Desert region
Islands	Over 100 islands. Major islands: Kamaran, Greater Hannish, Minor Hannish, Zaqar in the Red Sea, and Socotra in the Arabian Sea

Source: CIA World Factbook (https://www.cia.gov/library/publications/the-world-factbook).

TABLE D   Government Leaders

President	Abd Rabbuh Mansur al-Hadi
Vice president	
Prime minister	Muhammad Salim Basindawa
Ministry of Local Administration	Ali Mohamad al-Yazidi
Ministry of Planning and International Cooperation	Muhammad al-Sa'adi
Ministry of Defense	Muhammad Nasir Ahmed Ali
Ministry of Interior	Abdul Qader Muhammad Qahtan
Ministry of Finance	Sakhr Ahmed Abbas al-Wajih
Ministry of Foreign Affairs	Abu Bakr al-Qirbi
Ministry of Industry and Trade	Sa'ad al-Din Ali Salim bin Talib
Ministry of Justice	Murshed Ali al-Arashani
Ministry of Oil and Mineral Resources	Hisham Sharaf Abdullah
Ambassador to the United States	Abdul Wahhab Abdullah al-Hajri
Permanent representative to the United Nations, New York	Jamal Abdullah al-Sallal

Sources: U.S. Department of State, Bureau of Near Eastern Affairs 2012 and *CIA World Factbook* (https://www.cia.gov/library/publications/the-world-factbook).

TABLE E   Additional Economic Statistics

Currency	Yemeni rial
Poverty	34.8% (headcount ratio at national poverty line, 2005)
Exports	US $7.5 billion (2010)
Export goods	Crude petroleum, liquefied natural gas, refined oil products, seafood, fruits, vegetables, hides, and tobacco products
Major export markets	China, India, Thailand, South Africa, South Korea, the United States, and Switzerland
Imports	US $9.2 billion (2010)
Import goods	Petroleum products, cereal, feed grains, foodstuffs, machinery, transportation equipment, iron, sugar, and honey
Major import suppliers	United Arab Emirates, China, Saudi Arabia, India, Switzerland, and Kuwait
Merchandise trade	59.3% of gross domestic product (2010)
External debt stocks	25.6% of gross national income (2009)
Labor force by industry	Agriculture, 53%; public services, 17%; manufacturing, 4%; and construction, 7%

Sources: U.S. Department of State, Bureau of Near Eastern Affairs 2012 and *The World Bank 2012.*

TABLE F1   Agriculture: Estimated Area Planted (Hectares) in 2009 by Governorates

Governorates	Sorghum	Maize	Millet	Wheat	Barley	Total Cereals
'Amran	35,462	2,700	12,910	5,060	7,994	64,126
Sana'a City	1,600	177	31	478	479	2,765
Sana'a	28,600	5,002	660	26,010	13,595	73,867
Al-Hudaydah	115,337	2,510	51,565	0	0	169,412
Dhamar	33,835	8,490	915	24,802	5,244	73,286
Ibb	23,866	7,637	1,935	15,783	2,772	51,993
Taiz	34,126	5,830	7,088	106	163	47,313
Al Dhali'	6,120	1,351	2,082	109	131	9,793
Al-Mahwit	12,034	1,478	1,411	446	465	15,834
Hajjah	71,144	1,800	21,051	968	942	95,905
Al Baydha'	20,692	620	997	2,008	849	25,166
Sa'dah	12,704	1,125	600	1,705	1,501	17,635
Lahaj	8,282	947	2,575	97	48	11,948
Abyan	16,801	824	5,197	251	0	23,073
Hadhramawt	12,052	95	679	4,731	343	17,900
Al-Jawf	4,279	760	409	19,680	1,571	26,699
Shabwah	4,065	299	1,067	1,643	345	7,419
Al-Mahrah	489	4	30	17	0	540
Marib	3,914	554	316	4,878	816	10,478
Aden	158	35	95	0	0	288
Raymah	9,067	875	410	252	88	10,692
Yemen	**454,627**	**43,113**	**112,022**	**109,024**	**37,346**	**756,132**

Source: Special Report FAO/WFP Crop and Food Security Assessment Mission to Yemen, December 9, 2009, http://www.fao.org/docrep/012/ak342e/ak342e00.htm.

TABLE F2 Agriculture: Area (000 Hectares) and Production (000 Tonnes) of Main Noncereal Crops

Crops	2004		2005		2006		2007		2008	
	Area	Production	Area	Production	Area	Production	Area	Production	Area	Production
Qat	122.8	118.2	123.9	121.4	136.1	147.4	141.2	156.3	146.9	465.7
Cash crops	71.6	66.0	73.3	68.9	80.4	81.5	83.4	86.4	85.5	88.8
Vegetables	72.3	833.2	73.5	877.8	75.6	904.5	85.1	995.4	84.8	1,037.3
Fruits	80.8	742.4	82.8	764.8	85.2	862.0	87.8	922.4	90.7	959.0
Fodder crops	121.9	1,505.2	122.8	1,541.3	127.8	1,626.9	147.0	1,870.9	155.8	2,000.4

Source: Adapted from *Agricultural Statistics Year Book 2008*, Sana'a: Department of Statistics and Agricultural Information, Ministry of Agriculture and Irrigation, March 2009, http://www.fao.org/docrep/012/ak342e/ak342e00.htm.

TABLE F3   Agriculture: Livestock (Number of Heads)

Livestock	2004	2005	2006	2007	2008	2009
Sheep	6,712,366	7,723,973	8,197,024	8,588,782	8,889,389	9,324,969
Goats	7,423,621	7,695,661	8,041,955	8,413,602	808,078	8,969,320
Cattle	1,392,969	1,447,240	1,463,700	1,494,707	1,530,580	1,558,130
Camels	281,712	357,010	359,137	365,282	372,587	390,732
Total	**15,810,668**	**17,223,884**	**18,061,816**	**18,862,373**	**19,500,634**	**20,243,151**

Source: Adapted from *Agricultural Statistics Year Book 2008,* Sana'a: Department of Statistics and Agricultural Information, the Ministry of Agriculture and Irrigation, March 2009, http://www.fao.org/docrep/012/ak342e/ak342e00.htm.
Note: Data for 2009 are estimated by the mission.

TABLE G   Literacy

Total	63.9%
Men	81.2%
Women	46.8%

Source: CIA World Factbook.

TABLE H   Health

Smoking prevalence	18% (2006)
Population physician density	0.3 per 1,000 (2009)
Physicians	7,127 (2009)
Hospital bed density	0.7 per 1,000 (2010)
Dentists	2,375 (2009)
Prevalence of contraceptive use	28% (2006)
Healthcare personnel-assisted births	36% (2006)
Total health expenditures	5.6% of gross domestic product (72% private and 28% government) (2009)
Health expenditures per capita	US $64 (2009)
Government budget assigned to Ministry of Health	3.6 % (2010)
Children underweight (under 5 years old)	43.1% (2003)

(*continued*)

TABLE **H** Health (*continued*)

Major infectious diseases	Food- or water-borne: bacterial diarrhea, hepatitis A, and typhoid fever; vector-borne: dengue fever and malaria; and water contact: schistosomiasis

Disease Infection/Instance Rates

HIV/AIDS	23,000; 531 people receiving antiretroviral therapy (2010 estimates)
Malaria incidence	10.36 per 1,000 (2010)
Malaria cases	138,579 (2009)
Measles incidence	21.47 per 1,000 (2010)
Measles cases	130 (2009)
Mumps cases	5,243 (2009)
Tuberculosis notification rate (all forms)	38 per 100,000 (2010)
Tuberculosis incidence	49 per 100,000 (2010)
Tuberculosis prevalence	71 per 100,000 (2010)
Meningitis cases	356 (2010)
Cholera cases	300 (2010)
Leprosy cases	339 (2010)
Tetanus cases	93 (2010)
Pertussis cases	2,534 (2010)
Yellow fever	0 (2010)

Immunization Rates among One Year Olds (2010)

BCG	65%
DPT3	87%
Polio (OPV3)	88%
Hepatitis (HepB3)	87%
Measles (MCV)	73%
HBV3	87%

Sources: CIA World Factbook (https://www.cia.gov/library/publications/the-world-factbook), *World Health Organization 2011,* and *Ministry of Public Health and Population: Republic of Yemen 2012.*

TABLE I1   Climate: Average Monthly Temperatures

Month	Average Low	Average High
January	72	82
February	73	82
March	75	86
April	77	90
May	81	93
June	84	99
July	82	97
August	82	97
September	82	97
October	75	91
November	73	86
December	73	82

Source: www.yemen.climatemps.com.

TABLE I2   Climate: Average Monthly Rainfall

Month	Average Rainfall (in.)
January	0.3
February	0.1
March	0.2
April	0.0
May	0.0
June	0.0
July	0.1
August	0.1
September	0.3
October	0.0
November	0.1
December	0.2

Source: www.yemen.climatemps.com.

TABLE J   UNESCO World Heritage Sites in Yemen

Site	Type of Site	Year Admitted to UNESCO
Old Walled City of Shibam	Cultural	1982
Old City of Sana'a	Cultural	1986
Historic Town of Zabid	Cultural	1993
Socotra Archipelago	Natural	2008

Source: www.whc.unesco.org.

TABLE K   Environment

Threatened species	269 (2010)
Percentage of forested land area	1% (2008)
Carbon dioxide emissions (000 metric tons)	21,958 per capita (2007)
Energy consumption (kg oil equivalent)	287.0 per capita (2008)

Source: data.un.org.

Major Yemen Holidays

Note: Some holidays are fixed in the calendar; others vary because they are based on the lunar calendar.

September 26—It is the commemoration of the day the 1962 revolution began against the Imamate in the North.

May 22—It is the National Unity Day, to commemorate the unification of North and South Yemen in 1990.

'Id al-Fitr (End of Ramadan)—It varies depending on the lunar calendar.

'Id al-Adha (Feast of the Sacrifice)—It commemorates the ending of the Hajj and varies depending on the lunar calendar.

November 30—It commemorates the day southern Yemen became independent of the British.

Muharram (or Islamic New Year)—It varies depending on lunar calendar.

Mawlid (Birth) of the Prophet Muhammad—It varies according to the lunar calendar.

January 1—It is the New Year's Day, according to world reckoning.

Country-Related Organizations

GOVERNMENTAL ORGANIZATIONS

Parliament (Republic of Yemen)

Contact Information:

P.O. Box 623, Sana'a, Republic of Yemen
Phone: 967-1-274-961/967-1-272-671
Fax: 967-1-227-816
E-mail: parliament.ye@y.net.ye
Web site: http://www.yemenparliament.gov.ye

Federation of Yemen Chambers of Commerce and Industry

Contact Information:

P.O. Box 16992, Sana'a, Republic of Yemen
Phone: 967-1-232-445/967-1-232-361
Fax: 967-1-221-765/967-1-251-551
Web site: http://www.fycci.org.ye

Yemeni Ministries

Ministry of Foreign Affairs

Contact Information:

P.O. Box 1994, Sana'a, Republic of Yemen
Phone: 967-1-276-612/967-1-276-545
Fax: 967-1-286-618
Web site: http://www.mofa.gov.ye

Ministry of Industry and Trade

Contact Information:

P.O. Box 22210, Sana'a, Republic of Yemen
Phone: 967-1-252-345
Fax: 967-1-251-557
E-mail: info@moitye.net
Web site: http://www.moitye.net

Ministry of Finance

Contact Information:

P.O. Box 190, Sana'a, Republic of Yemen
Phone: 967-1-260-361
Fax: 967-1-263-040
Web site: http://www.mof.gov.ye

Ministry of Public Health and Population

Contact Information:

P.O. Box 274160, Sana'a, Republic of Yemen
Phone: 967-1-252-193/967-1-252-215
Fax: 967-1-252-247/967-1-1251610
Web site: http://www.moh.gov.ye

Ministry of Human Rights

Contact Information:

P.O. Box 16313, Sana'a, Republic of Yemen
Phone: 967-1-419-672
Fax: 967-1-419-555/967-1-419-700
Web site: http://www.mhryemen.org

Ministry of Culture and Tourism

Contact Information:

P.O. Box 129, Sana'a, Republic of Yemen
Phone: 967-1-235-114/967-1-213-092
Fax: 967-1-235-113/967-1-202-767
Web site: http://www.yementourism.com

Ministry of Information

Contact Information

P.O. Box 3040, Sana'a, Republic of Yemen
Phone: 967-1-274-009
Fax: 967-1-282-004
E-mail: Yemen-info@y.net.ye
Web site: http://www.infoyemen.net

Ministry of Social Affairs and Labor

Contact Information:

Phone: 967-1-274-921/967-1-262-809
Fax: 967-1-262-806/967-1-449-670

Ministry of Defense

Contact Information:

P.O. Box 1399, Sana'a, Republic of Yemen
Phone: 967-1-252-374
Fax: 967-1-252-378

Ministry of Education

Contact Information

Phone: 967-1-274-548/967-1-279-966
Fax: 967-1-274-555/967-1-274-487
Web site: http://www.moe.gov.ye

Geological Survey and Mineral Resources Board

Contact Information:

Phone: 967-1-211-818
Fax: 967-1-217-575
E-mail: gsmrb@y.net.ye
Web site: http://www.ygsmrb.org

Central Bank of Yemen

Contact Information:

P.O. Box 59, Sana'a, Republic of Yemen
Phone: 967-1-274-310
Fax: 967-1-274-360/967-1-274-131
E-mail: governor@cbyemen.com
Web site: http://www.centralbank.gov.ye

National Information Center

Contact Information:

P.O. Box 19560, Sana'a, Republic of Yemen
Phone: 967-1-215-116/967-1-215-117
Fax: 967-1-207-716
E-mail: info@yemen-nic.net
Web site: http://www.yemen-nic.net

Central Statistical Organization

Contact Information:

P.O. Box 13434, Sana'a, Republic of Yemen
Phone: 967-1-250-619/967-1-250-619
Fax: 967-1-250-664
E-mail: csoi@y.net.ye
Web site: http://www.cso-yemen.org

Social Fund for Development

Contact Information:

P.O. Box 15485, Sana'a, Republic of Yemen
Phone: 967-1-449-669
Fax: 967-1-449-670
E-mail: sfd@sfd-yemen.org
Web site: http://www.sfd-yemen.org

Yemen National Commission for Education, Culture, and Science

Contact Information:

Phone: 967-1-214-612/967-1-214-615
Fax: 967-1-214-613
E-mail: yncecs2@yncecs.gov.ye
Web site: http://www.yncecs.gov.ye

Embassy of the Republic of Yemen in the United States

Location: Washington, D.C., U.S.A.

Contact Information:

2319 Wyoming Ave., NW, Washington, D.C. 20008
Phone: 202-965-4760
Fax: 202-337-2017
E-mail:

General: information@yemenembassy.org
Ambassador's Office: counselor@yemenembassy.org
Political Affairs: political@yemenembassy.org

Web site: http://www.yemenembassy.org

U.S. Embassy in Yemen

Location: Sana'a

Contact Information:

P.O. Box 22347, Sa'awan Street, Sana'a, Republic of Yemen
Phone: 967-1-755-2000, ext. 2153–2266
Fax: 967-1-303-182
E-mail:

Public Affairs: passanaa@state.gov
Consular: consularsanaa@state.gov

Web site: http://yemen.usembassy.gov/about-us.html

General Authority of Tourism

Contact Information:

P.O. Box 129, Sana'a, Republic of Yemen
Phone: 967-1-252-319
Fax: 967-1-252-316
E-mail: gtda@gtda.gov.ye
Web site: http://www.gtda.gov.ye

Yemen Tourism Promotion Board (YTPB)

Contact Information:

P.O. Box 5607, Sana'a, Republic of Yemen
Phone: 967-1-209-265
Fax: 967-1-209-266

E-mail:

General: ytpb@yementourism.com

Assistant to Executive Director/Marketing Manager (Yasmin al-Hamdani): marketing@yementourism.com

Web site: http://www.yementourism.com

NONGOVERNMENTAL ORGANIZATIONS
American Institute for Yemeni Studies (AIYS)

Contact Information:

United States:

P.O. Box 311, Ardmore, PA, 19003-0311
Phone: 610-896-5412
Fax: 610-896-9049
E-mail: aiys@aiys.org
Web site: http://www.aiys.org/

Yemen:

P.O. Box 26458, Sana'a, Republic of Yemen
Phone: 967-1-278-816
Fax: 967-1-285-071
E-mail: aiysyem@y.net.ye
Web site: http://www.aiys.org

Comprehensive List of Yemeni Nongovernmental Organizations:[*]

http://www.yemenembassy.org/economic/The%20Directory%20of%20
the%20Yemeni%20NGOs.pdf

Comprehensive List of International Nongovernmental Organizations in Yemen:

http://www.yemenembassy.org/economic/NGOs%20%28bw%29.pdf

NEWSPAPERS/MEDIA
Saba News Agency

Contact Information:

Sana'a, Republic of Yemen
E-mail: info@sabanews.net
Web site: http://www.sabanews.net/en/

[*] As provided by the Yemeni embassy in the United States.

About:

- It is the official news agency of the Republic of Yemen.
- It was established in 1970 by Yemen Arab Republic (after unification, Saba combined with Aden News Agency to be Saba).
- It is a member of Federation of Arab News Agencies (FANA).

Yemen Times

Contact Information:

P.O. Box 2579, Sana'a, Republic of Yemen
Phone: 967-1-268-661/2/3
Fax: 967-1-268-276
E-mail: ytreaders.view@gmail.com (letters)
Web site: http://www.yementimes.com

About:

- It was founded by Abd al-Aziz al-Saqqaf in 1990, who was also a cofounder of the Arab Human Rights Organization (1983).
- It was the first English-language newspaper to be printed in Yemen, and is now the most widely read English-language newspaper of Yemeni origin.
- It became the first newspaper to appoint a woman as editor in Yemen when Nadia al-Saqqaf became editor-in-chief in 2005.
- It was given the 2006 Free Media Pioneer Award by the International Press Institute.

Almotamar

Contact Information:

Sana'a, Republic. of Yemen
Phone: 967-1-208-934
Fax: 967-1-402-983
E-mail:
Information or Suggestion: info@almotamar.net
Editor-in-chief: chief@almotamar.net
Editing Manager: editing@almotamar.net
Web site: http://www.almotamar.net/en/

About:

It is an online newspaper published by the General People Congress (GPC).

BUSINESSES

Yemen LNG

Contact Information:

P.O. Box 15347, Sana'a, Republic of Yemen
Phone: 967-1-438-000
Fax: 967-1-428-042
E-mail: pr@yemenlng.com (Public Relations)
Web site: http://www.yemenlng.com/ws/en

About:

- It was initiated in 2005 to commercialize and export Yemen's gas as liquefied natural gas.
- It was funded by the Yemeni government and shareholders such as Total, Hunt, Yemen Gas Company, SK Corporation, Kogas, Hyundai, and the General Authority of Social Security and Pensions.
- It was considered to be the largest industrial project undertaken by the country.

Annotated Bibliography

GENERAL WORKS

Geography

There is no synthetic work on the geography of Yemen. Below are key works on issues of having to do with water, a key problem for contemporary Yemen.

Handley, Chris D. *Water Stress: Some Symptoms and Causes: A Case Study of Taiz Yemen.* Burlington, VT: Ashgate, 2001.

It is an excellent study of political conflicts that can arise over water scarcity in Yemen.

Lichtenthäler, Gerhard. *Political Ecology and the Role of Water: Environment, Society and Economy in Northern Yemen.* Burlington, VT: Ashgate Publishing Ltd., 2003.

Written by a political geographer with years of fieldwork experience in northern Yemen, this is one of the few works to examine water shortage in Yemen. It is a superb study, detailed but quite accessible to the nonspecialist.

Maktari, Abdulla M. A. *Water Rights and Irrigation Practices in Lahj.* Cambridge: Cambridge University Press, 1971.

It is a classic study of customary water-use practices in Lahaj, immediately to the north of the port city of Aden. It is indispensable for anyone trying to understand sustainable water use in Yemen before the 1980s when water overdraft began.

Varisco, Daniel M. "Sayl and Ghayl: The Ecology of Water-allocation in Yemen." *Human Ecology* 11, no. 4 (1982): 365–83.

It is a classic article on water usage in highland Yemen.

Ward, Christopher S. *Yemen: Towards a Water Strategy.* Report No. 15718-YEM. Washington, D.C.: World Bank, 1999.

By one of the leading water development experts in the world, this is a sobering account of what Yemen must do to conserve its water resources.

World Bank. *Republic of Yemen: Country Water Resources Assistance Strategy.* Report No. 31779-YEMN, March 3, 2005.

It provides an overview of the water problem in Yemen from one of the most powerful agencies in the world dealing with it.

Prehistory

This section has mainly archaeological texts that refer to the history of Yemen before the advent of Islam (622 CE).

de Maigret, Alessandro. *Arabia Felix: An Exploration of the Archaeological History of Yemen.* London: Stacy International, 2002.

It is an accessible summary of findings from several Italian archaeological expeditions carried out in the 1980s in the region of Yemen known as Khawlan al-Tiyal, extending from just east of Sana'a to the outskirts of Marib. The findings relate to our understanding of the Paleolithic period in Yemen.

Gunter, Ann C., ed. *Caravan Kingdoms: Yemen and the Ancient Incense Trade.* Washington, D.C.: Arthur M. Sackler Gallery (Smithsonian Institution), 2005.

It is a beautifully produced book that is full of gorgeous photographs and illustrations, accompanied by a clear text on the history of South Arabia.

History

Burrowes, Robert D. *Historical Dictionary of Yemen.* Lanham, MD: Scarecrow, 1995.

It is a basic reference work on Yemen's history.

Daum, Werner, ed. *Yemen: 3000 Years of Art and Civilization in Arabia Felix.* Innsbruck: Pinguin, 1987.

This is the catalog that was published in conjunction with the 1987 exhibition by the same title at the State Museum for Folk Arts in Munich, Germany. It contains essays on a large array of topics by leading experts on Yemeni studies and includes beautiful illustrations and photographs.

Dresch, Paul. *A History of Modern Yemen.* Cambridge: Cambridge University Press, 2000.

This is the indispensable work on the modern history of Yemen. It is well written and readily accessible to nonspecialists. It is especially good tracking the histories of both northern and southern Yemen in conjunction with each other in the postindependence period. As such, it can be read as a companion volume to Stookey, *Yemen: The Politics of the Yemen Arab Republic.*

Margariti, Roxani Eleni. *Aden & the Indian Ocean Trade: 150 Years in the Life of a Medieval Arabian Port.* Chapel Hill, NC: The University of North Caroline Press, 2007.

Relatively little has been written about the medieval history of Yemen, and so this deeply researched book on the important port of Aden from the 11th to the 13th centuries is a welcome volume. An unusual array of sources is used—archaeological, geographic, maritime, and historical documents from the famed Geniza Documents of Cairo—to bring the social history of the port city to life. This study is part of a burgeoning historical scholarship on ports in the Indian Ocean and their importance over millennia in fostering a global trade that linked Asia and the European world.

Stookey, Robert W. *Yemen: The Politics of the Yemen Arab Republic.* Boulder, CO: Westview Press, 1978.

Until well into the 1980s, this was the indispensable general history of Yemen, starting with ancient Marib and ending with the independence of the two Yemens. Though it has been rendered outdated by subsequent scholarship, in many ways, it is still the most accessible account available in English.

Government and Politics

Burrowes, Robert D. *The Yemen Arab Republic: The Politics of Development, 1962–1986.* Boulder, CO: Westview Press, 1987.

Yemen was unique among Arab countries from the 1960s through the 1980s in that much of its development came from local initiatives in the form of local development associations, financed largely by remittance payments from Yemenis working overseas. The complex politics of this development, especially as the Yemeni state began to centralize, is expertly told in this book by one of the leading political scientists of Yemen.

Carapico, Sheila. *Civil Society in Yemen: The Political Economy of Activism in Modern Arabia.* Cambridge: Cambridge University Press, 1998.

This important and controversial book examines the modern history of civil society in Yemen from a political economic approach. It is important because it argues that Yemen has had a social participatory movement in its civil society that may be unique in the Arabian Peninsula and has been overlooked by political scientists searching for "democratic" practices. Anyone interested in the role of development and nongovernmental organizations in Yemen must read this book.

Gauss, F. Gregory, III. *Saudi-Yemeni Relations: Domestic Structure and Foreign Influence.* New York: Columbia University Press.

It is an indispensable work on the influence of Saudi Arabia on Yemeni affairs.

Peterson, John E. *Yemen: The Search for a Modern State.* Baltimore, MD: Johns Hopkins University Press, 1982.

Though a bit dated by now, this is still an analytically sharp and insightful look at the Yemeni state.

Phillips, Sarah. *Yemen's Democracy Experiment in Regional Perspective: Patronage and Pluralized Authoritarianism.* New York: Palgrave Macmillan, 2008.

This work of political science is a critique of the Saleh regime in Sana'a.

Salmoni, Barak A., Bryce Loidolt, and Madeleine Wells. *Regime and Periphery in Northern Yemen.* Santa Monica, CA: RAND, 2010.

This intelligence report is a must-read for anyone trying to understand the history and political dynamics of the Houthi rebellion in northern Yemen. It is exemplary in its efforts to place the rebellion in a set of contexts—tribal, ecological, and religious—that make it comprehensible and is judicious in its sifting of often unreliable or ambiguous data when it comes to its analysis.

Wedeen, Lisa. *Peripheral Visions: Publics, Power, and Performance in Yemen.* Chicago, IL: University of Chicago Press, 2008.

This superb study of the contemporary Yemeni state is refreshing in the way it stresses the more cultural and not just organizational aspects of Yemeni politics (parties, elections, and state bureaucracy). For those unconvinced that there is a tradition of democratic debate in Yemeni society, let alone that qat chewing has any redeeming social consequences, they should check out the wonderful chapter on the qat chew as spaces of public debate. Also illuminating are the chapters on what are called Islamic piety movements in Yemen and their political implications.

Wenner, Manfred W. *Modern Yemen: 1918–1916.* Baltimore, MD: The Johns Hopkins University Press, 1967.

This is a political history of modern Yemen, focusing almost entirely on the northern part of the country and the reigns of Imams Yahya and Ahmed. It is particularly good at explaining the foreign affairs of these leaders, and how they tried to use conflicts between outside states to their own advantage.

Economy

There is no comprehensive work on Yemen's economy, though there are works on special topics such as development economics, the oil industry, the agricultural sector, migration, small-scale local markets, and poverty reduction, written usually within the framework of political economy. The difficulty that might deter most specialists would be the dearth of reliable, long-term statistics.

Chaudhry, Kiren A. *The Price of Wealth: Economics and Institutions in the Middle East.* Ithaca, NY: Cornell University Press, 1997.

It is a comparative study of some nations in the Middle East with oil economies, including a detailed analysis of Yemen.

Economic Intelligence Unit (EIU). *Country Profile—Yemen and Oman.* London: EIU, various years.

It is a good source for statistical information.

El Mallakh, Ragaei. *The Economic Development of the Yemen Arab Republic.* Wolfeboro, NH: Croom Helm, 1986.

This work should be read in conjunction with the one by Lackner, *PDRY: Outpost of Socialist Development in Arabia,* to get a sense of how the two Yemens developed economically in different ways.

Lackner, Helen. *PDRY: Outpost of Socialist Development in Arabia.* London: Ithaca Press, 1985.

By a leading left-wing political economist, this is one of the few comprehensive studies of the Socialist economy of South Yemen, before it unified with the North.

Mahdi, Kamil A., Anna Würth, and Helen Lackner, eds. *Yemen into the Twenty-First Century: Continuity and Change.* London: Ithaca Press, 2007.

Though not an economics text per se, Part I is devoted to the important subject of structural readjustment programs and their impact on Yemen. Consult also Part III on water, the environment, and land tenure.

Morris, Tim. *The Despairing Developer: Diary of an Aid Worker in the Middle East.* London: I. B. Tauris, 1991.

The author spent part of his time in Yemen. This is a damning critique of the development world.

Pridham, B. R., ed. *Economy, Society and Culture in Contemporary Yemen.* Dover, NH: Croom Helm, 1985.

It is an excellent collection of essays that give a picture of Yemen in the mid-1980s.

Stevenson, Thomas. "Yemeni Workers Come Home: Reabsorbing One Million Migrants," *Middle East Report* 181 (March–April 1993): 15–20.

This piece is about the expulsion of Yemeni migrant workers from the Gulf after the first Iraq war, a signal event that had a devastating impact on the remittance economy of the country.

Swanson, John. *Emigration and Economic Development: The Case of the Yemen Arab Republic.* Boulder, CO: Westview Press, 1979.

Though this work is now dated, it is still valuable for its analysis of Yemeni migration abroad and its impact on local development through remittances. It is clear that development depended far more on this self-help model than on state-centralized development (but that would change with the oil economy in the 1980s).

Weir, Shelagh. *Qat in Yemen.* London: British Museum, 1985.

It is a good study of this popular plant in Yemen, and a companion piece to the book by Kennedy on the same subject, *Flower of Paradise.*

Society and Culture

Abraham, Nabeel and Andrew Shryock. *Arab Detroit: From Margin to Mainstream.* Detroit, MI: Wayne State University Press, 2000.

It is an interesting account of Yemenis in Detroit, an important immigrant population in the United States.

Caton, Steven C. *Yemen Chronicle: An Anthropology of War and Mediation.* New York: Hill & Wang, 2005.

Engagingly written as a memoir of the author's tumultuous fieldwork in a tribal area of northern Yemen in the late 1970s, it is also an account of an abduction of two tribal women by a young descendant of the Prophet Muhammad, and how it was eventually resolved through peaceful mediation. This should be read as a companion piece to Weir's book on tribal law, *A Tribal Order: Politics and Law in the Mountains of Yemen,* for it shows in detail the political process—and not just the laws—in which conflict is mediated. One of the more unusual aspects of this story is how poetry becomes a central communicative means in this political process. Dozens of such poems are included in the text.

Dahlgren, Susanne. *Contesting Realities: The Public Sphere and Morality in Southern Yemen.* Syracuse, NY: Syracuse University Press, 2010.

This is a political and social history of Aden from the late British colonial period until the present, which focuses on the cultural frameworks of propriety and ethics that have been used in judging and controlling behavior, both male and female. Dahlgren finds that despite a traditional patriarchal system, Adenis are flexible in the way they apply such ethical frameworks in concrete action, showing ingenuity and creativity in the way they constitute their persons or selves. It is a valuable glimpse into the little known world of South Yemeni women.

Dorsky, Susan. *Women of 'Amran: A Middle Eastern Ethnographic Study.* Salt Lake City, UT: University of Utah Press, 1986.

There are few studies of gender in Yemen and this one, though dated, is still one of the best. It's accessible to the nonspecialist and filled with interesting details.

Dresch, Paul. *The Rules of Barat: Tribal Documents from Yemen.* Sana'a: French Center for Archaeology and the Social Sciences, 2006.

It is a meticulously researched and carefully translated collection of documents having to do with tribal customary law in northern Yemen.

Dresch, Paul. *Tribes, Government and History in Yemen.* Oxford: Clarendon Press, 1989.

It is a detailed study of the northern tribes of Yemen that combines history and ethnography to elucidate their social system over the past one thousand years. Along with Shelagh Weir's book, *A Tribal Order: Politics and Law in the Mountains of Yemen,* it is indispensable for understanding tribal identities and tribal political processes in Yemen. This book is for specialists, but the stouthearted can glean a great deal from it with patience and fortitude.

Friedlander, Jonathan, ed. *Sojourners and Settlers: The Yemeni Emigrant Experience.* Salt Lake City, UT: University of Utah Press, 1988.

It is an excellent collection of essays on Yemeni emigrants in the world.

Kennedy, John. *Flower of Paradise: The Institutionalized Use of the Drug Qat in North Yemen.* Norwell, MA: D. Reidel, 1987.

Written by a medical anthropologist, this is a detailed and nonbiased account of qat use in Yemen, its medical side effects, and its social uses.

Leveau, Rémy, Franck Mermiet, and Udo Steinbach, eds. *Le Yemen Contemporain* [Contemporary Yemen]. Paris: Karthala, 1999.

It is an excellent collection of essays on the economy, politics, and culture.

Marchand, Trevor Hugh James. *Minaret Building and Apprenticeship in Yemen.* Richmond: Curzon, 2001.

It is an original and brilliant study, based on the author's apprenticeship to stone masons and builders in Sana'a, of architecture and the building trade in Yemen.

Meneley, Anne. *Tournaments of Value: Sociality and Hierarchy in a Yemeni Town.* Toronto, ON: University of Toronto Press, 1996.

It is an excellent and very readable anthropological account of women and gender relations in the Tihama region of Yemen, with a focus on households in the famous town of

Zabid. This study shows how gender and social status are performed through hospitality and reciprocal visiting of households.

Mundy, Martha. *Domestic Government: Kinship, Community and Polity in North Yemen.* New York: I. B. Tauris, 1995.

It is an important study of social organization in the perspective of women and their management of household resources. This will prove a challenging book for nonspecialists, however.

Serjeant, R. B. and Ronald Lewcock, eds. *Sana'a: An Arabian Islamic City.* London: The World of Islam Festival Trust, 1983.

A handsomely produced and lavishly illustrated volume, this is a multidisciplinary study of one of the oldest and most fascinating cities in the world. Most of the studies are architectural in nature but not all. Chapters include works by historians, philologists, archaeologists, social anthropologists, and geographers. In the absence of a comprehensive social history of the city, this volume will be the indispensable reference work on Sana'a.

Stevenson, Thomas B. *Social Change in a Yemeni Highlands Town.* Salt Lake City, UT: University of Utah Press, 1985.

Though somewhat dated, this study is still indispensable for understanding the forces of change at work in 1980s Yemen.

Stone, Francine, ed. *Studies on the Tihaamah: The Report of the Tihaamah Expedition 1982 and Related Papers.* Essex: Longman, 1985.

This book contains survey reports related to the geology, flora, fauna, history, archaeology, architecture, music, and ethnography of the northern Tihama in Yemen. Texts are accompanied by beautiful hand-drawn illustrations done by artists on the expedition.

Swagman, Charles F. *Development and Change in Highland Yemen.* Salt Lake City, UT: University of Utah Press, 1988.

This study focuses on the people in the rural western highlands of northern Yemen who developed their region through local associations. To be read in conjunction with Carapico's *Civil Society in Yemen.*

Weir, Shelagh. *A Tribal Order: Politics and Law in the Mountains of Yemen.* Austin, TX: University of Texas Press, 2007.

It is a superb account of the tribal system of law in Yemen and the ways in which political processes are dependent upon it. This book definitively refutes the mistaken view that territories outside the control of the central state are "lawless." It is an indispensable reading not only for social scientists but also policy-makers concerned with Yemen.

Jews in Yemen

Ahroni, Reuben. *The Jews of the British Crown Colony of Aden: History, Culture, and Ethnic Relations.* New York: E. J. Brill, 1994.

This book illustrates the history of Jewish settlement in Aden from ancient times through the end of the British occupation with a detailed discussion of economic roles, education, and religious institutions while in Aden and in the relocated community in England.

Goitein, Shelomo Dov, ed. *From the Land of Sheba: Tales of the Jews of Yemen.* New York: Schocken Books, 1947.

It is a delightful collection of stories about Jews in Yemen as told by Jews from Yemen, collected in Israel by the great Yemenite scholar S. D. Goitein.

Goitein, Shelomo Dov. "Portrait of a Yemenite Weavers' Village," *Jewish Social Studies* 17, no. 1 (1955): 3–26.

It is a case study of the Al-Gades Yemenite Jewish village in lower Yemen. Through interviews with former residents, Goitein follows the town's history detailing the economic, social, and religious practices of the villagers and their interactions with the surrounding Muslim population.

Goitein, Shelomo Dov. *The Yemenites: History, Communal Organization, Spiritual Life.* Jerusalem: Yad Ben-Zvi Institute, 1983.

It is a description of Yemenite Jewish culture, society, and history based on material from the Cairo Geniza. It focuses on Jewish intellectual and religious life and the community's interactions with the surrounding Muslim communities during the premodern era.

Muchawsky-Schnapper, Ester. *The Jews of Yemen: Highlights of the Israel Museum Collection.* Jerusalem: The Israel Museum, 1994.

Religion

Ho, Enseng. *The Graves of Tarim: Genealogy and Mobility across the Indian Ocean.* Berkeley, CA: University of California Press, 2006.

Covering a period of 600 years and a space of thousands of miles, this is a rich and complex study of how Sufi practitioners, descendants of the Prophet Muhammad, from the southern region of Hadhramawt, brought Islam to the Indian Ocean and beyond through trade and commerce. It is a story of diasporic Yemenis long before the global or transnational movements of the 20th century made diasporas as we have come to know them today. In addition to the historical account, this is also an ethnography of Sufism in Hadhramawt and how it has fared under the onslaught of both socialism and Wahhabi Salafism. Published accounts of non-Zaydi Islam are rare in the literature, and so this is a valuable book for that reason as well.

Messick, Brinkley. *The Calligraphic State: Textual Domination and History in a Muslim Society.* Berkeley, CA: University of California Press, 1993.

This important anthropological account of the traditional processes of Muslim learning, especially in regard to the law, is original for its focus on writing and the reading of texts (manuscript as well as printed, contracts as well as religious tracts) that for centuries has marked Yemen as a "book" culture. The author explores how this textual tradition was complexly related to government, especially in the Imamate state, which he calls a "calligraphic state." The book also explores how that traditional world changed with the printing press, new pedagogical methods in the schools, and new concepts of the nation-state.

Vom Bruck, Gabriele. *Islam, Memory, and Morality in Yemen.* New York: Palgrave Macmillan, 2005.

There are very few ethnographic accounts of the descendants of the Prophet Muhammad in Yemen, the elite that was overthrown by the 1962 revolution, and so this excellent study is exceptional. It sensitively explores their memory of their past and their sense of their ambiguous place in contemporary society where they are often stigmatized and occasionally discriminated against. Anyone who hopes to understand the long-standing Houthi rebellion in northern Yemen must read this book for necessary background.

Art and Architecture

Marchand, Trevor Hugh James. *Minaret Building and Apprenticeship in Yemen.* Richmond: Curzon, 2001.

It is a superb ethnography by a trained architect who apprenticed himself to master Yemeni builders in Sana'a to learn the art and trade of mud-brick building.

Language and Literature

Abdul-Wali, Mohammed. *They Die Strangers: A Novella and Stories from Yemen,* translated by Abubaker Bagader and Deborah Akers. Austin, TX: University of Texas Press, 2001.

It is a selection of Abdul-Wali's short stories, including "Abu Rubbiya," "Brother, Are You Going to Fight Them All," "The Land, Salma," and "On the Road to Asmara," as well as his novella *They Die Strangers.* Weir's introduction provides essential historical and biographical background as well as critical commentary on the selected texts.

Akers, Deborah and Abubaker Bagader, ed. *Oranges in the Sun: Short Stories from the Arabian Gulf.* Boulder, CO: Lynne Rienner, 2007.

It contains eight short stories by Yemeni writers, preceded by biographical sketches, as well as Akers' brief introduction to the history of the short story in Yemen, situated within the larger geographical context of the genre's history in the Arabian Peninsula. The Yemeni authors include Zayd Mutee' Dammaj, Wajdi al-Ahdal, Hamadan Dammaj, and Yassir Abdul Bagi.

Caton, Steven C. *"Peaks of Yemen I Summon": Poetry as Cultural Practice in a North Yemeni Tribe.* Berkeley: University of California Press, 1990.

This is the first comprehensive study of tribal oral poetry as a performance-based set of genres composed in a host of social occasions. It argues that this poetry is essentially a form of political rhetoric used to persuade actors to moral points of view, and that it is as important as coercive means for understanding tribal politics. It is an excellent source on language and aesthetics in Yemen.

Dammaj, Zayd Mutee'. *The Hostage,* translated by May Jayyusi and Christopher Tingley. New York: Interlink, 1994.

This translation of Dammaj's *The Hostage,* perhaps the best-known Yemeni novel, also provides an excellent introduction to the novel's historical background by Robert Burrowes and literary commentary by Yemeni poet Abd al-Aziz al-Maqalih.

Jayyusi, Salma Khadra, ed. *The Literature of Modern Arabia.* Austin, TX: University of Texas Press, 1990.

This anthology includes a dozen selections from Yemeni short story writers, including Aulaqi, Ba-Amer, Abdul-Wali, and al-Qadi. This text is also of interest for its compilation of authors' biographies, which notes their educational and professional experience as well as selected publications.

Liebhaber, Samuel. *The Diiwaan of Hajj Daakoon: A Collection of Mahri Poetry.* Ardmore, PA: American Institute for Yemeni Studies, 2011.

Mahri is a Semitic language that is distinct from Arabic and is spoken in southeastern Yemen (near the border with Oman). Very little is known about it, and so this collection of poetry by a linguist who did extensive fieldwork on the language is important to anyone interested in the folk literature of the country.

Miller, Flagg. *The Moral Resonance of Arab Media: Audiocassette Poetry and Culture in Yemen.* Cambridge, MA: Harvard University Press, 2007.

While we know a fair amount about tribal poetry in northern Yemen, this book is the first to explore this topic in the south, in a region to the north of the port city of Aden that has experienced a resurgence of tribalism since Yemeni unification in 1990. With this has also come a renaissance of tribal poetry (especially the ode known as the qasida) that is recorded on cassette tapes, sold in stereo stores, and sold all over Yemen, the Arabian Peninsula, and even the Yemeni diaspora.

Wagner, Mark S. *Like Joseph in Beauty: Yemeni Vernacular Poetry and Arab-Jewish Symbiosis.* Boston, MA: Brill, 2009.

This scholarly work focuses on Humayni poetry, the sung colloquial verse associated with the urban elite of Yemen. It is not so much concerned with its contemporary varieties (though there is a chapter on modern forms as represented by the poetry written in the late period of the Zaydi Imamate) as it is with its "Golden Age" in the 17th century, and is particularly valuable in its treatment of the great Jewish poets who wrote in Hebrew using Arabic script.

DOCUMENTARIES OF YEMEN

Borelli, Caterina. *The Architecture of Mud.* Watertown, MA: Documentary Educational Resources, 1999.

It is a beautifully photographed film about the craft of mud-brick building in the magnificent Wadi Hadhramawt, with special attention to the making and application of a lime plaster called nurah.

Borelli, Caterina. *Qudad: Reinventing a Tradition.* Watertown, MA: Documentary Educational Resources, 2004.

This features the equivalent of nurah in the south, though called qudad, used only for mosques and irrigation works. It is also about the reinvention of this lost art in the restoration of the magnificent 'Amariyyah school and mosque complex in Rada'.

About the Editor and Contributors

Steven C. Caton is professor of contemporary Arab studies at Harvard University. His research has focused on the Arabian Peninsula, especially Yemen, and has included topics such as Yemeni Arabic, tribal social organization, oral poetry, and contemporary issues of water sustainability. His primary publications on Yemen include two books, *"Peaks of Yemen I Summon": Poetry as Cultural Practice in a North Yemeni Tribe* (1990) and *Yemen Chronicle: An Anthropology of War and Mediation* (2005), in addition to numerous articles.

Ali Saif Hassan is executive director of the Political Development Forum, a nongovernmental organization that promotes sustainable political and economic reform, and works as a special adviser to Yemen's Ministry of Planning.

Katherine Hennessey, PhD, is a fellow and researcher in residence at the American Institute for Yemeni Studies in Sana'a. Her research focuses on Middle Eastern literature and drama, on contemporary theater on the Arabian Peninsula in particular. She has received two Fulbright awards, a Mellon grant, and a Beinecke fellowship. Her recent publications include articles entitled "Staging a Protest: Socio-political Criticism in Contemporary Yemeni Theater" and "The Inaugural Season of the Royal Opera House, Muscat," and she is currently completing a book entitled *A Century of Yemeni Theater.*

Asher Orkaby is a doctoral student in Middle Eastern history at Harvard University. He holds an MA in history from Harvard University and an MA in Middle

Eastern studies from Ben Gurion University. He has done research on the economic impact of the Jewish exodus from Yemen (1949–1951). He is currently working on the International History of the Yemeni Civil War (1962–68).

Charles Schmitz is professor of geography at Towson University in Baltimore, Maryland, where he has taught since 1999. He is a specialist on the Middle East and Yemen. He began his academic career as a Fulbright scholar and American Institute for Yemeni Studies fellow in Yemen in the early 1990s. His current research interests include the political economy of development in Yemen, international law and the counter terror policy, international governance and failing states, and the sociology of contemporary Yemeni society.

Mohammed Sharafuddin is associate professor of English at the Department of English, University of Sana'a, Sana'a, Yemen. Graduated with an MA from Kansas University and PhD from York University, England, in 1988, he has been teaching at a number of universities in Yemen, Kuwait, and the United States. After the publication of his book *Islam and Romantic Orientalism* (1994), he has been engaged in research covering a variety of topics including Orientalism, American transcendentalism, English romantic literature, Shakespeare, and Sufi literature. Most of the research published so far, and many still pending, is based on papers delivered at international conferences such as the International Wordsworth Conference (Grasmere, Cumbria, UK) and MESA Conference (United States), as well as keynote speeches at prominent universities such as Drew University, Harvard University, and St. Lawrence College.

Stacey Philbrick Yadav is assistant professor of political science and director of the Middle Eastern Studies program at Hobart and William Smith Colleges in Geneva, New York. She is the author of *Islamists and the State: Legitimacy and Institutions in Yemen and Lebanon* (2013), as well as a number of recent journal articles on the Joint Meeting Parties opposition alliance and the Islah party.

Thematic Index

POLITICS AND GOVERNMENT
Political Legacies from Yemen's History

Subject Index

economy in historical perspective,
114–121
 modern urban markets, 117–118
 political economy of agriculture,
 114–115
 republican government and economic
 transformation, 118–119
 rural markets, 115–117
 socialist government and economic
 transformation, 120
 United Yemen (Republic of Yemen)
 and challenges, 120–121
education, 202–208
 modern. *See* modern education
 possibilities and limits, 207–208
 traditional. *See* traditional education
Egyptian Fatimids, 51
emigration, 17
 consumer durables, import of, 134
 labor immigration, 135
 movement to British colony of Aden,
 133–134
 remittance economy, 133–135
 resource scarcity, 17
Empirical Research and Women's Studies
 Center, 110
ethnic groups, 18–19
 akhdam, 19
 badu, 18
 khaddam, 19
 other groups, 19
 qaba'il, 18
 religious differences, 19
 saadah or descendants of Prophet
 Muhammad, 19
 tribes, 18–19
etiquette, 218–229
 bargaining, 228
 challenging someone in public, 229
 conversation, 221–222
 friendship and hand-holding in public,
 228–229
 gift giving, 227–228
 greetings, 218–221
 hospitality toward stranger and guest, 222

meals, 222–224
 qat chew, 224–227
 transactions, 220–221
exceptional courts, 102
executive branch
 premier-presidential system, 99
 reelection won by Saleh, 100
 Yemeni Congregation for Reform
 (Islah), 99
Exodus and Operation Magic Carpet,
 163–164
 1839 British occupation of Aden, 163
 messianic community, 164
 1914 Balfour Declaration, 164
 1939 British White Paper restriction,
 164

family household (*bayt*), 166, 190–191
 biological family, 190
 dependents, women and children, 191
 educating children, 190–191
 establishing own household, 191
 working for larger family welfare, 191
Fatimid caliphates, 50–51, 150–152
female politicians, 111
feminism, Western-style, 201
fertility rate, 22
festivals or 'Ids, religious, 195
fiction, 247–250
 imaginative short-story collections,
 250
 important writers, 249
 novel, 249
 short stories, 248
 vibrant genre, 248
finance, 137
 debt service, 137
 oil revenues, declining, 137
 transfers, 137
fiqh (science of religious law), 203
First Gulf War, 75
fishing
 canning plants, 126
 export, 125–126
Fivers (Zaydis), 149